NOW THAT'S FUNNY!

THE ART AND CRAFT OF WRITING COMEDY

PETER DESBERG
JEFFREY DAVIS

SQUAREONE
PUBLISHERS

EDITOR: Caroline Smith
COVER DESIGNER: Jeannie Tudor
TYPESETTER: Gary A. Rosenberg

Square One Publishers
115 Herricks Road
Garden City Park, NY 11040
(516) 535-2010 • (877) 900-BOOK
www.squareonepublishers.com

Library of Congress Cataloging-in-Publication Data

Names: Desberg, Peter author. | Davis, Jeffrey .
Title: Now that's funny! : the art and science of writing comedy / Peter
Desberg and Jeffrey Davis.
Description: Garden City Park, NY : Square One Publishers, 2017. | Previous
edition, published in 2010, has other title information: at the writers'
table with Hollywood's top comedy writers. | Includes index.
Identifiers: LCCN 2016055985 | ISBN 9780757004452 (pbk.)
Subjects: LCSH: Television comedies—Authorship. | Comedy films—Authorship.
| Television comedy writers—United States—Interviews. |
Screenwriters—United States—Interviews.
Classification: LCC PN1992.8.C66 D37 2017 | DDC 808.2/523—dc23
LC record available at https://lccn.loc.gov/2016055985

Printed in Nutech Print Services - India

10 9 8 7 6 5 4 3 2 1

Contents

Acknowledgments

A serious "thank you" for a book about comedy writing

All books come together through the generosity of spirit of countless individuals, but a book of interviews, especially one that is by its nature a little offbeat, requires the kindness of friends, acquaintances, and sometimes even total strangers. From the inception of this project, people enthusiastically stepped up to assist us many times over, sometimes without our even having to beg. Without them, this book could never have been completed.

We would like to begin by expressing our gratitude to Bill Gladstone, our literary agent, whose enthusiasm for this project has never wavered. Without Bill's support, the book would never have dropped into the lap of our publisher Rudy Shur, whose gentle prodding helped to shape it. That shaping was further assisted by our watchful editor Caroline Smith. We also want to extend our thanks to our inventive publicist, Kathy Berardi, and to Square One's Anthony Pomes, for contributing his near-encyclopedic knowledge of all things pop-cultural and comedic to a final read of our material.

If we wrote a sentence or two about everyone who helped us with this book, we would deplete a forest, so we would like to thank all of these generous friends:

Barbara Alexander, Carolyn Bauer, Larry Brezner, Neal Dodson, Jay Douglas, Julie Fleischer, Stephen Galloway, Bill Gladstone, David Goldbeck, Mark Goldberg, Gary Grossman, Jack Heller, Peter Heller, Shirl Hendryx, Monica Horan, Deborah Langford, Jackie Oleeski, Julie Sayres, Bill Tanner, Bryna Weiss, and Frank Wuliger.

We'd also like to thank the following transcribers for their dedication, perseverance and creativity: Sal Cardoni, Diana Levy, Ivana Lyon, Ori Seron, and Lauren Wilson.

And we're putting our families at the end because the Principle of Recency says that you remember the last thing you hear best.

. . . and, of course, we'd like to thank all the writers we interviewed for giving us their time, talent, and tolerance.

We would like to dedicate this book to the memory of two legendary writers who graced its pages, Sherwood Schwartz and Leonard Stern.

About the Authors

Peter Desberg is a licensed clinical psychologist specializing in the area of stage fright, working with many top standup comedians who are regularly confronted with massive cases of flopsweat. After receiving his PhD from the University of Southern California, he began moonlighting as a university professor at California State University, Dominguez Hills. He has done extensive research on the psychology of humor and is a frequent consultant to business presenters on how to use humor persuasively. In the areas of humor and stage fright, he has done many radio and television interviews and is frequently quoted in national publications including *The Wall Street Journal, Reader's Digest, Psychology Today*, and *Cosmopolitan*. For a decade he hosted a cable TV show about technology. Peter's extensive academic research on the psychology of humor has significantly reduced the number of party invitations he has received over the years. In addition, he has authored six joke books along with sixteen other non-humorous titles.

Jeffrey Davis's earliest memories are of sitting around a table at Nate 'n Al's Delicatessen in Beverly Hills while his father and his comedy writer pals gathered over corn beef on rye and Dr. Brown's Cream Soda, telling war stories and trying to fix third acts. Jeffrey began his own career writing jokes for *Thicke of the Night*. Among his credits are *Love Boat, House Calls, Give Me a Break, Diff'rent Strokes, Night Court, Small Wonder*, and *America's Funniest People*. He has had film projects developed by Bette Midler's All Girl Productions, among others. He has also written for Discovery Channel and the National Geographic Channel, as well as a documentary on the history of presidential scandals, *If These Walls Could Talk*, for Weller/Grossman Productions and A&E. His play, *Speed Dating 101*, was published by JAC Publishing, Boston. It and other plays have been seen in New York and Los Angeles. Jeffrey holds an MFA from the University of Iowa Writers' Workshop. He is an associate professor of film and TV writing at Loyola Marymount University in Los Angeles. When cornered, he admits to having been the chair of its screenwriting department since 2009.

Preface

Years ago, I got a phone call from a woman named Susie who said she was getting her master's degree in psychology from Antioch West University. She said she was interested in the psychology of humor and had gotten my name from one of her professors. She asked if I would be willing to help with her thesis and serve on her thesis committee.

It was the tail end of a grueling day and the thought of working for no compensation was doing nothing for my mood. But being polite to a fault, I asked her to describe her thesis. In a droning voice she outlined a plan to write a chapter on the psychology of humor, a chapter on the sociology of humor, and a chapter on the anthropology of humor. I was about to cut her off, politely, of course, when she said she was going to interview a famous Hollywood comedy writer. I asked who the writer was. "Edmund Hartmann," she said. He was the first president of the Writers Guild of America. He'd written several classic Bob Hope movies, including *The Lemon Drop Kid, Sorrowful Jones, Paleface,* and *Fancy Pants.* He also wrote several movies for Abbott and Costello and much, much more. I asked how she knew him and she said offhandedly, "Oh, he's my dad."

I suggested that we drop the first three chapters and asked if her father would ask some of his comedy writer friends to be interviewed. This seemed like a once-in-a-lifetime opportunity. I had an idea that was different from books on the subject in which writers were asked, "How did you get into comedy writing?" Instead, we would give the comedy writers a task that they performed as part of their work. They would tell us how they solved comedy writing problems while our tape recorder was rolling.

We were lucky enough to get some of the top writers in Hollywood at that time, including people like Hal Kantor and Herbie Baker. We completed eight interviews and then I got a surprise call from Susie announcing that she was moving to Illinois. The project, which, by this time, had worked its way into my heart, was dead.

Fast-forward twenty years. Jeffrey was sitting in his car in front of my house. He had come to pick up his son, who had a playdate with my daughter. He was sulking in the front seat, waiting for his son to come out, knowing that if the youngster didn't come out soon, he would have to make small talk with yet another set of parents. His luck ran out, as often happens when you are waiting on fifteen-year-olds. He came in and we introduced ourselves.

Within a minute or two, we found out that we were both college professors and wallowed in a few minutes of commiseration. Jeffrey said he taught screenwriting, mostly comedy, at Loyola Marymount University. He had written many plays and sitcoms, but had never done any academic-type writing or research, which was now something that was expected of him if he wanted to continue down an academic path. He asked me if I had done much of it. I reluctantly admitted that I had. On a hunch, I told him about the comedy writer project I had begun so many years before. He asked me who some of the writers were. As I reeled off the names, his eyes began to open wider and he began to smile. "All those guys were around my crib . . . probably playing poker." Jeffrey's father was a well-known comedy writer from that era. He was a show runner for *Bewitched, That Girl,* and *The Odd Couple* and had credits a mile long. Jeffrey said, "Let's do it!"

We decided to start from scratch, and on Jeffrey's suggestion, we changed the task. We wrote a generic sitcom premise—reprinted in its entirety in the Introduction—which we gave each of our twenty-four writers. Then we asked each writer to develop it while we watched. Not only is the rest history, but you'll be reading this history very soon because it's the rest of this book.

We have been fortunate to work with some of the most talented and generous comedy writers in Hollywood. We want to thank them for opening up and sharing their artistic processes with us.

Peter Desberg and Jeffrey Davis

Introduction

JOIN US AS TOP COMEDY PROFESSIONALS CREATE

As veteran comedy writer Elliot Shoenman (*Maude, Home Improvement*) is retracing the cab ride his father took on the way to his suicide, he wonders how much his famously cheap old man tipped the cabbie.

Ken Daurio and his partner Cinco Paul are listening to notes on their film project *Bubble Boy* when the producer insists they lose the bubble after the first act. He wanted him out of the bubble at the end of Act I. The writers said, "The movie's called . . . *Bubble Boy*. He's a germ-a-phobe." Ken turned to Cinco and said, "Are we changing the name of the movie to *Boy*?"

These stories illustrate just how different comedy writers are from the rest of us. They notice character quirks and conflicts they can turn into interesting and often off-kilter situations. If there's no quirk or conflict, they think, "Yeah, but what if . . . ?" Then they create one. How do they do it?

That's the question *Now That's Funny!* sets out to answer in twenty-four unconventional interviews.

WE'RE IN HOLLYWOOD, NOT FRANCE

In Paris, people line up and pay to see the works at the Picasso Museum. What would it be worth to you to have been in Picasso's studio at Montmartre, sitting next to him on a bench, watching him *as* he created his paintings? Now, imagine if you could also have been in the studios of Monet, Renoir, Degas, Chagall, Cézanne, and Matisse—and you could have watched each of them as they painted. If that wasn't enough, imagine if you could also choose the object or model that all of them were to paint. Think about all you'd learn, seeing commonalities, differences, and unfurled creativity as they hit each canvas.

1

Well, we're not in France, but we are in Hollywood, and those painters are all dead anyway, but this book does something similar. It puts you in a seat at the table in the Writers' Room to see how some of the best comedy writers apply their brush strokes to their computers or to others in the room. If you're new to sitcoms, most shows have a gaggle of writers (around ten) who write each episode. Their process usually starts in the Writers' Room as they brainstorm a story. Sometimes they sit at a large table coming up with ideas; other times, they work in smaller teams. Generally, some are specialists in story construction and others are great joke writers. Some go both ways.

When Hollywood writers like Dan O'Shannon (*Modern Family* and *Frasier*), Sherwood Schwartz (creator of *Gilligan's Island* and *The Brady Bunch*), and Phil Rosenthal (creator of *Everybody Loves Raymond*) are interviewed, they're typically asked, "How *do* you create comedy?" But they're really being asked, "How *did* you do it?"

There's an old adage attributed variously to Euripides, Mark Twain, and George Bernard Shaw: "The autobiography is the highest form of fiction." In other words, when artists discuss their creative process, what we learn is more likely to be inaccurate.

We tried something different. We took a left turn from the standard interview book. We asked twenty-four comedy writers to *show* us what they do. We gave each of them the same generic premise about a mother and her adult daughter and asked them to develop it any way they wanted. We told them there were *no* rules, *no* boundaries, and *no* limits. That was just as well; they wouldn't have followed rules. They're comedy writers, not accountants.

Try and picture what we put them through. Each writer walked in cold, was handed the same premise, and was asked to begin the development process. Talk about being put on the spot! Many of them said that the interview felt like a stress test. They had to create on the fly, knowing that their work would be compared to their peers in this book. Yet each one not only succeeded . . . they sparkled.

Encouraging them to play with and develop the premise results in memorable new stories as unique as each of the writers in this book, proving that there is no "one size fits all" way to create comedy. The writers jump in, ask questions, develop characters, create conflicts, pitch jokes, and make casting suggestions.

Some of the writers stay with the original premise, while others turn it on its head. Several of the writers choose to ignore the main characters and build minor characters into a prominent part of the story. Almost all of the writers mention they write from experience and they write what they know. Not surprisingly, several of the writers choose to take our Mother/Daughter main characters and turn their stories into Father/Son stories; that's what they know best.

Some writers cast the roles with actors so they can visualize how the main characters might walk or speak. Some identify key people in their lives on whom they model their characters. Some create a story and then work the characters so they fit in comfortably.

In addition to the development process, you'll also read rare Hollywood anecdotes that flow naturally from each of the interviews. Many of the writers told us they give the same rehearsed answers in most interviews, but here they revealed themselves in a way they have never done before. A few told us that they planned to use material they came up with from this interview in their own work.

And it all happens in real time.

The writers featured in *Now That's Funny!* span the history of show business from the original Golden Age of Television, with legends like Sherwood Schwartz (creator, *Gilligan's Island* and *The Brady Bunch*) and Leonard Stern (co-creator, *Get Smart* and writer, *The Honeymooners*), to the generation who were influenced by them, represented by Peter Casey (co-creator, *Wings* and *Frasier*), Yvette Bowser (creator, *Living Single*), and Ed Decter (co-writer, *There's Something About Mary*), to some of today's hottest young movie and television writers, including Hank Nelken (co-writer, *Saving Silverman*) and Dan O'Shannon (writer, *Cheers*, *Frasier*, and executive producer, *Modern Family*). In addition, many are also show creators, show runners, producers, and directors.

ARTING AND *SCIENCING* IN COMEDY WRITING

There's an old saying: "Comedy writers are born, not made . . . that's a good argument for birth control." But it brings up an interesting question—can comedy writing be taught? We start with a core belief: You can't teach talent. Almost every writer we interviewed agreed that the gift of comedy creation is not distributed evenly.

On the other side of the equation is the science of comedy, known in the industry as craft. We went to several conferences put on by the International Society of Humor Studies, where academics really do—wait for it—investigate the "science of comedy." In the sessions, not one drop of actual humor was spilled.

On the other hand, a great deal is known about the craft of comedy writing, and the writers interviewed in this book share an abundance of it. As we begin our discussion of the craft of comedy writing, we thought we would open with a joke:

> *A couple is driving out in the country and as they pass a farm, they see a bunch of barnyard animals. The husband says, "Relatives of yours?"*

She says, "Yes, they're my in-laws."

Here's an alternate punchline to the same joke:

"Yes, they're my in-laws; just look at them."

It might look the same to you, but try telling the second version to somebody. When you get to the word "in-laws," sure, you'll still get a laugh—but it will be cut short because you're still talking. Your audience assumes something even funnier is coming and they don't want to miss it. But after they hear the word "in-laws," all you're giving them is, *". . . just look at them."*

You've violated one of the basic rules of comedy. The climactic word must always come at the end. You never want to step on your own laughs.

THE NEED FOR CRAFT

An interesting question came up in our interview with Dennis Klein (co-creator of *The Larry Sanders Show*): How often do writers create something completely original compared to the number of times they are given story ideas, characters, and constraints to develop? We're not going to be spoilers, so you can read Dennis's response yourself on page 123, but based on our interviews, the answer seems to be *rarely*. If you create a sitcom, you can go any way you want with it—at least until someone buys it. But if you work in a Writers' Room, the show and every character on that show has a history and a corresponding set of traits. Everything you create must fall within those constraints.

For example, say you're writing a spec script (an unsolicited script). If it's your idea, you can go wherever you want with it. But if you're a writer who is brought in later to work on a script, you're a writer for hire, and you have to please the director, producer, and the stars—if you last that long.

The ratio of writers who begin with a blank slate is tiny compared with the number of writers who are given their starting point. This is why *Now That's Funny!* has so much to share with writers and anyone who is interested in comedy. It mirrors the process that most professional writers do on a daily basis.

When interviewing Hank Nelken (*Saving Silverman*), he told us that he is frequently brought in by producers and executives, handed a premise, and asked to develop it. He also knew that a bunch of other writers were brought in to do the same thing; he always wondered what they came up with. He said he couldn't wait until *Now That's Funny!* is published so he can read what the other writers do with the same premise.

ARTS AND CRAFT

When *you* hear a funny story or joke, you remember it and retell it. How well you do this may determine the course of your social life. But imagine if someone walks up to you and says, *"Quick, I need a joke about how fast some restaurants go out of business, yet the ones I like, I can never get into."* Most people couldn't come up with that joke right away, or ever. The people interviewed in this book can come up with that joke, and as they do, they can tailor it to millennials, pro football players, middle-aged families, or their in-laws. How do they do it? In a word . . . *craft.*

Here's a useful tip. If you meet a comedy writer, don't tell her a joke. That will annoy her because she already knows them all, just like every other comedy writer she works with. So if you ask a comedy writer to create the joke like the one we needed about restaurants closing and she can't think of something, one of the major tools of her craft is to take an old joke and switch it. Switching a joke means taking an existing joke and reusing it for a different purpose.

Switching a joke is more involved than inserting an old joke when she can't think of a new one. First, she must find an appropriate joke from the thousands that she knows. Then she must disguise it so that it will fit into the script and appear fresh. That way, only every other comedy writer will know its origins. This is just one important part of the craft of comedy writing. It's hard to find a script without any switched jokes in it. Here's an example of a switched joke:

> **Original:** *A man at a cemetery sees a tombstone that reads, "Here lies a lawyer and an honest man." He goes up to a caretaker and says, "Hey, since when have you been burying people two at a time?"*

If someone came up to you and said, "Quick, I need a joke about a bank president," you could easily switch this joke.

> **Switched joke:** *A man at a cemetery sees a tombstone that reads, "Here lies a bank president and an honest man." He goes up to a caretaker and says, "Hey, since when have you been burying people two at a time?"*

THE MOTIVATION TO BE FUNNY

We hate to use the F word, but Freud wrote a book called *Jokes and Their Relation to the Unconscious.* In that book, he explains how and why people use humor. He identifies several types of comedy. The first deals with using hostility. The joker "attacks" the butt of the joke and if his audience laughs, he's made a funny joke at someone else's expense. But if that audience recognizes the hostility and doesn't laugh, he is busted, and he and his joke are naked and exposed.

Most of us have been in a situation where one person is making fun of another: *"Hey, that's a nice tie . . . did you have to wear it because you lost a bet?"* In addition to using these jokes as a way to express "friendly" hostility between buddies, we often see such jokes on sitcoms dealing with high-profile individuals, religion, political races, different nationalities, and other easily identifiable groups. Comedy writers must be careful. Careers have ended because of one inappropriate hostile joke told in the wrong setting.

Since Freud loved puns, he slipped in another category of jokes that didn't contain hostility that he referred to as "harmless." These include puns and abstract jokes. Although they don't get the big laughs that hostile humor gets, to many people, they are not only funny, but they're witty. Here are two puns to show that they don't get big laughs: *"No one can love me like my old tomato can."* Or, *"No matter how high you put an awning, it'll just be a shade over the street."*

There are some notable comedians, like Steven Wright and Mitch Hedberg, who use abstract humor brilliantly to get laughs. One of our favorite Steven Wright jokes is, *"I woke up this morning and someone had stolen everything from my apartment and replaced it with an exact replica."*

Another type of humor Freud identifies has to do with making an audience feel superior at someone else's expense. Dumb jokes, blonde jokes, racial jokes, and jokes about children's misinterpretations are examples. We, as the audience, feel good about ourselves because we would never make the silly mistake the person or associated group in the joke has displayed. Freud's idea was that with hostile jokes, you get pleasure from attacking someone else with the joke. In this type of humor, you feel good about yourself because you feel superior to someone.

> *A nine-year-old girl was attending her first wedding. She leaned over to her mother and whispered, "Mom, what does fornication mean?"*
> *Her mother said, "Honey, where did you hear that word?"*
> *"In the back of the hall. I heard the bride say to the groom, 'Fornication like this, we should have had champagne.'"*

The final category of humor Freud talks about is using humor to deal with painful emotions. In interview after interview, you read about people who were picked on as kids until they learned to deflect the pressure by being funny. We all remember the kid in grade school who made the bully laugh, or the kid who deflected a teacher's annoyance when someone didn't know an answer. When he cracked up the class, the awkward moment passed. People who can use tension-relieving humor are prized in almost any situation.

Freud believes that this type of humor reduces the effects of emotional pain. Successful performers with disabilities or known problems use humor to downplay them and make their audiences feel more comfortable. Ray Charles once told an audience, *"My new lawyer has so much juice. Man, he just got me a driver's license."*

WHAT MAKES THAT FUNNY!

Freud talks about what motivates people to use humor. Other psychologists have looked into what makes something funny. In their view, comedy is based on *expectancy violation*. Comedy writers are good at creating distractions in the same way magicians are. You think one thing will happen (expectancy) and all of a sudden, what you expected didn't happen (violation), but something funny caught you off guard and made you laugh. You are diverted with a setup, and then they get you with the punch. In an interview, Stephen King once said the secret to his writing was, *"I have the heart of a small boy . . . I keep it in a jar on my desk."* Freud said reducing tension was the basis of pleasure.

Here is an old joke from Henny Youngman, king of the one-liners: *"My wife just ran away with my best friend . . . boy, do I miss him."* Most people think the man misses his wife who ran away, and that he must be even more upset because it was with his best friend. He was betrayed. That's what you'd expect, but something is wrong here. Finally, he reveals that it's his best friend that he'll miss, not his wife. First, the expectancy was violated, and now it has a resolution that makes sense.

Larry Gelbart (creator of *M*A*S*H*) once was asked how many rules of writing comedy there are. With his accustomed lightning-fast wit, he answered, "Fifty-five." He took a long beat, then, "Unfortunately, nobody knows what they are."

If you sat down with most comedy writers, it's doubtful that they could explain these theories. They are reserved for academics who study humor. But through their craft, comedy writers "internally" understand all this and *use it to create comedy*. So when one of them has to come up with an insult joke, he has heard just about every frame for an insult joke ever created. So he just has to slip in a new topic: *"How many _____ does it take to screw in a light bulb?"* And, if he needs to, he can probably come up with a new frame, because it was he and his kind that created it.

A "joke-joke" is a stand-alone joke that doesn't need a story or character reference. Through the 1980s, it was common for producers to tell writers they needed three jokes per page. These forced jokes found their way into many TV shows: *"Oh, look, there's Barbie Cantrell out on the beach almost wearing that bikini."* (In the early '90s, Jeffrey was forced to write sexist jokes. Aside from being dumb and pointless, these jokes break an important rule of comedy. Danny Simon, older brother of Neil Simon and the man who Woody Allen credits with teaching him how to write comedy, said, "Never set up a straight line to accommodate a punchline." He also said, "Cut your joke-jokes. Jokes are worthless unless they fit the occasion and character.")

A BAG OF CRAFT

Sooner or later, every stand-up comedian gets "flopsweat." They're scared; they've all experienced going on stage and bombing. That's why they hold back a "saver," a joke or bit they can use before the audience starts to feel sorry for them. Once the audience feels sorry for a stand-up, he's lost it. With that "saver," comedians look at its *probability of getting a laugh*. The more craft you learn, the higher the return.

It's the same with comedy writers. As they prove over and over again in these pages, they have the ability to create hilarious original material—but when it's not flowing, they can reach into their knowledge of craft and come up with something funny.

Writer Herbie Baker (*The Danny Kaye Show* and *The Flip Wilson Show*) has said, "If you need a laugh, have the telephone ring." The more inopportune the time, the funnier the ringing phone is. When a character is under serious stress and the phone rings, who is the worst person for him to hear on the other end of the phone? His mother. Whatever he is trying to get done under all this pressure is made funnier by his mother saying, "Don't you think you've wasted enough time trying to become a writer? Shouldn't you go back to pharmacy school?"

When she's up against it, Heide Perlman (*The Tracey Ullman Show, Cheers*) goes toward darker, even cartoonish conflict and says she's rarely in the mood for "nice" moments. On the other hand, Leonard Stern told us that although conflict is the basis for all of his comedy, that conflict always comes out of love rather than hostility. You just read a sample above with the mom's call to her stressed-out son. A similar kind of conflict was present in almost every *I Love Lucy* episode. Lucy and Ricky loved each other, but had conflicting ways of approaching their situations.

WHY YOU MUST READ THE PREMISE FIRST

You can read this book any way you want, with one *big* exception. *Make sure that you read the Premise at the end of this Introduction first!* Each writer was given this premise, and you need to read it to be able to follow what they do as they develop it. However you plan to read this book, whether from beginning to end, or in any order you want . . . read the damn Premise first.

If you're a daring type, here are a few additional suggestions. Whether you are an aspiring writer, seasoned professional, or anthropologically inclined (a student of history of the entertainment industry), you can try to identify similarities and differences in these writers' approaches. If you are really adventurous, try your own hand at developing this premise and then compare your efforts with the pros. Have a look at the Premise we used in the interviews that will follow throughout this book.

THE PREMISE

If you want something done, give it to SARAH. She will do it creatively, thoroughly, and have it done a week early. Her problem is her boss is afraid there's only room for one woman vice-president . . . *her*. Sarah is so focused on her work, she is unaware that she is relationship-challenged where men are concerned.

In a generation where it isn't fashionable, Sarah has a great relationship with her parents. Of course, it helps that they live two thousand miles away. At their end of the country, her parents had a great life. Stylish apartment, expensive car, beautiful clothes and jewelry. Her father made sure of all that. When he suddenly dies, Sarah's mother, MOLLY, is stunned to find that their financial situation is not an iceberg with a firm 80 percent below the water level. He was obsessed with appearances. He made it . . . they spent it. What she sees is all she has.

Molly is fiftyish, broke, unprepared for even the most unskilled job. Sarah invites her mother to move in with her. Molly reluctantly agrees . . . if it's just for a few weeks. A few weeks turns into a permanent arrangement as Molly decides Sarah's apartment, friends and lifestyle are the perfect launching pad for her new life. To complicate things even further, Molly's mother and father both have a strong work ethic and find their free-spirited daughter baffling. Sarah is actually the daughter they never had and always wanted.

Molly may not have any work skills, but she has a gift with people, especially men. She wants to help her daughter's social life, but somehow she always ends up stealing the show. Sarah wants Molly to get a job or go back to school. Molly wants to "examine all her options," which she now has for the first time in her life. Sarah wants the mother-daughter relationship she never had. Molly wants to be best friends.

An Interview with
Walter Bennett

A partial list of Walter Bennett's credits as a writer and producer includes: *The Cosby Show, The Steve Harvey Show, In the House, Here and Now, Buddies,* and *Contradictions of the Heart.*

Walter Bennett has an infectious kettle-drum laugh that comes from somewhere deep inside. Combined with his generous and unpretentious demeanor, this laugh makes it easy to forget that he is a graduate of the Yale School of Drama and an accomplished, award-winning writer. But Walter's laugh is something much more. It is his comedic barometer. He uses it to test out material, breaking himself up when he hits a line or a character bit that pleases him. His laugh is his personal transition from writer to audience.

In the way Walter approaches the process, he reminds us of great jazz improvisers like Miles Davis, who said, "There are no mistakes." As he moves from idea to idea, Walter's "playing" is so beautiful and his technique so pure that all you hear is the lovely, lilting music, accompanied by his laughter.

PD (Peter Desberg): As we've explained in our Premise [see page 9], how would you go about developing the show's plot lines?

WB (Walter Bennett): The first thing I usually do is try to put myself in the place of Sarah. I try to figure out, whose story is this? What's this really about? You've got your mom, she's got to be "out there." But, I feel kind of bad for her, but the crazy thing is you think you have a great relationship, until they're a block away. And then, when they're in the house with you, I want to make it as bad as I can for Sarah. I think she's doing okay. I guess I'm trying to figure out what her job is. It's not good enough that she has a room. Sarah is saving money so that they're in an apartment, but, where they're right on top of each other. I see a moving van pulling up to this single, efficiency, one-bedroom apartment. The story's about their proximity. So that's where I start. And then you can't go any farther without really knowing who these people are.

I'm thinking Sarah takes on a few of the traits of her father, meaning that her life is 80 percent under water, and only 20 percent is above, and Molly only really knows the 20 percent. Maybe some discovery on the daughter's part because she's not really aware of guys. I would say that she's finally taken notice of somebody, and in a perfect world, while she starts to figure this out, she doesn't need her mom around. This has got to be the worst time that her mom could show up, so I'm trying to figure out what would be the absolute worst time.

PD: Well, in your own life, what would be the worst time for a parent to show up?

WB: Unannounced. Maybe she didn't call and say, "I'm shutting down the house." Maybe the phone call was on a message machine, like, "One of these days maybe I should get out there." That was the whole message. "Call me, we'll talk about it," or something like that. So Sarah finally meets this guy. I just see her coming to the door in a towel, you know, and there's a van outside. And Mom's had Cousin Derrick drive it, you know, Derrick with a lisp—but you've got to be able to understand him. Meanwhile, the guy that [Sarah's] just started going out with is in the other room. They've just . . . you know.

The worst time. And so Mom's here, and she's looking at the 20 percent. But, the 80 percent is represented by what just went on in the room there. And you've got this guy with the lisp, "What you want off the twuck?" Sarah says, "That's not going to fit," you know, and Derrick keeps moving things in. And so Sarah's going back and forth. She whispers into the bedroom, "You've got to get out of here." He whispers back, "I thought you said your mom was cool."

So Mom is actually leaving a situation where financially, it was not what it appeared to be, and now she's coming into a relationship with her daughter that's not what it seems. So now we need to know, how often did they visit each other? Did Sarah want to move out because Molly was a little bit overbearing? And [her date's] got to be in the bathroom, trying to make it a one-room kind of situation. Maybe Sarah shoved him into the bathroom, and her mom says, "You just got up? Whose shoes are these?"

JD (Jeffrey Davis): So it's a way of using the confined space to make conflict?

"Comedy is drama, but the worst-moment drama."

WB: To make conflict. When I start to look at it, I say, "Okay, that's surface. That can only go for so long." Let's get some laughs, but now we've got to talk about their needs, which is not really funny sometimes. Comedy is drama, but the worst-moment drama. And surprise. Our laughter gives us a chance to be one step removed from drama.

JD: Do you think comedy is harder to write?

WB: It's harder to write. I break it down as an actor, because I was an actor for ten years, off-Broadway. And so, what I need to know as an actor is what happens just before the doorbell rings. And some of these are writing things, too. "Who am I expecting?" And then I take that back a little bit: "What was I doing, what was going on, what was the last conversation, or relationship I had with Mom? What was she trying to get me to do?" Or, "What did I promise her I was doing, and why?"

So now I've got to get into: What does Sarah do for a living? Her job makes her a fish out of water. So whoever she is, she's in a situation where she's working around cool people, or her work partner is Salma Hayek. Somebody who she thinks she could never be like. But when she looks into the mirror at home, she's saying, "Me gusta que miro . . ."

I'm going to put Sarah at Target. She's a manager at Target. No, no, she's a trainee at Target. And she told Molly she was a VP. And the boyfriend works in the popcorn thing. And the Salma Hayek woman is at Register 4. So Sarah came from this splendid background, and she was two thousand miles [away], and this is the way she lives now. And her mom said, "Your dad passed away," whatever, ". . . and the money's tied up." I don't know if she can break it to her daughter.

PD: They're all living at 20 percent.

WB: Yeah, we start to find out who this family is. And so, there's constantly layers every time there's something new that comes out. And I think Sarah gets found out. I think her mother becomes a secret shopper. "I've got a job." "What are you doing here?" But then, story-wise, I've got to know my ending here. It's about closing a gap. The big thing is they're too far away, they're two thousand miles away. They come together, and what do they get out of that? What are they avoiding? What are they afraid of? And why are they afraid to close this gap?

PD: When you close the gap you go from 20 to 40 percent? Or, 20 to 90 percent?

WB: I think in the end Molly and Sarah may stay at 20 to 80, but they know they're at 20/80. They respect the gap, and that's where you get the juice from.

PD: You get stories there.

WB: You get stories about Sarah saying, "I've just been promoted." And Molly asking, "To what?" "And where?" Mom is like 50–55.

JD: What would you have to do to sex Molly up and keep it commercial?

WB: You know what they did to Fran Drescher? They made her a young, hot mom. That's going too far. I think I would look at actresses that we generally don't see as a mom, like Sharon Stone. The other question is, an overpowering mom?

PD: Does it help you to find a person to do it?

WB: Yeah, it helps me to start thinking of a person. Then I go to who in my life, which helps me. I go, "Oh, man, I remember . . ." Sometimes it's not even like a mom. It was a teacher, or it was a cousin, or a friend's mom, a friend's cousin. But nowadays, you really—even in the studios, you really have to think, who do you know? Shirley MacLaine. Yeah, Shirley MacLaine might be good at something like this. In fact, she would be.

I think the mom has a daughter who's out there. "My daughter lives two thousand miles away, and she is the vice president of such-and-such. And by golly, I may only have what I see here financially, and that 80 percent isn't here, but hey, you know who's out there, Sarah. She's my 80 percent."

It's like someone telling you, "You want to become a dealer in Vegas?" and someone saying, "Well, I'm a big guy at this big casino, and one day when you get here"— thinking they'll never get here—"When you get here, I'll introduce you to Steve Wynn." You show up and you find out he's at the end of the Strip, doing a little lounge act. He also has to bus tables. And this is who the Debra Messing character is. I think her character has a personal flaw with regard to almost getting somewhere. And she's scared, and she's always had the potential, and Mom is living through the eyes of the potential, rather than reality.

PD: So Sarah was on the fast track a few times and got knocked off.

WB: Yeah, or knocked herself off. She's presented herself in one way but she's really at Target! And that's a dead end unless you're in the executive training program, which she's constantly trying to get into. Again, at one point I go, "Where did Molly settle?" She met a man who provided a lavish lifestyle. Well, let's just say upper-middle class, not exceedingly rich, or anything like that, but I think the downside of that is it can make a person lazy, it can make them complacent. "Do I have to do this anymore?" or, "Why am I doing this?" "I'm just happy raising my daughter." And at a point, the dad starts to realize that this is what she expected, because I don't think it's all his fault that he didn't come to her and say, "I'm broke, we've got to downsize." I don't think he ever said that to her because this was her world, it would crumble around her, and since Sarah was now out of the house, why do that now?

But the question is, how long had they been living like that? Did the dad leave every morning with a briefcase and then change clothes to do whatever kind of work he really did, and then put his suit back on and come back home? I think the father's side of it was the true drama side of it.

PD: Would you actually bring him on in flashbacks, or in her recollections?

WB: I've got another way. Molly says she sees him and the daughter's sitting there, "Mom, what's wrong?" I think the daughter's teaching her how to drive. She's never had to drive. And she says, "I just saw your father." "No, Mom, it was closed casket." "Well, it could have been your father."

PD: So is it a vision? A wish fulfillment? Or is it really him?

WB: It's left open. And I think throughout the piece, she keeps seeing her husband. And at some point, we've got to come to, "Does she see her husband?" And the hard thing is that if she did, then what really happened? But if she didn't, but she meets this guy who just looks like him, and she brings him home, and Sarah is shocked. "It's crazy!" But maybe he is everything her father wasn't.

I think if we have this element, we have the family album. In comedy, there's that element of reliving a relationship, keeping the funny there. But, through that story line, we get a chance to find out what was her relationship with Dad. I think there would then be a point where the guy who looks like her father stumbles across a picture. He hasn't seen a picture of all this and he stumbles across a picture, and he realizes what's going on here.

I would love to do a story where both Molly and Sarah pull jury duty. They each have different versions, so other people who are dealing in the 100/100s have to deal with these two. So we have times where they're far apart, but when they're in the regular . . . "These guys are nuts. These two are just, what are you . . . ?" And then to see them move on different sides of the street . . . in that kind of setting.

JD: What do you think it is about jury stories that make them work?

WB: I think because it's confined. And I think it taps into what you really have to get to in comedy for it to work, and that's character. You're in that room. I was working on a show. There was one episode I wanted to do that was kind of like *The Breakfast Club* with our main characters, and they come in on a Saturday . . . you know, it's a cabin story, it's Lucy, Ethel, stuck in the cabin, and she crinkles a candy wrapper, and you go, "Oh, my God, who has food?" I think it breaks everything down, and it's what the action pictures do. It breaks everything down to its essence, its common denominator. It's who these people are to each other. And they become each other's conflicts and barriers.

PD: You established a conflict within the character right away, so they were always going to get into conflicts because of who their characters are. When you're writing comedy, how do you know when something's funny?

WB: Usually the first thing that comes out is funny. Then you go, "Oh, I'll tweak it here, I'll tweak it there." Then there's a point where I go past it, and I go, "No." But first, it's got to make me laugh.

PD: You have this infectious laugh and you have a really nice meter inside that says, "That would be funny."

WB: I do it so fast now, it's like, "No, no, no, yeah." And sometimes I don't even know what the "no" was.

PD: How do you go about making stuff funnier when you get feedback that you need more laughs?

"If it's not funny, it's usually because it's not the worst thing that can happen."

WB: First, I'd look at what the original joke is, and a lot of times when it doesn't work, it's because there's no surprise in the joke; it's expected. If it's not funny, it's usually because it's not the worst thing that can happen. There's something worse that can happen. And you can't get any worse than this. Let me give you an example. "Well, the camera fell over." And I go, "Wow, now that's bad," but where did it fall? But, it's not specific enough. And a lot of times, it will be something specific that plays into the fear of your character that you've built up. You can get comedy out of that.

PD: How did you get into writing?

WB: Actually, when I was fourteen, I had an eighth/ninth grade teacher. We were doing *Pearly Victorious.* So they're reading *Pearly Victorious*, which I'd never read. So she said, "I want you to read the part of Pearly." I had no clue who Pearly was, I did not know it was the lead, I did not care. We had been reading *Beowulf.*

So we're doing this and I said, "Alright, alright, I'll read it." So I start reading this thing, and the class is rolling. They're cracking up, and I'm imitating the character.

Many of the writers we interviewed stunned us by saying that they wrote from experience. Phil Rosenthal changed Sarah and Molly to a father and son because he revealed to us that he had never been a daughter. He said he never could have written *Everybody Loves Deborah*. (See page 252 for Phil's interview.)

A number of the writers in this book were attracted to the secondary characters of the father and the grandparents. Lew Schneider (see page 265) builds an entire story around them, including a scene in which Molly, in her fifties, gets a driving lesson from her eighty-year-old father. Sherwood and Lloyd Schwartz (see page 280) begin by thinking of the father as a ghost and end up creating a two-timeframe story involving the grandparents at Molly's age, all done in sepia, while Charlie Peters (see page 222) plays with the notion of Sarah's father and grandmother being dead and running off together.

Walter Bennett takes a different route. In his take on the story, Sarah's father is dead, but Molly keeps seeing him in the side-view mirror. Walter is interested in ambiguities. He wants to keep the characters and the audience guessing. Is the father real

And I'm just playing around, goofing, having a good time, and the teacher said, "Okay, we'll finish this tomorrow," and she comes to me, "You don't know this, but you really have something here." And I said, "Eh?" And finally she said, "We're going to enter . . ." and what I realize now, she did this on my account. My class wasn't prone to doing theatre and things like that, but she entered our class in the New Jersey Teen Arts Festival, and she said to me, "Well, we're going to do a class play," because we'd been studying playwriting, and I said, "That's great," and she said, "And you're going to write it." I said, "I'm going to write a play for the class?" She said, "Yes. You're going to write the play and I want you to do something on your own also."

"'I only know how to do two things: talk and write.'"

So I wrote this play, called *Walt's Bad Trip*, and of course I'm playing the part of Walt. I wrote the thing. So I'm playing this thing, and it goes to the Teen Arts Festival, and it's a dud. But I'd written a monologue for myself, and I performed this monologue, and got back to school and later on, we got a letter from New Jersey Teen Arts Festival. We weren't selected to represent. But Walter was. And everyone applauded, and I was like, "What am I supposed to do?" My teacher said, "Everyone from all over the state will come to perform in the Capitol, and you're going to represent this region." And when I left high school, they asked me, "What are you going to do now?" And I said, "I only know how to do two things: talk and write."

PD: How did you get schooled in comedy writing?

WB: My first school in comedy writing was television. Watching Norman Lear at the time *Good Times* was on, and *Maude,* it was the heyday of half-hour comedy. I used to think of half-hour sitcoms as a play. Where I went to school, a small Black school, traditional African-American school in North Carolina called Shaw University. We had sixteen majors, and in order to get out if you were a theatre major, we had to write one one-act, and one full one, you couldn't graduate without writing two. The first one I wrote was great; it was a sitcom script. I didn't know. I was just trying to figure out how to make it work, and after that, I was instructed on structure. But in comedy, I always thought whatever I thought was funny, that was how I did it.

PD: So you picked it up by watching it.

WB: By watching it, and whatever I thought was funny, I would put down on paper. And going back to the "what if" idea, I would put down what happened. And a lot of it I learned along the way. It started to turn into a curiosity because I started to get my own books on comedy. In theatre, for some reason, drama is king, and you're trying to be Oscar Wilde. I was drama all the way to Yale. I was known for writing drama and social criticism. And then I wrote a piece in New York called *Snapshots, An American Slide Show,* and it was done as part of a performance at Lincoln Center and Alice Tully Hall. I had to direct this thing, and I just said it was social commentary. I thought it was kind of funny, but I think the worst thing for a writer to hear is laughter. Live laughter.

JD: It's habit-forming.

WB: It's habit-forming. They roared, the audience roared, and then stood up and gave this standing ovation, and called me out on the stage and I took a bow with the actors. And I said, "Oh, this is good."

JD: Did Norman Lear mentor you?

WB: No, actually we worked together for a brief time on the show *704 Hauser.*
I've spent time with Bill Cosby. Cosby said, "Let me help you out here." And so he would talk about his take on comedy. I remember what he told me, he said, "Don't go for the joke," that's what he kept saying, "Don't go for the joke, go for what's real. If it's real, you can always build off of something that's real, but it's more difficult to

try to build off of a joke, because that's not real. And everybody sees, everybody laughs because they relate to it, it's something real to them."

A problem I had in the beginning was trying to emulate the joke I'd seen on television, and it wasn't very good. But when I started to learn, it's like Cosby was saying, it's real, it's real, keep these people real and you can keep coming back to the well.

JD: What are your feelings about Writing Rooms, and the politics of a Room?

WB: I like the Writers' Room; I hate the politics. When I first went to *The Cosby Show*, I came in, I had never written for a sitcom, never. In fact, it was embarrassing. I didn't know how a sitcom script lined up on the page. I only knew plays and screenplays. When I got the job, I told one of the writer's assistants, "Can you get me a script?" I said, "Okay, between you and I, I don't know what one looks like." And they laughed. What they said to me was, "Do you know what it's like to be at a table?" And this is my interview, and I go, "Ah . . . yeah, yeah . . ."

"No, no, no . . ." It's writers who sit around the table, and they explained it to me. And I went, "You mean like improv, you mean working off of somebody." And they went, "Yeah." And I said I could work off of somebody, I said, "We can really go back and forth, and whatever you say, it's true, and I just . . . it's like improv." And they hired me.

"Now it's counting jokes, how many they get in a script."

I really loved working off the other writers. It felt comfortable. That became like my strong suit. And I had three scripts my first job, which was pretty much unheard of. As a staff writer, from what I found out, you usually just sit and listen, and go write cold openings, or something like that. It was a great experience. And at that point, there was no politics, and I look back at my staff writer days and go, "Man, you could say you didn't know something, and people go, 'Oh, he's a staff writer.'" But as you move up into the ranks, those who want to be heard, those who, you know, how many scripts did this person get, versus this person? Who's the funny person at the table? You're no longer the new guy, where everyone can just laugh. Now it's counting jokes, how many they get in a script.

Another one, counting jokes, oh, making an incredible pitch, and everyone goes, "Oh, no, that's not it," and then someone else says the exact same thing that you said, and someone says, "That was brilliant," and then saying, "I just said that." "Oh, come on now, let's not get that way."

Some of the writers we interviewed for this book love the experience of the Writers' Room, while others, notably Michael Elias (see page 89), couldn't wait to break out and write alone. Everyone agrees that Rooms come in two categories: Functional, like the ones Yvette Bowser (see page 21) and Bob Myer (see page 141) ran; and extremely dysfunctional, like the ones Paul Chitlik and Marc Sheffler (see page 298) were trapped in.

Walter Bennett loves the collaborative nature of the Room and feels he grew from the process. However, his initial entry wasn't so smooth. He recalls being the new writer around the table and pitching a joke. It was greeted with silence. Later, a more experienced writer pitched the exact same joke later that day and everyone thought it was hysterical. When he pointed out this discrepancy, they said, "C'mon Walt, don't be that way." Compare this to Elliot Shoenman's experience on *Maude,* where Bob Schiller and Bob Weiskopf were his mentors, helping him out and guiding him—even after he ripped off a joke from *The Honeymooners,* a classic TV series. (See page 317 for Elliot's interview.)

It's crazy. The other thing that starts to happen is the money. Factions start on both staffs in the room, then it's, "Whenever they say a joke, don't laugh." I was on *The Cosby Show.* I was sitting at the table and we were working all these hours. One of our writers wore a tie all the time to the table and to work, and it's really a casual thing, and this is like two or three months in. We're working, and we're trying to find a button on the joke, or something like that, and one of the producer/writers looks across the table and goes, "Why the hell do you always wear that tie?" And I'm going, "Hmm," thinking, "Okay, maybe that's the way to go." Now I'm thinking about the joke. The other writer said, "Excuse me?" And she says, "Why the hell do you always wear that tie? I mean, here we are, everybody's casual, and you're wearing a tie."

And now suddenly my mind is going, "Oh, wait a minute, we're not on the script right here. We're having a moment here, over a tie." And they go, "Well, I don't care." And it escalated over this tie 'til the show runner pretty much had to say, "Okay, let's take a break." And everyone left the room. And again, that was my first job, so I'm sitting there at the table by myself going, "Did we just . . . was that . . . ?" So one of the writer's assistants comes in and says, "What happened?" I said, "I really don't know. There was a tie, she didn't like it, he asked what?" It's a wonder sometimes that good shows make it. There's a huge minefield. It's more that a show doesn't make, than makes, it, because of all the clashes in personalities and the politics.

PD: The family you came from, were they artistic?

WB: No. I come from a whole generation of teachers on my mother's side. My mother and father were divorced when I was seven years old, so I was basically raised by my mom, and my sister's a teacher. My sister taught in the same classroom she went to kindergarten in. And it was the original school that my mother taught in. And my grandmother taught. And her brother taught. And so when they said, "What do you want to do?" I would—we'd go in the basement and just pull out school supplies.

PD: Did they have a good sense of humor? Was there a lot of joking in the house?

WB: One thing that my mother as a teacher was really into was the arts, and she would take me to plays. We always went to Radio City [Music Hall]. I said, "Why are you taking me to these plays? This is something I will never, ever do! Why are you doing this to me?" And I don't know how, but she just knew.

An Interview with
Yvette Bowser

A partial list of Yvette Bowser's credits as a creator, show runner, and writer includes: *Living Single*, *A Different World*, *Half & Half*, and *Hangin' with Mr. Cooper*.

Imagine graduating from college and calling Bill Cosby for a writing job—and getting it. **Yvette Bowser** imagined it, did it, and has moved forward to create her own shows—and she did it their way. While many comedy writers struggle with the constraints of writing for network television, Yvette took on this challenge and won. She uses her background in psychology and political science to tap into the ebb and flow of everyday conflicts that have a universal theme, which enables her to make a statement without having to ruffle feathers and be edgy. While many writers deal with the outer 5 percent fringes of life to find their comedy, Yvette has gladly accepted the remaining 95 percent of life to draw her material from. She has made a career of tackling the situations that meet her criteria of being important, entertaining, and that go with the flow, rather than fighting to swim upstream. The result has been the creation of shows like *Living Single*.

PD (Peter Desberg): As we've explained in our Premise [see page 9], how would you go about developing the show's plot lines?

YB (Yvette Bowser): I would break down each of the characters and give them different attributes. *You want me to do that?!* Now you want me to do what I do over the course of weeks.

PD: Pick a character.

YB: I would start with Sarah. Obviously, she's the lead, she's the center. I would kind of break it down. I'd do a little list, what's her take on relationships, what's her take on financial success?

PD: So, give her some attributes.

YB: Well, I think relationships are very low on the totem pole for her. But I think that financial success is something that gives her a sense of worth, so I would write that down.

PD: So she defines herself by her financial status?

YB: Absolutely, financial status, I think, is important to her. I think that gives her a sense of worth because I think that's also something that she's come from. Sometimes people feel that way because they haven't come from means, but I think she's someone who's determined to kind of stay on par with where her parents raised her. But also, I would try to think of, well, where is she politically, in terms of her position? I think . . . she's a little bit of a conservative, which is also not that popular to be right now. But I think she's secure enough in herself that she would kind of go against the grain. She's still young, but I think she has very firm opinions.

She's going to protect her money. And as I said, I think her relationships are going to be kind of secondary. She's going to climb up the ladder as quickly as she can and secure her spot there. And then, whenever *he* fits in, she'll fit him into the picture. What else? Let's see.

PD: You're dimensionalizing the character first.

"If you have multi-dimensional characters, then the situations will come, because you always know what they will do in whatever scenario you give them."

YB: And that's what I do. If you have multi-dimensional characters, then the situations will come, because you always know what they will do in whatever scenario you give them. There are only a certain number of plots and certain curves that you can throw at these people, but if you know what they'll do, that's the thing that makes them unique. That's why we can have a hundred different family sitcoms, but they each have their own point of view, but the point of view comes from who those individual characters are, who those kids are, who their parents are, who their grandparents are.

PD: What other dimensions do you look at?

YB: What are some other dimensions? I mean, those are kind of the main ones. And then I usually do a list of quirks. Do they have any quirks? Are they superstitious? Are they kind of guided by their horoscopes? I also do where they are spiritually.

PD: So where do you place her?

YB: [*Spoken with a hint of sarcasm.*] Oh, this is so fun! You know, that's an interesting question. I'm not really sure. I don't have an immediate vibe on her. I think she'd like to live right. I'm sure she believes in God, but I'm not really sure if she follows the tenets of the Bible. How about that? Yeah, I think there's temptation, there's compromise, but I think her spiritual growth kind of keeps her on the most right path, which I think would create more comedic fodder. I think it kind of creates more comedic conflict, if you have that groundedness that's pulling you back, even though you want to do the wrong thing, even though you might want to do what's best for you.

PD: So when she's faced with a spiritual conflict—like, move ahead, but screw your friend over—what does she do?

YB: I think she tries to do the move ahead, without screwing the friend over, which may not be entirely possible.

PD: You end up with some great conflicts.

YB: Exactly, exactly. So that's kind of my model.

PD: What other quirks would you look for?

YB: I think she probably has a really bad sense of direction. There are people who are incredibly charming, or book smart, who just have no sense of direction. I know some of those people. There are a lot. There's a saying, "God does not give with both hands." And so I try to apply that pretty much to every character, you know, where they're strong in one area, I try to give them a weakness, you know, like a real crutch, in the other.

JD (Jeffrey Davis): What about the mother?

YB: Molly's a mess, because Molly's been spoiled. She's never had to do anything on her own. She's that character who would probably, in many ways, be very quickly labeled "the breakout," because she knows nothing. She knows nothing about taking care of herself. She doesn't know that much about being a mom, really, because I think she's really been just about herself, and her possessions, and her lifestyle, and her social status. So, in a way, the mother becomes the child, which is a very common dynamic. I'm not unfamiliar with that.

My mother's certainly not spoiled, but very often the children kind of rise above the parents, in terms of responsibility. Maybe that's really the way it should be. But again, you've got to find those things that are also universal about the dynamics, so I'm saying even though we might not all have a very kind of pampered and privileged mother, we would have a mother who needs us more than we ever thought our mother would need us. So that would be the universal dynamic. And then we'd get the comedy from the fact that there's this woman who's in her early fifties.

PD: That's universal, and really pulls any kind of audience in and says, "I resonate with that, I get that."

YB: Right, right, because that's what you've got to find. You've got to find your specifics for your situation, and know all the dimensions of all the characters, and then find what's universal in that. Why is it going to entertain anybody other than myself? That's the key. Why is what I'm doing going to be of interest to anyone but me and my family? "Here, everyone, read my script. Everybody in the kitchen, do you like it?"

JD: Where do you think that comes from?

YB: I try to put my degree to use. I have degrees in psychology and political science from Stanford. And so, life is very political, and how we deal with people is all very psychological and sociological, so I really try to observe people. Most people in my life circle are like, "Careful what you say around Yvette," because I always change the names to protect the guilty. So I don't really create that much. I really just take from life and put it down on paper. It's kind of my own admission to the world that I don't make that much up, I just really take my own observation and funnel it into concepts and story lines.

PD: What you really do is the hardest thing in life—to put all these elements together.

YB: Wow, I've done something difficult. It's actually the only way I know how to do it. And certainly the way I've succeeded, when I've succeeded. When I haven't succeeded, I actually can look at it and say, "You know what, there was something in here." Well, there's always the politics of it, and who wants a certain star in their show that you don't have for your project, but I think that where the concepts haven't totally stood up, it's where there was something that tried to be too quirky for its own good, or some central character who just wasn't relatable enough.

PD: You've found a way to hold people's interest, and that's a real gift. And then to be able to stitch them together.

YB: I really do perceive it as a gift. It's kind of like, okay, it's on loan, use it while you've still got it. You don't really know. And I think that's the thing that keeps me driven and hungry to do it, because I know it is a gift, and if you don't use it then you've really kind of wasted your time here on the planet.

PD: Would you do a little more with Molly like you did with Sarah?

YB: Molly is very much about the money. She also, I think, came from money and from privilege, and thought she married into it, and kind of did, but then only to discover that there wasn't enough of it to sustain her after her husband's passing. I think her ethical and moral lines are very fuzzy. I think there's very little she wouldn't do to get ahead, or put herself in a better financial or social position.

PD: So she's not really as spiritually grounded as her daughter.

YB: Right. I think her daughter's just more aware. She's just come up at a different time, and just has developed her own set of values from perhaps her college experience, and who her friends became then, and how she met different people from different socio-economic backgrounds. And I think that influenced Sarah, where Molly was kind of isolated, perhaps, more in the higher socio-economic background. So, she's fifty and she's broke.

Okay, I think it's really interesting, given her former social status, that she decides that her daughter's apartment is the perfect place for her. So again, that's one of the reasons I gave Sarah a certain amount of value on her finances and her career, because it is certainly where she came from, but her apartment's got to be certainly nice enough that Molly would say, "I'm setting up camp here." She's not living in some tenement somewhere. She's living in a really nice place. Otherwise, Molly would find another friend, a socialite, or someone who might take her in 'til she could figure out what she was going to do, how she was going to rewrite the will, or come up with something to turn around her financial circumstances. I think clearly, to a certain degree, she was in love with her husband, so when we talk about romance now, I think she was in love with her husband, but maybe more in love with his money. And now she'd like to find someone else so she could love his money, and maybe love him too. Which I think is very different from her daughter's approach, which is . . . she'd like to have her own money and then find real love, and if he happens to have money, then that can work out as well. I suggest it's easy to love a rich man. It really is.

JD: When you go in to pitch a show, do they want you to talk about the arc of the first season? Do they want you to go past the pilot and really talk to them about what you think people will be watching a year from now?

"I don't want to advance someone's social or financial status that far in the first season."

YB: I always do. Again, I start out very simply with what it is that I want to examine, or talk about in this series, and then what are the best group of characters to kind of approach that topic through, or with, and then I kind of come up with . . . I don't go on a pitch unless I have twenty story areas. Now, every show that I've sold thus far I probably have used, on average, six or seven of those twenty that I have when I go into the pitch. I've used six or seven of those twenty in the first season. By the time the series has come to its end, four or five years later, I probably have used all of them at some point. But you know what I'm saying, you can come up with a really funny story that you know already in your gut is a great episode, but it's not a Season One episode.

But when you're pitching a series and you're trying to sell it, just for them to know that you have a multitude of stories and places to go beyond Episode One, you don't really have to draw that line so hard for yourself because you also have to know where do you go beyond Season Two, and that's when you're working in production, that's what you figure out: What are all the Season One episodes? And I do a lot of talking to the staff about giving them feedback, when they're pitching me something, I'll be very clear about whether or not I feel that's actually a Season One, or Season Two episode, because sometimes people will pitch something, and you go, "That's like Season Five; we don't know these characters well enough." You know what I'm saying, I don't want to advance someone's social or financial status that far in the first season, because there are so many baby steps we can take to get great episodes out of. And I don't like to go in and pitch without those, because the worst thing I think that can happen to someone is that you sell an idea and you don't know what episodes two, three, four, five, and six are. That, to me, would be the scariest thing ever.

I hear people talk about it all the time: "I wrote this phenomenal pilot," and we see lots of great pilots, and I don't know how these people actually get a show on the air without having pitched, but somebody goes, "You know what, this is so bizarre, it's so quirky, it's so funny, it's a live-action cartoon, wow, it made me laugh so hard." But now what? You know what I'm saying? I just saw a pilot last week and thought, "This is a cute pilot, but I don't see this for five years," and I'm really intrigued to watch subsequent episodes, because I don't think they're going to do it. But if they pull it off, they're brilliant. But nine times out of ten, they won't pull it off. There really won't be a series. You know, you can see, sometimes they have . . . there are series that are developed and they have these great devices, and I can actually watch it and tell that the writers were getting very tired by Episode Three or Four, in trying to incorporate that device of telling the story backwards, and sideways, and trying to manipulate the form. There's a reason why a certain story structure has worked since the beginning of time. And it's not like it shouldn't be broken, but I really do feel like you need to know the structure, in order to break the structure in a way that works, you know, like the anti-structure.

JD: What would make us want to watch this as a series?

YB: I think this show could be an interesting exploration of where women are in the millennium, now trying to be executives in the ranks with men, as well as balance these multi-generational issues with our mothers, and perhaps our younger siblings. I might even give Sarah a younger sibling who is different from her, in terms of her desires and wants, and maybe more like her mother, and so she kind of finds herself in this sandwich. And just have it be a show about where we are as women, and where we've maybe taken on too much, and maybe where we need to take on more. Again, that would be like the seed of it.

And then there's also the grandmother, correct? There are the grandparents. So the grandmother, obviously, was probably a very '50s housewife, so she did what she was supposed to do in her little cubby, and they provided very well for this daughter, who had a very comfortable life, and then she married this man, and she had a comfortable, fabulous life, and never really learned to do much of anything for herself—but now Sarah's coming up at this time when women are really doing it for themselves, I mean, we can't have "the movement" be in vain. So we're trying to do it all. And then the question is, have we taken on too much, just as individuals, and then also as members of our family, because I think the family element is a really interesting element.

JD: If you didn't have to worry about any constraints from networks and you could do anything you wanted to give it the Bowser touch, what would you do?

"I wouldn't say, 'You know what, I just want to make it a cable show,' and suddenly she's naked."

YB: If there was one element I could put into it . . . just giving Sarah more dimension, and making her represent women like me as much as possible, in as many different facets of her life as possible, I mean, that would really be it. I wouldn't say, "You know what, I just want to make it a cable show," and suddenly she's naked. I think, for me personally, I pitched a show to cable and I think when I left I really wondered, "When they want to have these sex scenes, or certain kinds of things that go against my personal, spiritual grain, I don't know that I'm really ready to do this." I think maybe there'll be a time and a place, but I kept thinking, you know, when I'm ready to tell the secrets and stories yet untold. I've told so many stories on network TV, and then I pitched this idea to cable, and then I just thought, "Am I really ready for them to be naked?" I don't know. Or, whatever, same-sex scenes, or rough sex scenes, or any of the stuff that cable might impose on an idea, I don't know if that's really who I am.

"To me, there's a challenge in kind of keeping it clean, and knowing where those lines are for network television, and I think it's harder."

YB: . . . To me, there's a challenge in kind of keeping it clean, and knowing where those lines are for network television, and I think it's harder. I curse like a sailor sometimes, but I don't necessarily know that it's what I want to put in.

JD: So what problems do you find with the networks?

"Executives like to try to guide your vision too much."

YB: Executives like to try to guide your vision too much. This recent process that I've been involved in has been really pretty good. There's been very little tampering. But I do find that executives either have a sensibility that leads toward the extremely quirky, or toward the extremely conventional. If you give them a story that kind of *just* goes to the left of what they've seen before, they will almost always try to bring you back to that one story that they've seen a thousand times. And it worked twenty-five of those thousand times. But, it's not fresh. And actually, I find for myself, having been in the business now nineteen years, and then I've been a show creator and show runner for the last thirteen years, I probably challenge myself more than executives do, because I just have a strong desire to keep it fresh, to just make the material somehow new for myself. You have to go and sit in a room all by yourself and face your pad of paper, or face your computer, and it's like, "Blue Sky." I don't want to feel like I'm just writing the same thing I wrote and succeeded with thirteen years ago. I have to contribute to my own evolution, as a person and as a writer.

So, I have certainly done the pilot that focused on a young woman and her mother and the relationship ended in the pilot. We've seen it a thousand times, haven't we? So when writing another show that focuses on a young woman, I'm not opposed to having the story have something to do with her romantic life and the conflict there, but I just don't want to do: She's in a relationship, he breaks up with her, or he cheats on her, she discovers the pictures on the Internet, she discovers a text message, or something. I barely want to see it again, let alone write it. So it is mostly about keeping it fresh for myself, and thinking that, quite frankly, that's what the audience wants. The audience doesn't want to see the same old pilot again. It's not 1970, when we've only had twenty years of television. Now the audience has higher expectations. And they don't just want wacky, single-camera comedies that look like live-action cartoons, where people suspend each other from the tops of buildings. We still crave the basic humor and premise of *I Love Lucy*. Characters—and we know so purely what their motivation is, and we have our own expectation, and we're humored by our expectation of what they'll do, and we're also humored by their violation of our expectation of what they'll do.

Satellite radio offers several comedy channels, but only one of them is a clean one. Unless you listen to that clean one, you will never hear any material from Jerry Seinfeld. He is bright, creative, and often hostile. He's never dirty, and proud of it. If you read Leonard Stern's interview in this book (see page 361), you will be impressed by the way he avoids hostility while still creating conflict. Yvette Bowser is in this clean tradition. She is one of the few writers we've interviewed who enjoys taking on the challenge of working within network constraints without feeling like she has to compromise. She still manages to infuse her comedy with real characters working their way through real situations while still making serious psychological and sociological statements about contemporary culture.

PD: Using the "F" word, as a female writer, you've worked with lots of male writers. How was that experience?

"I called my agent, I said, 'Get me off this plantation.' . . . I wasn't going to allow them to put me in a little cubby."

YB: Well, let's see, I'm not only the "F" word, I'm the "B" word, which is Black. So my experience is again, the double minority, which I decided to take what could be a double negative and make it into a double positive, and have made very much a career out of that. I have certainly experienced sexism along the way, and racism along the way. And it wasn't necessarily covert racism. But the inequities that I experienced really drove me to create my own show.

I was on one show, and I called my agent, I said, "Get me off this plantation." They didn't know what they were doing. And they were treating me badly, (a) because I was a girl, and (b) because I was Black. And I had come from a very nurturing environment, where what I had to say as a woman and, particularly as a Black woman who was just out of college, was very relevant to the show that I was working on, which was *A Different World,* and I earned my way into those ranks and I earned my way onto my next job, but [at my next job] I wasn't treated as though I belonged there, and I wasn't going to allow them to put me in a little cubby. It was a reality check for me because I felt like, wow, I spent the first five years of my career in this very kind of insulated and unique situation. Bill Cosby was at the helm, and it was female-friendly, and it was African-American friendly, and it was also a situation where it welcomed people who were intelligent.

And I think the next situation I was in was just the antithesis of that, where they resented that I had lived life as a Black person and dared to offer some things that might be culturally specific but weren't necessarily alienating, but were like, could be fun—a little bit of vernacular here, a wardrobe suggestion there. I'm not like a hip-hop person, so trust me, when I'm talking about vernacular, it's like phrases like, "busting suds," I think they use it in the Navy . . . you're washing dishes. So I would be told things like that, and everyone in the room would laugh whenever the punch line was about "busting suds," and then the show runner would go, "Hmm, no, I don't think so."

"Really? Well, everybody laughed."

"No, look who laughed," indicating the other two Black people in the room at the time, who were baby, baby writers, and here I was coming off the number-two television show, as one of the top two writers on that show. So I'm like, I know that I've written things that millions of people have watched and plugged into, so I'm not sure who you are, or what you've worked on, but I just pitched something that everyone in the room laughed at, not just the Black people. So that's why I had to call my agent and tell him to "get me off this plantation." So anyway, that's when I started pursuing development very aggressively, because I felt like if that particular situation was much more reflective of standard Hollywood experience, I wasn't going to last long. I was not going to be long for this business.

PD: I had a friend named Isabel, born in Mexico, college professor . . . she had a lot of trouble with her young, male Latino students, being a female Latina telling them what to do. When you became a show runner and then a creator, was it sometimes difficult to be the boss?

"I think there's been a fine line between 'teacher' and 'mentor.'"

YB: You know, it's interesting, because I think I've always tried to be a really good mentor to people, and I think there's been a fine line between "teacher" and "mentor," but I think mentor is a little bit more like, "I'm trying to help you be my equal," as opposed to, "I'm teaching you something that you need to know, little person," so I think that's probably the difference. And I haven't really had problems. Let me tell you about the biggest problem I had in my first season of running a show. I was twenty-seven years old. I'd never run a show before. I assigned a show runner, a guy who'd worked on a show that was a well-oiled machine, and he and his partner ran the show in Seasons Ten and Eleven. So he had no knowledge of how to start a show, and really how to run a show, because it was already kind of all in place for him. It was like he'd inherited it. So it was a real trial by fire, so somehow the report was I made it look easy. So by the spring of that first season, three-quarters of my staff was actually developing their own show, so I'm sitting in a room with three people, "Hi, everyone, let's crank out these last six episodes," because people were like, "It was so much fun, and you made it look easy, and I have no idea what I did."

"It's a lottery, and you just have to pray that they call your number."

YB: You've got to have stick-to-it-iv-ness and luck. It's a lottery. So each time I sell a concept, a script, or shoot a pilot, I just always have to remember in the back of my mind, "It's a lottery, and you just have to pray that they call your number."

JD: I'm assuming that Bill Cosby mentored you.

YB: You imagined that.

JD: So were you mentored?

YB: Truly, no. Interesting. I'm a weirdo, in that sense. I tend to try to be a lot of things that I wish I had had coming up. That's kind of been my approach to life. Neither of my parents went to college. I made a point to go. They couldn't, for various reasons. My mother had to drop out, actually, two years in. So I was the first person in my family to graduate from college, and I didn't really have mentors. I had people who were in place who could have certainly mentored me, but they were a little preoccupied with kind of finding their own niche at the time. So no one really [said], "Okay, come under my wing, little one, I'm going to show you what's behind the curtain." That really wasn't there for me. Opportunities were made available to me through Bill Cosby and several of the writers who were on *A Different World* that year. But there were enough things that were done to me during that hazing time, that pledging, pay-your-dues time, that I would say totally counter-balanced any one act of mentorship that any one of them might actually think they provided me. So I do feel very much like I was mentorless. I'm not saying I was friendless, but I was mentorless.

JD: You were hazed? Without mentioning any names, do you have a story about being hazed?

YB: Here's an interesting one. I'm twenty-two years old, "Doctor" Cosby sends us on a research trip to Atlanta, right around the time, kind of still within that window of time, where the whole Atlanta murders thing was happening. And I'd never been to this city before, and I wasn't a baby, but I was still a young woman. So, myself, and my two would-be mentors were sent on a research trip, and the two of them, one about five years older, and the other about fifteen years older than I, we all met up at the airport 'cause we took different flights in, and one other female and myself arrive at the same time, and our older writer friend, who was a guy, came in a car and picked her up at the airport, and they left me at the airport to get a cab to the same hotel. What?! Now here I am in the City of Death. I thought that was pretty cold. "Fend for yourself, Kiddo!" I also happened to be the poorest one of the bunch. If I have to use my little stipend for the cab, then I guess I'll eat tomatoes for dinner. That was interesting. That was very telling. It was kind of like, I still respected them completely as writers and as people, but I also knew that I had me, me, and only me, to rely on to get wherever I was going next. I mean, to get wherever you're going next. It's all on you.

"... I begged Cosby for a job. 'I'll get coffee,
I'll get sandwiches, I'll do whatever I have to do,'
just to see what it is, because I didn't even
know what writing for TV was."

PD: You get out of college as a psych major, how do you make this transition into comedy?

YB: Once upon a time, I lived somewhere right around these parts in a building where our neighbor was a really good friend of Mister Cosby's. So during my senior year of college, I was having a "pity party" with my best friend, and we were watching *The Cosby Show*, and I saw the name of that person on the credits, and I tracked him down. And it just so happened that he was on his way to the Bay Area to do some music for a movie that Cosby was shooting in Oakland, and we met up on the set and I begged Cosby for a job. "I'll get coffee, I'll get sandwiches, I'll do whatever I have to do," just to see what it is, because I didn't even know what writing for TV was.

PD: Have you always had a good sense of humor?

YB: Yeah, I mean, I wasn't voted Class Clown, but yeah, I think so, I think people have found me amusing, so I just decided, "Oh, then I must be." But I don't kind of hold myself out as like the funniest person, and I try to really have a diversified staff, when I'm staffing a show, and I try to make myself *not* the funniest person in the room, because that's a lot of pressure. I try to find people who I think are actually funnier than I am, smarter than I am. I try to always find someone who knows TV history better than I do, because I like to have people in the room who knew, "You know what, they did that on *The Mary Tyler Moore Show*," "You know, that was in an *I Love Lucy* episode, and let me tell you how it went," so we can go, "Oh, okay, how do we make this situation work for us?" and not . . . because there are staffs where they'll sit around and talk about, "Okay, what retread can we do this week?" And that just drives me nuts.

PD: Did you learn all your comedy writing craft on the job?

YB: Yeah, on the job, just watching other people do it, seeing how they did it. Again, part of that hazing process that first year of being an apprentice was contributing ideas for characters and story lines, and actual episodes that other people ended up writing and putting their names on, that had actually been generated by me. So once I saw that I could do it, that I was actually doing it, like, I was saying it, and the writer's assistant was writing it down, and then the actors were saying it, I realized, "Oh, I have a gift for this." And basically, again, I went back and spoke at the Stanford graduation, and I realized, "I'm sorry, gang, I've told all your stories on my show." It was a hugely popular show back at Stanford, because, particularly, the Black community had seen a lot of their stories told. We had some Black sorority and fraternity stories, and things like that, and people were like, "We know who was doing that."

JD: What was it like working with Queen Latifah on *Living Single,* particularly because she didn't come in with an acting background?

"... she was wielding a spoon on the stage like a scepter..."

YB: But she was a big star in the rap world. She was a personality and she's always been larger than life. She was very cool. In 118 episodes, there were probably two instances when I felt like, "Oh, gosh, I have to go face 'The Queen,' and it's not going to be easy because I'm strong, and she's strong, and I don't think she's going to necessarily fold on this one, and I know I'm not going to fold on this one, so I've got to find some compromise." And I remained open, and she remained open the whole time. There was one day when she was wielding a spoon on the stage like a scepter, and the whole cast was just not happy with a particular scene, and I think they weren't sure because they were all still so green. They weren't sure how they could just express their frustration and get some response to their concerns.

PD: I get the sense that when you say you're strong, it doesn't come from a place of ego; you approached it with reason and said, "And here's why."

YB: Absolutely. I don't respond to people who try to shove their agenda down my throat, so I wouldn't imagine that someone would respond well to that being my approach.

JD: Have you ever backed down on a piece of writing, something you felt should go into a show, and then later said, "Shouldn't have done that."

YB: Maybe where the network was concerned, but I don't really think so. Well, they're the people paying the bills, and at the end of the day, particularly when you're doing a pilot, if you don't kind of take the notes, find a way to make them your own, and really at least convince them that you're giving them what they've asked for, you'll be sitting at home watching your pilot in your robe.

PD: Some of the writers we spoke to haven't shared your eagerness to work with networks. Some came right out and said, "I will never write something again if I can't produce or direct it." And still others have said, "I'm just so tired of having to have my outline approved, and then my story approved, and the characters approved," and you were saying that's part of the challenge.

YB: I think people forget the salesman part of the job, and that's part of it. Unless you're paying for it yourself, when someone else is paying for it, you have an obligation to sell it to them . . . and you just continue to sell them on your point of view, on your approach to a given story, and your approach to a particular scene. That's part of the job, and I think people forget that. And it's one of the things that we're teaching people in the show runner's training program that we've started at the Writers Guild a year ago. We just started our second session . . . a big leap from being a writer to being a manager, which also includes being a salesperson.

They're really separate skills. And I do feel I've been blessed with both. I'm a pretty good writer. And I feel like I'm a really, really good manager. And I don't know if I'm better at one than the other, but I know once the writing really gets started, the production really gets started, there's a lot more to manage. My approach has also changed over the years, because the first year of *Living Single,* I took home every script, and every script went through my typewriter, which was a computer at the time. It's evolved, but we still say that.

But now I have a husband and two children, and I'm always on a show, or developing a show, or on a show and developing three shows. And I also feel much more comfortable financially, and so, where the staff is like, "Are we going to get two scripts, are we going to get three scripts apiece, are we going to get one script?" I'm just like, you know what, I'm not going to take five episodes for myself, because there are people on that staff who really need that money to sustain them through the hiatus, and it's not as significant to me, as it was way back then, where I was like, "Omigod, I may never make money again. Let me make as much as I can." Even when I was taking the scripts home the first season of *Living Single,* I wasn't putting my name on them. I created the show. And so I just wanted to make sure that the voice was consistent. It worked out, so, that for me, it was the thing to do at that time. I feel now, I can more clearly articulate to my staff early on what it is that I want them to put in their drafts, so I feel much more at ease and less pressured to take it home and write it all.

JD: Do you bring in some freelancers to see if they have any fresh ideas?

YB: We do bring in freelancers, the Writers Guild requires it, at least two. And I try to use four or five a year. The thing is that usually, you hire someone who is very talented that you can't put on staff, and you hire them as a writer's assistant, because they're still coming up, and then you give a couple of those scripts to your writer's assistant. That's happening more and more, and I certainly have done that, but they're not on staff. It's a way to grow writers.

It's really nurturing writers' positions, but we also use friends. I've worked with writers who are on staff, or just temporarily out of work, or whatever. Yeah, people need to keep their insurance. It's interesting because as salaries seem to have been cut back, the staff does get a little bit more antsy when they're not getting two and three assignments each. Then you just have to have that conversation, where your moral and ethical standards come into play, and you say, "You know what, you guys have a check every week. These other people are going to lose their insurance, so some of you are not going to get three episodes this year, because we're going to give them to people who need the money, people who need the insurance."

JD: Stephen Sondheim suggests the more specific something is, ironically, the more universal it will be. Do you find that in your work?

YB: I do. I completely find that to be true. Unless it gets to be *so* inside some specific dynamic. There was a show on TV recently, which I actually thought had an interesting pilot, and it dealt with people who were in therapy, but as the series developed, the people who were in therapy, their issues, or their neuroses became so unrelatable to me that I disconnected. But what was relatable to me initially was, there was a group of human beings who had very different circumstances, but who were somehow bound together and looking to each other for help, and then it just went in a different direction. So I saw a tremendous potential from the pilot, but it wasn't really fleshed out in the series.

PD: You take a story and make it pass a litmus test of universality.

YB: Right, it's like the core values have to be universal, so that you're not just writing it for yourself. It can come in so many ways. The show *24* is a show that everybody, from its inception, was saying, "Omigosh, we can't miss an episode." And I kept saying, "I refuse to watch it, because it sounds really good, and I'm going to get addicted, I can't afford another hour of TV." And this year I watched Seasons One to Five, and I am a complete junkie even though the situations are ridiculous, they're preposterous, and yet on an emotional level they pull me in every week. There's something there that I can see myself in that set of circumstances. I get passionate about what's going on. And there's a formula. I know when Jack Bauer's going to say, "You're lying." I know it. I know when it's coming, and yet it still grips me.

PD: Talking about formulas . . . you have a very precise paradigm for how you go about writing, dimensionalizing the characters . . . has that evolved much over the years? Has it been pretty constant, or do you keep adding wrinkles and changing it?

YB: I say, "If it ain't broke, don't fix it." So, no, I haven't changed it much. I really start out with my list of things. I can also go beyond the romantic, and the spiritual, and the financial, and the political. What do they think of holidays? Any topic. Sometimes I'll take headlines from the news and say, "How does this character feel about this? How would this news article play out in this situation?" Just to see if I have enough different points of view in a series idea.

For example, I like to dress down when I go shopping in Beverly Hills, just to see how the salespeople treat me. And the ones who treat me right, I give them my business with my black American Express card, and those who don't, I don't patronize them. It's my little game. And I wrote an episode about it on *A Different World*, and, actually, we got a Humanitas Award for that one.

An Interview with
David Breckman

A partial list of David Breckman's credits as a writer and executive producer includes: *Monk, Saturday Night Live, Pic Six, Underfunded,* and *Pulled Over.*

Unlike some of the other writers in this book, David Breckman never had to worry about showing up at the breakfast table with a zinger. He grew up in a supportive environment where books were treasured and humor was gold. He spent "forty-five minutes" attending college and then began his real education. He signed up for courses with Woody Allen, Monty Python, and his older brother Andy Breckman, who preceded him on *Saturday Night Live* by ten years, and who David calls "the funniest man alive." He funded his education by earning as he was learning.

David Breckman has an innate sense of what's funny, but is uncompromising in his pursuit of what makes a story work. As he develops this Premise, he moves from a wide view to something very specific that tips toward the dark side of the color spectrum without diminishing the commercial aspects of his project.

PD (Peter Desberg): As we've explained in our Premise [see page 9], how would you go about developing the show's plot lines?

DB (David Breckman): Well, my first-blush reaction is that it's clearly a sitcom. The Premise is great for a sitcom because it's loose. Sitcoms are primarily about the characters, and then each individual episode can be very tightly written, and very premise-driven. But the premise of the show itself is typically very loose. *Seinfeld* is just a bunch of neurotic New Yorkers hanging out and having adventures. I don't agree that show was about nothing, because, particularly in the later years, it was the most plot-driven show of all time. Often, there were three plots going on simultaneously and they would all dovetail at the end. The whole thing about the show about nothing, that was true for the first year or two.

I would want to do Molly and Sarah's story as a feature, but with a feature you'd have to have a very specific log line. Molly, who's lost her husband, and perhaps lost her anchor and is probably, to some degree, rudderless now and also is struggling with the idea of being middle-aged, maybe starts competing with her daughter Sarah who she's just moved in with, for the attentions of a guy. I don't know who that would be, but that's another way to go with it. And that's something that certainly, I think, a lot of people, myself included, can relate to: The fact that we're trying to hold on to our youth, and are feeling threatened by every succeeding generation.

PD: They've got a whole new category for these women. They call them "cougars."

DB: That would certainly inform this idea. You could do it as a feature where you could . . . just the idea of a woman, it'd be more compelling: Molly the mother was the heavy, and doing it from Sarah's point of view. Sarah would be faced with the prospect of having her own mother competing with her, and indeed, trying to undermine her, as they're competing for the attentions of a guy. And it could be funny, but there's also something heartbreaking about it, knowing that your own mother is sabotaging your efforts at seducing or romancing this guy. And there could be scenes with Sarah as this realization first dawns on her, as it's first sinking in: "Holy crap, the tires on my car were slashed. I couldn't figure out who would do that. I thought it was my creepy neighbor, Jack, but I think I'm seeing evidence now. I think it was my mother."

So, that kind of dawning realization would be harrowing. Your "frenemy" is your mother, of all things. So that's another way to go. But one problem—one of the reoccurring flaws of that premise—is that although mothers and daughters traditionally are at odds with each other, I don't think this situation I'm describing happens very often. So I don't know if there's a lot of relate-ability there. You can talk about a mother being stifling, you can talk about a mother being smothering or intrusive, but a mother sabotaging you, and whatever the female equivalent of "cock-blocking" is in your efforts to romance a guy—well, God forbid, if it happened. But I do think it's a funny way of going.

PD: It's a funny idea. I'm just thinking Molly has convinced herself this guy's not really right for her daughter.

DB: That's great. That's great. She could be rationalizing these atrocious things she's doing. Because even people who do the most dastardly things don't ever think of themselves as evil. No one thinks that what they're doing is malicious. They're always rationalizing everything they do. Stalin, Hitler. Rationalizing everything. Rationalizing everything and so, yes, I guess both parties would feel justified in what they're doing, although Sarah, I think, with a lot more justice.

If this is a feature, the central character is Sarah coming to terms with the fact that she is competing with her mother for the attention of a guy. Or a job. Her mother moves to town and throws her hat in the ring for the same job Sarah's going for. Molly starts sabotaging her. And then there could be a guy at the company they can both be competing for. This is an easy way. What if it's the boss? I guess the basis of the story would be realizing that you have to compete with your mother. Which is alternately funny and harrowing. How outrageous can I get?

JD: (Jeffrey Davis): As outrageous as you like.

"'My mother might be a c–nt.'"

DB: At a certain point, Sarah could say to her best friend, "Omigod, my mother's sabotaging me," which is a bitter pill to swallow because your psyche is denying this the whole time. "Okay, she's going out with Ted. I love Ted, but she's dating him and she's spending the night at his chalet. I'm sure with the best of intentions. Just wait a minute, I'm sure she had a reason, but she slashed my tires. But I'm sure it was with the best of intentions." At a certain point, all of her defenses would be down; the fire-walls have been penetrated, and there's just no conclusion left except, "My mother might be a c–nt." Which, in a sense, makes this almost a horror movie.

Yeah, I think that might be the way to go with it, and it would just be sort of this creeping realization. I don't quite have a resolution for that. There's any number of ways. Focus groups would probably want a comeuppance for the mother, but then it also depends on what studio you're doing it for. There might be a reconciliation of sorts.

PD: You can also come up with three or four endings.

DB: Right, which is sort of how it's being done now. They ultimately end up with three or four. The focus audiences will reject the first ending, and the studio will very hastily demand a new ending, and they'll re-shoot the last ten or fifteen minutes. And typically, the new ending is much blander and more by-the-numbers and unsatisfying.

PD: Composers have false cadences where you think you're going to the ending, but they're setting up for a different ending.

DB: That's my favorite kind of storytelling. It should be the goal of any ending. It should be satisfying, but surprising at the same time. That's a difficult nexus to find. But you're right; ideally, you're going for something like that. What you end up with is something usually much more unsurprising, unfortunately, and cliché.

PD: How would you handle the question of the mother's likability?

DB: You'd have to decide if you want the mother to have a tenable argument. You'd have to decide if the audience would be called upon to sympathize with Molly. I don't know if that would make for as entertaining a movie. If it was more from Sarah's point of view, the mother could be more of a heavy, and you wouldn't have to make her as likable. As a writer, I'm inclined to make it about Sarah, and to make the mother this villain, which I think is just more interesting. But maybe if you wanted to attract Jessica Lange, or some really talented fifty-something actress, you'd have to end up making the mom more sympathetic, which frankly, I'll say, for me, just won't be as fun. If you're talking about a fun ninety minutes, this should be a perverse sort of horror movie. But instead of, "Oh, my God, my mother is a werewolf," it's, "Oh, my God, my mother is a bitch!" And so to keep this as entertaining as it can be, I would not feel obligated to make Molly sympathetic.

The other thing is this: Sarah we like. She's your protagonist. You would like her. I'm not a marketing person, but I suspect that young women, twenty-something girls, would really spark to the idea of a woman who is at odds and fighting for her life against her mother. Of course we'd be pandering, but . . .

PD: You've come up with some very good film "noirish" dark comedy elements. Is that something that interests you?

DB: It's funny you should say that. One spec I wrote a long time ago and I'm retooling is actually a dark comedy. It's a riff on the Hitchcockian premise of the innocent man falsely accused, and then having to go on the run and establish his innocence. *North by Northwest* is a classic example of that, but Hitchcock did that a lot. He did it in a movie called *Saboteur*. He remade that movie at least three or four times.

I tried to think of what would be the most horrible thing you could be accused of, but still maintaining a comedic tone, that you would then have to establish you were innocent of. And it occurred to me that if there was a spate of killing of grandmothers—in America, we love mothers, but we *really* love grandmothers. So if you were accused of that crime, and the people that were framing you . . . in my story, this guy is being meticulously framed. It looks for all the world like he's doing it. The cops show up at his apartment when he's not there and they find five dead old women on the floor. And they were summoned there because of a phone call that he apparently made. The cops had his voice coming from his apartment. They come in and find five dead grandmothers on his carpet. It looks very incriminating. Think David Schwimmer in the first couple seasons of *Friends*. "I did *not* do this. I am not the grandmother killer." But no one believes him. And this guy would never survive eleven minutes in prison because a lot of convicts were raised by their grandmothers. So he escapes his captors and he goes on the run, and he's trying to find out who's doing this, who's setting him up, who framed him. So that, I think, falls under the heading of "dark comedy."

But like we do with *Monk*, I want the mystery elements to make sense. It shouldn't just be an excuse to have gags; hopefully, the comedy works. But the mystery should make sense. One of my favorite movies is *Silver Streak,* which is a really good comedy-thriller.

PD: How would you take those elements and integrate them into Sarah and Molly's story?

"The more perverse part of me, which is the dominant part of me, thinks you can't go far enough."

DB: Well, this is not a thriller. Hopefully there'd be moments of suspense, I think it's dark comedy, but not a thriller. It has that sort of an "enemy within" feel. You don't know how far the mother will go. You'd have to decide how far you'd want this mother to go and exactly what she's willing to do. The more perverse part of me, which is the dominant part of me, thinks you can't go far enough. Molly would *literally* end up ruining Sarah's life to get what she wants. But then you are limiting yourself, as far as your wrap-up or resolution is concerned. You can't have reconciliation at the end, and to have them hug and everything's forgotten, as you roll the credits.

But if you were to explore that aspect, you could have the mother ruining her daughter's life. Near the end of the film, the end of the second act, where the main character is typically at a low point. God forgive me for breaking out the Robert McKee algebra, because you can't reduce it to calculus. But one problem is every executive has taken these courses and believes this stuff like it's the Talmud. So they talk in these terms. At these meetings, they say, "Tell me your inciting incident, what's your page 30 incident?" And you just want to say, "It's not algebra!" Thank God, because I failed algebra. But if you were to borrow that template, Sarah's low point would have to be where she's completely undone. She would have to be out of work. Her relationship with the guy, we'll make him Dermot Mulroney, is in shambles.

PD: Would Sarah figure out it was Molly?

DB: Oh yeah, absolutely, by the end of Act Two. Without question. She knows, but there's nothing she can do about it. She's impotent at that point. She knows. And then in Act Three, she strikes back. And in Act Three, the wrap-up is some kind of public comeuppance. I don't know what that would be yet. The easier way, almost a

When David Breckman says, "God forgive me for breaking out the Robert McKee algebra," he is talking about screenwriting coach Robert McKee. But he's really referring to the legions of books, coaches, and courses that provide templates for screenplays in general. They proclaim rules about what should occur by what page number in every script. These "experts" have created the fiction that creativity has strict rules and that there is a one-size-fits-all method for writing movies in general, and comedies in particular. This book, through the interviews, shows the fallacy in this kind of thinking. David laments that too many movie executives have read one or two of these books and, he says, "believe this stuff like it's the Talmud."

Let's just say the cast consists of Reese Witherspoon, Dermot Mulroney, and Jessica Lange. So, what if Dermot Mulroney has a schnauzer? Dermot Mulroney hates Reese because it looks for all the world like she backed over the dog in her car and killed it. Of course, it was Jessica Lange who did it. Jessica Lange undermined Reese Witherspoon at work and took credit for it. And she's the one who came up with the new account at the advertising firm where they both work.

cliché, is some kind of a videotape of Mom being thrown up on a jumbotron in a public place. We would see this compromising thing that would undo the mother entirely. It would expose her as a fraud . . . the monster that she is. And it would vindicate Reese [Sarah]. And of course it would reestablish Reese in Dermot Mulroney's good graces and allow her to get her job back. But that's kind of a cliché, but maybe for commercial purposes, the best way to go. I don't know what that footage of Mom on the jumbotron would look like.

PD: When you say that, where would you take it instead?

DB: I'm not sure that the public comeuppance scene is necessarily awful if it was clever and surprising. If it was just entertaining, that could be great. I guess we'd have some fun lunches just trying to talk about what that climax would involve.

PD: One of the things you alluded to before; you could try and find a resolution in this idea: Jessica [Molly] turns out to be okay. It was all a huge misunderstanding.

DB: Right, but you'd have to soften all of her actions that precede that moment. She can't, at least intentionally, completely ruin her daughter's life that way. The problem with that is if she does it unintentionally, and she's aware of it, and doesn't do anything to make restitution or to put the pieces back together, then she's a monster. So what you have to do then if she's doing it intentionally—and that's the only way it's interesting to me, if she's doing it intentionally—and you want some kind of reconciliation, then you've got to soften the actions and whatever she's doing prior to that. It just can't be as extreme. It's more of a subtler, nuanced James L. Brooks kind of comedy. Your way is less broad, which may not be the worst thing.

I think my taste, probably because of my background as a sketch writer, tends to run toward broad comedy, and I tend to take things to extremes. I think there's less of an appetite for that, at least among executives. Most people, certainly directors like Mike Nichols and James L. Brooks, would want something that's more grounded in reality.

PD: What if Molly did the wrong thing, thinking it was the right thing, and then being reeducated?

DB: Then you're imposing restraints on your character's behavior. You can talk about reeducation, but again, that only works if the mother's behavior is more moderate. And I don't know what she'd be doing, unwittingly or half-unwittingly. I think doing intentional harm is less commercial, but I think it might be funnier and more satisfying.

PD: Maybe it is commercial. Earlier you mentioned this twenty-something demographic: "My parents are my antagonists."

DB: I wish you guys were running Warner Brothers. Yeah, it's relatable to some degree. But again the overriding question is still, how restrained is the behavior of the mother? Is her behavior moderate? Is she unwitting in her behavior, or is this calculated? Does she know what she's doing, and is she truly trying to sabotage her daughter's life?

PD: If you said, okay, the things she did were a little more on the benign side, what would it be?

DB: Well, if you want benign, you want to talk to someone else. Where do you go from tire slasher and dog killer? But some of the more outrageous things might be if Jessica Lange is trying to undermine Reese Witherspoon's nascent relationship with Dermot Mulroney, she can, a la Iago, place things in Dermot's line of vision. It's far more persuasive if the person you're trying to con or dupe appears to discover them for himself. If I tell you that something is amiss, you might believe me; you might not. But if you seem to uncover that on your own, you're more apt to believe it. So I would have Jessica Lange leaving evidence for Dermot Mulroney to discover that Reese Witherspoon has chlamydia.

JD: Do you think Molly is insane?

DB: It almost meets the definition of a sociopath. "My mother is a sociopath. The wrong parent died."

PD: The new term for it is "antisocial personality."

DB: That just doesn't have the same ring to it as, "My mother is David Berkowitz." The movie would be a continuous campaign of undermining Reese Witherspoon.

PD: I like the insidiousness of it. Leaving just enough evidence to create a doubt.

"If you guys haven't read anything by this guy Shakespeare, you should. He's really good."

DB: So the other person is convinced of it. Like the handkerchief in *Othello*. If you guys haven't read anything by this guy Shakespeare, you should. He's really good. What's so great about Iago? What's great is that Iago is brilliant. He sticks up for Cassio a little bit. He sticks up for the guy he's undermining. He's saying, "I'm telling you, Cassio is a great guy. He would never have done what you say. He would never have done that." And, of course, this raises Othello's suspicions. "What are you talking about? What did he do?" Iago says, "It doesn't matter. He's a great guy. Forget I said anything. Let's play cards."

"No, go back to what you said about Cassio."

And so, what would be very insidious would be if Jessica Lange was pretending to stick up for her daughter vociferously, just saying to Dermot, "My daughter is great. This thing about this positive lab slip she got, tear it up, it means nothing."

"What positive lab slip?"

"You didn't hear?"

"No, I didn't hear that."

"Doesn't even matter. Nothing. No positive lab slip. My daughter is great."

That's always more interesting to me. So not only is she undermining her, she's pretending to stick up for her. This makes her evil, and, to me, interesting. And so . . . that would be the mother's campaign. A campaign of terror.

"I didn't finish college; I didn't quite have the temperament for college. I went to Wagner College for forty-five minutes."

JD: Tell us a little bit about how you started.

DB: I started in the '90s. I didn't finish college; I didn't quite have the temperament for college. I went to Wagner College for forty-five minutes. I guess I was kind of a depressive sort. So I was just knocking around, doing odd jobs and minimum wage jobs throughout my twenties. But I always wanted to write and I always loved film and was working at a South Jersey bistro working in the kitchen, making salads and mopping the floor and writing as much as I could in my spare time. I was just trying to learn how to do it, teaching myself the craft. At that time I was working on a screenplay, and also writing sketch comedy.

My brother wrote for *Saturday Night Live* in the '80s and introduced me to Jim Downey after I'd written a lot of sketches and tried to send them in without any agent's letterhead. And, of course, I was roundly rejected. I got frustrated because I thought the sketches I was writing were pretty good. I managed to get them to Jim Downey, who has been with *SNL* since '77. He's a brilliant comedy writer, one of the best ever, and was one of the first ones to storm the beaches, and set up a beachhead for other guys like him coming out of the *Harvard Lampoon*.

He liked what I gave him and he asked for more. He recommended me to a couple of the producers there who wanted to see more work, and then there was a round of interviews. After several months I ended up on staff there in '96. So I'd gone from working in the back of a restaurant in South Jersey, to writing at *SNL*, which was great, and also terrible. Again, I refer to this as the best and worst job I've ever had; it was just alternatively wonderful and harrowing.

"Dennis Miller has compared *SNL* to Gladiator School."

Dennis Miller has compared *SNL* to Gladiator School. And if you've ever worked there, you'll know that's an understatement. It's fiercely competitive. It's twenty writers competing for a certain number of slots every week. When I was there, it was even harder because of those eight or nine sketches that were available, most of them were being filled with sketches that featured recurring characters. The Cheerleaders, The Ladies' Man, and Mary Catherine Gallagher. Because Lorne Michaels had been spinning these characters off into feature films, and it was lucrative for a while.

But I'm saying as far as sketches are concerned, I like Pythonesque, premise-driven sketches. That's just what I've always loved and what I've always written. But there was only room for one or two of those per week. As a rookie writer, I was being held to one sketch per week. I could turn in one sketch every week. So it was very difficult, but it was also equally educational and instructive and because it was so competitive, I'm now ready for anything.

PD: Did people work together?

DB: Yes, a lot of time they did. I was kind of writing on my own, which on reflection, may have been a mistake. But I don't regret it, because the kind of sketches I was writing are the only kind of sketches I like to watch.

PD: Once you came in with a sketch that they liked, would other people work on it with you?

DB: The sketches were rewritten collectively, usually on Thursdays around the big table.

PD: How was the rewriting process for you on *SNL*?

DB: Frustrating, of course, but generally the sketches got better. But you did lose the singular voice that you had going in, which is always unfortunate, I think. But there were very talented people there, so the sketches got better. And I did some things I was proud of. And the only reason we're talking now is because I was at *SNL,* and that led to other things, and I have a career because of it. So I have no regrets. But, again, it was a nerve-racking year. I suspect a lot of writers who worked there would say much the same thing.

PD: Were you a funny kid growing up?

DB: I always tried to be. It was sort of my default setting. I wasn't always successful. I don't know, you hear these stories. When you were sitting around the table, you were jockeying for attention and you always hear kind of the same story. If you weren't fast with a zinger, boy, you were in trouble. It wasn't like that; it really wasn't. Thank God. It would've been terrifying, just waking up in the morning, "Do I have a zinger for breakfast? Holy f–ck, I'm a dead man." That would've been terrifying. But I wasn't a very happy kid, and I think that's almost a prerequisite for getting into this business.

JD: Were you mentored?

DB: By my brother, Andy Breckman, who was and remains the funniest guy I've ever met. He is eleven years older than me. Certainly he mentored me during the eight years I've been on *Monk.* We never worked together before the show. But he's the show runner, he created the show, and I've learned as much about writing from him as from anyone, particularly comedy writing. He didn't set out to do that. It wasn't like a tutorial, but just through osmosis, just watching him work.

PD: Were your parents artistic?

DB: I didn't know my father very well. He died when I was very young. I was seven. He was an engineer, but apparently, a very funny guy. My mother is very bright and has always loved theatre and film and literature. I was surrounded by that growing up. What was valuable was that this kind of pursuit wasn't really frowned upon. I was never discouraged from pursuing it. One thing I do remember is my mother was very slow to buy me toys. When Chanukah rolled around, maybe I'd get one or two of the things I wanted. I'd be mostly disappointed. But she was very willing to buy me books. There was always money for books, which I think is telling. And most people in my family, and certainly it's true of my brother, are very good storytellers. So that was sort of treasured. That facility was encouraged.

PD: How formal was your schooling?

DB: It couldn't have been less formal. It involved a lot of reading and watching movies. But above all, just planting the ass in the chair and writing.

PD: How did you learn the technique of writing comedy?

DB: Well, unfortunately for me, some of the technique had to wait. It was almost like when I was at *SNL*. Earn while you learn.

JD: How long were you on *SNL*?

DB: I was only there for a year. It was my first job in show business. I was there in '96–'97.

PD: But even there, you'd already been writing sketches.

DB: Yeah, it's true. I kind of got better as I went along. I really came in kind of raw. How did I learn? I don't know, frankly, if there's a real, a ready answer for that. I guess it was just, you learn by doing, and you learn by observing. I'd always been a huge fan of Woody Allen and Monty Python . . . John Cleese, in particular. I am a huge admirer of how John Cleese structures sketches. They always started with a very strong premise. "The Argument Clinic," in particular. It was one of the best sketches I've ever seen. Just a brilliant sketch, and it had a great premise, and so I was watching and paying close attention to the work I admired.

PD: Were you analytic about it?

DB: I think eventually I was. Especially when I would sit down and try and structure my own sketches. Obviously, a lot of it's instinctive. Who are we kidding? A premise is funny, or it's not. The joke is funny, or it's not. And a lot of that, I think is about a sensibility, and it's who you are. But as far as just structuring things goes, I was trying to be as economical as possible. I was trying to be as disciplined as possible, and not be afraid of losing a joke if it was funny, but was interfering with the whole piece. So, I probably was, in my own haphazard way, trying to be analytic about it.

JD: What's the Writers' Room on *Monk* look like?

DB: It's mostly comedy writers. It's seven or eight of us. Most of us have comedy backgrounds. But there are exceptions. Hy Conrad has been on staff for years. Hy has a mystery background. He wrote a lot of one-minute anthologies . . . collections of one-minute, or five-minute mysteries, like *Encyclopedia Brown,* remember those stories? He wrote stories in a similar vein. He still does. And they're very well-crafted, and you are called upon to solve the crime along with the detective. "How did Inspector Sullivan know that the waiter shot the gun?"

So he was hired for his mystery chops, but the happy surprise was, he is really funny, and a really good writer of dialogue. He has also written plays. One of our writers was on *The Tonight Show* and worked for David Letterman.

JD: You're describing some older writers.

DB: With great enthusiasm.

JD: So Andy selected older experienced people, as well as young people.

DB: Well, I didn't mention Tiny Kid Baxter, who's nine and a prodigy. I would say the median age is about forty.

JD: How do you work in the room? Do you break out stories?

DB: Here's how it works: Andy [Andy Breckman, *Monk* creator] will approve a story nugget. They're called nuggets, a kernel of an idea. Typically, we start with the mystery kernel. And Andy generates some of the ideas, just as often, if not more often, he's approving ideas, usually they're shot down. For every idea that he approves, there are ninety-nine more that are shot down. And a mystery nugget might be this: A man is murdered twelve hours before he is due to be executed in the electric chair. Someone killed the guy on death row twelve hours before he was going to die anyway. Why on earth would anyone want to do that? What could possibly be a motive for them? That's an intriguing question. So we would just break our ass trying to come up with a satisfying answer. That's intriguing, and it also gets you Monk in a prison, which is, we hope, fun. This guy is very uptight, and a nervous guy, persnickety guy, finding himself dropped in the middle of San Quentin. We thought it was a funny notion, and so we ran with it. We had a solution that was a little more surprising, but, hopefully, logical. That's typically how we begin a story, with a premise like that, and then the question is, how does Monk get into this? And is it fun? It might be a great mystery, but it may not be fun. It has to be a fun ride for the viewer, and what's Monk doing?

And then there's another question that has become more important to my brother over the years. It's, what is the emotional core of the episode? What's Monk going through in this episode? We've had episodes where, in the course of the story, Monk is coming to terms with his own mortality; or Monk has to overcome a specific fear; Monk starts to date again . . . that kind of thing. And Monk is very faithful to the memory of his late wife, but in an episode we did, he's feeling a romantic yearning for a woman who might be guilty of murder. And so we have a clever mystery going on, but we are also addressing Monk having these feelings.

PD: Do you develop these ideas around the table?

DB: Yes, absolutely. When Andy approves a story, we typically spend five or six work-days outlining these stories, and putting note cards up. It's five cards per act. Four acts, roughly twenty sequences. And you've got to bring the funny, but you've got to also bring the heart, although "heart" is a word I despise when it's bandied around Writers' Rooms and executives' offices because there's something almost calculated about it. "Where's the heart?" If you have to impose it like that, if it's artificial, like you're talking about a bottle of Excedrin, you're talking about an artificial heart. But you have to bring comedic and emotional elements and hopefully, it works as a mystery. So there are all these things that have to work together.

PD: Is it collaborative rather than competitive?

DB: People who have worked in other rooms, who end up in ours, say it's one of the best environments they've ever been in. Obviously, it's competitive to the extent that everybody wants to shine and we all have egos . . . who doesn't? But it's mostly supportive. We love the comedy and we love writing it, but we break our asses getting the mysteries right. Because we all have comedy backgrounds, it's easier for us to do that than it is to write the mysteries, which we're really proud of. Mysteries are very hard to structure; they're very intricate if you're going to do them right. They have to have a tantalizing puzzle at the beginning, and then a satisfying solution. But before we're through, everything goes through Andy's typewriter. Andy's antiquated writing software . . . WordStar, actually. Think Hoover Administration.

An Interview with
Peter Casey

A partial list of Peter Casey's credits as creator/show runner and writer includes: *Frasier, Wings, Cheers, The Jeffersons,* and *Encore! Encore!*

Peter Casey is insightful, demanding, and *nice.* Some of the writers we've interviewed would say that's an unlikely blend of characteristics to be found in the co-creator of two of television's most successful situation comedies. But it's Peter's work experience that tells the story. He and his partner David Lee started out on a show where writers were encouraged to compete with each other in unproductive ways, where there was little camaraderie—where very often, second-best was good enough. Then Peter and David had the good fortune to move to *Cheers,* where they were mentored by the Charles brothers, two guys who are poster children for toughness, never settling for second-best, and being nice. The staff on *Cheers* worked hard, because they were treated well and their ideas mattered. Even working into the early hours of the morning and not settling for the first joke or story idea that came along became an opportunity for celebration. It was all about *esprit de corps.*

Peter saw firsthand the success this approach created. Following in his mentors' footsteps, he ran with this idea and, judging by the fruit it bore, he made a good call. His shows have won Golden Globes, Peabodys, Humanitas Awards, and Emmys—over thirty in all. Spending time with Peter Casey, you realize Leo Durocher was wrong. Nice guys *can* finish first.

PD (Peter Desberg): As we've explained in our Premise [see page 9], how would you go about developing the show's plot lines?

PC (Peter Casey): This Premise does have elements of *Frasier* in it. You have this daughter, Sarah, who is on her own, and she's got this independent life, and she's on the opposite coast from her parents. *Frasier* started that way, with Frasier being in Boston at *Cheers,* and the rest of his family in Seattle. Now it happens that he's the oldest one and he moved west, where in this case, the mother moves in. But when Frasier did get out west, he was starting this brand new life where he says, "I'm going to have it the way I always wanted it. I have my apartment the way I want it, I have this new, exciting career." Everything is perfectly set in place and then the dad moves in, and the dad brings the dog, and because of his condition, the health care worker moves in. And suddenly, this sort of idyllic life that Frasier had set up for himself is kaput.

PD: And the chair . . . ?

PC: The chair was a character. When our set designer came in, we said we want a barcalounger and it's got to be pretty hideous. We want some duct tape on it. And he comes in with this book of fabrics, and I swear the book was this thick, and it was that pattern of fabric, just in various colors. It was literally that same striped pattern, but with different hideous combinations of color that he obviously thought, "These are great." I can't imagine somebody actively going out to make an ugly chair. So we just picked the worst one in the book, and there we go.

"The more different they are, the more chance you have of disagreements and conflict . . ."

But yes, this Premise has certain elements that are reminiscent of *Frasier*. It could benefit from Molly and Sarah being a little more different from each other. The more different they are, the more chance you have of disagreements and conflict, and that's where you get fun in the family. Molly might be trying to get Sarah involved with someone, while I could see Sarah thinking, "If I can get Mom hooked up with someone, I don't have to have her in the house anymore." So I think you have a whole array of stories that can work that back-and-forth way.

It also seems like you need, I think, if Sarah had a confidante she could express her frustration with whatever's going on with Molly, whatever difficulty she's having with her mom. If she has a confidante that she can express those things to, then you can really state them very clearly to the audience. It could be a girlfriend, it could be a guy friend. You could make it a guy at work, and maybe the mother's always thinking, "Well, he's such a nice guy, you should go out with him." And Sarah's always going, "No, he's just a friend."

"Oh, honey, that's the way your dad and I started out."

Molly is fiftyish, and broke, and probably constantly telling Sarah, "Your father, God rest his soul, I loved him so much, but the bastard left me dead broke." And it also seems like you have the possibility of a lot of stories where you're trying to get Molly work-ready. Sarah might say, "Oh, maybe you need to look for a little job." And Molly answers, "Well, what am I skilled at?" "Well, you're not really skilled at anything, but let's find something for you, even if it's volunteer work." Or, Molly's decided to take some classes at night school and is trying to expand and explore her life. So those could be stories. In fact, it might be funny if Sarah's decided to take a class, and when the mom hears about that, she says, "That's a great idea." And then the next thing you know, Molly shows up at the class too.

This sets up conflict of another kind. Sarah's feelings are, "My dad's just died. My mom's got issues. I've got to be pretty sensitive toward her." And maybe Molly, in turn, is being very insensitive to Sarah. So those strike me as some possibilities that you could do a lot with. That's just stuff off the top of my head. Short interview, huh?

PD: You've set up a whole bunch of potentially interesting conflicts.

PC: But that's always the thing. You want as many types of conflict as you can find. If you look at any comedy, that's ultimately what you end up having. That's what I think makes any story funny.

Molly being a little older, and being a mother, may look at certain things in Sarah's lifestyle that she may not agree with. Maybe that's the way kids are dating now. She also could be one of those, it's kind of clichéd and traditional, "Why do you have this career going? You really need to settle down and have a family." And maybe there's something funny in the idea that Sarah just can't bring herself to tell her mother, "You're the reason why I don't want to have children, because I saw what you did to me." So those are the kinds of differences you'd want.

PD: Sarah's very sensitive to her mother's feelings of loss and dependence. So she's constantly in conflict with herself.

PC: "She's making me crazy." There could easily be feelings of resentment on Sarah's part, in the sense that, "You've not only invaded my life, but I've been doing something very nice for you, and you don't seem to look at it that way. You can be completely insensitive to me, and I have to take it because you're the one mourning the loss of your husband."

You know, there's also something I was thinking about. If Sarah lived in an apartment building, it might be one of those things where—I remember sometimes when we'd have my mom down here from the Bay Area, after my dad died, and we'd go out to some place in public, and my mother would just strike up conversations with strangers, and I'd start thinking, "Oh, God, I didn't come to this restaurant to sort of chat with these people." And it may be the kind of thing where Molly's trying to make friends. "Well, you told me I need to go out and make friends." And every time Sarah's coming home, somebody else from the apartment building is in the apartment. It's like, "Well, who's this?" It seems like you could have some fun with that, too.

". . . and it doesn't hurt if she starts wearing some hot clothes . . . the least amount of clothes she can get away with."

There is an issue here. It's not just the character of Molly who's old. It's *me* that's old. So it might be tough getting networks interested in me. But the obvious solution is, you've got to make Sarah incredibly hot, and it doesn't hurt if she starts wearing some hot clothes . . . the least amount of clothes she can get away with.

It's tough. It's interesting when you stop and look at something as great as *Everybody Loves Raymond*. This show had two older actors in very prominent roles, but they were great, they were gold. The younger the network executives get, the harder it is to convince them that there's fun to be had there. We had John Mahoney on our show, and interestingly enough, people didn't realize John's about ten years older than Kelsey [Grammer], that's all. Yet he played his dad. But we never had a problem with that. I think that problem has started rising up of late. Look, it all boils down to demographics. They keep wanting this eighteen-to-thirty-five age group. The thirty-five-to-fifty-five age group doesn't matter that much to them, which is very sad, because they're the people who have the money to spend. But when you ask the executives about that, they say, "Well, that's not what we're looking at. The advertisers are looking at future buyers. Eighteen to thirty-five is where they're forming their buying habits, and if they decide they want to buy Crest toothpaste, they're going to buy Crest toothpaste until they're fifty-five, so we don't have to worry about selling Crest to the forty-five-year-old people. Their buying habits are set." It's not every eighteen-year-old who can buy a BMW. "Buying habits . . . we're looking to get those, as soon as they have that money to buy it. At about twenty-eight, maybe."

I think some of it also has to do with casting. If you get somebody who's really terrific as Molly, that'll make a difference. And it also has to be how good the character is. If you look at Peter Boyle's character [on *Everybody Loves Raymond*], he was a fun character because he was so cantankerous. If he was sort of warm and cuddly, I don't know how particularly interesting that would have been to the network and advertisers. So I think it's a matter of how you make this work. And you really are kind of treading a fine line, too, because you don't have a lot of room between making them interesting as an older person, and making them unlikable. If you make them too soft and fuzzy, they're probably not that interesting. So you try to put a little more edge into them. But you can also make that go over the line into, "I really don't like watching this." So you don't have a lot of room for error, I think, with an older character like Molly.

JD (Jeffrey Davis): If you could do anything to this Premise you wanted, what would it be?

PC: I'd change it to two men. First of all, I know that better than I know women. I also think that viewing audiences are more apt to watch a show with men in the lead than women. That isn't to say that you can't have great shows that feature women in the lead. *The Mary Tyler Moore Show* was a pretty good show, but I just think that, if not both of them, certainly I think Sarah should be a man. And also part of the reason is in my experience the only thing harder to find than a really attractive, young, funny guy, is a really young, attractive, funny woman. It's just really hard casting. When we were doing *Wings*, we had lots and lots of casting sessions out here that were unsuccessful, and we finally had to go back to New York, and we found both Tim Daly and Steven Weber in New York casting sessions. But finding attractive, funny women? Really hard.

For *Wings*, we were going crazy trying to cast the lead part of Helen, and finally the network called and said Crystal Bernard. Well, the character was originally Greek, so when Crystal finally came in and read for us, and she was far and away the best person we'd seen, we said, "Look, we'll rewrite it to Texas." So long Greece, hello Texas. Just had to do that because the casting was so hard to find. And then, she had already had a pilot that she had shot, so we were in second position. And we were just sitting there praying that her pilot fell through so we could get her to do ours. And it did.

Well, again, to me, it feels like you have sort of a classic *Odd Couple* situation set up here. That's, in a way, what we did with *Wings*. We had this sort of button-down brother who owned the business, Tim Daly, and then the completely wild-haired other brother. And they had a long history of animosity with each other. But as their father's dying wish, he wanted them to work together. And that's how that came about. So if we changed Molly and Sarah to a father having to move in with his son, you could even do the kind of thing where the father doesn't necessarily want to be there with the son, and each believes this is all going to be a very temporary thing. In fact, maybe what I would do is, the father has not let the son know that there's any kind of financial problems, or that he's broke. He's just too proud to let him know that. And the son, this is just like me, "Okay, he's going to come for a visit. Let's just put up with this for a few days, and then he'll be gone." And then it comes out that they could have had a strained relationship. That's one way of doing it, I think.

JD: Did people come to you near the end of *Frasier* and say, "Spin-offs?"

PC: No, interestingly enough, they didn't. But on the other hand, we always said, whenever a hot show came on, usually the following development season, you would see people doing variations of it. And we never saw anybody attempt to do something like *Frasier*.

PD: If you had a chance to play with this and not have to worry about networks, and oversight, and could take this anywhere you wanted, and make it as outrageous as you wanted, what would you do with it?

PC: I've come to really enjoy edgy. We didn't always do a lot of edgy on *Frasier*. I thought we did very smart humor. I remember how we used to talk about the difference between us and the Charles brothers. Besides their being just incredibly brilliant writers. But with *Cheers* they never kind of came off the cynical end of the show, and we usually would. We'd usually show a little heart at the end of our episodes of our shows. So that was a difference we had. But I like shows that are a little darker humor. My favorite show on the air right now is *The Office*. I'm so in love with that show. I can't wait to watch it. It really is the best show I've seen in years. And those characters, as quirky as they are, they're so real to me. And I like "real."

When we created *Frasier*, we spoke with our writers, especially during that first season, and we said, "We'd rather have a page of good dialogue without jokes, than to have two or three mediocre jokes on the page." And we said, "Look, we've got the horses here in the stable, that if you want to write a good, dramatic scene between Kelsey Grammer, David Hyde Pierce, and John Mahoney, you've really got the capacity to do that. So let's try to be real about this sort of dysfunctional family we have here. And don't feel like you have to cram jokes in."

JD: How was the Writers' Room on *Frasier*? Was it as great as everybody says it was?

PC: Yeah, it was. And it was constantly changing because we were like a sports team that constantly has some of your best players going up for free agency. They'd be plucked out from under us, and we'd have to find new people who fit in. But yeah, it was a great room. You'd hear from different writers when they'd first come on, they'd talk about how intimidated they were in the room. But it was never one of those rooms where if your joke bombed, people jumped all over you. Of course, the silence could be pretty brutal. But it was fun. It was a good room. And there were a lot of different personalities in that room. Chris Lloyd was sort of the driving force in the room. He was the show runner for us, and he and Joe Keenan were the dominant forces in the Room, when they were there. What I always enjoyed was the fact that our writers' drafts came in very, very good shape. There's nothing worse than having worked out a story, and then given it to a writer, and you wait for a week and a half or two weeks for that first draft, and you go, "This is a train wreck. We've got to push this whole thing." And that happened a couple of times in the first season, because you're feeling your way.

"Almost always, a train wreck is a story problem. It's a structure problem. And that's our fault. We're the ones that came up with the stories . . ."

JD: How do you fix a train wreck?

PC: Almost always, a train wreck is a story problem. It's a structure problem. And that's our fault. We're the ones that came up with the stories and then we would try to construct them, and then farm them out to the writer. And it's the same thing, even when sometimes when you'd get the drafts and you'd think, "Oh, this should be great." And you'd have a bad reading. It wasn't the actors' fault. You'd have to go back to the story. You can't just go back to the script and say, "Oh, well, we just need to punch it up and make it funnier." No. You've got to go back to the story, to the structure of this thing, and why are we having problems with it? I always hate to use that phrase, "Somebody has to have something at stake." That's the phrase that sends chills down a writer's spine because it's what every network executive says. But the fact of the matter is, is that you do. In *Frasier*, even when a story was built around Niles, you had to go back and say, "Well, what's Frasier have at stake in this thing? What is he looking for out of this?" Because even if it was Niles's story or a story about the dad, you had to bring your star into it.

The show's called *Frasier*, so he's got to have some very strong point of view in any given situation. And it's always great if every character has a point of view. You can't have everybody meandering along, and reacting to one person talking. Give them all a point of view. When David and I were creating the show, we really made a conscious effort not only to show how Frasier related to the other four characters in there, we made sure that every single character had specific feelings toward each of the other characters. So that if you needed to do a little side scene with Niles and Roz, there was a relationship that was set up there. They happened to have a very antagonistic relationship early in the show, got better as they grew, but that's how it should be. There are many people you meet that you may not particularly like when you first meet them, and then over time you begin to get along. But very early on? Oh, they couldn't stand each other.

What I'd try to do with this Premise is, I'd look for little, quirky things that you can play between the father and son, again and again. One of the things that we did the entire first season, which I always loved, was every time Niles would come into the coffee shop, or over to Frasier's house, and Roz was there, he'd walk over and say, "Oh, hi, I'm Niles." And she'd go, "We've met!" "We have?" It's like she made so little impression on him that he completely forgot her when he left, and then every time he'd see her, he'd re-introduce himself, and it would just piss her off. And that gives you an attitude, right there. It gives you something to play all the time. And she had no problem calling him an "uptight prig," and he would make constant comments about the fact that she'd slept with everybody in Seattle.

You want to have those things, and on *Frasier,* what we wanted to do was isolate Frasier. The dog irritated him; his father irritated him; Daphne irritated him. And Daphne and the father got along great. She's the one person that really sort of brought out the sunshine in the father. And yet, that just irritated the hell out of Frasier, too. You also look for the things that your actors can do well, and Kelsey explodes well. He's just very funny when he does that. So I'd look for values like this in the father and son who are stuck together.

I remember when Kirstie Alley first came onto *Cheers.* Shelley Long was brilliant, and it was very hard to see her go because it was such a well-established relationship. When Kirstie first came on the show, we were having trouble finding what is the thing that makes her funny. And for the first few episodes after the episode that introduced her, we were doing stuff where she would walk in, say a couple of lines, and go out into the office. And it was like, "Okay, now we've got our other guys that we're comfortable with." Then we did a story where she'd asked Norm to paint her office. Norm was out of work as an accountant so he'd started doing house painting to make money. So while he's in there painting, she comes in and starts kind of opening up a little to Norm, and what you find out, what you realize is that this very hard exterior of hers is a façade. She's a completely insecure person underneath, and she's very frightened about taking over this job, and during this conversation, she breaks down and cries. Kirstie was really funny when she cried, and we said, "Okay, now we have something that can play." And so anytime we could get her to get all sniffle-y and cry, we would. So once we cast this father and son show we're talking about, it might take some time to discover what's funny. What the actors can do.

With Shelley, it was the total opposites attract kind of thing. But with Kirstie, it was all about, "This woman's incredibly hot and she doesn't seem to be attracted to me. Aren't all hot women attracted to me?" You see this guy, the guy who usually is the cocksman of Boston, and he's suddenly doubting himself.

PD: Was that a conscious decision to say, "This can no longer be a boy/girl show?"

PC: We were there when this transition was made, but it was the Charles brothers who created Kirstie's character, and they wrote the episode where she was introduced. But I think they still wanted to have this sexual attraction going on, but they didn't want it to be in the same way, the same configuration with Shelley. I mean, in a way, you lost a certain amount of intellectual aspect of the character when Shelley left, because she was just really book-smart. And that's not necessarily Rebecca's character, but they were just trying to find a different way of making sure they still had the sexual tension. And they still had Sam being able to be Sam.

JD: Were there people around you as a kid who were funny?

PC: My dad was funny. My dad was a policeman, believe it or not. But he was a funny guy. He used to make me laugh. And he loved Jackie Gleason. I grew up watching *The Honeymooners,* and *The Jackie Gleason Show,* from Miami Beach: "The entertainment capital of the world."

JD: Elliot Shoenman got his start on *Maude*. He pitched a story from *The Honeymooners,* and Bob Schiller said to him, "That's great, Elliot, except . . . "

PC: "We've seen it!" I remember one of the things that used to make us crazy on *Cheers,* when we'd be sitting in story sessions with the Charles brothers, and you're sitting there thinking, thinking, and somebody would pitch something, and they'd go, "That was an episode of *Phyllis."* And I'd go, *"Phyllis?* Can't we just change it?" To their credit, I tip my hat to them, they would not do something they had seen before. But it made it tougher. They raised the bar incredibly for David Lee and myself, because we had started out on *The Jeffersons,* and *The Jeffersons* was just a very different type of show, and the jokes were easier, and the jokes were a little more on the nose, and in your face.

In the Room with *The Jeffersons,* there was almost a sense of panic if it got quiet when all the writers were together. So people were constantly talking, even if there wasn't something funny in the story. You just made sure you had some noise in the Room, and pencils going in the ceiling. And there always had to be activity and noise going on, and I remember when we got *Cheers,* and we sat in the Room with the Charles brothers when they brought David and me in to pitch story ideas. We pitched our first idea, and they'd sit there and they'd just be very silent. It was like going to confession and watching the priest. Glen Charles would sit over in his chair, and he'd have his hand out the window with the cigar, and he'd be looking out the window, and you're just going, "Oh, my God, what's going on here? Is anybody going to talk?" And there'd be like five, ten minutes of silence, and then they'd start talking about story. But they gave themselves time, a lot of time to just think, and kind of put it together. There never seemed to be any urgency.

JD: We're in a period where there aren't many situation comedies making it onto the schedule. Do you see this as a cyclical problem?

PC: I think it is. My first year at *Cheers,* believe it or not, there were literally stories in *Time* magazine about how the sitcom was dead. And then the second year, *Cosby* came on and that changed everything. The sitcom was alive again. But the sitcom was really suffering. So I think it'll probably be back, but I don't know if we'll see the sort of four-camera, before a live audience style the way it was. Everyone seems to be enamored of the one-camera show. *Scrubs, The Office.*

"'. . . when you create a television series, you're creating an open-ended movie.'"

PD: What's fascinating for us as you were doing it was watching the procedure that you had; you're really interested in people's relationships, and that's the first thing that you went for.

PC: Okay, how can I take these people that like each other and make them collide? Or, how can you get another twenty more episodes here? Okay, well, let's look at Sarah. We'll get Molly to get socially involved.

I remember somebody once said, "When you write a movie, it's two hours from a beginning, to a middle, to an end. And when you create a television series, you're creating an open-ended movie." When you create it, you have no idea when it's going to end. And if you're lucky, you get to end it, as we did. You don't get a call at the end of the season and they say, "You're not coming back." And you're kind of left up in the air. And you don't know if that's going to be three seasons, or six seasons, or, in our case, eleven seasons that you're going to be on the air, but you want to make sure that you've given yourself enough possibilities to keep generating stories.

PD: How did you get into comedy?

PC: I moved down here in 1975, three days after I got out of college. I studied broadcasting. I was actually thinking I was going to be a TV news guy. But I met David Lee not long after I moved down here, and we started writing together. But we were writing hour shows like *Petrocelli,* which was a detective show. Then we started doing some *Barnaby Jones,* and we weren't selling these, we were just strictly spec. David had two friends who had been struggling actors, who had just sold a script to *The Mary Tyler Moore Show,* and then we started noticing that we were throwing jokes into our drama scripts, and we thought, "Well, maybe we should try to write a half-hour sitcom."

The first script we ever tried to write was a *M*A*S*H*. That didn't get us any work. We actually wasted a year writing a pilot, thinking, "Well, let's create our own show," and that was just this really stupid mistake, because when you're unsold, and unknown, the last thing a network's going to do is trust you with doing your own show. They want you to run a show. You better have experience to do that. So after we wasted that year, our agent said, "Look, write an episode for the show that you like the best, that's on the air right now. It should be a really popular show, so that other producers will know the show." So we did a *Barney Miller*. And the *Barney Miller* was rejected, but it got us into *The Jeffersons*. So it took three and a half years to finally get our first pitch session.

"'. . . they're going to get their jokes into the show; we're going to be left out,' and it really became kind of a cannibalistic thing."

PD: There's a lot of craft to writing comedy. How did you pick this up?

PC: I spent six years on *The Jeffersons*. When I started, it was the only way I knew that this is how things were done. Mike Milligan and Jay Moriarty were there for the first year or two years I was there. And then Ron Leavitt (co-creator of *Married With Children*) came in to run the show, and he had been over at Garry Marshall's company doing some of the shows over at Paramount. Mike and Jay were more the Norman Lear style, and when Ron came in, he kind of changed the way we did things. The way Mike and Jay did things is was to have David Lee and myself go in to work on a story with Mike and Jay. There would just be the four of us in a room. And we would work and work and work, until we got a story.

Once we got a story, we would go out and we would write the story outline, then we would meet with the two of them, and they would give us notes. Next, we would do our draft, and then we'd get notes on the first draft, and do a second draft. When the show was on the stage being produced, when we'd watch rehearsals, their style, and it's a style now that I think was really counterproductive, we wouldn't go down to the stage, we would sit in their office and watch it on the monitor because the show was done on tape. So we'd watch the rehearsal on a monitor, and when the show was over, with all the writing staff in the room, they'd say, "We need a new joke on page 8. We need another new joke on 13." They'd point out where all the new jokes were, and they'd say, "Alright, come back when you've got something." And you would see the writers go out of the Room, everybody would go to their separate offices. The last thing you wanted to hear was a door open and close down the hall, and hear people walking by your door, because it's like, "Oh, shit, they're going to get their jokes into the show; we're going to be left out," and it really became kind of a cannibalistic thing.

And so what Ron did was have everybody in the Room, kind of working on the story, before you figured out the story, they would've decided, "Okay, it's going to be your assignment." So then everybody starts working on the story. And they would literally work on it almost line-for-line, so you're just sitting there kind of writing stuff out, making sure that you're getting everything down, and there's obviously places where you're going to get your material in too. They can't have everything, you've got to cobble it all together. When you walked out of those meetings, you would have 70 percent of the script written already. So we tended to work more as a group under Ron, but there was still some of that pitting elements of the writing staff against each other.

When we went over to *Cheers*, what we found from the Charles brothers was, first of all, they didn't settle for the first thing that was pitched, even if it was funny. They'd say, "Well, let's see if we can do better than that." That was never the case at *The Jeffersons*. If somebody pitched something that got a laugh, "Okay, let's move on to the next thing." And then the other thing is, they always had the staff work together as a staff. No matter whose story it was, they had everybody come in for a story session. The Charles brothers' philosophy was, "Get as many minds working on one problem as you can." They gave you much more of a chance as a writer to do your thing. When they would pitch the story out, they'd pitch the beats of the story. When they'd start cobbling a story together, you'd get the beats of the story and you'd get the occasional joke; they'd toss you a shiny, gold coin, and you'd make sure you caught that and got that written down.

The other thing about Ron Leavitt—you'd never do a story outline. You turned in your first draft, and that was it. Then they'd do some brush-up on it and then they'd send it off to the stage. But with the Charles brothers, they had you do a story outline, a very clear, concise story outline, then gave you notes. Once the story was broken and it was your assignment, then they worked with you, just you, the writer and the Charles brothers. But then when it came time during the week of production, we would be down on the stage with the actors. At the end of every scene, the director, James Burrows, would stop and the actors and the writers would talk about the scene. And we would say, "What works for you? What doesn't work for you? Are you comfortable with this? Do you feel this isn't like your character?" And there was a

What do you think the most important factor is in job satisfaction? If you said "money," you'd be wrong. The *Harvard Business Review* points out that the most important elements people look for are *creativity* and *autonomy*. James Brooks, co-creator of *The Mary Tyler Moore Show* and *Taxi*, was legendary for getting the most out of his writers by treating them with dignity and respect. They didn't feel like "hired guns." They felt like vital members of a team. Two of the writers on *Taxi* were Glen and Les Charles. They embraced this view and carried it with them when they created and staffed *Cheers*. When Peter Casey and his partner David Lee moved from *The Jeffersons* to *Cheers*, they not only saw the difference, they felt it. Peter carried this tradition into his shows and made his writers feel valued. This tradition was evident on *Everybody Loves Raymond*, which you can read about in Phil Rosenthal's interview on page 252. Read Dennis Klein's interview on page 123 for a contrasting view. He believes that many writers in a Room are "corralled" when working on shows they didn't create.

wonderful exchange of ideas, and then you'd move on to the next scene. And when you were finished with the rehearsal, the whole staff would go back to the Charles brothers' office, and we would all work as a group on the rewrite. So it just became sort of a community banquet. And that was the style the Charles brothers learned from James Brooks, when they were on *Taxi*. That's the style we took with us to *Wings* and to *Frasier*. That's the way we wanted it to be. We said, "Let's all pull in the same direction. We're all in this together."

> "There are certain jokes that we do that we call 10 percenters. You figure, 'Look, it's a little sophisticated, who knows, maybe only 10 percent of the audience gets it, but we don't care.'"

JD: What are your feelings about jokes? How do they best fit into a script?

PC: What we used to say was, there are certain jokes that we do that we call "10 percenters." You figure, "Look, it's a little sophisticated, who knows, maybe only 10 percent of the audience gets it, but we don't care. Let's put it in there." And it was inevitably, like when you'd do it in front of the live audience, almost everybody got it anyway. So what it basically told us, very early in, don't write down to your audience; give them credit. If it happens to be something they don't get, that's okay. If you really love the line, leave it in for your own pleasure. If it happens to be something they don't get, you go, "You know what? We were wrong. That shouldn't be in there." Take it out or rewrite it. But don't dismiss something before you even give it a chance, because you think they're not going to get it. One of the things that we felt was a solution to a lot of problems [was] simply, "I'm trimming it down; it's too long. Cut, cut, cut, and then clarify."

Another thing about the Room was that the Charles brothers had worked with *The Mary Tyler Moore Show* guys on *Taxi* and they told these legendary stories about their times there, most of them incredibly great. This one famous writer/producer, who shall remain nameless but who is a screamer and a yeller, he's just incredibly highly critical of writers' work. They talked about it in a way that was semi-amusing, but you could tell it was miserable. David Angell (producer, *Cheers*), David Lee, and I had sort of similar personalities, and we always felt, "Don't you attract more bees with honey than with vinegar?" Especially if you're going to be in a Room with a bunch of people late at night? I doubt I ever stayed past 7 o'clock at *The Jeffersons*, except on shooting night.

"I ate more dinners at *Cheers* my first year than I ate in six years at *The Jeffersons*."

I got a very early baptism of fire on *Cheers*. We were staying for three, four nights in a row until one or two in the morning, doing rewrites, because the Charles brothers were very exacting and demanding, and perfectionists. Their whole thing was, "We stay until we get it done." We would never change the story in mid-week at *The Jeffersons*. With the Charles brothers, after the table reading, if the second act didn't work, you threw out the whole second act, and you rewrote it that afternoon, and evening and early into the morning. I ate more dinners at *Cheers* my first year than I ate in six years at *The Jeffersons*.

In our shows, we really believed in trying to promote a happy atmosphere on the show. The Charles brothers were great mentors to us, because they did that. They threw great parties at Christmas time, and they used to do a premiere party every season, which we'd never experienced on *The Jeffersons*. What they did for the premiere party was, they rented out the top room at Chasen's, and they would have the cast, and all the writer/producers and their spouses, and they would do a big dinner and then the TV monitors would be set up and we'd watch the show, and then after the show, there'd be cheers, applause, champagne. They'd break out Cuban cigars. What a great way to kick off the year.

And so we kept that tradition. We would always have a premiere party on *Wings* and *Frasier*. The *Cheers* Christmas party was always held on the set because you had a bar. And you had a big, open space. So they made the bar operational for the Christmas party. They'd bring in bartenders, and that's where you'd get your drinks. We learned from Glen and Les. We always tried to make sure our people knew that we appreciated them, and throw a great party for them. In fact, when we had *Wings* and *Frasier* on the air at the same time, we did a combined Christmas party.

PD: You had a long and successful collaboration with David Lee. What is the nature of a good partnership?

PC: Comradeship. I'll tell you what it isn't. I can't remember who these two writers were, but they walked in to pitch an idea to the Charles brothers and when one partner is pitching the story, he makes a story point and one of the Charles brothers says, "I don't think our characters would ever do that." And the other partner turns to the first guy and he says, "See?" Oh, man! That's not the best partner you want to be with.

> "... he calls in the production assistant to bring him the menus, but he called them Lunch Goons. 'Hey, Lunch Goon, we need a Lunch Goon in here.'"

You know, it's funny, too, I remember, again, having not eaten dinner at work much on *The Jeffersons,* and we started eating meals at *Cheers.* The first thing that was amazing was I remember when we were at *The Jeffersons,* you had to buy your lunch. There was actually a little kitchen and there was a woman who would come in, and she would make a big lunch every day. It cost you five bucks. And you'd give her five bucks and you could eat the lunch. Or, you went out to lunch somewhere, to Denny's. We were at Metro Media at that time. They've torn it down to build a high school. But when we went in to pitch to the Charles brothers the first time, the very first day we go in, and I guess the meeting probably started about 11 o'clock, and so we're talking. It's kind of a "get-to-know-you" kind of session, and then we were just starting to get into the pitching, and Glen says, "Well, let's order lunch."

I love both of those guys so much. They're both really funny, but Glen had this way about him, and he calls in the production assistant to bring him the menus, but he called them "Lunch Goons." "Hey, Lunch Goon, we need a Lunch Goon in here." And so a kid would come in with a bunch of menus, and Glen would decide where they were going to go. And so we ordered what we were going to have for lunch, and they'd go out to get it. David and I both took out our wallets. One of us said, "How much is that?" "What are you talking about? When you're here, we buy lunch. Nobody buys lunch but us," Les said. And every day they bought lunch for the whole staff, and office staff. Everybody ordered lunch, they bought lunch, and then at night, when you had to stay late, you'd have things like Marino's, and all these really good restaurants. And they said, "Look, if we're keeping you from your home, and we're keeping you from your family, you're going to have a good meal here." And then they'd say, "You guys want to order a couple bottles of wine?" There've been some awfully funny, half-in-the-bag rewrites I've been in on that were great.

We really appreciated that, and we kept that absolute same policy on *Wings* and *Frasier*. Although we did have to temper it a bit at *Frasier* one year when Chris Lloyd was on the show. One night when neither David Angell, David Lee, nor myself were at the rewrite session, Chris ordered crabs flown in from Joe's Stone Crab House in Miami. After that we said, "Let's try to keep it at least within the Los Angeles City limits."

An Interview with
Ed Decter

A partial list of Ed Decter's credits as a screen and television writer includes: *There's Something About Mary, The Lizzie McGuire Movie, The Santa Clause 2, The Santa Clause 3, Senior Class, Boy Meets World,* and *The Closer.*

It's a good thing we taped this interview; otherwise, we would have been like students frantically taking notes on the fine points of comedy writing. If there was a Ph.D. in comedy, Ed Decter would not only have one, he'd be the chair of the department that granted it. As he effortlessly takes us through premise development, he cites movies and sitcoms that reflect his ideas, or identifies the comedy principles behind them. Two interviews in this book—this one and Charlie Peters's (see page 222)—stand out as great teaching interviews as well as brilliant comedy creations. In Ed's hands, industry terms like "middle-slice pilots," "four-box demographics," and "pipes" become as understandable as if you'd spent your life around the Writers' Table. He can give you the rationale for every setup he creates, but instead of making it sound academic, he makes it sound funny.

PD (Peter Desberg): As we've explained in our Premise [see page 9], how would you go about developing the show's plot lines?

ED (Ed Decter): The first thing is, for me, it's not a feature because these days, a feature needs to be played out on a bigger palette. It could be an independent feature, a really well-done independent feature for a small market. But these days the criteria that they have for movies, at least the kind that I work on for the studios, is what they call *four-box movies.* That means that it has to have almost every demographic; the studios want them to be huge. And this would make sort of a delightful, small feature, something the British do very well. But it does seem to be a television premise. I come from sitcom, and it lends itself to sitcom.

I don't like sitcom any longer. I don't believe in it anymore, but I do believe in the half-hour film comedy. An executive would tell you that this is one of the premises that lends itself well to three-camera because it's not like Sarah's a private eye or something that has to be taken out of her home and out of her apartment a lot. So it could lend itself to three-camera. So, assuming that you're going to do it this way, the first thing you have to say to yourself is, "Why is it funny? Why do we care about these women?" And then you have to go about conceiving a pilot. And a pilot is different than anything else on earth, because in a pilot you have to think forward and backward at all times. You have to think, "What's a good story? What's a good story for the pilot?" And, "What would make a very good episode?" And plus, it is the trend these days to do what they call a *middle-slice pilot,* meaning that it's a run-of-the-mill episode that could be aired any week, and yet, it still has to set up all of the characters, and all of the story you need to know to set up the show, so that people understand what they are seeing. Even more importantly, what the advertisers are going to see at the upfront and decide to support. So that means that your pilot has to be burdened with an enormous amount of what they call backstory, or *pipe,* we call it, which is information about why these women are living together, who they are, and what their relationship is, and all that.

". . . a pilot is different than anything else on earth, because in a pilot you have to think forward and backward . . ."

And then you need to tell that story in twenty-three and a half minutes. You have to tell a story that entertains you here, has to also tease you, so you say, "Oh, I would really like to see next week's episode." And it has to also say that these people have known each other a long time. What's more, it also has to say this will be a good, long-enduring franchise. That's why pilots are so, so, so difficult. And that's why those of us who do a lot of pilots get hired to think backwards and forwards at all times. What's really difficult is that a pilot should really be two episodes. It should be the backstory episode about how these women came together, and it should also be the episode that we wanted to watch—but they won't produce that. They won't make that. They believe that it should exist, that it should be like any episode. So, you have to do it in a half-hour, or exactly twenty-three and a half minutes.

Now, say you did this as a single-camera film pilot, you could show the scenes where Molly's grieving, or start at the funeral and set up what's the lock of the situation. The other thing is that every single one of these shows, every single show that has a concept, you have to present to the audience what the lock is of the concept, or else the audience isn't going to buy it over the length of time.

The lock means, why does Molly have no other option but to live with her daughter? You have to show it, right? You have to show. . . and by behavior, and by comedy . . . why she has no other option but to live with her daughter. If the audience feels she wasn't that badly off, as with what we've got here, it seems to me she has many other options. They're not going to buy the fabric of the series. And so the first thing you would do is develop a pilot episode that shows that somehow, some way, these women can't live without each other even though Sarah was doing well [*Ed makes quote marks in the air around the word "well"*] in her life before this. But something about Molly's arrival would have to point out to Sarah immediately that by the end of the episode, of course, not at the top because there has to be conflict, but at the end, that there's something about having Molly there that is incredibly helpful to her, or needed in her life at this point.

So you have to design the story backwards from that point. You would say, "What is that moment that Sarah realizes that it's not just a burden to have Molly?" Because that would be like hitting someone over the head with an axe every week, if it's the same joke. So there's got to be something that Sarah gets out of this relationship with Molly, and if it's that moment of humanity where she realizes that it's sometimes good to have a mother around, then the audience will say, "Oh, that's very sweet, I understand what's funny about it, but I also understand what's fulfilling about it." The next thing you have to do is try to find what will hook the audience into what's relatable about this Premise, because most people, maybe just the people I know, wouldn't want to have their mother living with them. And if Sarah's successful enough, there's a whole bunch of situations that I would imagine she might suggest, "Let me rent you an apartment." See, again, you have to think backwards and forwards. If Sarah's rich enough, or successful enough, to rent her mom an apartment, well then the show is over, right?

So it occurs to me that one of the ways you can do this show is to have the mother-in-law apartment, or the mother-in-law guest house behind the main house that you often see advertised, so that the mom is there, but you understand that it's an adult relationship where they're trying to keep their separate spaces. Because otherwise, it's an incredibly old-fashioned Premise. And then again, if Sarah isn't successful enough to have some place like that, where she could have her mom, you know, like for instance, in *Frasier* where the dad lived with him, and the first thing that they did was made him injured and he had a cane, so it was never a question why he lived there. That was the first thing that they did. Those are incredibly bright people and what do we do, why is Martin living there? Right, so here you have a fairly successful young woman on a good career track, why is this her only option? So the first thing I would do is build in a lock where maybe she has that little converted garage in the back of her house, so that Mom is always around, always watching what's going on.

There was a show called *In-Laws*. It was about two families living next door to each other. They had converted a garage for their kids, and you understood that beautifully. It was a good lock because the kids couldn't afford to have their own place, and they converted a garage for them. Now they had both sets of parents meddling in their lives. So this could work the same way. There's the little house in the back and then, of course, you could do a whole bunch of things where in getting that house ready for her mom, it's disaster, after disaster, after disaster, and the mom has to stay in the house. That would be a good thing for the pilot because then they'd be smashed together, in really close quarters. And then the other thing is, if the father had left a lot of debts, not just no money, but debt, that now was burdening Molly, so that she really had a pressing need to take care of this or else somehow it can crush down on her. And in some way, if Sarah were impacted by this, Molly could be homeless, or worse, then it builds in the lock. However, everything I described to you takes pages and pages of exposition.

Now, if you did it single-camera, you could help yourself visually. You could see the funeral. You would show the funeral, then you'd show the meeting with Molly and her husband's CPA. The CPA would say, "I've got to tell you, you're in a volcano of badness, a sucking abyss of badness." So, Molly finds out all this, and then she comes to stay with Sarah temporarily and she's looking for a job, and trying to get her life started, and that's how she would ingratiate herself. And there's another thing that they do now where they have a hybrid pilot. In a hybrid pilot, there are certain scenes that are filmed out of the studio, and certain scenes that are on a soundstage. The most famous of these would be *Seinfeld*. So assuming you could accomplish that lock very quickly now, again, that lock of why she's there, and why she has to be there, and what their prior relationship was. Again, it takes pages, and those pages eat away from your current, present story of what's going to be entertaining about that thing, which would be, obviously, something about Sarah and her love life, or her professional life, or her lack of love life because of her professional life.

And the problem with that is, it's a story we've seen 10 million times. It's the woman who's got a career, and her love life interferes with the career. I mean, it is the fodder for almost every show on television. Look at *Grey's Anatomy*, which is a fantastic show, but it's about that every week. It's about how much sacrifice do we make for our dreams, and our professional careers, and how much time do we set aside for love. So the first thing you would do in the Writers' Room, or when you sit down to write this, would be how do you flip that story where it's fresh and interesting? And then all of that has to service the bigger issue, which is that how, at the end of this—with all the funny conflict that's going to happen and all the intrusion into Sarah's life—how, at the end of that, do you make it where they almost discover that they really need each other? But, of course, they can't really discover that or else your show's over. I mean, so that discovery of the fact that they need each other has to be fought over a long time if you're going to do a comedy, because if they both say, "I really need you. It's really great that you're here," there's not a lot of conflict after that, if they're in accord.

"Writing a comedy pilot is a little bit closer to poetry. I'm not talking about the highfalutin' concept of poetry, but every single word makes a difference because it's taking away from another word."

Here's the classic example: If you made Archie Bunker say, "You know, I've been wrong about so many things, and people are all the same. I've made a lot of mistakes, and I really love all races," that would be the end of the show. So in a sitcom, and in any comedy, or in any good drama, you have to leave a lot there for the show to explore. And then, we haven't even discussed what other characters are populating the show, and those people eat up pages, and you have to service those people so everybody in there has to be very important. Writing a comedy pilot is a little bit closer to poetry. I'm not talking about the highfalutin' concept of poetry, but every single word makes a difference because it's taking away from another word. I do drama pilots, as well, and I'm not saying it's easier to do a drama pilot, but you can have a scene that adds a lot of character, or suggests something else, but you can't in a comedy pilot. In a comedy pilot, you need every single thing to work for you in a certain way, and you can't have a little dangling edge, except for maybe the last scene that sort of suggests what maybe next week's episode is going to be. So the tenets of what you need are a really great beginning that hooks you about why Molly's coming to live with her daughter, quickly gets into the current story about Sarah's life and what she's actually lacking in her life. Show how, in a funny way, her mother tries to solve it, makes it worse, and how then they come to some partial truce at the end that suggests many funny things to happen later in the series. And again, not being critical of the premise, but the problem is this treads on a lot of familiar ground that you have to find a very fresh way to turn over.

So the first thing I would do is look at that classic story of Sarah's spending so much time at work, and she is not devoting herself even a little bit to this very good guy in her life. I would try to find a way to flip that. That, in fact, Sarah is distracted by some very hot guy at work, and her work is actually suffering. I'd do anything that flips what you'd expect to see. Or, the fact that her dual pursuits of both a love life and a career leave her ignoring her mother at this very difficult time, and her mother is vying for her attention. Her mother needs someone, and maybe they've never had that relationship before where the mother seems needy, and of course, the thing that's relatable to everyone is that when you become an adult, ultimately your parents become your kids. That is something that I think an audience will relate to.

Now the other big question is about the audience. In other words, is the audience relating to that idea, the people who you want to be watching this comedy? Because you'll find that a network will say, we want the *Heroes* crowd—the people who are watching *Heroes*—to be watching these comedies, and not the *Everybody Loves Raymond* crowd, because maybe the *Raymond* crowd doesn't spend a lot of money. So one of the things that you would imagine when you're doing these shows is what's best for the show. It's not always that. A lot of times you'll be sitting in the room saying, "How do we make this demographic younger, and younger, and younger?" And so, it's very possible that a network would not buy this show because there's a middle-aged woman in the show. Now, one of the most successful sitcoms of all times was *Everybody Loves Raymond,* and it was all about middle-aged people and older people. But it's not necessarily true that the current network wants that demographic. For instance, the only successful sitcom on the air right now is *Two and a Half Men.* It's the only successful sitcom in the top twenty. No one even talks about it. No one mentions it. It's not hip in any way, although it's a very solid, very good show. But no one talks about it. It's not water-cooler stuff.

They're talking about all the other shows: *Grey's Anatomy, American Idol, Lost,* shows that cover much fresher territory. That's not to say that the people who would do this show aren't going to reap tremendous rewards, or the network's not going to reap tremendous rewards, but you'll notice that there's no sitcom up in that area, so that's why the networks, and everybody else, are searching desperately to find a way to freshen that genre. And *The Office,* for all its acclaim, and for all its brilliance, is still not doing that well.

PD: Why do you think that is?

ED: I think that in this cycle, they're wanting to do something like *Ugly Betty. Ugly Betty* gives you the soap aspects that people like, but it also gives you a fresh, energetic, fast-paced comedy, and it's an hour, and that's fantastic. Now what syndicators like is *Seinfeld.* So everybody's still looking for that half-hour that really works. *30 Rock* is a brilliant, fantastic half-hour comedy. It's incredibly low-rated and it's just barely hanging on, but it couldn't be better, it couldn't be funnier. And that's all fresh and new and applies to a younger demographic, a hipper demographic, and all the things that they want. [*Since this interview, Ed's instinct has been proven correct. 30 Rock was picked up for another season and performed better in the ratings.*]

So, not only are you writing a show, and telling the best possible story for that show, and trying to find a fresh way to do it, and trying to find a way to set up all the pipe at the beginning, and the story in the middle, and the teaser at the end, not only are you doing that, but then, you're also being asked to think like a marketing strategist. By the way, no one is immune to this. I mean, David Kelley [creator, *Ally McBeal*], who's about as good a writer as anybody in the world, his shows go off the air after four episodes. Some of them last for a long time, but he just had one that didn't even air the full season. No one's better than David Kelley, and no one's funnier, no one's more energetic; no one has fresher things going on. But it's a very cruel and succinct world. You don't succeed for three episodes, you don't get any numbers at all, they don't see any growth happening there, and you're off. So all of that fear and business stuff creeps into what you need to do for a pilot. Your show doesn't exist without it.

PD: Do you think some of that is coming from cable competition?

ED: No. There are cycles, always. You remember how there were no Westerns, then Clint Eastwood does a Western, and then there's a lot of Westerns, and then a few Westerns that work, and there are no Westerns for a while. When I came into the sitcom world, they were dead, and nobody's making sitcoms anymore. There's never going to be another Gary David Goldberg [creator, *Family Ties*] again, one of those big show runners with those successful shows, and then *The Cosby Show* happened, and then there was this surge in sitcoms, and then there was *Seinfeld*. After that, there was the phenomenon of *Friends*. I think its creators, Marta Kauffman and David Crane, are the best at what they do. That show had no premise, which is lovely. The premise was, "You can't choose your family, but you can choose your friends," right? And this group of people . . . it was devoid of a premise, which is fantastic. This one, you have to service. You have to service the Molly/Sarah Premise. You have to have this backstory creep into your current story. But with *Friends* you can introduce them, and it was clear that they were friends. The only backstory they had was Rachel escaping from her wedding. But the reason why I think David Crane is the best show runner that ever lived is because he found a way to make everything fresh, current, serialized, but not too serialized. So, you can still enjoy the episode of the week without having seen the other twenty-five shows of the season. And that's why it was such a phenomenon.

At the end of the day, they had this unbelievable cast, all of whom had been on other shows that had failed, but somehow the chemistry of that cast worked. The best example I can give you is that if you have a show that's running and working, you don't have to do anything to set up a joke. I can go back to Jack Benny to describe this, but the best way is with *Friends,* which people know much better. You could start the series after it had been going for a while, and if you just showed the apartment and showed a horrible mess on the table, things dripping, and glue, and something had fallen and it's disgusting, and you started the episode with no characters there, and you saw the apartment, you'd start to laugh. You'd know that Monica was coming in the door. . . . and as soon as the door opened, you'd get another laugh in anticipation of the fact that it was incredibly messy, and she's so anal and neat, and then—so you'd get a laugh on the setup, you'd get a laugh on the anticipation—and then you'd get a laugh on whatever brilliant line David Crane would put in for her to do at that moment.

And so that's really great comedy writing. But that's an up-and-running show. That same situation with a *new* show, with friends and the same character, she's very anal, but now you've lost everything when it opens and there's a mess, you don't know who's walking in, you don't know whose apartment it is, you don't know why that's funny, or not funny. And then when the character walks in and sees it and reacts to it, and is anal about it, you go, "Well, that's bad storytelling," because you've set up a joke that really isn't happening. You don't know the character that's coming in. You would only set up a scene that way when you know Monica's coming in, and you know that she's going to be there, and it's going to be a mess. So then you get that anticipation. In this other one, you'd have to show Monica's character through a conflict that shows how anal she is. There was a great episode where she was describing folding the ends of the toilet paper, and how it makes everything so neat in the bathroom. That's very funny just in description, right?

And so, getting back to this Premise. I say, "Okay, who is Molly, and how is she this outside force in the life of Sarah?" And, "Who is Sarah?" And then again, the whole thing would be to *not* make Sarah that stock character who nobody wants to play, which is just the career woman who misses out on love, you know what I mean? That's the first thing I would work on because my brain goes blank thinking about that, because I've seen it so often. And the other thing is, how do you make that fresh? How do you make the summer breeze of Molly be irritating, funny, and sustaining, so that you're looking forward to seeing what she does every week? And then, thinking business-wise, you have to say, "Well, who wants to play Sarah? Is she the straight person for love?" And nobody wants to be the straight person. The greatest straight person in the history of comedy was Bob Newhart. Bob had no problem with other people being funny, and he knew that his face, when you cut to it, would get a laugh at his disbelief, and his beleaguered expression would get a laugh. And that's why he was able to do the phone bits in his standup routines.

Okay, so, who's Sarah, and what makes her funny? Why is she funny, even if Molly never came into the story? So you might do it that she was the hypertensive, neurotic, organization person. The first thing that comes to mind is that she's the ultra, ultra-organized one, and Molly comes in and she's Bohemian, and you would think, "Well, that's a switch because Molly's older." But we've seen that, too. So you'd have to come up with a fresh way to do that, and maybe Molly, for all her Bohemian ways, kept a tidy house. And Sarah, for all her organization and killer instincts at work, is a slob. And obviously, you're treading right on a show that your [interviewer Jeffrey Davis] dad worked on. You're treading right on *The Odd Couple*. And so that's inherently relatable, because *The Odd Couple*'s the ultimate, relatable story: Everybody has that friend. Everybody has that opposite. And then again, how do you make that fresh, how do you make *The Odd Couple* fresh, when Neil Simon did it better than anybody's ever going to do it? And so did Garry Marshall, do it better than anybody's going to do it. How do you make that *Odd Couple* thing fresh? And yet, it still can work. If you find the two characters appealing, because it is an infinitely renewable premise, *The Odd Couple*. *Two and a Half Men*. It is the central theme of a bulk of stories. I'm not an expert on that Joseph Campbell guy, but one of the archetypes of comedy is that *Odd Couple* thing. And even before Neil Simon did it, somebody did it.

JD (Jeffrey Davis): Your knowledge of the industry is impressive. You mentioned Jack Benny. Were you going to do the "Your Money or Your Life" routine?

ED: It's not the "Your Money or Your Life" joke, but the classic Jack Benny joke that fits here would be the one where somebody would say to Jack Benny, "Well, we could fix your car, but it's going to be $400." So that's a straight line. You'd laugh at the straight line, at the anticipation of Jack Benny thinking, because he would take this long pause, and you'd be thinking, "What can he possibly say?" Or, "How is he going to try to get it not for $400?" And then he would say the joke. Then the amazing thing is, he would say the funny line about how maybe there's something that he could do . . . he'd offer to perform at a benefit for this guy to not pay that $400. And then there'd be a wait while that guy was thinking, and it would be funny, because you'd be thinking about how Jack would respond. That's the classic melding of what's best about comedy, which is surprise, and then great character. A character that is inherently comic, which means a character that inherently causes conflict. And that's what you'd have to find with both Molly and Sarah to make it live. And also, you'll find that almost everybody who's doing comedy has a good sense of the history of back and forth, because everybody, usually, who's in comedy started the same way. In my era, it was the Carl Reiner/Mel Brooks record, *The 2000 Year Old Man*. And the people who work for me now, young people who work for me who come from shows like *South Park*, which is also unbelievably, enormously funny, there's usually a sense of the past. There's some reason that you didn't become a hedge fund manager—the only smart thing to have done in the last twenty years. And any of us who didn't, had to have some crazy reason why we didn't do that. So, anyway, that's what I would do with this.

"I had a friend who made a beautiful distinction. He said, 'Features are like war, and television shows are like government.'"

JD: You've done both. What's the difference between working in television and features?

ED: I had a friend who made a beautiful distinction. He said, "Features are like war, and television shows are like government." There's a line, and they deserve it. The Marty Scorseses, the Clint Eastwoods, the Steven Spielbergs, they have well-established, creative freedoms, and then there's everyone else. And it's completely changed. A maverick filmmaker like John Ford, who said, "Oh, we're behind in the script . . . you're worried about we're behind . . . we'll take the script and rip four pages out and throw them . . . now we're caught up," that guy does not really exist anymore.

There are certain people, like David Kelley, who keep doing it, but he certainly isn't like those of us who have to work and support families. That's why you keep going, but then the other thing is that in the transition from television, if you're the show runner and the show creator, you were actually a very important person . . . very, very, very important. And before they fire you, they have to think hard, not too hard, but pretty hard. But in film, when you're writing a film, even if you're Scott Frank [screenwriter, *Out of Sight, Minority Report*], even if you're the best guy out there, they *can* and *will* fire you.

"'CBS Productions'—which is not CBS, the network— 'CBS Productions wants the woman to enter first, and Warner Brothers, who's paying most of the money, wants the guy to enter. And the network doesn't think anyone should enter but the dog.'"

To be a show runner, you have to be very present because it's a lot of work. Your day gets divided. Only 10 percent of your day is necessarily working on the script for the show, and 80 percent of the day is dealing with the network and studio. Say Warner Brothers is the studio making the show and is paying your salary. They will often partner with a network's production arm, say, NBC Productions, or CBS Productions, because those shows get picked up a little bit easier by the networks. So then you have two production companies involved. That means two companies who are writing the checks for the show, and have creative input. So now you've got NBC, or CBS, or ABC. That means there's a lot of sitcom writers for the show runner to deal with. You can say what you want, but they're fast and funny, and can do stuff really quickly. It's amazing, when I do a feature rewrite now, I sort of laugh. I mean, people think it's going to be weeks, and it doesn't have to be. But, when you're in that room, most of the time you're going, "Okay, CBS Productions"—which is not CBS, the network—"CBS Productions wants the woman to enter first, and Warner Brothers, who's paying most of the money, wants the guy to enter. And the network doesn't think anyone should enter but the dog." You know what I mean?

So, I have a writing partner, and he's very patient. He'll get on the phone and say, "Well, you know, the network was thinking the dog could enter first, and that could work and get you what you want . . . I think the same, if the next person to enter was the wife, quickly followed by the husband, and then it seems like they all enter together, but . . ." and not a lot of funny comes out of that. And that is what your day-to-day life is. So, people always say, "Why is there so much bad stuff on television?" And then, one time I went to the Upfronts [sponsors] and met a lot of people from Coca-Cola, and Chevrolet, and all those people who advertise, and who pay our checks. And to them, the show was the gray thing that happened in between the commercials. So that gray thing just had to provide the right people to sit there looking at the TV until that commercial came on, and the really important thing happened. So it depends on what your point of view is.

"'Good storytelling is looking the truth in the face and sometimes taking a little step to the left.'"

JD: If you didn't have to think about the networks and the suits, is there anything in this Premise that speaks to you?

ED: Well, unfettered, I mean . . . to me, there is a relatable part. My mom passed away, but before she passed away, my dad had passed away. So for twenty years, even though she was technically my mom, I felt like I was her dad. My mom didn't know how to write checks; she had never written a check in forty-five years. To me, those types of things are interesting. But again, my show biz-entertainment senses are saying, "Well, my mom was much older than Molly is and she was not out there dating," and everything like that, but to me, that interests me, and I know a lot of people go through that when one of their parents dies. And now that person is sort of newly revealed to you as who they are. So that's what I connect to, and relate to this, and that's what I would bring to this. I once had a fiction teacher in college who said, "Good storytelling is looking the truth in the face and sometimes taking a little step to the left." So the truth of this is there's a tremendous sadness, which a lot of times runs under good comedy. There's a sadness, because obviously her father's passed away. I would connect with the parenting of the parent. How do you launch that person back into the world after they've been sheltered inside of a long-term relationship? That's what interests me.

PD: But that's a great situation. I remember a friend of mine's father passed away, and he realized his parents were like this. Although his mother was really developed in a lot of areas, she was now out there alone. She had never written a check, so shopping, cooking, cleaning were easy for her, but all of a sudden, she realized that she couldn't do some of the most basic things.

ED: This would be a scene between Molly and Sarah in one of the episodes. I remember that my mom couldn't watch movies I had done because they're not making videotapes anymore, and she had a videotape machine, and so I would send her the DVDs of the movies I had written. She didn't have a DVD player. So I sent her, through Amazon, a DVD player. And then I got the call, "Okay, it's here, it's in a box, I'm never going to hook it up." "Well, why not?" "Because I don't know how to." I say, "It's the easiest thing in the world." And then on the phone, like in one of those movies where the pilot dies, and somebody has to land the plane, I say, "See, there's a yellow, red, and white plug." "I don't see it." "It's in the back there, it's yellow, red, and white, and there's three things, and all you have to do is take the yellow, red, and white plugs and put them in the yellow, red, and white spaces." You know what I mean? And so that could be a scene. Now the funny thing is, I immediately would flip it and make it that Sarah's been so focused on her career, and all that kind of stuff, that she doesn't work with things technical, and that her Blackberry, and everything technological, confuses her. I mean, something to make that fresh, so that she's not Ms. Blackberry, and all that kind of stuff. And maybe somehow Molly, who had more leisure time when she was with her husband, was able to have all those gadgets, and when he died, they were all taken away from her.

JD: How many pilots do you do a year?

ED: We're doing a drama pilot this summer, and this will be my eleventh produced pilot, and I've had four series. The thing you get very quick and good at is how to get the people into the room because all sitcoms, all television shows, are family shows. They're all family shows, whether they take place in the workplace, or they take place on an island, as in *Lost* or *Seinfeld.* Or they take place on *American Idol.* They're all family shows. If you think about *American Idol,* it's a family show. It is our four main characters are our judges, and Ryan [Seacrest], and they're there every week. We like them, we get to know about them, our family, through their interaction, and then we get to know our contestants. They're our new characters, and then we go to their hometowns.

The reason why *American Idol* is better and more popular than current sitcoms is because it's real, and even though it's *created* real. We go to their hometowns, and we go to Alabama, and we see somebody delivering mail, and it turns out that that person can sing, and there's our backstory. That's an episode of the television show. And so, what we would have is somebody from Alabama as our lead character. Then, somebody comes to visit them from their hometown, and they say, "Hey, how come you don't sing anymore? You used to be such a good singer." And then we would come up with some sort of phony set piece where they would sing at some club, and reconnect with something that they used to do in their past. Well, that's really phony, and really stage-y, and that's a bad example, but when you go and you see Vonzell, the woman post office worker delivering mail, and then singing with a beautiful gown on and all dressed up, that's a better story than anything you could tell in a sitcom. And that's why things like *Ugly Betty,* they said, "You know what, we could do this differently and better." And they did. And so it delivers you all the punch of a sitcom without the laugh track, gives you all that good serial drama, and has fresh high-stakes stories.

We're asked to make multi-ethnic casts, it's very important, obviously, but that's not why people turn it on. They turn it on because very simply, everyone has had a job, and everyone has been beleaguered in their job, and she is a "working girl." She's the girl who's smarter, more sensitive, and better than the people that she works for, but she's hidden by the fact that she's a nobody. And then the other lovely complication is she's not as physically appealing as the people that she works around on the surface. But, of course, after two episodes, you want to see Betty more than you want to see all the glamorous supermodels. But nevertheless, it's everyone's story; everyone's had a job. And what you do when you create a show, you find that thing.

You asked what I would do with Molly and Sarah were I not concerned about demographics. I went through raising my mom after my father died, and so I connect with that very deeply, and it is an *Odd Couple* situation. When my mom would come to visit me, I would only have about a ten-minute patience level. And from that point on, it was kind of hellish. But nevertheless, that could be done very funny. And the way I dealt with it with my mom was to keep her moving. Playing golf, activity, so we wouldn't have to just sit and talk. And I think that the reason why you laugh is because it's very relatable. Because people deal with their parents that way.

PD: Listening to you talk, I get the image of the plate-spinner on *The Ed Sullivan Show*. You're saying, "Okay, got to get the lock here, a good grasp of the characters there . . . "

ED: My partner and I use this example. We use the Sabre Dance song . . . *Da-da-da-da-da-da-da* . . . we use that in the Room all the time; that exact example we use in the Room all the time. You always want to throw up your hands and give up, because you go, "Well, if we can't have any character older than fifty years old" . . . and you want to say, "Hey, did you see *Raymond?*" It was a phenomenal show, but it was an old-fashioned show. They only had six scenes, maybe four scenes, it was as old-fashioned as *The Dick Van Dyke Show*, which is the highest compliment you could ever give it, but it was the same structure as *The Dick Van Dyke Show*. You sit with these long scenes in the living room, and yet it was brilliant, because all the characters crackled.

"The less successful your sitcom is, the longer your scripts have to be, and the more successful it is, the shorter your scripts have to be."

They had the exact same thing. Raymond's wife would be cooking, Patricia Heaton would be cooking, and you'd see her struggling and just getting a little frustrated, throw some spice in, and at that moment, at the door, you would see Raymond's mother looking through the door at Patricia. And then, there'd be this huge, anticipatory laugh, and friends of mine who worked on that show told me that scripts were very short, much shorter than your average sitcom, because the spread of the laughs was so great on every episode. They couldn't fit in more story. So the less successful your sitcom is, the longer your scripts have to be, and the more successful it is, the shorter your scripts have to be.

JD: Nobody ever left. They enjoyed being in that Room, right?

ED: Why wouldn't you? Phil [Rosenthal] actually cared about feeding people. Yeah, Phil is a great show runner, and you know, he's one of those guys who proves you don't have to be a jerk to be successful.

JD: Can you elaborate a little more on the four-box demographic idea the studios operate on now?

ED: There's [ages] eleven to eighteen, and eighteen to twenty-five, and then twenty-five to forty-nine, and then forty-nine to . . . And so, there're these boxes of demographics. They are obsessed with which box the movie's in. Now, you can make a movie for one box, but it'd have to be at a certain price, you know what I mean? You can't make *Shrek* just to appeal to kids two to eleven. If you did that, you would fail miserably, because somebody has to take those kids to the movies, and so there has to be something entertaining for the parents, and then when everything's working, like *Shrek*, it appeals to everybody. Teenagers will go to that movie. It became hip to go see an animated movie because of *Shrek*. So that's when it hits all the boxes. That's what they said. So obviously, if you're going to do a $100 million movie it has to hit as many boxes as it can. You can't just make a movie, like you'd think, for teenage boys. It has to appeal to other people. You *can* make a movie for teenage boys if you make it for $20 million, or $30 million. You can make a movie, and if that returns $80 million, you're a big hero. But you can't make a $100 million movie for one sector of the population, because, like *Indiana Jones*, it'd have to hit everybody. A movie that you make for $100 million, the theatres keep half the money, right?

So to get that $100 million back, you have to make $200 million at the movie theatre to get the $100 million back. But then you've spent $35 or $40 million promoting it, so you need to get that money back too. So that's another $100 million you need to get back, because you have to split it with the theatres. And as you go, you have to make more and more and more money. So obviously, to cover costs, that's why some-

Ed Decter is sensitive to the forces driving the commercial film marketplace. As he defines the four-box demographic, he demonstrates how to create a script that will appeal to the most diverse audience. He points out how elements can be added to movies so that they will appeal to both younger and older audiences. Citing *Shrek* as an example, he points out that because adults bring kids to a movie, it has a chance of doing better if the filmmakers add elements to the story that will appeal to this older demographic.

body like Tom Hanks, that is one of those Jimmy Stewart, Henry Fonda guys, that's why they would pay them so much money to be in a movie. It gives them a guaranteed lock on a certain audience. But occasionally, Tom Hanks's movies fail. Even Tom Cruise movies sometimes fail, not often, but they do. So that's why you have to care about those boxes.

"... girls have dials, and guys have dials ... and when something's funny, they turn the dial, like that, and when somebody's not funny, when there's something that they don't like, they turn it the other way."

In television, I mean, if people knew what went on, in the sense that the second you finish your pilot, they start to test it. And you've heard about testing; it's the oddest thing in the world. You can go and see your pilot and they put it in a room in front of people, and the people have dials, and girls have dials, and guys have dials, and everybody has dials, and when something's funny, they turn the dial, like that, and when somebody's not funny, when there's something that they don't like, they turn it the other way. And the guys are blue lines, and the girls are pink lines, and you

One of the most engrossing parts of this interview is Ed's amusing dissection of the way that network television has turned upside down and backward since Sherwood Schwartz and Leonard Stern started in the business. This is because corporations have taken over. Notice we said corporations. *Plural.* A network and two studios are likely to share ownership of a single show and lock themselves into a perpetual duel over content, which means a show runner and her writers have to jump through a series of hoops to get something on the air. When you read Heide Perlman's interview, you'll see how this battlefield is laid out. A few of these hoops include focus groups, re-shoots, and contradictory notes from the three owners and the sponsor to get a show through. When you read Sherwood Schwartz and Leonard Stern's interviews, you'll notice that, although there was always interference, the Golden Age was a time when the creative people were not second-guessed and the originality of the product mattered most.

Multiplatform outlets are changing this model. With the advent of companies like Netflix and Amazon, content that is more original is finding an easier entry into the marketplace. We were gratified to discover that in 2017, TV pioneer Norman Lear got a reboot of his series *One Day at a Time* on Netflix at the tender age of ninety-three.

see an average of those lines as the show is being projected to you in your little secret room that you're in. As it's being projected to you, you see a graph being projected of the pink and blue lines.

And obviously, what you'd like to see is a very happy line that goes infinitely up to the top of this band of funny. That means they turned the dials all the way, and you'd like to see it not go to the top early, but you'd like to see it go higher, higher, higher, higher, and end in a beautiful two lines at the top of the chart. But you never see that. And then the funny thing is, you'll do a joke and you would think that guys would like that joke, and the guys go up, and the girls don't like that joke, and then they start going [up], and then the guys plummet. The whole process of testing is being influenced by various notes to "service this" and "service that" about things that aren't necessarily what's funniest, or what's best for the show. Because of that, what you get is a very tepid little line going back and forth like that. And then they say, "Well, you know, it didn't test very strongly." And then they'll say, "Let's do a re-shoot," or "Let's add some things to the editing, to make it spike." People who are experienced know how to make it spike at the end a little bit. If you have somebody dancing at the end of your show, dancing and singing, dancing to a piece of music, people like that and it spikes. So you would tend to do that.

". . . you would see that they had laughed from beginning to middle, and end, they laughed the whole time, but when they came out, they felt that they should say it was disgusting."

There are embarrassed laughs. In *Something About Mary*, you'd go to the theatre and it looked like a revival meeting. People were laughing so hard that their hands were going down, and coming up, almost like a horror film. The audience moved around a lot. Then you'd hear people come out, now most people were, luckily, very pleased with it. But you'd hear people say, "That was disgusting," and you would see that they had laughed from beginning to middle, and end, they laughed the whole time, but when they came out, they felt that they should say it was disgusting.

JD: What was the germ of *There's Something About Mary*?

ED: Well, my partner John Strauss lived in an apartment that overlooked a condo, and his apartment faced the bedrooms of all these condos. There was this one really, really attractive girl who would come home each night. It sounds like I'm making this up, but it's really true. She would come home, she was an aerobics instructor, and she would get undressed, take a shower, and then stand naked in front of her mirror. She'd try on various outfits that she was going to go out to clubs in. This was a long time ago, and I was a very young man, so it was way before I was married. But nevertheless, when she would come home, we didn't want to get caught staring at her, so if it was night out, we would turn off the lights in the apartment and we would watch. And, of course, I think it was my partner, John, said, "We're stalkers at this point. This is bad. We can't do this." And I said, "No, you know, maybe we're not stalkers, maybe we're detectives thinking about what women do in their private moments, and we could bring this knowledge to bear on all of our lives and the lives of our friends." This is the rationalization for being creepy. So then we said, "Well, what if some guy couldn't find somebody and they sent a private eye to do that. The private eye would fall in love with her, and the first thing the private eye would say, 'Oh, she's horrible, she's fat, she's ugly, you don't want to have anything to do with her.' Then he'd take that woman for himself." And then the next thing we thought was, "Well, by having followed her, he'd know everything about her, so it's the perfect setup to get her. He would know everything she was interested in, and everything she did wrong, and everything, so you'd have all this information." So that's how it was born. And then came the Farrelly brothers, who were the single greatest guys. If you ever get to meet them, they're the greatest guys ever. They're like the Irish brothers that you would want to have.

"They engage in The *Raiders-of-the-Lost-Ark* School of Production. They get this huge ball rolling, and they get it rolling so fast nobody can stop it."

So we start the script with the Ben Stiller character endlessly talking to his friends about this girl, Mary, that he knew in high school. One of the Farrelly brothers said, "We need to see that." But we said, "The problem is that Ben's going to be in his thirties, so are you going to have another actor play young Ben?" And he says, "No, no, no, we're going to have Ben play Ben when he's in high school." And we said, "That could look really goofy." And he says, "Yeah, it's going to be hilarious." And, in fact, I think that single thing was why the movie was successful. Because as soon as you saw Ben with his braces, and being clearly a thirty-year-old guy playing a high school kid, the audience relaxed and said, "Oh, all these funny things are going to happen." And you had a guy up in a tree singing. Of course, the studio absolutely was going to cut the guy singing in the tree, and the troubadour, the troubadour thing, and they were going to cut the hair gel scene, and the dog, the dog was clearly an animal activist's nightmare, and they didn't want the mentally challenged brother . . . everything. They didn't want Cameron Diaz, and everything that you can imagine.

In retrospect, it all worked, right, but I mean, Cameron Diaz had been in *The Mask,* so she had been the hot girl in *The Mask.* And Ben had a television show and wasn't that well known, and Matt Dillon was at that time the boyfriend of Cameron, and was a bigger star than any of the other two. And so, they didn't want any of those people. They didn't want any of them.

PD: How did you prevail?

ED: Well, I didn't do anything. It's the Farrelly brothers. They engage in The *Raiders-of-the-Lost-Ark* School of Production. They get this huge ball rolling, and they get it rolling so fast nobody can stop it. And that's what they do, and they agree and they're jovial so they always say, "Oh, absolutely, yeah, we're changing that. We're getting on that." And they don't. And they do *exactly* what they think is funny. And the greatest thing about the Farrelly brothers is the other alternatives that most of us agonize over, that are not the funny things you ultimately land on what you hope is the funny thing, those other not-funny things don't occur to them. So they're incredibly efficient, and they only shoot things one way. They always choose the funniest one. It doesn't occur to them to do it another way. I once talked about it to Peter [Farrelly] about *Dumb and Dumber.* There was this very funny shot where you're tracking with Jim Carrey, and he cuts away from the camera, and runs down the gangplank to the airplane, and then the camera keeps going to the window, and he falls out of the end of the tube where there's no plane, and you just see that in the distance. And I said to him, "That is just hilarious. There would be about five ways to do that shot. You could track with him and he could open the door and fall, and have no plane there, or you could be below the thing." And he looked at me in the strangest way, like he couldn't even have imagined those other ways, just because he just naturally went to the funniest one. And it was so much funnier than any of the ways that I would've thought of.

PD: Did you study writing in school?

ED: Yeah, I went to a really famous film program at Wesleyan in Connecticut. It had this really famous film teacher named Jeanine Basinger. Michael Bay, Dana Delany, Paul White, Miguel Ortega, Larry Mark, and Jeffrey Lane went there. The list of the people who've come from there is long. Then I went to AFI [American Film Institute], and when I left there I wrote a script. I was the first independent filmmaker from AFI, and when I made like twenty minutes of the film, I got hired as someone's assistant here. This guy was a very famous screamer in the angry sense. A really nasty guy. And he fired me after three weeks, so I was out here and then I started writing. I've been in the [Writers] Guild for twenty-eight years.

JD: When did you meet your partner?

ED: About three years after I moved out here. I ran into a guy I went to college with, and we started playing in a regular softball game. This guy went to high school with my partner, so that's how I met my partner. John was film editing at the time, and he says, "I have this idea for a film." I say, "Yeah, that'll be great if you did this, this, this, this." The hilarious thing is that script we wrote, we wrote for Taylor Hackford, the director, the first script that we wrote together, we're going back to sell that script again, after all these years. *Mary,* we wrote ten years before it got made, before the Farrelly brothers made it. My partner and I were going to do it as an independent film, and we used that clause in the Writers Guild contract that you can get material back to you after a certain amount of time. Our lawyer said, "We're going to go through this whole thing and nothing's going to happen and it's going to be a long process." I said, "Can we just do it, because I think it makes a good, independent film?" And finally, the day I got the piece of paper from Interscope that *Mary* was released back to us, I happened to run into Peter Farrelly. He and I were both doing a favor for another friend who had done a movie and wanted to get notes. Peter's unbelievably generous with his time and expertise. He said to me, "Whatever happened to *There's Something About Mary?*" I said, "That's so weird that you brought that up after all these years, because I just today got . . ." He says, "We'll do it!" He says, "When I teach screenwriting, I teach that script." I say, "That's very kind of you, but you haven't seen it in many years, so I'll give it to you." He called me the next day after he read it, and he said, "We'll set it up at Fox, and we're going to do it." And he says, "And here's the eight things that we're going to do." And from that point on, it just rolled. So no project ever really dies.

PD: Were you interested in comedy from early on?

ED: Yeah, yeah, from four years old. I would watch Johnny Carson. My parents would put me to bed, and as soon as I heard them sleeping, I would turn on *The Tonight Show.* Always. It was Don Rickles coming on. I remember when Johnny Carson and Don Rickles traded places. Johnny Carson said, "It's so much easier to be in your chair." Don Rickles, Mr. Put-Down and Mr. Zinger, got behind the chair, and Johnny Carson sat in the guest chair, and Johnny Carson shredded Rickles. And it was one of the funniest things ever. And I said to myself, "I don't know what this is, but I want to be part of it." I didn't even know that there was that kind of a job in show business. My family used to drive back from New York City after seeing a play. I lived in New Jersey, and we would drive across the George Washington Bridge, and my dad would stop at this neighborhood in a bedroom community of New York, and he'd just stop in front of this home. It was just like a regular house, and he would say, "You know who used to live in that house? Buddy Hackett." And we would just sit there in the car and look at this tract home, and we'd imagine Buddy Hackett being on Johnny Carson. And that made us feel close to show business, looking at Buddy Hackett's former house.

PD: Did your father have a great sense of humor?

ED: Yes, he had a great sense of humor, and he was a great storyteller. And he wrote really funny letters, too. I certainly got that gene from him.

JD: What do you consider your greatest skill?

ED: There are all these different skills, and the structuring of what you care about and the long-term thinking, I believe that's my true strength. I'm funny. I write good jokes. But I have friends who are just extraordinary, who can't say anything unfunny.

PD: What's the relationship between the writers in the Room and the network?

ED: You have two production companies, and then the network, and so there's too much workload. For instance, they'll say to you, "Here are the promos we wrote for your show." You look at them, and they do it on purpose, because you look at them and you say, "Ah, this doesn't sell the show at all." They'll have your characters, your actors saying lines like, "Hey, come watch next week because . . ." or whatever promo it is, right, and then so you go, "Well, we can't do that. We have to protect our show. We have to sell our show." So you write them. Now you have a staff that's got to produce a show for the next morning, and something's got to be on the table for the actors to read, and they have to do these promos. So then you say to your three young writers, "Okay, you guys go off and do these promos." Then you have to go in there, like a honeybee, you have to go in that room, "How are the promos going?" And they say, "Well, we're doing this," and you go, "Well, no, you can't do that because that reveals the joke, the central surprise of the show. You can't do that." Now the networks also want you to write Internet material that's exclusive, meaning that's new. So they want you to write new scenes for the Internet, and they would prefer not to pay for them.

JD: Were you mentored?

ED: Sure, I mean, I think you get mentored. My film professor at college, Jeanine Basinger, is the ultimate mentor, in the most positive sense. And then I've also had mentors who were sort of crazy, lunatic people who taught me a lot of what *not* to do. Absolutely to remain nameless, but I worked for an executive producer who was one of the last of the dinosaurs. He said to the network, "Let me tell you five reasons why you're wrong." Were you to mentor yourself in that direction, you would mentor yourself out of a career. But he was of that era where he would walk around saying, "I'm going to call the network and tell them that we're not only *not* going to do their notes, I need to explain to them why they're wrong." And that does not fly anymore. It can't happen unless you have the raging, unbelievable success of all time. Most of those guys are not working because you have to be a bit of a politician today. They'll root against you. Again, to remain nameless, but there was an unbelievably huge show runner at ABC who did dramas, but had that kind of a deal where there was no network interference. The network couldn't give him notes, and ultimately they rooted against him in a very, very, very big way, and now he's not that guy anymore. And that's the current state of the industry. There are only five corporations now. That's it.

An Interview with
Michael Elias

A partial list of Michael Elias's credits as a television writer and screenwriter includes: *The Jerk, The Frisco Kid, Head of the Class, The Cosby Show, The Mary Tyler Moore Show, The New Dick Van Dyke Show,* and *Lush Life.*

Michael Elias wanted to wear a tweed jacket with leather elbow patches . . . which means he wanted to be a serious writer. His first writing job was creating the material for his own comedy duo. After success in clubs and television, including *The Tonight Show,* he was called out to the West Coast by William Morris and began earning a living as a writer. His stand-up comedy background served as his training ground. It's where he honed his instincts about what was funny and what he wouldn't want to face an audience with.

PD (Peter Desberg): As we've explained in our Premise [see page 9], how would you go about developing the show's plot lines?

ME (Michael Elias): It's kind of old-fashioned. A parent moving in with the daughter, and wants to start a new life. This has been done before, I suppose with some success, more or less. But I'll stay within the parameters of this Premise.

PD: Do what you have to do.

ME: No, I don't want to turn it into a war movie.

PD: Make it funnier.

ME: It's funny only in the execution, but what I'm thinking is . . . so you've got a woman, Sarah, who seems to be like a personal assistant type. She's creative, but she's not going to go anywhere in her life, or the job. She's so focused on her work she's unaware that she's relationship-challenged where men are concerned. I don't know how you're unaware of that, so she's gotta be aware of it, or it's not true, so let's figure out what would work better. Anyway, let's see if you can make a movie out of this. And how can we make it more contemporary? And who's going to be a star. So it's the mother and the daughter—actually, the mother interests me more than the daughter—and they come together at the same point in their lives. That is, they're both single, sharing an apartment, and relationship-challenged, so dating should be a big thing. How do a mother and daughter date together and search the Internet or the world for men? It might be interesting if the mother is actually much more successful than the daughter at dating men. Cast her kind of sexy, still attractive, and I'm thinking the Gail Godwin novel about a woman who rediscovers her sexuality at sixty-three and is just going to do nothing but have sex, and sex, and sex, and is having a great time at it. That might be an interesting thing for this striving young woman who finds herself saddled with a sexually active older woman.

So I think the mother would embarrass the daughter, and maybe the mother's got a guy. Molly's got a guy who's crazy about her. It's about her relationship with this guy that she met online. At the beginning it's about how this relationship develops, and then she's living with a guy. I mean, the daughter is living with her mother, who's dating a guy who might be a no-goodnik, or he might be younger than her, or he might be a criminal. That might be interesting if he's sort of criminal. And, not only does the mother want to have a real relationship with him, maybe she wants to rehabilitate him and get him out of his life of crime . . . could be white-collar. And so Sarah's watching this all going on around her. Her mother's having an incredible time; Sarah's embarrassed. The mother's trying to get the daughter's life turned around. So maybe the daughter is very conservative, so there's real conflict there. So the daughter works as a librarian in a private library in New York City. A medical library, or something, and she's got a very settled life, and she expects her mother to come in and have a very settled life with her. And they would do all kinds of cultural things. Instead, her mother is now hanging out with a Dominican dope dealer. She's got an uptown, or maybe a Brooklyn-Haitian boyfriend, or a Brooklyn guy, and it's all exciting.

"'Why can't you be more like the person you write about instead of the person you are?'"

Her grandparents, that is, Molly's parents, can come in and complicate things . . . screwy, too. Maybe there's a guy who's with Sarah. They've had this long, sexless, dumb relationship, where they do all these terrific things, you know, go to lectures and it's all very fine and non-sexual, and the mother is telling her daughter, "Get rid of this guy," and she keeps bringing Hector's friends and cousins to meet Sarah and take her out. Maybe that's the beginning.

Or maybe Sarah could be a writer, too. She could be a writer like the Kathleen Turner character in *Romancing the Stone*, you know, stays home and writes her books.

So the mother is an interruption at home. Yeah, if she works at home, if she's a writer and works at home, then having this mother who's bringing all this fancy life and fun into her apartment is a drag, and then you can have the mother . . . and what she writes could be a reflection on her life, I mean, maybe she writes spinster-detective stories, where she's got this alter ego. Oh, yeah, she's got an alter ego who she writes about, which is nothing like her. That would be better. Nothing like her, and her mother keeps saying, "Why can't you be more like the person you write about instead of the person you are?" "I can write about her because I'm not her." "Well, if you can write about her, why don't you just be her?" "It's not easy." So she's not afraid, she's not shy. She's all those things . . . so that could be interesting. Yeah, and maybe her boyfriend is her editor. It's kind of skewing old. I'm thinking of the commercialism of it. Now you've got a fifty-year-old mother. But then again, there are a lot of actresses who could play this and be sexy and funny, and the younger daughter . . . she wouldn't be Lindsay Lohan, but she would be of age, and I think you could have a lot of fun with that.

What else about mothers and daughters? I don't have much experience with that, but you could also have a relationship. Maybe have her . . . she's a widow, so the dead husband . . . there's a lot to be learned in, what was their marriage like? "Your father didn't touch me for the last ten years of our marriage." And "I didn't know what I was missing . . . I forgot what an animal I was." You can do a nice thing here, where the mother talks to the father. She's got a picture of him, and she says, "George, I know you're not approving of this, but he's a great dancer, he's this, and this," and she turns the picture to the wall every time Hector comes in, and Hector says, "Who is it?" and she says, "It was a guy who sold me insurance a long time ago." She won't admit to her past.

Yeah, so you could have parallel love stories, what's going on in the mother's life, what's going on in the daughter's life. Neighbors. You could keep it traditional. If it's an apartment, you've got a neighbor downstairs, across the hall, 4F, 4G, she's never seen in thirty years, whatever. Life in New York. It might be funny to bring in a character who's a lawyer, who deals with Molly's estate, the father's estate . . . it's going to be one of those Dickensian estates that's going to be tied up in probate for the next fifty years and every once in a while this guy comes in and says, "We've made some progress. Turns out your ex-sister-in-law, if we can give her X amount of dollars, she won't sue for this." It's like the guy died, and the inheritance is basically trouble . . . and lawyers.

PD: You started with her as a librarian and then you got her to be a writer who writes about crime, while her mother is dating a criminal. So how did you get to that point?

ME: I once wrote a pilot about a woman who was the victim of a crime, and so crime is on my mind. I was just reading *The New York Times* about old con games, and sort of con games and crime. So crime was really on my mind, and the hero of my story was a petty thief. A woman comes home and finds her apartment's been robbed. And the thief steals her purse that had a script in it. She's a TV writer. And he reads her script and he decides that there's something interesting about this woman. He sees her picture from her license; she's kind of cute. The thief comes back to her apartment and returns the purse. He says he found it in the garbage. Unfortunately, all the money was taken; they took her money, but they threw the purse in the garbage, and he's returning it to her . . . maybe he can get a reward . . . and he wants to meet her, and she says, "Oh, my God, thank you, this is fantastic," and she says, "There was a million dollars in that purse. Thank God it wasn't lost." And she holds up the script. "This is my pilot, my pilot script I'm turning in. This could make me a million dollars." And he likes her. He also read her date book and remembered that she was going to the theatre, to the Hollywood Bowl with her agent. And then he makes a mental note to rob the agent that night.

JD (Jeffrey Davis): If you could do anything you wanted with this Premise, if you didn't have to think about commercial constraints, what would you do?

ME: What fascinates me is that she's young. She's fifty. If I went out with her, I'd be scoring a young chick. I think the age is interesting. How a person can be really hip. If I was going to put this woman, make this woman me, which I would probably get to. How people can be old in age, but their heads are young . . . and deep down, we're all sixteen. And we all just keep going through the same stuff, whatever it is. So, thematically, that's always interesting. I did this movie, *Lush Life*, about jazz musicians, and it was Forest Whitaker and Jeff Goldblum.

Originally, they were, I guess, in their forties, or late thirties, when they did it, but originally, I wanted these guys to be in their mid-sixties, still smoking dope, still chasing girls, still hanging out, because there are guys like that. They were still doing that, and that's what interests me. But then on the other hand, I have to say that this Premise . . . and you've been generous—said I could do anything I want with it.

Would I really want to develop a show about a mother and daughter living together? And even if I could do whatever I wanted with it, I'm not sure, even knowing some men, just not sure that's something I'd want to develop. That's what I'm saying. But, as a member of the writing community, that's what you're asked to do a lot of times. So you come up with something and say, "This could be it." But I have to say, people on the edge of criminality, in a way, interests me. Maybe because I've lived here so long.

"'If I can find a way not to screw you on this deal, I won't.'"

PD: As opposed to New York, where it's safe.

ME: Yeah, where it's safe. I once had an executive say to me, "If I can find a way not to screw you on this deal, I won't." "God bless."

JD: Charlie Peters [see page 222] told us a story about an executive who asked him, at the very beginning of his pitch, to predict how this movie would open. Does that sort of thing affect how you work?

"'Okay, that's the pilot. Tell me what happens in the twenty-second episode.'"

ME: Not me. It used to be in movies, it was, "What's the poster going to look like?" And television guys would say, "Okay, that's the pilot. Tell me what happens in the twenty-second episode." "I don't know, you got me." I remember when my partner, Rich Eustis, taped the pilot of *Head of the Class,* and afterwards, one of the network executives came by and said, "This was great. You're going to get picked up. You're going to get it on the air. Don't worry." Later, I said, "Rich, I can't think up another story. Can you?" and he said, "No." So we just went, "What are we going to do if they pick us up? I can't do it." He said, "I'm not going to do a hundred episodes." We did 150 episodes.

I think they're all scared now. Not just the writers, but all these executives. I think they're all terrified. And the stakes are high for everybody. But I don't want to be one of those guys who says, "In the old days . . ." Because if I said, "In the old days," one of these guys is going to say, "No, no, in the old, old days . . ." and then another guy would say, "No, in the old, old, *old* days . . ."

JD: Want to talk a little bit about what a Writing Room is like? What was your experience of it?

"There was no personality, no voice. It was talking, it wasn't writing."

ME: Well, I gave up on them, at some point. The last one I ran . . . Rich and I were on *Head of the Class* . . . on sitcoms, it's three jobs: This week's show, next week's show, and last week's show. Rich was very good on post-production. He liked it, I hated it. So, he would take care of last week's show, and I would be working. Together, we would work on this week's show, and then I would work on the Writers' Room. But Writers' Rooms used to be—well, if I go back a long time, the Writers' Room, for instance, on *The Cosby Show,* was myself and Ed. Weinberger. That was the Writers' Room. It was because you hired a lot of freelance writers, and they delivered a script, and you only needed one person, who was called the story editor then, which was a really big job. There were two people to work out a script, an outline, whatever it was, to break a story. And that writer would go away, write the script and come back, and you'd have a draft. So the Writers' Room—and by the way, that writer would usually go away; maybe he'd get a second draft out of it, but that writer would go away—so the Writers' Room was now you and the story editor. I was assistant story editor, and we would rewrite the script. And simply make it conform with all the previous scripts and characters that we had. That's the job, basically, of the story editor, is to make sure that each chapter in the novel of a sitcom resembles the previous one, and is consistent with it.

"'I don't want to do it anymore. I'm not going in there.'"

So then they stopped giving out scripts to freelance writers, and you had all the writers on your staff. And now the staff is eight, ten, twelve, you know, and the deal was each writer, or team, would get a job as a story editor, or associate producer . . . you know, all the titles . . . and write one or two scripts, and then he used to rewrite all the others. But what it evolved into was almost starting from the beginning, and writing scripts with a bunch of writers. Or one of the writers on the staff comes in and the script is not finished, or it's not good, whatever it is, so everybody would pitch in and write line by line. And I hated it! I hated it because it wasn't writing, it was writing by committee. There was no personality, no voice. It was talking, it wasn't writing. And then you have this assistant who, I saw this on the last job I had, who has a computer, only it's on the television screen. So everybody can look up and say, "Change this, change that," or, "Here's a better line," and so forth. And I said to Rich, the last show we did together, "I don't want to do it anymore. I'm not going in there." "So I'll rewrite with you," which we used to do anyway. We would take the script on Sunday, and rewrite it so we would have it on Monday. But I hated it. I hated it. It

In the beginning was the Writers' Room. It started with the fabled *Your Show of Shows* and is portrayed in Neil Simon's play, *Laughter on the 23rd Floor*. Writers worked alone or in teams. The work this produced had a clear, distinct voice. You could tell a Larry Gelbart sketch from one written by the Simon brothers. As television comedy evolved, shows were principally written by freelancers. A now-extinct species, the story editor was employed by producers to make sure all the episodes written by different writers conformed to the constraints of the series. Starting in the mid-1970s, beginning with shows like *Happy Days,* the story editor and the freelancer morphed into a new kind of Writers' Room, where staffs worked by committee.

Some writers believe that while this new Writers' Room may help a script's jokes become stronger, what is lost on many shows is a single voice, the very thing Sid Caesars's Writers' Room was famous for.

could be funny, because you've got funny guys and women, you know, spritzing. But, in terms of actually being a writer, it doesn't resemble writing as far as I'm concerned. How do you write a monologue for a character who wants to pour his heart out? How can five or six people write that?

JD: How is writing for a movie different from television?

ME: You don't have anybody, until you turn it in, looking over your shoulder. Especially if you're writing a spec script.

JD: Was *The Jerk* a spec?

> **"'You know, you can write novels, and get Pulitzer Prizes for plays, but still, on your tombstone they're going to write, *Here Lies The Jerk.*'"**

ME: No, no. *The Jerk* was written first for Paramount, and they turned it down. And it was very different. I mean, the story is . . . Carl Gottlieb and Steve Martin wrote a first draft. They gave it to Paramount. Paramount rejected it, said, "We don't want to make this." They took it to Universal, Universal said, "Yeah, but it needs a rewrite." Carl said, "I don't want to work on it." He went on to do other things. Steve called me up and said, "I've got to rewrite *The Jerk.*" At that time it was called *Easy Money* then. "Would you come and write it with me?" And I said, "Yeah, sure." So we rewrote the whole thing, and the three of us got credit, because we were the original writers.

I was the third writer. Universal liked it, and made it. That's the whole story. I said to Steve [Martin, who starred in *The Jerk*], "You know, you can write novels, and get Pulitzer Prizes for plays, and you can be a great art collector, and everything, but still, on your tombstone they're going to write, *Here Lies The Jerk.*"

PD: I know you come from a creative family. How did you get started in comedy writing?

"I was this radical, renegade, criminal actor."

ME: I wanted to be a writer, a serious writer with leather elbow patches on a tweed jacket, and a pipe. And then I decided in my last year of college that I wanted to be an actor. So I went to New York and I tried to be an actor, and I was. And they had all these improv classes and I took one and I met this guy, Frank Shaw, and we were very funny together. And I said, "Okay, let's be a comedy act." And we started doing a comedy act, and we had some success. We were on *The Johnny Carson Show*, and we opened for rock 'n' roll groups, and toured the country, and nightclubs, and we had a kind of smart, Nichols-and-May act that went over some places, and didn't go over in others. But we played all these little clubs, at The Upstairs at The Downstairs, and Julius Monk, and did that whole circuit. And at the same time, I kept up my acting career, and I was in a group called The Living Theatre.

I was this radical, renegade, criminal actor. We were arrested, and all that stuff. That was very exciting. And then, we were on *Johnny Carson*. And somebody called from William Morris [a talent agency] and said, "Who wrote your material? We want to hire him." And we said, "We did." "Okay, we want to hire *you* to come to California, and there are two guys, Wilson and Chambers, they saw your act and they wanted to know who the writers were." So, anyway, we said, "Okay, great," and we gave up performing, pretty much, came out here, and became writers. I remember the first day we were in this office, and a secretary came in and said, "How many typewriters do you want?" And we went like, "I don't know, two?" And then we just did variety shows, in those days, and sitcoms, and movies, movie scripts. And we split up. I partnered with Rich [Eustis]. By then, I was firmly established as a comedy writer. But, for the last ten years, I haven't worked in television. We're divorced. I have nothing against it. I like it. But whatever you want to say about ageism . . . maybe it is a young person's game, certain aspects of it. I don't want to work the hours I worked anyway, so I'm happy.

What I do now is, I read books, I option books and adapt them. And the genres are not comedy anymore. My main interest at the moment is completing the financing for a book I optioned by Anthony Burgess, on the life of Christopher Marlowe. So I wrote a screenplay and I'm going to direct that when the rest of the money comes in, any minute. And another one is a science fiction novel by Robert Silverberg, which I have with a producer, and I wrote the screenplay for that. I'm more interested in those things now. I'm not saying I left comedy behind. I have a comedy screenplay I wrote, and I'm still funny in person.

I'm interested in expressing my real interests, which include Elizabethan literature, science fiction, English crime novels, and Stalin. I'm very big on Stalin. I'm writing a play about Stalin and the Moscow Art Theatre.

JD: How do you balance all these projects?

ME: No balance. I get overwhelmed; it's all at different stages. I wrote a play and I'm fooling around with it, you know, I go back. We had a reading. Paul Mazursky wants to direct it. It's a play about the Catskills, about a Communist hotel in the Catskills. I'm really from the Borscht Belt. So, I have a lot of stuff; I go from one to the other. Somebody reads it and they say, "Well, we can talk about it . . ." maybe change a few things, go through various drafts . . . you know art is never finished, it's merely abandoned.

JD: Who have you mentored?

ME: Well, I don't know if I'd use such a fancy word, but a lot of people have worked for us. One of the actors on *Head of the Class* is Brian Robbins, although we never encouraged him. Let's see. I read screenplays that people send me. "My friend and I wrote a screenplay; would you read it?" So I do that. I teach . . . every year I teach a course at Screenwriter Expo called "The Art of Collaboration." And another one called "Adapting the Novel." I taught at a few institutes around the country. I started as a junior high school math teacher. That was my first job. Bill Lawrence, the guy who created *Scrubs,* was on our staff at *Head of the Class.* Danny Smith, who was on *Family Guy,* the animated series, he was one of our first hires.

PD: Was wit a big part of growing up in your family?

"My father made fun of everything, including us . . ."

ME: I have an incredible family; we're all funny. My father liked to really turn things on their head. It's like this Jack Benny writer I once worked with. He said, "Just for argument's sake, what if we make him a chimpanzee?" And that was always great. It would start you thinking completely differently. My father made fun of everything, including us, and we learned to be funny. My whole family has a good, ironic sense of humor. Nobody's allowed to take anything too seriously.

JD: Do you think you carried that into the improv and the writing?

ME: Yeah. But, more and more, I liked improv as its own art form. What I didn't like when I became a writer and director, I certainly didn't like people improvising any of my words. And I would say, as a director, I always say, "I want to hear it the way I wrote it. Then we'll talk." But I want to hear it first the way I wrote it. Television is the writer's medium, because in television, you're in charge. They need you more than they need the director, and you can say to the actors, "This is the way you say it," or, "This is what you say." Then, at a certain point, the actor gets a lot of power.

> ## "It's a schizophrenic occupation because you make something, and then on the other hand you have to make it better, and in order to make it better, you have to realize that it's not good enough yet."

PD: How can you tell when something you create is funny?

ME: You mean before it's tried out by an actor? It's experience. I think good comedy writers are . . . It's a schizophrenic occupation because you make something, and then on the other hand you have to make it better, and in order to make it better, you have to realize that it's not good enough yet. And that's the mark—for me, that's always the mark of a really professional writer. He's skeptical of his work. And it's also the reason why comedy writers do better as teams because the other partner, you can make him laugh, or they say, "Not so funny."

PD: Do you think that writers with a stand-up or an acting background develop a survival skill for what's funny?

ME: That's absolutely true. My years as a comedian, and thinking something's funny, and staring out into 200 faces, you better make sure it's funny. Or, this is what not being funny feels like. So I don't mind telling actors, "Don't worry, it's funny. Just do it, it's funny, you'll see." I want to have the confidence, know that the actor's going to help make it funny. My experience as a comedian, I think, really helped me, because people would say, "This is going to be funny." And I'd say, "No, it's not; I'm telling you it's not." The hidden part of that sentence is—because I couldn't go up there—

In the first incarnation of this book, we asked writers how they knew if their material was funny. (If you haven't read the Introduction on page 1, now might be a good time.) We thought it was just a throwaway question and were surprised by the interest it evoked. Hal Kantor, a well-known writer/director from the 1950s to the 1980s, said, "I've had the same secretary for twelve years. I would write something and then walk out of my office and read it to her and say, 'Do you think this is funny?' Without changing her expression or tone, she would say, 'Yeah, that's real funny.'"

He would often have to wait six months to a year until he heard an audience respond before he got his answer. All of the writers who didn't have stand-up comedy experience said they had a lot of doubts about knowing if their material was funny. On the other hand, those who had stand-up experience seemed more confident because they had frontline experience and kept referring to it as "a survival skill."

"If I had to go up on stage, I couldn't make people laugh at this piece of crap, so don't tell me it's funny."

PD: We did an interview with a joke writer for Bob Hope, who said, "Hope is so infallible. When you give him ten jokes, he says, 'These four are funny, I can get laughs with these two.'" He knew. And he was right.

ME: Right. See, there are guys . . . yeah, but then there are guys like Cosby, for instance, when I wrote on *The Bill Cosby Show*, this is the first one when he was a teacher, and then I did his variety show. Cosby was different. You couldn't make Cosby say a line any way. He would never say exactly what you wrote. That's why you had to write situationally . . . you had to give him an attitude; you had to give him a situation that was funny, and he would approximate the line. It didn't matter . . . and he would make it funny. So you knew going in, he's not going to hit the word, making it funny, he's not going to take a beat and say the word, whatever it was. But he knew how to make it funny in his own style. So that was a different kind of comedian.

PD: How did you pick up skills like how to write a setup, how to pause a beat, when to do that?

ME: Well, I had teachers, and through experience being a comedian, writing our own material, and doing it all the time and finding out, "This didn't work, this didn't work . . ." "Hey, if you take a beat here, it'll work." So I got a pretty good experiential grounding, but I never took a writing course, which I regret.

One of the first desk jobs I had was working with Ed. Weinberger on *The Bill*

Cosby Show. He really taught me a lot, just by being with him and writing with him, and he was great. I really learned a lot from him.

JD: Are you ever in conflict when you direct something you've written?

ME: Something happens when you're the writer and the director with actors who are really good, like Forest Whitaker, Jeff Goldblum, and Kathy Baker. I mean, writers have inhibition levels that go to here [*Michael holds his hand at chest level*]. Actors have them up here [*he holds his hand at forehead level*], right. They leave you in the dust, so when they read something you wrote, you're like, "Wow, did I even write that? I have no memory of that because I didn't think about the guy shouting, or acting," or whatever. So that's one thing. The other thing is, you have to look and say, "The scene doesn't work." If the scene doesn't work, you can't say, "As a writer I love the scene," you have to say as the director, "Hey, this scene doesn't work." Now you have to call on the writer, yourself, and say, "How do I fix this?" If you can't be self-critical, not to the point that you're indecisive, or completely negative, but you have to be self-critical so you can repair what has to be repaired. And that's the good thing about television. You don't have to do it on the spot, because you've got five days. So if the scene isn't working, and I guess that's a place where the Writers' Room could be effective. Sometimes you just need more jokes; it has to be funnier. So that group writing can help there.

". . . I realized that I was going to meetings with the writer's personality."

A writer's attitude, a producer, a director, an actor . . . they're all different personalities. I became aware of this when I wrote the screenplay for *Lush Life*. When I started out talking to people who were interested in producing it, I was going to be the director. And at one point I realized that I was going to meetings with the writer's personality, not the director's personality, because they would say, "We really love the script." "Oh, thank you, thanks." "But we're a little unsure about maybe the ending, or whatever it is," and I said, "Yeah, sure, we can talk about that," or, "No, that has to be the way it is." And I came out of these meetings, and I said, "Something's wrong here. I know what it is. I'm going there as a writer." Because a director wouldn't go in and say, "You know, I really love the script," the director would say, "Yeah, so? Let's talk about schedule, casting. What do you mean, you love the script? We're talking about . . . I don't care, we're getting another writer to rewrite it, anyway."

An Interview with
Heather Hach

A partial list of Heather Hach's credits as a writer includes *Freaky Friday* (2003), *Legally Blonde: The Musical* (2007), and *Freaky Monday*.

Heather Hach's sensibility in comedy was shaped by milestone events, like her father insisting that the entire family walk out on *Cannonball Run*. Her taste runs toward the dark side, which is a surprise, since she looks like a cheerleader and got her big break as a Disney fellow. Despite her pull toward the dark side, she is versatile enough to have written the 2003 remake of *Freaky Friday* and the book for the stage version of *Legally Blonde*.

PD (Peter Desberg): As we've explained in our Premise [see page 9], how would you go about developing the show's plot lines?

HH (Heather Hach): I think there is something interesting about this idea of the delaying of aging. People are telling themselves that sixty is the new forty and forty is the new thirty. It seems as if women, in particular, are looking younger. I think about what my grandma looked like at sixty. She was what we think of as a classic grandmother. My mom won't be called "Grandma." She's glamorous, and she's fabulous, and she looks forty. There could be a really interesting relationship here between the mother and daughter, especially if the mother is reverting more to a daughter-like persona, especially if she's a free spirit. But, you have the restraint of not having any money. I might get rid of that aspect of the Premise.

Sarah's a workaholic with a guesthouse above her garage that's unused. What if Molly comes to live there? I think the fun of it is Sarah thinks that her mother is in a really bad place. She tells someone at work, "My dad died a year ago, she's totally destroyed. I've had to talk to her on the phone every day." So she goes to pick her up at the airport, thinking she's going to find a grief-stricken woman in a shawl, but instead, Molly steps out and she just happens to mention she's into Pilates. She looks fabulous. And maybe she says, "Everything I thought I needed, I don't need. I'm starting over."

The fun is the shock Sarah feels when she finds out that her mother isn't like who she was expecting. She was prepared to help her grief-stricken mother, when in actuality, the mother could be helping her daughter find her sense of fun. Since Molly looks fantastic and is into Pilates, what if she opens up a Pilates studio that's really successful, and fabulous, and fuels her kind of craziness? Here's an idea for that kind of craziness. She's having an affair with the pool guy. I think that's a funny juxtaposition, especially if you have it in your mind that it's going to be one way, but it's so completely the opposite.

It's funny if tunnel-vision Sarah is freaked out that her mother is way hotter than she is, and has a much better social life than she does. Molly's the one on Match.com, and she's the one setting Sarah up on dates, and she's the one with a second lease on life. She tells her daughter, "I'm not going to apologize for being sexual." Automatic conflict.

It could be a series, but frankly, there is so little TV that I respond to that I always go toward film. The first act would be the revelation that Molly is not in this grief-stricken, devastated place. She's been so busy that she just kind of hears what she wants to hear. And maybe the movie is also about destroying the myth around Sarah's father. And maybe it's Molly who does the destroying. He was supposed to be this stallion when it came to finances. But it was a complete lie, and he invested all his money with a Madoff-like guy. So where's the truth? "Mom isn't living for a man, as I always assumed she was." We've seen workaholic women like Sarah ad nauseam, but if you have it playing off her mother as a free spirit, I think it can be fun.

PD: She's a free spirit, but is she also smart?

HH: Not in a traditional way. I think she's clever. She's always lived her life for other people, and now suddenly for the first time, she says, "Well, what about me? Someone forgot to put me on the checklist." And Sarah says, "Oh, my God, my mother has gone crazy." It would be funny if Sarah works herself past exhaustion, and her mother comes home and says, "The Pilates studio has taken off."

"Everyone thinks I must watch *Sleeping Beauty*."

Maybe at the same time, Sarah fumbles in her own career. She screwed up at work. Made a bad decision. Maybe they join up and the solution is that Sarah becomes the CEO of Molly's company. Together they open up this really successful juice bar, Pilates workout studio. And what happens is that Sarah realizes she needed a timeout from the corporate fast track. She needed a re-jigger of her own life as well. Fun. It's a really fun movie!

JD (Jeffrey Davis): What personal element would you add to this story?

HH: Honestly, my taste for film is always much darker than what people expect of Heather Hach. Everyone thinks I must watch *Sleeping Beauty*.

PD: How would you darken this?

HH: I would give it a more *Flirting with Disaster* edge as opposed to the Goldie Hawn route. You know, make Molly more Mary Tyler Moore, with a drinking problem. Because there are a lot of people who are healthy and yet they drink a bottle of Chardonnay a night. There is some fun to be had with that kind of mom, someone who is completely obsessed with her appearance. They pretend it's all about health, when health has nothing to do with it. It's all about vanity. I can't watch ten minutes of TV without seeing wrinkle remover and injectable facelifts. There's so much comedy in that world and in that reality. Let's be honest, there's comedy in how much pressure there is on women not to age. I'd like to explore that aspect of the story.

PD: What ends up happening to Molly as a consequence of her drinking?

HH: She bottoms out. She has to face the drinking. Or does she? This is a part of the problem with movies. You always have to have everything completely fixed at the end. Not every movie, but commercial, studio-driven movies. I always loved the end of *Election*. It's just stunningly perfect. I think *Election* is also one of the best political movies ever made. It's also very human. At the end, when Matthew Broderick is at the museum and there is the new little Tracy Flick, Reese Witherspoon's character, with her hand in the air, it says that nothing changes, which I love, because nothing does really change.

I like a happy ending, too. I don't want to walk out of the theatre absolutely, morbidly depressed. But I like movies that have a darker edge and feel more real. If her mom is an alcoholic, at some point, Sarah has to find out about it and confront it.

Maybe Molly makes a sloppy agreement. She says, "I'll only drink on the weekends." And even then, her drinking is completely out of control. I'll tell you what I wouldn't want to see in this story. I don't want dialogue from Molly like, "You're right. Thank you for illuminating the truth. I do need to stop drinking." You want it to be real. Of course we go to the movies to see people who look better than we do and have better romantic lives. But what is so satisfying is when a film also reflects what we feel and didn't know we felt.

"... one of my friends said, 'You are a very dark blonde.'"

Frankly, I had much darker impulses earlier on in my career. What really started my career was this script like *Heathers*, about a sorority where they kill a lesbian and they cover it up. But then I got *Freaky Friday*, and that's not exactly a sad day at Auschwitz. They always want you to make it sweet and happy. But one of my friends said, "You are a very dark blonde." I would like to see Molly still drinking at the end.

JD: Would the audience find this out at the same time as Sarah?

HH: Probably as Sarah discovers it. How about this? No one ever talks about the fact that people who drink tend to be more fun. I'm sorry, I'll take the drinkers over the non-drinkers almost any day. I'll find the people who like wine like I do at the party. So what if Molly does stop drinking, and she becomes a complete pain in the ass? And then Sarah is begging her, "Please start drinking again!" I think that could be really fun. I do like the lesson in moderation. It's a valuable lesson when there is a happy medium where you still get to be a little bit bad, but it's still kind of satisfying at the same time.

PD: So she goes from drunk to sober to moderately sober?

HH: Moderate to occasionally sloppy. Because isn't that more interesting and real?

JD: Where would you take their relationship?

HH: I think it's got to be tied to the business, because everything starts to collapse for Sarah at the time that everything's going really well for Molly's new Pilates studio. So they start to work together, and you can have this wonderful montage of everything going so great, and then the drinking and all the other things start to snowball and drive it all down. Maybe that's what makes Sarah say, "I gave up my job for your Pilates studio, and you're more focused on guys and dates than work, and you're still a booze-hound."

Sarah has been on this delusional path of working, working, working, and that's why she didn't see the truth about her father. Maybe Sarah is so driven because her father was so driven. She's modeled herself on him. She didn't see the truth about her mother either, and says, "I'm not seeing the truth about myself." She's putting everything into it and it collapses.

PD: Does Sarah change as she goes through this experience with Molly?

HH: I think she's got to wake up and face the fact that she's been on this hamster wheel. She's got to be honest about herself, and her mom and her dad. She's got to realize that her life is passing her by. She sees clearly that her mom has a better social life than she does. She's never made time for it. This could be a fun movie, especially if it was done with a little bit of a subversive edge. You need a little complication. What if Molly starts dating Sarah's boyfriend from high school? That's creepy, right? This is the guy Sarah always pined for.

PD: Did he dump her?

"... the only satire that works is satire that has a soft heart towards what it's satirizing."

HH: Yeah, in high school. But this is about how Molly and Sarah don't communicate, so Molly doesn't know the truth about anything. Sarah never told her mom how much he meant to her. And her mom doesn't even remember this guy, and he comes to the Pilates studio. They start dating. Sarah finds out about it and reverts to the high school girl who had a crush on this guy.

No matter how sophisticated you are, or what you accomplish in your life, you're always just two emotional beats away from being the girl who didn't get asked to dance. It never goes away.

I would do this as satire, but I think the only satire that works is satire that has a soft heart towards what it's satirizing. You can't do it with malicious intent. There has to be a little bit of empathy and emotion.

PD: It has that feeling, especially if neither the ex-boyfriend nor Molly has such a great memory. She innocently stumbles upon it.

HH: Sarah never confided in her, but she's enraged anyway. "You don't remember my prom date?" That's kind of funny. "No, I don't. It was a long time ago." "There were pictures. More than one." You thought your mom was so checked in and completely there for you, and she had no job, and she was just out to lunch, and Sarah didn't see the drinking growing up.

PD: So she starts dating him. Where does that go? That's going to bring up a huge conflict.

HH: He doesn't know that this is Sarah's mother. So when he sees Sarah at the Pilates studio, "Oh, my God, it's Sarah." Suddenly he's in the middle of a crisis. "Your mom is so hot." "Stop saying that!"

PD: Who does he end up with?

HH: Maybe neither. It's too loaded. Once you've made out with Mom, you can't date

Heather provides an inspired example of a non-hostile conflict when she has Molly inadvertently dating Sarah's old boyfriend. Sarah and Molly are not out to get one another. This is an accidental situation. The old boyfriend is a clever example of what Charlie Peters refers to as a "third object." As we see how each reacts to the introduction of this character from the past re-entering their lives, we learn more about Sarah and Molly than we do about him. He disappears in the next scene, but their reactions to him reveal a lot about who they are.

the daughter anymore. I think he should just go away. He could be the catalyst to bring them to a greater disclosure about the drinking and all the other secrets they've kept over the years.

PD: Who are the secondary characters in the movie?

HH: I think you've got to populate the world with the Pilates clients and the other instructors. It's such a funny, self-centered world. "We're really going to focus on those glutes." There's just so much fun to be had in that world. It's therapy. We don't talk to the closest people in our lives about the truth of what's going on. And you end up sitting next to someone on a plane and they know more about your life than your parents. It's the same thing with Pilates. It's a weird dynamic. It's intimate. People spill things to Molly they'd never tell their husbands.

PD: Did you act before you started writing?

HH: I did improv comedy. I was with a troupe for years. The Comedy Sports. It was such great training for what I do now. I also did forensics in high school. I did Lincoln/Douglass debate and Humor Competition. You took source material and you wrote a little bit. I had such success doing it, and I wrote to my forensics teacher, "I would not be doing what I'm doing had it not been for you." Everyone went to the finals in Humor at these competitions, and most people were eliminated throughout the course of the day. All the schools from Colorado attended, so it was this huge forum. You would be competing in front of a packed auditorium. At sixteen. And then to win, it was just so thrilling. It made me feel like, "This is who I am."

"The best thing that happened to me was bad vision and bad teeth."

PD: Were you always a funny kid?

HH: I was always a liar. I would tell horrible lies. My best friend's mother in preschool thought my parents weren't married for a year. "That's not my real dad." Now my three-year-old daughter is doing it. Her teacher pulled me aside and said, "Harper's been telling everyone at school she's pregnant and she's going to name the baby Drake." And the kids believe her. Here we go again! And my daughter is so cute. I'm hoping to God that her teeth come in crooked. I had glasses and I had horrible teeth. I'm so glad I did because if I had been the cute girl in class, I don't think I would have had to be the funny one. The best thing that happened to me was bad vision and bad teeth.

JD: Well, that has definitely been corrected.

HH: Thanks. Good skin care products.

JD: How did *Legally Blonde: The Musical* come about?

HH: The producers saw *Freaky Friday* and thought I might have the right voice for it. I was very dubious about it because I love movie musicals, but I had no experience with them. I used to listen to *Little Shop of Horrors* soundtrack in the car in high school, which not a lot of girls were doing.

JD: Who mentored you?

HH: I was assigned to Andrew Gunn as my producer when I won the Disney Fellowship. He's the one who got my career going. He was a great mentor and got me *Freaky Friday*, and I'm working with him now on *Freaky Monday*. But I've had lots of mentors in different arenas that aren't a part of show business. I worked at *The New York Times*, Denver Bureau, right out of college doing research.

PD: What did you study in college?

HH: Journalism. I didn't think I could write movies. This was beyond the scope of my imagination. I was always a writer, but I just thought I had to be practical about it, and make a living. I didn't know anyone in Hollywood. Even though movies and comedy were my passion, it just seemed abstract.

> **"I really think that studios should pick five top candidates and pay them at least a couple thousand for the amount of work they do . . ."**

JD: You've spent time in development?

HH: There are things that are so great about what we do as writers, but the thing that is so frustrating is the amount of work you do for nothing. I put in hours, and hours, and hours figuring out a whole movie. Rehearsing it, really thinking about it. It's not easy to come up with a movie. And then you go into a studio. I really think that studios should pick five top candidates and pay them at least a couple thousand for the amount of work they do, because the amount of work we do for free is just absurd.

Then you pitch, and they always come back with, "We want it like this." It's like everything is another movie that reminds them of something else. "Okay, yes, we know you've seen that great film." Or, "Yes, we all love *Tootsie*, but this is a different movie." It's just frustrating that there seems to be no other headspace beyond, "It's *like* this." I have a movie right now, *French Women Don't Get Fat*, that's trying to get a director. And people have said, "Oh, it's kind of similar to *Julie and Julia*."

JD: Were your parents funny?

HH: My dad is very subversive and very funny. My mom is "Miss Show Tunes." I didn't think she was as funny as I've come to see. She's a big personality and always singing. My dad was always like David Letterman, always at the expense of someone else, which most comedy is. We'll drive by somebody running really slow and he'll say, "There's somebody I could beat in a race!" Just that kind of mean comedy. They have great taste. They showed me great comedy.

JD: For example?

HH: People think I'm making this story up, but before *Plan 9 from Outer Space* was a huge cult favorite, Ed Wood's worst film ever, they saw it and they thought it was so hilarious. My first night back from college and they were so excited to be together and said, "We have *Plan 9 from Outer Space* to watch!" I just don't think that's a really common back-from-college-reunion-for-the-whole-family story. They have good taste in film. As a young kid I watched *Harold and Maude*. I remember we went to *Cannonball Run*. It was such a hit. Everyone loves *Cannonball Run*. So we're in the middle of a packed theatre in Colorado and my dad says, "I can't take it! I gotta get out of here!" Everyone's dying of laughter, and we had to creep over everybody and I was like, "This is funny, I think. I don't know what's going on." My dad's like, "Get outta there. My God, it was awful." So I was always aware of good comedy versus cheap laughs.

An Interview with

Mitch Klebanoff

A partial list of Mitch Klebanoff's credits includes: *Disorderlies,*
Beverly Hills Ninja, The Jersey, and *Swap Meet.*

Mitch Klebanoff is a study in contrasts. By turns screwy, off-the-wall, and adolescent as he comes up with original jokes, he then turns into an adult who makes use of his math and science background through his attention to story structure and detail. This rare balance of oddball comedy and well-crafted cause-and-effect relationships makes the most outlandish situation become plausible and produces some extraordinarily original work. Mitch's placement of a mother-daughter relationship against the backdrop of punk rock is one of the most unusual stories we've seen in these interviews.

PD (Peter Desberg): As we've explained in our Premise [see page 9], how would you go about developing the show's plot lines?

MK (Mitch Klebanoff): The first thing I would do to make this Premise seem different is do it single-camera. It would change the whole nature of how you'd go about it because I would be bored with the idea that you have a living room with a wacky mother and daughter. I'd find a way to make it more like a movie. In the movie world, you're following the action and you're going to watch and see everything that's relevant. In the sitcom world, a lot of things are going to happen off-screen and you're then going to see everyone's reaction to it. I like those shows where you're using the visual medium much more than just doing some dialogue-based comedy.

So what are the visuals of this show? Where's Molly? Molly being in a living room is not a particularly visual idea. The visual would be how we get her into a place where she's trying to work or trying to do something. Each week I would probably try to do a new task of figuring out what she wants. And we'd be following her, going with her, whether it was an interview or starting a new job. And they would be silly or visual, or something like that, as opposed to . . . she goes off and she does those things and then comes home and tells Sarah about them. I'd like to see her *do* all those things, and if that means she sells lemonade in the mall with one of those funny hats, that's what she's doing. I don't know if that's the best of all jokes. The wackier, the more it would grate on Sarah's nerves. Because if Sarah's very officious and she's got this—you know, she's going to be V.P. Actually, the more lowbrow Molly's job is, the more it would grate on Sarah because she's a V.P., so she's not going to want to see her mom working at a lemonade stand at the mall. I would start out and I would probably do a bunch of different shows where the mom's not working at a level that the daughter would find satisfying. At some point, you might want to do the reverse: Have the mother get a job that the daughter would be jealous of. Working with male models?

If Molly got a job as a photographer, or an assistant to a photographer, now she's working with all these hot male models, who are not gay. And so, Sarah might be attracted to that, she would find that to be something she might find interesting. But I wouldn't want that one joke to define the show, because it could end up throwing the whole show off in a direction that wouldn't be worthwhile.

Another thought that just crossed my mind is that Molly starts a dating service, but not just a regular dating service, but like eHarmony, where she's actually really successful at it and all her friends now look up to her. The oldest way of telling that joke is she's a matchmaker. The modern way of telling that joke is she's working at eHarmony. They're pretty much the same thing. And the goal is to set her daughter up. One could start a whole multi-million-dollar business just simply trying to get her daughter laid.

It seems to me Sarah is going to stay who Sarah is and Molly's just going to go off the wall. And she's going to be the person that fuels the comedy every week. There are a lot of great fifty-year-old comediennes. Probably very underused and really hysterical.

PD: How do you go about defining the characters?

"I know everyone says you start from the character, right? I start with whatever comes to mind."

MK: I know everyone says you start from the character, right? I start with whatever comes to mind. And so in trying to solve logic problems, ideas emerge. Like anyone else, no matter how creative, I'll get hung up on the logic of it and I won't be able to think of anything until I understand the premise and make sure that it's really solid. Everything has to be believable within some world you're creating. Even with *Beverly Hills Ninja*, it's the silliest premise in the world, but something has to ground it enough to say okay, yes, he washed ashore on a Japanese island, he was brought up by ninjas, so obviously he wanted to be one of them. Well, that defined who he was. Just that desire. If all your brothers and sisters are running around throwing nunchucks, you're going to want to throw one, too. So, there's nothing more basic than that. The character is going to grow from there.

So we start fleshing out Molly and Sarah because we wanted to know why Molly wants Sarah to date. Molly works around male models. Maybe she sees how desperate Sarah is to get ahead. Maybe Sarah's an ass-kisser. Now, that's not very heroic, so that's a tough call. You have to decide right there. Okay, would I be willing to make Sarah an ass-kisser, which means she's not attractive? She could be beautiful, but she could be an ass-kisser and that's going to be funny, but usually you would give that role to some other character. You wouldn't give that to your hero or your heroine. So, if you wanted to go that way, that would be a difficult choice and you'd want to think it through. She has a reason to be an ass-kisser on this. Here's where my logic comes in. Something kicked off her need to be an ass-kisser. So Mom then came and had some job that was similar and started thinking, "Oh, she's an ass-kisser." It's not as grounded that way because if she really was one, what Mom had to say would be truthful.

PD: If Sarah's an ass-kisser at work and then lectures Molly about the kind of work she's doing, she'd be awfully hypocritical.

MK: Which creates the bringing back 4 billion conversations they had when Sarah was sixteen and when Molly was thirty-two. Obviously, all teenagers do is pick out all the possibilities for hypocrisy, which we all are filled with. It brings up the issue if you do that episode, which is the *hypocrisy* show, which of course would be really attractive to all our teenage viewers, is it like *Rashomon?* Do you go back and re-tell the story, and do you go into a flashback? And you have to try and make Sarah look like she's sixteen and Mom look like she's thirty-two, which is a casting problem. That would define the problem with that episode, which is that you probably couldn't do that show. Or you'd have to come up with a funny way to do it so that we could buy the fact that Sarah's going to play herself at fourteen. Because do we really want to bring another actress in to play that role that day? Not likely. But it would be funny to do *Rashomon.* You always want to show how nobody remembers anything the way it's supposed to be. And the hypocrisy is certainly going to be an issue that is going to come up over and over again. It's not just going to be one show, it's going to be many shows, and it's going to flip back and forth between them.

PD: That's also a really funny idea to develop. That you're dealing with each other as adults, but the same conflicts have been there all through their history.

MK: Yeah, that doesn't change. But actually they flip to some extent because—well, it's possible that they may flip, where Sarah is acting the adult and Molly is actually the child, but the truth is that it might have been true when they were fourteen and thirty-two. And as a matter of fact, in terms of fleshing out the characters, now that I think about it, she might have been born adult, you know, right from the beginning. She always knew. Molly may have always been the wayward mom, if she was a hippie.

Actually at this point, she wouldn't have to be a hippie, she could actually be a punk rocker. In other words, Mom was a punk rocker, but she's now a mom. Okay, I think we've gotten enough years past punk rock, which probably started as early as 1974. So '74, okay, so that means today that's thirty-two years ago, and she would have been fourteen then . . . yeah, Molly could have been a punk rocker. So that's funnier. That's better than being a hippie because that's already too old. And we've seen that idea. But I'm not sure we've seen the idea of a mom who used to be a punk rocker. That would be good.

PD: Would you ever play around with the idea that in business situations, Sarah is mature, but when it comes to relationships, they would change roles?

MK: I think that I would always do it. It's a matter of fact. Most anybody who's going to be as protected as Sarah is, is going to have her vulnerable side. And the question is, how often does she let you see it; what button gets pushed? And how often do you want to push it? I mean, it would be repetitive if you constantly played it that way, where she has this veneer that's really tough. She's officious, but she's got this other thing going. I mean, it's in her. It wouldn't be repetitive if it was there all the time. But it would be repetitive if you were making a point of the series showing this.

"What show is not a one-joke series?"

PD: You'd have to work really hard to not make it a one-joke series.

MK: What show is not a one-joke series? Let's talk about *Seinfeld.* It's four jokes. One for each character and they get repeated every time. I didn't watch it every season for that reason. I got bored with it at some point. The safety of the formula is also its potential downfall. Some people don't have that problem with it. There's this theory out there that audiences want to see the joke repeated.

JD (Jeffrey Davis): What would you do if this was a comedic movie?

MK: It could be an indie movie if you made it really quirky and you didn't try to make it mainstream. Then it would make more sense to me. The punk rock idea not played cheesy could *quirk* it up. If you did it in the comedy vein of *Office Space*, which I don't see as a mainstream movie. If you found really offbeat comedy having to do with some of these places Molly worked at, and odd characters that were quirky and bizarre, and you were able to have her meet a lot of people along the way.

PD: The people in the punk rock movement believed in what that movement was about. They were intense social critics and they expressed themselves in really shocking ways.

MK: I don't know if I've thought it through that far. Now that I think about it, it would be an interesting thing to do with this mom, because that mom may have already dampened all her intensity. That may not be what she's been doing for the last twenty years, and then her husband dies and she's out on her own. All of a sudden, maybe the real Molly suddenly starts to reappear. And that person is not just a person who has punk rock in her background, she has punk rock in her spirit. And that's different.

PD: I remember walking through the streets of New York in the 1970s with them yelling, "Die Yuppie Scum."

MK: I remember that phrase.

PD: And here's Sarah, who is Yuppie scum, and Molly raised her.

MK: I tell you what *wouldn't* make it quirky is if she picked up a guitar. Then it would be like *Freaky Friday* or *My Mom Is a Rockstar.* That's not what I meant. It would be more the behavior of a . . .

PD: . . . the philosophy . . .

MK: Yeah, the philosophy and that kind of thing. Think of how embarrassing the political activism would be for Sarah. The punk rockers were kind of nihilistic, they weren't even trying to make the world a better place. "Die Yuppie Scum" was purely a gut reaction. I don't think there was a "Let's do this" part. They didn't care about what people thought of them. If people walked out and said this is horrible music, they could give a shit. Which would actually be an amazing thing. I mean, that would be a whole different tone if that mother really felt that way. I mean, Molly, fifty years old, all of a sudden gets back in touch with that music. That's not even a comedy anymore, necessarily. That's actually something else.

PD: Especially if it was done suddenly, where she's not going to pierce her lip with a safety pin. It's more the attitude than the accoutrements.

MK: But with that attitude, she would probably start to hate her daughter. All of a sudden she's watching Sarah and she's basically saying, "Die Yuppie Scum," and her daughter is the Yuppie scum she's going to end up hating. Or, I guess there's a comedic form of that hate. But if it's played real, it wouldn't be a comedy anymore. We're going into drama now. Molly is a mom who is bitter about her husband's death. She actually blames all the institutions that have caused it. And then you start to explore that part of it, which is Sarah asking, "Why did Dad die?" That's drama. Then it would be like a French film, or German, or something like that. It wouldn't be American. There's got to be a conflict, there's got to be something at the core of it. The question is how close you cut to feeling like it's a drama versus masking it and really holding it together with the dramatic push of the movie. I run into this problem all the time. I fall in love with a joke so I go, joke, joke, joke, joke, story's gone. So now I go, joke, joke, story, joke, joke.

JD: Is this something you do when you're writing a rough draft?

"I do that in my fiftieth draft."

MK: I do that in my fiftieth draft. It comes up all the time. Lately, what I do is scene lists. I pretty much write down every scene prior to writing the script. That doesn't mean I do those scenes if something new happens. But I've found if I don't do that, usually the story goes awry. Probably my logical mind is working on the scene list, and then my right-brain mind takes over when I'm writing the scenes. Then, instead of ending the scene where I expected to end it, I get some new idea, and then the next four scenes go off in another direction. Then all of a sudden, I have to pull it back somehow. And if I love those four scenes, that's worse. Because then I have to figure out a way to make them work and then I'm re-tooling everything. And that's really the problem.

JD: You talked about *joke, joke, story, joke, joke.* What does that mean?

MK: What I mean is pretty much when I'm writing a comedy, I'm always insecure about how funny it is, so I'm always pushing to see where I can find humor. But sometimes that's a mistake. You just can't push. I'm not saying they're not funny, but I am saying that people's response to comedy on paper, at least in the reading process, you're not going to get everybody who is going to get the joke. So you really better get the story working well because if they don't get two of those four jokes, they've really lost the story. If they get all four of those jokes, they'll wait for the story to come back around, but that's a risk. You know the reading process of Hollywood. The linearity of the plot is relative to the short attention span of the reader. You don't know that those four jokes will work on everybody. I mean, that's a risk that is tough when people are reading.

"The linearity of the plot is relative to the short attention span of the reader."

I think when you're shooting a movie, it's less of a risk. Because I think that your audience is already there. They're there watching the movie and they'll give you some more leeway to do a couple of scenes that might be funny, but make you feel as though the plot is not really pushing forward all the time. I guess it doesn't really make sense to have a philosophy about writing spec scripts or scripts in general, because each one will be different creatively. But I have learned over the years that you can't get too far away for too long from the plot because no matter what you think it is, or how funny even five out of ten people think it is, because the chance of you getting it read by enough people in a row that are of those five out of ten are pretty slim. It almost sounds like a mathematical formula, but it's kind of true.

PD: How do you know if what you're writing is funny?

MK: I don't. I make judgments for the moment and then basically, it's a consensus operation. I used to say, when I was writing with my partner, that if one person was writing alone, they would have no idea if it was funny. The fact that we were working together meant we had twice as good a chance at thinking it might be funny. But that was the only shot we had. We all know that until you go and give it to other people, it's just like a vacuum, you just can't tell. You have your own spark. I tend, historically, to write or come up with comedy that has a wide range of appeal. So I can tend to think it might be funny because I have been able to make a larger group of people laugh. But on any one given joke? No. There's no way of knowing. My intuition is probably ultimately pretty good, but I've written plenty of clunky scripts. Sometimes you find yourself in the middle of a script and it's like finding your way out of a paper bag.

JD: How soon do you think you should show a draft?

MK: I'll show it right away as long as it makes sense, at least in my mind makes sense.

Especially if I think there's enough for a person to be able to help me judge it, and tell me what's good and what's working and what's not good. Show it to your agent? I'd wait quite a long time. Show it to your studio? I'd wait even longer. I won't show a draft to a studio that's not at least six drafts, and that's only if I was lucky.

"I won't show a draft to a studio that's not at least six drafts, and that's only if I was lucky."

Yeah, it's really hard to judge your own work. And if anybody tells you, "Oh, and that's funny," that's a problem. You'll know in the way they respond if it's funny. It's an energy thing. It's a transfer of energy. You tell somebody something. If the energy surges, you know it's funny. If the energy is, "Oh, yeah, that's funny," you've lost.

PD: When it comes down to actual joke construction, how did you learn to build a good set-up, a payoff?

MK: It's all mimicry. Ultimately, it's like learning how to speak English. You're experiencing it and you absorb it through some form of osmosis, and then eventually, you regurgitate it. Here's just a little thing. I'm watching your eyes, what you're responding to, the things that get you excited. I'm like a dog. I'll put in more of those. I think that's really what it is. It's like a behavior modification concept. Which is that ultimately, I guess, I have a humor gene. I like things to be funny. I like to laugh. And somehow in my youth it started and then I just fed it more. But it's really mimicry in the beginning, I mean, certainly.

PD: As a kid, did you tell a lot of jokes?

"I was voted class chatterbox."

MK: I was voted class chatterbox. I wanted to look at it as a positive thing, that I was a joke teller, but it could have meant that I was extremely talkative. Partially, it's self-entertainment. We entertain ourselves. And then we try to entertain other people by being clever or witty, and then you get accused of not being engaged in the reality of what's going on in the moment because you're trying to be funny. I never read a book about screenwriting either, by the way, which some people might say would have been a good idea. But, I did eventually read those books. I read my first screenwriting book when I went into a development meeting and I was told about one. Like how my work didn't really correspond to something that they thought was important, and that's when I read the book.

But I basically taught myself. Literally, the first thing I ever did was copy my version of *Raiders of the Lost Ark*. I loved the movie. Basically, you know, tried to write a new version of it with completely different characters and completely different situations, but really, I tried to mimic it. And so I think that I've always used that technique.

PD: You're analytic in the way you approach things.

MK: I was a much better math student than I was an English student. I mean, I was a decent student in both, but math was my thing, and especially visual math. Geometry. That's why having partners is good. Because when you lose track of story and structure, there's somebody to reel you in and tell you that you've gone off the deep end. I've been in comedy rooms and some people don't have that piece. There's just that freewheeling thing. And you become like the cop, where you have to bring it in and say, "Well, could you help me with the context of this material, could you tell me how I would possibly throw it into this scene?" But sometimes, you really want that freewheeling thing because it's brilliant. If they had five people to choose, they will get two people who are completely off-the-wall, no logic, but brilliantly funny [their strong point is joke writing] and two logic people [their strength is in story construction]. And then somebody who actually has a heart. Somebody throws out the gem, and then somebody else has to be smart enough to know how to catch it. And I don't know that it would matter if they worked off of each other in terms of the moment. Like improv.

If he's too grounded where he's in denial of the brilliance simply because it doesn't quite fit at the moment, he won't be effective. You have to be able to go with the path and realize that maybe something so freaking unbelievably funny will happen.

PD: It seems that would take an awful lot of self-knowledge.

MK: But I bet you a lot of these comedy guys, the really good people, have it. Who in the room is self-aware? Which is a whole different level of writing. Not to be threatened. Not to be working off your ego. Some people are just fueled by that, there's nothing else that's going to motivate them. But nirvana, I guess, would be where you had everybody in the Room feeling really secure enough to not be motivated by proving anything to anybody.

PD: How do you deal with people in a Room one-upping one another?

MK: Well, in some shows, I'm sure gold came out of that competition. I don't think that would be the best motivator. The way it works in improv is people really have to give themselves up for the moment to their partners. One way of working in the Room is to have people improvising off each other. Here's another way. People take role positions. The person who's nutty and off-the-wall needs the logic person to throw out the logic situation to start them off. It may not be something that would have ever occurred to them, that the logic of the situation is Sarah would act one way and Molly would act another. That's the given.

PD: It sounds like to make it really work, you would have to have awfully selfless people.

MK: That's why it doesn't work.

JD: Were people in your family interested in the arts?

"My mother and father did *Guys and Dolls* . . . It was Temple Theatre."

MK: Nobody in my family comes from an artistic background. No, I shouldn't say that. I'm going to totally contradict myself. My mother and father did *Guys and Dolls*. They did a little bit of theatre. They acted. I was an audience. It was Temple Theatre.

PD: What did your parents do?

MK: My dad is a personal injury lawyer. My mom always worked primarily as a secretary or as an assistant, and she always had projects. You know, like the Cambria Heights chapter of Weight Watchers or something like that. She always had something she was doing. They owned stores sometimes, too. Greeting card stores. Bookstores.

The best part of that as a kid was—do you remember in the late sixties when buttons were big? Where every catchy saying was put on a button? Well, my parents had every one of those. They sold them. They gave them to us. I guess I would say they both had a sense of humor. Neither of them are stoic people in any way. But my mom likes to tell jokes that she hears. My father's just a character. He's an unusual person. He was an ambulance chaser when he was young. He had that sort of "New York City, I'm a lawyer but I'm kind of a businessman, I get stuff done," thing. He was also a great guy, a man-of-the-people type of a guy. All his clients were Haitian and Puerto Rican.

Mel Brooks says there are two basic kinds of comedy: One in which an unusual person is placed in an everyday situation or setting, like the black sheriff in *Blazing Saddles,* and the other, in which an average person is placed in an unusual setting, such as Bob Hoskins's character in *Who Framed Roger Rabbit?.*

Mitch talks about how being one of the few Jewish students in a mostly black junior high school added to his ability to write multi-racial characters. This experience was enhanced because his father was an attorney with many Haitian and Puerto Rican clients. Mitch came into contact with many of them. *Beverly Hills Ninja* is a good example of this "fish out of water" setting.

He brought a lot of cultures into our house. Because I was a city kid, but beyond just being a city kid, my dad's business exposed me to a lot of cultures. Which is probably why I wrote *Disorderlies* and literally every movie I'm working on right now is an urban movie with a black lead in it, because growing up in Queens, I felt I was part of that culture.

PD: Where did you go to high school?

MK: I grew up in Queens until I was thirteen and then by the time I got to high school, I had then moved farther out onto Long Island, which was completely the opposite. It was a completely white community. The junior high I went to [in Queens] was 95 percent black, and so between that school and my dad's professional life, I probably picked up a lot of ethnic humor beyond just Jewish humor. And it's actually the cornerstone of my life right now.

"I'm writing myself into a corner every minute of the day."

JD: What do you when you write yourself into a corner?

MK: I'm writing myself into a corner every minute of the day. It's always writing myself into a corner and then writing myself out of a corner. Every once in a while, I follow what I'm doing and it all unfolds as I would expect. But most often, I'm a little bit ADD and I'm going off on tangents and I need to write myself back into where I need to be.

Yeah, the way I would define writing myself into a corner is by going off on a tangent that's comedic, generally. Because most of the time, my logic stuff I plan out and so I've covered most of the logic points, and it's only where I go off and I have to change the logic where I end up in trouble. But most of the time, I kind of know what it is before I get started. Or, I started at the wrong place, where I just made a mistake with the way the script was going to be mounted, which happens sometimes.

PD: If you didn't create a character, what do you do to get into his head?

MK: Well, I have also adapted novels, so I've done that. I mean, it's kind of a sense memory concept, like any actor would. He's trying to picture who that person is and try and get into what his internal monologue is. You know, what's in their head. What are they saying to themselves as they're doing everything that they're doing? But I won't do that with every character. Some characters are props and they're there for the purpose of making my main character accomplish what they want to accomplish and they're the person who I'm absorbed with. So I won't do that with most of the characters. And especially if I'm doing a story where it's just one character you're following all the time—then it's easy because you're always in their head. You're them and you're maneuvering through. Things get more problematic when you create scenes that start with other characters other than that main character. That's a structural issue.

PD: Is it difficult for you if the character is unlike you? What about a really quirky character?

MK: No. It's not at all difficult. It's probably easier, actually. Obviously, Chris Farley in *Beverly Hills Ninja* is nothing like me. But there came a time where I knew his language pattern. I knew his sense of being orphaned, or what he felt like. I knew who he wanted to please and who he didn't want to please. Who he wanted to boast to and who he didn't want to boast to. And once I answer those basic questions, I'm there. Or if you were writing for Inspector Clouseau, how deep does that have to cut? There's a certain amount of things that you know you want to do. Yes, if it gets repetitive, you might have to add and re-think that. But mostly, it's being a chameleon. Where you're just being able to place yourself in another person's body and think the way they think. Specificity is crucial, *absolutely* crucial. In a movie like *Ninja*, the givens are limited. Not limited, but the concept is so high-concept that you don't know how much detail you'll need. Like, did the ninjas pick on him and that kind of thing?

PD: You didn't use any of those details in your screenplay?

MK: No, it just helped me understand Chris Farley's character.

PD: How is writing alone different from writing with a partner?

MK: For years I wrote with a partner, but that eventually played itself out and I started writing by myself, which was very, very difficult. One reason was the reason you brought up, which was not knowing what's funny or not even knowing *who* was funny in our original relationship. And not feeling completely secure in what part I played in it and whether I could do it on my own.

And then I went onto a television show, and I didn't have to solve that problem right away because I had a bunch of partners again in a room. When that ended, it took me a while to figure out what I could do by myself. And partially, it was by going back and doing the sequel to *Beverly Hills Ninja,* because it was familiar territory. The character was different in the new one, but it was a joke I knew how to tell really well. It helped me, in a sense, gain more confidence and go back and be really funny again.

PD: Do you have a preference between writing alone or with a partner?

MK: Now, I really like working by myself but I need a lot of support, so I use a lot of people in different ways for help. Here's an example: I have a student who was really funny, and I used him to polish dialogue. He'd tell me what he thought was funny. When he'd give me fairly immediate feedback, it was really helpful to me. And I need more people and I need to get the stuff out there quicker. For a little bit more feedback.

JD: When your world is being ruled by the clock, how do you deal with it?

"... when it comes to writing screenplays ... there's all the time in the world. It's a business for dilettantes."

MK: It doesn't work in screenplays, let me tell you that. There's too much time for people to fret over the development process for you to do a half-ass job because you've got a time crunch. There's no such thing as a time crunch. I mean, yes, maybe when we were shooting *Ninja* and we had to re-write a scene or something like that. But anybody who hides behind time when it comes to writing screenplays is making a mistake. Because there's all the time in the world. It's a business for dilettantes.

JD: What about your work on the series *The Jersey*? [A Disney Channel series.]

MK: In television, you know, you fight the battles you're fighting and you're keyed up and you're working on it, and you get done what you can get done, and the scheduled shooting day comes and you're there. There's nothing you can do about it.

PD: Do you have skills where, if you're not feeling a divine inspiration, you can still put out something that's competent?

MK: I write every day, pretty much from the morning until the end of the day, unless I'm goofing off. Some days are better than others, but you've always got stuff to say and stuff to do and stuff to spit out there. Will it really resonate? I don't know about *every time.* Sometimes the premise is kind of screwed up, and so it's never going to really sing. Sometimes this was the case on *The Jersey.* The characters you were dealing with weren't giving you a lot of comedic spin, so it was harder to make them really funny. Or, you were on your fiftieth episode. So it was hard because there were limitations to *The Jersey* that you wouldn't have on a lot of sitcoms. You had to have professional athletes involved in every show. The premise of the show was a boy magically being body-switched with a professional athlete every week. So you always had that same concept. You always had to be working with the athlete who was coming in as your guest star, and sometimes the day before the show was about basketball and they cancelled on you, and it became about figure skating. And it was the same show.

PD: You set things up so logically, even though the ideas you come up with are really funny, off-the-wall ideas.

MK: I certainly feel at this stage of my career I've come to accept myself more. I trust wherever my mind is going to go and then eventually, most problems will get solved. And they will probably be kind of funny in the end. Will they match up with what Hollywood wants at the moment to put out on a Friday night? I don't know. Most of the time, probably not. I focus on Friday night because that's what screenwriters do . . . movies that we do. It's all like, what will they sell on a Friday night and will it match up?

And that's just matching up. I mean, you could try to match that purposefully. There are people who are probably really good at that. And there are probably times in my life when it was all a big contrivance, and I was good at that when I was selling things. But it's the way I approach it now. I just happen to have very adolescent taste. But that is part of the sell. The stuff that I've been able to get people to get behind is the stuff that matches with that boy energy, that adolescent thing that I can still tap into. When I try to do a genre-thriller, they're very competently done, they're pretty good scripts too. Have I been able to get someone to match that up with what is happening movie-wise? No. Not always. It brings up a really interesting question. Is something genuine at the core of everything that gets made? And I would say that's probably not true.

An Interview with
Dennis Klein

A partial list of Dennis Klein's credits as a creator, show runner, and writer includes: *The Larry Sanders Show, Cosby, Grace Under Fire, Buffalo Bill, The Odd Couple, Laverne and Shirley, Beverly Hills Cop II,* and *Love, American Style.*

In the other interviews in this book, we asked questions; the writers gave answers. Sometimes we discussed things. They developed the Premise. They left the conflict on paper. From the moment we walked into **Dennis Klein**'s house and began setting up, we knew this interview would be different. In our other interviews, we asked the writers where they would be comfortable sitting, and they told us. Dennis took charge, arranging the pillows, the lighting, the backdrop, and kept moving the camera around until he liked what he saw. And he hadn't even looked at the Premise yet.

Good writing is all about showing, not telling. It's what makes for great drama, and great drama is what you get with Dennis Klein. If you've seen *The Larry Sanders Show* (which Dennis co-created), you know it had a unique edge to it. Characters clash and always show strong emotions. Dennis hates bland comedy. He likes things to be unpredictable and uncomfortable in the extreme. More than anything else, he's got to feel passion for an idea. To prove this point as no other writer in this book has done, as he develops the Premise, he points out that he doesn't like doing it, and that it's an irrelevant task anyway. When that doesn't get the intense reaction he's looking for, he goes after us directly. He creates the climate that others only talk about. It is a brilliant example of theatre within an interview. You will not just see what Dennis believes . . . you will *feel* it.

PD (Peter Desberg): As we've explained in our Premise [see page 9], how would you go about developing the show's plot lines?

DK (Dennis Klein): By the way, profanity? You wish I didn't use it?

JD (Jeffrey Davis): Absolutely not. Use it. Use it to your heart's content.

DK: I haven't said it at all. Now when I loosen up a little, because my daughter's ten, and I accidentally say, "Oh, shit," and she'll say, "Dad!"

JD: That's okay, by eighteen she'll be saying it to you.

DK: Yeah, I hope so. This Premise is really written like a television show. It seems that it all takes place in Sarah's apartment, and there isn't anything about it that says, "movie."

PD: You can immediately buy a trailer and have them start going across the country.

DK: That's true. That's very, very true. Well, gee, immediately, there's one thing about this that is at all interesting to me. To some extent, I hate it, but I'm trying to see if there is anything that I kind of like, or could kind of like in it.

PD: A good place to start would be: What elements would you change to like it more?

DK: But to like it more, I mean, it is sort of the same as dislike it less. There's something that's really exciting to me, and if this works, you could go on the air with this tomorrow.

"At some cost to me in terms of money and friends, I have chosen to never, never work on anything that I don't have an excitement about."

DK: I'll tell you something. At some cost to me in terms of money and friends, I have chosen to never, never work on anything that I don't have an excitement about. So this falls into that category so far. When I started in television, people were still doing their show imitating *Sgt. Bilko.* And even when I was working with your [Jeffrey Davis's] father on *The Odd Couple,* there were writers who had done *The Honeymooners* maybe a decade before, and they were still working.

What I noticed about them was that they weren't excited about writing. They only wanted to be producers, not writers. They wanted to supervise writing, but they didn't want to do any writing themselves. And they were bitter and cynical and they hated everything, and they weren't even available to be turned on by an idea. Not that they didn't think it was possible, they just weren't looking for that. They were really burned out. I thought, "Well, gee, these guys are in their late thirties, some of them, some of them in their forties, and I want to be doing this for a long, long time." I didn't want to be bitter. They were unhappy people. And I realized that the shows I was excited to be writing on, *The Partridge Family,* and *Love, American Style,* that kind of stuff, was a comedown for them. And for me it was great. I had just been writing jokes for comedians. It was really actually exciting, even beyond, not just the paycheck.

Early in his career, Dennis worked closely with talented writers who had been associated with seminal television like *The Honeymooners* and *The Phil Silvers Show (Sgt. Bilko)*. In the late sixties and early seventies, these writers were now writing for *The Partridge Family, Love, American Style,* and *Laverne & Shirley*. What Dennis noticed—which he says changed the direction his career took from that time forward—was that they wanted to produce and not write. It seemed to him that these shows were beneath their abilities. It burned them out. Dennis realized then that because he wanted to stick around the business for the long haul, he had to feel passionate about whatever he took on. He jokes that it has cost him personally and professionally. He knew even back in the *Laverne & Shirley* days that without passion, he would turn bitter sooner or later. Leonard Stern, whose interview is also in this book (see page 361), was a writer who has remained optimistic and enthusiastic from his early days on *The Honeymooners* to the present.

You write for characters, they're on film. You're watching them do their thing and suddenly it's funny. That was all great. But for these writers, they had done great work and now they were sort of taking the paycheck. It seemed to me that just the act, for them, of writing something that they didn't love, and that they weren't excited about, had corrupted them, probably forever. Maybe I was wrong. So I decided at that point, I just needed to be strict and really kind of turn down almost everything that wasn't exciting to me. So I wouldn't be saying, "Well, this isn't too bad, and I guess I don't mind it too much." Although that's tough, especially when you're just trying to break in, to be kind of picky like that and annoy a lot of people.

PD: Imagine if we said to you, "We bought the rights to this thing, but what we really want is you, so you can change any aspect of it."

DK: I understand the rules to this thing. Alright, so I'm going to see if there's something about this that I can actually love.

JD: If you can get to like—

DK: —no, no, no, has to be love. I won't get to like. I don't care about like. The only thing that's sort of exciting is the thing about where Sarah is. "There's only room for one woman vice president, and the vice president is a woman," and I guess that's for television or a movie. I don't know where that goes, but I love that. I must say I like the idea that this Sarah character is confused. She's not confused, actually; I like the idea that she's torn in all these different worlds. I don't like any of the different worlds, even the woman vice president, then we're into feminism stuff, and the politics of that, which is okay, but it's more head stuff. But emotionally, Sarah is a person who is trying to be alive in the world, and be herself. And she's being crushed by this other woman. I don't consider it so much like the focus of the thing, but it's constantly happening to her. And she can't do anything about it, as long as she wants to stay at that company, she's stuck.

So I don't think that's a fun thing to explore, but as a small other character in the show, which is how you have it, I like it. And then she has a mother who's a pain in the ass. And she has a father who is dead and has f–ked them by not taking care of them properly, and now he's dead. I guess Molly's better off with him dead, isn't she? Was she better off when he was alive, fiscally speaking?

PD: Molly thought she'd be taken care of, and was stunned to find out . . .

DK: Are you going to finish every sentence? So when he died, then the income stream stopped and it wasn't replaced by anything. So when he was still alive, the income stream would go because he was actually earning money. So that's the problem, he had nothing but an income stream going, and that was enough for them. They didn't need more than that, right? They were living fine. Now he has left nothing to replace it with. It's too bad there isn't more happening. The grandparents are just in this one sentence, and so they are whatever you want to make them. See, that's the problem with this thing, it's wafer-thin. There's nothing here, really, for me, anyway, or possibly for others. So the question is, what can be added or changed to this? Boy, it's amazingly uninspiring. With all due respect to whoever came up with it . . . You know, my daughter started using that phrase, "All due respect," and she realized what an insult it was. For a couple of weeks she was saying, "Now, Dad, with all due respect . . ." and it just was always kind of a knife into my heart. And that made her want to do it more.

JD: I love the thing you came up with about what's going on at the office with the female boss—we never see that. It's been mostly ignored. In fact, you're the first person who's brought it up.

DK: I would throw away the whole lifestyle thing, and the mother living with the daughter. Jesus Christ, that is dull and boring, and there's no way that I can think of that that becomes interesting or fun. And then, I keep trying *not* to cast Diane Keaton as the mother. There's a possibility that I could like it and that Gyllenhaal girl as the daughter.

I just keep thinking somewhere there will be a word or a syllable that will pop out at me that will suggest comedy, or drama. Even if it's drama, the comedy will be easy. That's just the icing on the cake, but the drama has to be there. It seems to me there has to be something that's interesting. So Sarah is working for a woman who's envious of her. If that were a series, then the problem would be to stay with the mother. Then, there'd just have to be more because the boss/employee relationship would have to be richer. But it couldn't really happen without sort of destroying the fun, or the premise that they're in competition. Because at a certain point you say, "Well, why doesn't the boss fire her, or why doesn't she quit?" You really have to say, "What is she doing there?" She has to be doing something else that doesn't have anything to do with the boss, because that's a questionable relationship.

So the problem is, if you really examine that relationship, Sarah and her boss, it doesn't make any sense in a continuing way for her to stay there. See, if it's a series, then it has to be five years' worth of somebody staying somewhere where they shouldn't be. Then if it breaks up, you don't have a series anymore. So if you really want to have that be any kind of a meaningful part, and I'm trying to make it be a meaningful part of the story, because that's the only sliver that's there. Otherwise, I have to leave your Premise behind completely. But, part of this is a challenge. I mean, it's easy to just throw it away and start over again. The challenge is not to make this work, or to make it palatable, to make it okay, to make it not horrible. The challenge would be to make it great and still maintain some semblance of what you have there.

"But if you come up with funny and compelling things about somebody, why do you need all the unfunny, un-compelling things, anyway?"

DK: So it seems like you're talking about a movie, at that point. It's a contained amount of time, and you would sort of think that at the end of it, something would be done about this relationship, either Sarah would quit, Sarah would be fired, Sarah would be hired by a higher-up to replace the woman who's jealous of her. Whatever it is, that could happen in a movie. It couldn't really happen in a series, without destroying the integrity of the series. But still, I don't like it as a central premise, but it's one of many things that are happening to Sarah. So then, one would have to invent a lot of things that are happening to Sarah, and then one would have to actually figure out, which your Premise has not done, why do I give a shit about Sarah at all? So that's what your Premise has done. If I may, with all due respect, your Premise has come up with all the unfunny, uninteresting, un-compelling things about Sarah and her life and the people around her. Leaving the, hopefully, funny and compelling things for somebody else to come up with. But if you come up with funny and compelling things about somebody, why do you need all the unfunny, un-compelling things, anyway?

JD: What's funny to you?

DK: In general? We're not talking about this project?

JD: If you didn't have to take any of this, or just take that one little sliver.

DK: I'm interested in the troubles that people can get into that are not containable, and are not usually where people get their entertainment from. There's something on the air about a sleeper cell, or something, I don't know, but I remember somebody told me the premise, and it seems like they've made it into something more probable. But I'm interested in the horrors of that, not just the horrors of what they do when they blow people up. If your life is your sleeper cell, that means you are sitting around waiting for some order from somebody. But I guess that's how we all spend our life, to some extent. But then, you're just an absolute victim, and what must that be like? Getting up every morning and being at the behest of other people.

I'm just interested in whatever it is that people do that is disgusting and horrible, like that *Woodsman* movie with Kevin Bacon, where he's a child molester, and he's not the bad guy. He is the bad guy, of course, he's a child molester, but he's not the bad guy in the movie. The hero is like somebody who's trying to catch him, or stop him, or doctors trying to help him. I like things that make people uncomfortable, make *me* uncomfortable.

JD: You feel that same way about comedy, right?

DK: I *am* talking about comedy.

PD: When you first came up with the idea of saying, "I like this relationship. That's the one thing that interests me here." I like the way you described it as a constant pressure. It's not huge, it's not overwhelming, but it's ever-present.

DK: Yeah. James Cagney gave a young actor some advice. Cagney was a very self-effacing guy, and his advice was, "Never relax." And the thing about James Cagney was in everything he did, he never was relaxed. And I think that's good advice. And honestly, that's the way I feel about drama and comedy, is that there should be some kind of a tension, some kind of an issue, even if I were writing about two people who are totally relaxed, two people like . . . just a husband and wife lying in bed, ready to go to sleep. What could be more relaxing? I think some people make a mistake. They put people in conflict, and I think that's easy and contrived. Everybody's kind of in conflict, but to me, I like to see people who aren't in conflict, because the truth is everybody's in conflict all the time. Everybody has conflicting needs with one another, so you don't have to invent conflict, like, "I like chocolate pie," and "I like vanilla, so what are we going to order?" "We both like chocolate pie, isn't that great?" And yet, when it comes, there's a problem, because one of them wants to cut it this way, or dig in. If I have a cake, I like to eat it with a fork. I don't want anybody around me. And if somebody wants to eat with me, I'll say, "Well, you order your cake and you can have it any way you want, and I'll just eat my cake with a fork."

PD: So as long as you get your way, it's okay. Should we censure you for that?

DK: That'd be the day, when I could get one of you to say something critical, because honestly there's glad-handing happening.

PD: With all due respect.

DK: The point is, you guys are being as nice as can be, and there's a tremendous amount of conflict here. I don't know, you have to be thinking critical thoughts and yet you're not expressing them, so there's internal conflict in both of you, unless you're really, literally as bland as you seem, which I don't believe.

PD: It's a harder skill than it looks.

DK: Fine. A young married couple are about to go to sleep, and one says to the other, maybe it's their first night together, or whatever, I don't know, and one says to the other, "You know, I think if we ever do get mad . . ." Such is the lack of conflict in this relationship. "If we ever get really angry and have a problem, then we shouldn't go to sleep angry." And the other person says, "Yeah, I think you're right," and then they start to go to sleep, and the other person says, "Why wouldn't we go to bed angry?" "Well, I just think it's not a good idea," and before you know it, there's a major battle going on, for maybe the first time that they've ever fought, and very early in the relationship. I don't know what they're doing in bed, if it's very early in the relationship, although I actually do know what they're doing in bed, and I don't want my daughter to know that. When I decided to get married and stop dating, one of the last dates I had, this woman—okay, this may not have anything to do with comedy . . . and maybe it does.

We're in bed together, and she gets up to go to the bathroom, and I'd never met her before and we had a great time and all that stuff. I'm glad I own this stuff, this interview you said on the paper. And so, all of a sudden I see a little bit of metal under her pillow, just a glint of metal, and I said, "What is this?" I think it's odd something got left there, or whatever. And I lift the pillow up and the biggest hatchet that I've seen is under her pillow, which I thought then, and I still think, is there for self-defense. Understandably, picking up guys in a bar. But what if it wasn't? So as soon as she got out of the bathroom, I said, "You know something, I actually have an appointment, I know it's three in the morning, it's crazy . . ." And I got out of there really, really swiftly.

I told my therapist about this, and she said, "Do you think possibly now, now might be the time in your late thirties that you might actually think about having a stable relationship?" and I said, "Yeah, there's a signal here." So anyway, the point is, conflict is essential, but does not have to be contrived. So if this is a movie, I'm still answering your question, I'm looking for the stuff that isn't overtly thought. This is, by the way, why I have trouble convincing anybody to do my stuff. It isn't overtly thought to be comedic, or thought to be about people in conflict, or even thought to be interesting by people. I'm not searching for it. But I'm saying I want to be discovering that. I want to find out what that is, but not arbitrarily. I want to find out if I'm interested in it. And what interests me a lot of times is the stuff that's underneath the bland realities of life, because I don't think anything is bland, I really don't. I'm excited and interested in a lot of stuff, in almost anything except contrived situations, because they're phony. Like, for example, Peter. Now, and again, with all due respect, you seem somewhat bland . . . actually, you seem even blander.

PD: Thanks.

DK: You're welcome. But you couldn't be *that* bland. So I'm wondering, even now, now I'm talking to you, and I'm theoretically insulting you, but you're smiling and laughing, but underneath that, there's got to be, I'm not saying rage, but there's got to be something happening that you're not revealing to me. But then who are you going to reveal it to?

PD: You've already put your finger on it. You said, "You guys are on polite behavior," which we are. Of course we are. And we're not friends, long-term friends, so it would be very bizarre to start being combative, or pushy.

DK: No, no, it wouldn't be bizarre, Peter. It's only bizarre because of your version of the way people should be with each other. Why can't you be combative? Why can't you say, again, with all due respect, why couldn't you say in a nice way, "If you have a problem with something I say," and we could right away leap to a different level of intimacy. So why are you going to wait five years?

PD: Let me answer that question. I think with you I could, but with a lot of people that I meet they'd say, "Hey, wait a minute, you come into my house . . ."

DK: That's right, that's right.

PD: ". . . and you're arguing with me. There's the door!" You have made it clear that you're looking for that, which is something more interesting than what we've done here so far.

DK: Fine, exactly.

JD: I understand how you could come up with *Larry Sanders,* because that's what that show is all about. It's all about things that aren't said, even when they're saying it, there's so much under the surface.

DK: It's all about false. Everybody's being false. We've got the camera, so we know the truth, we find out the truth, as everybody is being false.

PD: We're saying the conflict in the room is more interesting than the conflict on the paper.

DK: Well, anything's more interesting than the conflict on the paper, and I say that with all due immense amount of respect. But here's the thing. You say, I just want to go back to it, but that's right because I'm interested in what's real, and isn't contrived. Even if this was good, which it isn't, I think, it can't even pass for bad, but even if this were exciting to me, which it isn't, I could say that. I do say that. It's still just a piece of paper. There's nothing on here. Nobody has their heart in this piece of paper. In other words, this was contrived. Even if I say this is great, which I'm not, believe me, I want to make that crystal clear—but even if this were great . . .

JD: To you?

DK: No, I'm going to say something even that if this were great then, by the way, what I want to know is now that, Peter, I'm interrupting myself . . . well, you say in this situation, you've said it's okay for us to not be . . . that we can be combative and not bland, and still I haven't heard anything—not that I'm looking for it—and honestly, I'm afraid that we'll never crack that façade on either of you, I might go back to the hatchet. But you're still not doing it. And I'm not complaining about that, and I'm not criticizing you, I'm saying, you're still not doing it, which is what interests me. That's what interests me is that there's something still stopping . . .

JD: . . . something unsaid?

DK: Something unsaid, and something unsettlingly horrible beneath our bland affability with each other. So that interests me. Now here, nobody wrote anything on this that their heart was into. I don't know. I'm assuming you guys came up with it, but maybe you didn't. But maybe some retarded person came up with it, but I don't think—I bet that there isn't anything in here that anybody can say, "You can take this as a challenge?" There isn't anything in this paper, I know I'm interrupting, but you're interrupting me. There isn't anything on this piece of paper that anybody gives a f–k about, let alone people who read it, so people are reading something that nobody . . . So why are we reading stuff that nobody gives a f–k about, right? . . . not beyond this moment, but right now I do because you're sitting in front of me.

PD: I'll give you the answer to that one, though it's a little arcane, but an answer, nonetheless.

DK: I would expect nothing less from you.

PD: Since you're on the couch, are you a fan of Freud?

DK: Yeah.

PD: Here's how he did therapy. He believed that the therapist should keep his mouth shut and be a blank screen for the patient to project not just his thoughts, but his relationships as well. That's how the idea of transference came about. Just as a patient can view a therapist as anyone he wants him to be, our intention here was to make a premise as open-ended as possible so that anyone could take it in any direction he wanted. So there's the beginning of conflicts, and it's up to you to do anything you want with it.

If we had written something brilliant and funny, there'd be nothing left for anybody to do. So the intent is to leave lots of room for, as you said, "to do stuff."

DK: Okay, I hear you, I get it, I get it. I got it, even when I interrupted you because I was trying to save you from having to say seventeen more sentences. I like using the "F" word. So, sometimes a premise is just a premise. Here's the problem. You haven't done it. I agree with what you set out with, but you haven't created a blank screen. It's not blank. It's an idea that exists. It's an idea. It's an ostensible idea.

And that's the problem. If you wanted to get a little closer to what you're saying you want to do, which I think is—I don't know about admirable—might be an admirable thing to do, it might not be. I have to think about it. Then, instead of this thing that you've written, you would get an article from a newspaper, or some description of something that actually happened, or a picture, a photograph. That's where you get into the Rorschach test stuff, you know. A picture of a guy, or some photographs of something. Something that is completely not, I guess, just not made up. Something that isn't made up . . . non-fiction. The minute you put a piece of *fiction* on paper, it is not blank anymore. And now, somebody has to work with *your* piece of fiction. So, it already puts the creative person in a bind, in a box. Let me tell you something, I've been presented with horseshit like this, and said, "Oh, you can do anything you want with it." Well, I'm already sickened by it, and so there's . . . what do you do? What do you do? "Oh, you can depart from it." Then why did you put it down there? Why'd you put *anything* down there? Why didn't you say, "Start from scratch." So this sinks me. This sinks anybody, anybody in your book is sunk by this. And maybe you mean to sink these people. And maybe that's the anger beneath the blandness, the glad-handing and all that.

JD: The little piece that you did find interesting was the relationship in the office.

DK: It's the only thing that interested me, yeah. I wouldn't necessarily make it more than a sliver. Well, no, no, let's change that. It could be the whole movie. It could be the whole movie, that whole thing and that relationship. I have no problem with that, but what couldn't be the whole movie is her dilemma, like, "I got the job." That gets boring really fast. But as a piece of the movie, it is, to use your word, "fascinating." If you keep it, then the question is: How small do you make it so it's the right size and it doesn't become boring, and how small do you make it before it doesn't even exist?

Here's a person who's in conflict with the person that she depends upon and admires. See, I would throw that in. This is a job she's always wanted. And this is a boss she admires and respects. She is saddened somehow, and angered by the fact that her hero has a head of clay. That this woman could be so territorial, because that's what's ugly about the boss. That the boss would do that, and tie it into gender is really unenlightened. If you got Sarah just fighting an unenlightened person, and Sarah is terrific, and the unenlightened person is a devil, and she's fighting her, and it just gets really kind of concocted.

But for example, what if this woman, the boss, is admirable, and has this problem. And it is even maybe a problem for the boss herself that she didn't even realize. And then you have Sarah fighting the battle. The boss is fighting a battle within herself, and Sarah is fighting a battle within herself, because she wants to maintain her respect for this person, even beyond rising within the organization. But then the question for Sarah becomes, "How much do I want to rise?" In other words, "I can't just be fascinated with this woman and trying to change her, or concerned with my own hero worship at the expense of rising. I'm screwed if I stay here because I can't count on this. How can I count on this person changing?" That's the whole emotion of counting on somebody else changing, or something happening outside myself for me to feel good about myself. Any of that is really disgusting and ugly. Which would be something that Sarah, being a young person, might discover about herself in the process.

She wouldn't be in a television series, because characters don't change. But in a movie, she might. She might see through this relationship. How she wastes her time and her energy doing all the stuff, like hero-worshipping this person, if you add that. In other words, what's funny and interesting to me is that Sarah is royally screwed. She is in a job that is hopeless. She wants to rise. And by the very definition that this woman has set up, who is her boss, she can't rise. And yet she's there. Then why would she stay there longer than a precious day of her life? That's something that she has to wrestle with, even beyond the fact that she should quit in the next minute. What actually happens when she's in the office?

I'm interested in Sarah noticing that she's capable of screwing herself, and then looking at every other aspect of her life and questioning it, including her boyfriend and where she lives. "Why did I choose this?" "Why do I dress like this?" But then I'm describing a nervous breakdown and it starts to become a little bit less interesting. What Sarah ultimately would have to find out is that she carries those seeds within herself. There is something about her nature that will force her to always screw herself. So even if she gets out of this situation and quits here, and even if she changes her life and doesn't make the same choices, aren't these new choices something that is encapsulating her "Sarah-ness"? So, it creates a harrowing situation for Sarah because there's no possible way that she can do anything without screwing herself. It makes her paralyzed. But then paralysis is yet another way of screwing herself.

"There's a harsh reality to life. I guess that's what I like to write."

DK: So maybe she does get paralyzed. You know, I worked for a while with John Callahan, the cartoonist, he's a quadriplegic, and he's a very funny guy. He's a very funny cartoonist, and darkly, ruefully funny. He writes books and stuff, and his cartoons are everywhere. In one of his cartoons in the *San Francisco Examiner,* he had Laurel and Hardy in an AIDS ward. Hardy is saying to Laurel, "This is another fine mess you've gotten us into." So, John Callahan finds humor in his quadriplegia. In fact, one time I was talking to him on the phone and he said, "Do you hear a buzz?" And I said, "No, I don't." He lives in Seattle so it was cold, and he said, "I've got a hair dryer on." And I said, "Just wash your hair?" He said, "No, it's just cold, and . . . it's a quad thing." And then I realized he's a quadriplegic, he doesn't have to turn the heat on in the house. The hair dryer is all he needs. There's a harsh reality to life. I guess that's what I like to write.

But I do want to say something. What you guys have done here to me and the rest of the writers is very telling. You've caged the writer. Everybody has an urge to control writers, and control creative people. I'm not being paranoid here, but there's an impulse to not take what the writer thinks is interesting and funny and put it on the screen, but to somehow control it, shape it, shift it, for good commercial reasons, or bad commercial reasons. Stupid people do it stupidly. Smart people do it amazingly. And then all of a sudden, I've seen it, when a writer gets famous off something that I've done a rewrite on. I've seen this stuff. It stinks. And the movie comes out and it's amazing and brilliant, and that writer gets *complete* credit, not just Writers Guild credit. That corrupts the process. I'm sure I've been doctored, but you know, he thinks he's brilliant. So I see that process can work or not work. But it is an attempt to deal a death to the sanctity of a writer's singular, let's just say, not sanctity . . . the singularity of a writer's vision.

You guys couldn't go to a writer—you wouldn't go to a writer and say, "What's on your mind, let's see you create. Let's photograph you creating." You didn't trust that, and maybe rightly so, and probably rightly so, and you would've gotten like blank tape. So instead, you've moved down this road, and you tried to make it as tiny a move as possible, but it doesn't matter how tiny or big the road is, you moved down the road towards corralling the writer, and then you said, "Oh, we're corralling you, but you don't have to stay in the corral, you can go graze over here, and graze over there." Well, yeah, try that, then . . . here's a piece of paper. And that's what's made this process and your entire book, in my opinion, with all due respect, bogus.

Now your book is about, with all the taped interviews that you've done, and I hope I'm not bumming you out in any way, now your book suddenly is about how you can take comedy writers, even comedy writers who have done big things, and all that, but you can take really creative writers and turn them into puppets, or sheep. You watch how these sheep manage to have bowel movements that are so interesting, and you're going to photograph those bowel movements of the sheep that we have shorn and . . . I don't know, this metaphor is breaking down as I speak . . . but that's what you've done. Rather than film the creative process of a writer, you've filmed the destruction of a writer's originality.

There were times when we had difficulty knowing when Dennis was angry and venting about his views of our project and his views of the industry, and when he was creating theatre in the room. We're not sure if Dennis always knew, either. He was engaged. That's why this was such an interesting interview to us. He lives what he believes. We're not sure where the calculation ended and control ended with it. Only Dennis knew—perhaps.

PD: It's an interesting view, and here's what I think is interesting about this. We've read about studies where people have done what you said. They go to the artist and say, "Go and create." And frankly, a lot of what happened is nothing, unless you're willing to do it over a period of weeks and sometimes months.

DK: It doesn't work! That's why writers are corralled. It doesn't work.

PD: There's a wonderful parody that Monty Python did years ago. They're watching Thomas Hardy write a novel and broadcasting it on the radio as sportscasters. There's another way to look at this. It may be odious to you, but interesting to me. I'm kind of a science guy, and what you do in science is separate and control variables.

What's interesting is that everybody starts off at the *same* place. It's interesting to see how their approaches are different. What's been fascinating about this is that some people have begun, and said, "Yeah, this is easy, I could do this, I would cast this person." And we've had some people say, "This could never be done; I'd have to change this and this and this," and we've had some people say, "Gosh, this just gets me so pissed, this is why I don't write anymore, unless I get either direction or production in my contract, because I don't want people to change what I do," we've had people say, "I love the network system. I really thrive under it. I like the challenge of them giving me something to do." Your response has been the most extreme by far, that's why it's so fascinating.

DK: Mine's been the most extreme?

PD: Yours has been the most extreme view, in terms of not liking the task. And that's all great for us, because it's another viewpoint. So this is really valuable for us.

DK: I understand.

PD: You and I clearly don't agree on the nature of the task, and that's okay, because you're not right or wrong.

DK: It's not even that we don't agree. Maybe we agree, and maybe we don't, and probably we don't, it seems beyond that. We don't even agree on the morality of giving writers this task. The whole idea of it is . . . I want to hear you guys, what you say, but I do want to say that you have corralled these writers. A person, like a scientist seen as a business person, and people in charge of all kinds of stuff, and they want it for their own purposes, they don't want to have something be exciting and interesting in and of its own nature. So the first thing they want to do is confine it. And so now you have a premise, you've taken however many writers, twenty or thirty writers, and you've reduced them to become little gerbils in your study. So you've got this writer here pulling his pants down, and they're all different, but it's not really creative, even though I might be interested in reading the book.

PD: If I created a show and I hired five writers to help me write it, have I corralled them?

DK: Yeah, so we have to hire the five writers. But you don't have to pretend that you've done a great thing, "Gee, we're all of one mind, and we're all marching . . ." We're getting into an argument now about what's art, which is good. It's always a good argument to have. But, the five guys in there that you've hired to work on your show, I don't think they're prostitutes, and whores, and they're *not* artists, because you've corralled them. They have skills, they have talent. I'm just saying, to whatever extent you've done that. You're destroying their creative output.

PD: You're the one that's saying if they haven't chosen it, then they're corralled. You're saying there aren't even degrees of corralling.

DK: No, no, then I take that back. I'll change that. But to the extent that they haven't chosen it, they're corralled. You know, it's not that black and white.

JD: I'll just disagree with you to this extent, I saw you doing it anyway, and I saw Dennis Klein come out near the end of this, and that was what we got excited about.

DK: Thank you. I was glad to be able to provide that.

JD: I think it just took you a while.

DK: It took me a while because you guys . . .

JD: . . . pissed you off. Dennis, what's the difference between the freedom you have at HBO, and what you have at the networks, which you obviously didn't like? And you've had a lot of freedom at HBO.

DK: Garry Shandling had a lot of freedom.

JD: You didn't?

DK: Well, I had the freedom to please Garry. All I care about as a writer, what I care about is, just like in a sex act, just being turned on. It's like eating. I don't care what I eat in the morning. I have turnips and radishes, and I get into that, because now I try to eat healthy, but I'm not a vegetarian. But, when I eat that stuff, I enjoy it. And maybe I dip it into a little bit of that Chinese mustard sauce, give it a little zing.

Early in my life, I was confused and mixed up, and screwed up, but you know, finally, by the time I reached my late thirties, and to this day, all I care about is being really passionate about what I'm doing, whatever that is. And I don't care what it is. And I learned that from having a daughter and being passionate. Even if I'm not passionate about what we're doing together, I'm passionate about the fact that she's growing and I'm helping her kind of . . . or even just keeping her company. She's got a dad there. That's exciting to me. And so the same goes for television.

There were some jobs I really loved, like *Buffalo Bill*. That was a show where I was turned on to every aspect of it. Accidentally, I was in complete control of it, but I didn't need to be in complete control. I guess, maybe I did, but I'm kidding myself. I've been in situations where they needed a joke. I was rewriting *Cocoon*, and Ron Howard needed a joke. Instead of writing a joke for this spot, I wrote forty jokes, and then he picked six and shot them, and ultimately, one found its way into the movie. I had written the scenes and felt ownership of the characters. But basically, the premise wasn't mine. Everything was kind of handed to me, and controlled by the others. Ron was going to pick what he shot, and the producers were going to do focus groups. And so it was completely out of my hands, except for writing those jokes. Writing those jokes was great. And writing jokes *is* great. Coming up with ideas is great, for me. It's enjoyable, just like everything that I try. I try to make sure that everything that's on the menu of my restaurant, where I'm the only customer, is a tasty, delightful dish for me at that time, at that moment. So that's what I try to do, just keep myself excited, and not do anything that isn't exciting.

At one point, Garry Shandling was not sure about the premise of *The Larry Sanders Show*. He was very uncomfortable, and he thought, "Maybe there isn't a series here," and he wanted to discuss how there isn't a series here. And I found that tremendously productive, and he didn't mean it to be productive. That was just his angst, and it didn't really help him. I thought, "Can't we work today?" So I said, "I'll come up with forty ideas . . . stories for this series . . . not bland, not clichéd ideas for episodes, tonight. So, let's table this discussion. Let's just do work. And tomorrow, I promise you, I swear to you, I'll have forty ideas." So the next day I came in and I wrote them, handwritten on yellow legal pad, all the ideas. And again, like the forty jokes—I don't know . . . Biblical?

". . . there's unpleasantness in everything I've done, in show business, and not show business . . ."

So Garry looks at the forty pages; the first page has eight ideas on it. Five pages later, as I recall, and he said [*Dennis murmurs, as if reading to himself*], on the fourth page, he says, "I have to tell you, number forty-one I don't think is a story. I just really don't . . ."

The fact is that you can look at television and you can see some wonderful, wonderful moments on television. And you can look at movies and you can see some great moments, and great movies. Independent movies are also amazing and great, mostly. But there's a lot of great stuff, so that tells you that the system isn't better or worse. There's just a lot more entertainment, and a lot more horrible stuff. But I would bet, pound for pound, off the top of my head, there's exactly the same amount of good and great stuff today as there was ten years ago, twenty years ago, thirty years ago, forty years ago. And the system mitigates against it as much as it ever did, and as little as it ever did. And there are as many great writers, which is a very limited amount now, as there were in the 1800s and 1700s. Everybody's writing novels, but how many *Candide*s and other amazing works were there, even then? So at any given time, there are a finite number of writers. There are a finite number of people who want to see something great.

My mother kept trying to get me to read. She had all these novels. "You need to read novels. You're reading about Nazis and gangsters," and she would hide those books and burn them. I said, "You know, you're burning books about Nazis. Don't you understand? Don't you see the irony of that?" So my mother . . . there was a million times more of my mother in the world than there are Margaret Meads, who wants to go somewhere, do something challenging. Before you know it, you're sitting in an empty movie theatre saying, "Hey, this is wonderful, anybody watching it?" This is my most deeply held belief for the moment. People can get mesmerized by crap, and people's reactions to crap, and people who are getting rich doing crap.

I'll see these other movies, or plays, and they're crappy, and people say they're great and I want to kill them. I have those moments. But it's just an important discipline to focus on what's great. I've been saying all kinds of bullshit and you guys are going to cut it down, and you're going to cut it down, and hopefully, you're going to do a good job. There's a couple of minutes there where it was really worth something, and part of your thing, and it really worked, and that's nice. That's nice to have that as part of the writing thing, and the rewriting. You write a lot, and you whittle it down, and that's, I think, our job in writing.

We just try to focus, and forget about the stuff that we're cutting. We're cutting. Don't worry about that. They're the thirty-nine jokes that weren't in that one spot. It won't matter. Much of it was freeing because I could write forty jokes and they could be crap. Most of them probably were crap. But it doesn't matter, and if anybody's stupid enough to judge me on any one of them, and they have, and they say, "Well, what about this?" I say, "Yeah, you can focus on that, but that's ridiculous." That's all I have to say.

A funny thing happened on the way out of our interview. As Peter was putting the recording equipment in the car, Dennis took Jeffrey aside. He told Jeffrey about working with his father, producer Jerry Davis, on The Odd Couple *in the early 1970s. Dennis remembered Jeffrey's dad wore a suit and tie to work every day, and there was always a white handkerchief in his breast pocket. Dennis said, "Your dad regularly invited the writers to lunch. He never left anyone out. Not even the new kids like me." Then Dennis said he hoped we understood that during the interview, he'd been doing "shtick" so it would be more interesting. He wanted to leave no doubt that his interview was theatre.*

When Peter got home that night there was a voicemail from Dennis emphasizing how much he enjoyed doing the interview, and thanking him for asking him to be a part of this book. He found the process interesting.

An Interview with
Bob Myer

A partial list of Bob Myer's credits as a show runner and writer includes: *Mike & Molly, Happily Divorced, Roseanne, Cybill, The Facts of Life, Living with Fran, The Gregory Hines Show, Rodney, My Two Dads, The Charmings, 227,* and *Who's the Boss?.*

As a child, **Bob Myer** caught on to jokes more quickly than other kids his age. By adolescence, he realized that comedy could protect him from being beaten up by bullies, and as an adult, he has managed to get big paychecks for writing it. As a show runner on series like *Roseanne*, Bob created environments where people were never bullied, and everyone's talents flourished. As a writer, Bob has the ability to put people in situations where collisions will occur and laughter will result. His use of situations and character traits generates comedy that fits seamlessly within the story he is telling.

PD (Peter Desberg): As we've explained in our Premise [see page 9], how would you go about developing the show's plot lines?

BM (Bob Myer): Well, if you were the network and you came to me with that idea and said, "Do it," or you were pitching it as a pilot, or something like that, the first thing I'd say—because, as you have characterized it yourself, it's a generic idea—so the first thing I'd say is, "Who's in it? Who've you got?"

PD: And we'd say, "Who would you like?"

BM: Right. This is just the way my mind works. I file back to anything that was similar to it, because the first thing . . . in a comedy room, your first instinct, your first

The writers in this book are all successful professionals. When you compare the meanings of the words "amateur" and "professional," the difference isn't necessarily talent, although they often go together. The difference is success in the marketplace. Bob's marketplace instincts have been so finely honed that he seems to say, at the beginning, if we're going to spend time on it, let's make sure that someone is going to buy it.

pitch is something you've probably heard before, or has been derived off of something before, so you're always looking for your second and third pitch. So I'm always looking at the first pitch; it sounds a little like *Judging Amy*. A driven daughter and a mother who moves in and is trying to get her to settle down. So the first thing you say, when you see a generic idea, is, "Who do you have that's going to make this special?" So failing that, if the casting makes it special, that's the concept. If the casting doesn't make it special, now you have work to do.

Now you have to figure out, what is it about? This is going to draw the viewer away; another thing that has to be considered is, what are they buying? What are you going to be up against? What are you going to be compared to? And this is an era of *My Name is Earl*—very high-concept shows that the theme carries from week to week. It's like we just had a family show period; it's over, and now we're going back to high concepts. So this sounds like a high concept, but it's basically a family show. So now you have to dress it up somehow or other, so that it reads a little bit more like what's contemporary. So those are the things that would go through my head—not necessarily creative thoughts; those are marketing thoughts.

So, given those parameters, the first thing you start to pitch is: What does the daughter do? Did the mother have a history of doing anything ever? Whose influence is bigger on whom? It seems to read like a story about the mother coming in and teaching the daughter the values of home life. Maybe lay back a little on the job, find a guy. Be less driven. And the daughter, getting the mother out there, back in circulation. So you have, essentially, a buddy comedy where both of them are having an impact on each other.

". . . she's just opened an Ed's Coffee franchise, and across the street is Starbucks."

So what does the daughter do? If she's a lawyer, her mother can't be involved in that work. But if she's running a store, a coffee shop, or something like that, that she is trying to franchise, that she's trying to expand, now you can bring the mother into that arena. And that's what I would suggest. I would go to something where Mom is not just at home, because then it's a story about the daughter. So I would suggest that she open something that is growing, something that we can see, something that we can watch, and something that her mother, in getting involved in, can create situations down at the store.

So she's just opened a Starbucks franchise, or, better yet, she's just opened an Ed's Coffee franchise, and across the street is Starbucks. And she's got to work, work,

work, work, work, so that she can compete with Starbucks. And her mother comes in and adds touches: Cupcakes that she baked at home, or things like that. So that the pilot would wind up being the two of them in a somewhat uncomfortable but, for the daughter, a begrudgingly beneficial partnership down at Ed's Coffee. And the homey touches that the mother brings, versus the marketing experience and the driven energy that the daughter brings, are in combination [and] can make the business work.

Since they work down at the business, and they work at home, they're never away from each other, which is another source of conflict: "Where are you going?" "Can I come?" "But you want me to meet a man." "Are you meeting a man?" "Well, can he come in?" The typical disruptions that a mother would have in a daughter's life, I think, are magnified here by the fact that she can't get away from the mother, not only because she lives at home, but also because she works with her. So that would make it a story about both of them, so that—back to the business—your casting potential is that there's no real "second banana." So that if you were going, for example, to CBS, which skews a little older, and you could get Jean Smart, and you don't know who the younger girl is, you can get Jean Smart by saying, "It's not a secondary character, the mother; the mother's very primary." Or if you're going to Fox, or NBC, and you can get Courteney Cox, you can say to her, "No, this is not a story about the mother and her transitioning her arc from the East Coast to the West Coast. It's a story about you and your mother." That's basically what I'd do. Couple of funny neighbors. Some music. Some laughter. Some sweetening.

PD: How would you get a guy into this?

BM: First of all, it's easy to put a guy in at work. This is the guy who clearly has a crush on her, which Mom can see, but the daughter can't see the forest for the trees. So the sexual tension can come from him. He's not as driven. He's much more the mother's taste; he's much more what the mother would look for in a son-in-law. And the daughter has never even considered this guy. In the meantime, she's dating other guys, all of whom, in her mother's view, are wrong.

Let's go!!! [*Pounds the table.*] Let's go pitch to some fourteen-year-old executive.

"I'm sitting before one of these baby executives, and I pitch my heart out, and I'm waiting."

My greatest nightmare is that I'm an aging writer—even "age-ier" than I am now—and I go into the network to pitch something, and I'm sitting before one of these baby executives, and I pitch my heart out, and I'm waiting. The executive looks at me and says, "You know, Dad . . ."

JD (Jeffrey Davis): What would you do with this Premise that would put your stamp on it if you weren't constrained by selling it in today's marketplace?

BM: How do you turn it into a higher concept, the kind of thing that they won't look at right now and say, "Well, it's been done; it feels ordinary; it feels yesterday?" I would probably look for that. Not only to satisfy my own challenge, but also to satisfy what is right now, the network's need for something that is radically different; even though most of those are doomed to failure because on a week-to-week basis, you can't be radically different. You have to come back to character relationships and things like that. So how would I make it something that I would love? How big is my paycheck? That's the first question I ask.

Well, I would probably add a character to it that really created the imbalance in what is pretty much a very balanced concept. You asked before how would I get a male character into this. I would probably add a character. I've written a pilot on spec where the character's ex-husband is just coming out of jail. And I would probably throw in a variable like that, where somebody's coming in who has a brother, or an ex of the younger woman, of the daughter, who is coming in from left field . . . just to crank the story up a little bit, just to get in her life. So maybe instead of the guy down at Starbucks, I'd bring this guy out of nowhere. He was a philanderer, or he was in jail, or he was an addict, or something like that. A guy who has had a struggle and is trying to turn his life around, who her mother always loved. And Sarah can't stand him. So that we can get him over, with the relationship with both of the women that will skew the women's relationship to each other. And I think this guy coming out of a psych ward—something really a little bit out there; something you don't see on mainstream TV.

PD: He's not just "chicanerous," he's a loose cannon?

Steven Spielberg said, "I like ideas, especially movie ideas, that you can hold in your hand. If a person can tell me the idea in twenty-five words or less, it's going to make a pretty good movie." This is another way of saying "high-concept." In Bob's interview, he points out a balance beam a writer has to walk. The more "high-concept" a project is, the more unique it seems to be, but the more difficult it is to sustain from week to week on a comedy series. And, of course, it's what the networks want: A perfect blend of stable relationships with high concept that is almost impossible to deliver.

BM: Yes, he is. He's not just a funny neighbor; he's somebody who has a life of his own that impacts your life, as opposed to, he is leeching off of your life.

PD: He's very unpredictable.

BM: He could be very unpredictable, right, yes. He could be, if you really wanted to go in a direction that I think many network executives could relate to, but I don't know how the heartland would respond. You know, this is a guy who's switching from one anti-psychotic, or anti-depressant, to another. Or, he can just be a guy who had a real bad past, a really bad past. And he's got a parole officer; he's got friends that are a little questionable. And so all of these things, I think, get dragged into her life. And if you separate the two women so that they have opposite feelings about him, that for some reason the mother sees through the veneer—the daughter does too, she loves him, obviously it's sexual tension, obviously the series is heading toward somehow or other testing that relationship, getting them back together in some way. But the mother has always liked him, which gives the daughter an attitude, "But he stole cars . . . he killed somebody . . . " "We all make mistakes." Molly likes him.

Molly says, "Who else is asking you out, who else is so great out there for you?" And then the actual sensible, "You loved him once; there's got to be a little of that left." And, of course, the guy's got to be redeeming; he's struggling. He's coming out of rehab, or he's coming out of a psych ward, or he's coming out of jail, which I particularly love. But whatever that test was, it converted him in enough of a way that he is trying to establish a normal life, a better life than he was leading before. Sarah just isn't buying it. [*At this moment, Bob's face lights up.*]

If you took Sarah, and had her coming out of jail, or Molly, and have her coming out of rehab, or something like that, week-in and week-out, you'd have to remind the audience . . . it isn't the nature of their relationship; it doesn't impact upon them anymore. It's something that she's already moved past. After a while, you don't want to have to answer that question; you just want it to be a study of the characters and their interplay. But if you take the third character, and it's because of his being a wild card that it impacts them, it's much easier to describe: "I see you're here without your car-stripping friends today," Sarah says. It's much easier to describe how he gets in there. He's a two-and-a-half dimensional character, so it's a lot to get him in. And I forgot to tell you, he wears his pants up to here [*Bob points to the middle of his chest*].

PD: You seem like you can just twist a dial and make the work go in the direction you like. How would you go about making it darker?

BM: What I would do is make the profession darker so she would be surrounded by darker characters. Not prostitution—we're talking about the marketplace again. If you're doing it for Showtime, you could go there. That's actually a good idea.

"They put a lighter person in a darker arena."

I don't love this, but she could be on the crime beat of a newspaper. You know they do this on USA Network a lot, they take a crime show and put a funny character on it to lighten it up. They did it with *Monk.* They made Monk [have] OCD [Obsessive Compulsive Disorder]. They put a lighter person in a darker arena. I'd try to find an uglier arena. Something where there's a darker side to the arena . . . or, I would try to find the ghosts of the past. If it were darker, and an hour show, I would make it a ghost of her own past. I'd make it something she is trying to overcome. What if she was still fighting a drug habit? If she actually had one, and was trying to fight through it? That would darken it up considerably. I like that, actually. I don't know how the mother fits in, but you take a thirty-year-old woman, who's had a rough-ish past and is trying to become a professional writer, for example. She works on the newspaper and her deep, dark secret is her habit, which she just can't kick. That darkens it up a little.

PD: That's like what they had in *Cheers* with Sam being an alcoholic.

BM: Yeah, and *Murphy Brown,* too, but they never explored it. That's what happens to high concepts—"Wouldn't it be interesting . . . ?" Only ultimately, it's not. Because people like that ultimately grow. Like I said, the husband is a better person when he comes out of jail, not her, because she's trying to grow and if you hold her back, you hold up the drive of the series. It's the same thing with *Murphy Brown.* My thought about *Murphy Brown* is, what would you do with Candice Bergen? Here's a woman who is beautiful, and seems very upper-crust, and coming out of the movies, and how do I sympathize with her? She's kind of cold, how do I sympathize with her? So they

When we interviewed Bob Myer, show runner on *Roseanne,* he showed himself to be a consummate pro. He told us that as soon as he finished reading the Premise, he cast it and in about six minutes gave us a perfect network sitcom episode. Jeffrey asked him if he could darken it. Bob smiled and said, "How dark do you want it?" Picture someone with his hand on a dial about to turn it. He took our efficient, corporate Sarah and turned her into a drug-addicted private eye. Within a few minutes, he turned the story on its head. He laughed at the end and told us he just might try to use his new version.

gave her, right out of rehab, coming back to her old job and finding that there is a younger, prettier girl competing with her. And so they gave her a real struggle. This struggle lasted two episodes and then the show was just about this curmudgeonly woman reporter, a woman anchor in this arena with a bunch of crazies.

"She'd have to be funny out of her darkness . . ."

So if you're on Showtime, and Sarah was a private detective, good at her work, a minor Sherlock Holmes . . . Holmes was a drug addict, so you actually give her the cocaine or heroin habit that she's trying to fight. Take it to a place where she goes through withdrawal and relapses. That's how you darken it up. She'd have to be funny out of her darkness, out of her self-loathing would be comedy. You know, when you hate yourself, you hate the world. So, she would just hate everyone around her. Anger is funny. The negative emotions are the funny emotions.

PD: So once you develop a character like this, how would you flesh it out?

BM: In the pilot episode, I would probably start with a first act where you had no idea of her addiction. You just saw her at work and saw how good she was. And at the end of a quarter of an hour or half an hour, you'd see her make up all the chemicals she would shoot up. And you would go "Whoaaaa!"

Then you'd go to her psychiatrist and see her lie to her psychiatrist, saying that the habit . . . "I haven't done it in days." You know she did it the night before and she probably did it on her way [to the appointment]. So you see her lie. And only the audience knows the whole truth. And that way she becomes as dark as you want her to be. And especially if she hates the world. She has no respect for the world. She'll lie her way through anything, and that could be very funny. Trying to get into the evidence room, for example, and she's just a private detective. And how does she lie her way into that because she just doesn't care? Here's a woman who, because of her drug habit, her life is shit, and she doesn't care if she dies tomorrow. But the one thing that keeps her moving is this, what she's good at. And this is something that she can't suppress.

PD: And how do you make her likable?

BM: I think her dependency makes her likable and she's funny. And we like funny people. Second of all, she's pretty. You like pretty people. But she's also got a struggle and you're rooting for her. You want her to survive, you want her to pull out of this. And she's good enough about what she does and entertaining enough in how she behaves that just how she can keep her friends strung along, her friends haven't given up on her yet, and you don't either. You still feel like there's something of value there. You probably need a Jiminy Cricket in the show. You probably need a sister who knows enough about her, who's constantly sitting on her shoulder. And someone she lies to, but somebody who probably knows about the lies.

JD: Do you take the mother and transform her into someone else?

BM: I would take the mother and make her into a contemporary, because the mother not taking really fast action makes her very weak. And that's not a character you would really love, but take a character who was a very dear friend, a sister, someone who knows her well, and there would obviously be an intervention show right in the middle of an investigation. So she walks into her home, she's got the reports of the latent prints, the DNA evidence, she's coming home to pick up her hat, or whatever it is she needs, but it's obviously her cocaine. She's got an interview with the guy she's got to meet, and he's the Deep Throat. And she walks in and . . . INTERVENTION!

There's comedy in that. I'm thinking of pitching it now!

PD: It looks like you develop a character by creating a property list. "Okay, I need this trait to make her quirky, I need this trait to make her dangerous, and I need a trait to make her likable, and I need a trait to make her unpredictable." The functions derive the character.

JD: How much of what Peter just described is conscious for you? How much of it are you aware of?

"'Don't ever make Louie likable.'"

BM: Well, a lot of it was prompted by Peter's questions. Like, how do you make this person likable? And a lot of it is years of having it ground in by the networks, unlikable leads just don't work. You just have to find a way to make a lead likable. The classic example is *Buffalo Bill* with Dabney Coleman. Now if you could find a more entertaining rogue than Dabney Coleman at that time, I don't know who it was. But *Buffalo Bill* was one of the best-written shows on television at the time. I, and most of the comedy writers of that time, were rooting for it because it would have broken the mold, but it didn't.

You can make Louie de Palma [in *Taxi*], Danny DeVito, totally unlikable, but he's not the central character. You can laugh at him because you just know that he's never going to stop being grouchy and mean. And it's great for your secondary character.

Later, when the show matured and they needed to go other places for stories, they made him sort of likable. There was a studio executive named Glenn Padnick [co-founder, with Rob Reiner, of Castle Rock Entertainment] who said, "Don't ever make Louie likable. The minute you make Louie likable, you've lost your character." But a lead, it's kind of a knee-jerk reaction, has got to be likable in some way.

This takes us back to Candice Bergen. There's nothing innate in Candice Bergen's character [in *Murphy Brown*] that suggests vulnerability. She was very strong, with her voice, in her appearance; she was beautiful; carried a lot of authority . . . how are you going to feel for her? You've got to give her a struggle.

Roseanne created her own struggle. She was a struggling mother trying to hold a family together, in spite of her microcosmic economic disaster. Their situation was constantly never having two nickels to rub together. And that allowed her to be unattractive. Which I never felt she was. I always thought she was adorable.

PD: You're so skilled at the craft of setting up a joke. Like solving the crime and walking into the intervention. Where did you learn that set of skills?

BM: I don't know. When they staff you, they try to put you into some type of category. Are you a *story* guy or a *line* guy . . . and I am only a competent line guy. If I had to make my living just writing jokes, you know, I wouldn't be in the business. My mind works in juxtapositions and ironies. It just works that way. I can see situations better than I can see lines. And, I can punch up lines and I can re-phrase lines, and occasionally I will make myself very proud and come up with a line that the audience occasionally laughs at. But it's not the thing I do best.

JD: You've had a lot of experience in Writers' Rooms. What are the politics of a good and bad Room?

"As the head writer, you're still gonna spend 90 percent of your time in the Writers' Room and the other 90 percent in the editing room."

BM: Well, I've certainly had experience in both. I've had to learn a lot. Writers' Rooms are kind of an organism. They're made up of the personalities in the Room and how they get along, so it isn't just putting a bunch of funny people together, because some of the most horrible people in the business are the funniest. And they can work alone, but you can't put them into the Writers' Room. They're the ones that you give a script to and say, "Come back in a week, come back with a script, come back with a story,

The best way to describe Bob's character is through his view of the Writers' Room. In running a Room, he uses both his heart and his head: They tell him that every writer has to be appreciated and recognized. He is equally kind and nurturing to cooperative writers, and harsh with disruptive ones who have big egos. His Rooms are well-known for being harmonious.

As we interviewed Bob, he made us feel as if we were part of one of his Rooms. As you read his interview, you will see why he was such a successful show runner.

punch this thing up, but until then, don't show your face." In assembling a Writers' Room, you have to look at the dynamic of the individual personalities and make sure that they're all going to get along . . . 'cause that will absolutely kill a Writers' Room, and any comedy that can come out of it. Nothing good happens when two people don't like each other, or if one person has an attitude that's too big for the Room.

So I've been in good Rooms and really bad ones, and bad ones are a really horrible experience. 'Cause if you're a writer you will spend 90 percent of your time in the Writers' Room, even if you're running the show, even if you're the executive producer. As the head writer, you're still gonna spend 90 percent of your time in the Writers' Room and the other 90 percent in the editing room.

PD: So if you're a show runner, how do you deal with that?

"Ageism has had a lot to do with bad staffs."

BM: Well, you kinda have the opportunity to put together your own staff. If you didn't have that opportunity and you have made a couple of mistakes . . . on *Roseanne*, I had a couple of writers; they were oil and water. They just hated each other. One of them was perceived as my guy and the other was perceived as their guy . . . it was awful. And I tried to get them to sit down and air it all out. Go to a bar, have a drink, and talk it all out. I basically ordered them to do it. And now I know, you don't do that. You just sit down and you basically say, "This can't work. So, you either get along or one of you is going. You can decide if you're both staying, or by your behavior, decide which one is going." That's why there are options in contracts. So you can fire someone after the first few episodes.

Ageism has had a lot to do with bad staffs. I was on one staff where I was the executive producer running the show, this was the worst staff I was ever on, but the show runner and I . . . the show runner was the creator, with a great deal of power, he created another show that was in its fourth year of syndication. He got a tremendous amount of money from it. He was the darling of the production company. He could do no wrong. And at that time he had multiple shows on the air. So in order to run his various shows he selected show runners, people of show-runner rank, to run the Rooms when he wasn't there.

But when he was there, he was the boss and that was the understanding. So I was selected to run this first-season show with him. He pretty much put together the staff. I was just there as a kind of a rubber stamp. If he liked the person, that person was going to get hired. Not only did he put together a bad staff, but he put together a bad staff that was never there. So he hired the staff, but I was running it. And they owed no allegiance to me 'cause I was working all day on stories and he would come in at 11 o'clock and say, "No, no, no." That was a bad staff. Not only were the personalities haphazardly thrown together, and certain references overlooked, because he had other shows to run and he wanted to take care of the staff, but I was constantly undermined because he was never there and we didn't do any meaningful work unless he was there.

I had to wrangle the staff. I was, by ten years, the oldest guy in the room. There's a lot of belief in the business that if you're older, then you are not fresh. You can't understand. You can't write *Friends*. You know, you can't write *Will & Grace*. If you are older, because you are not hip enough, if you say "hip," you're not hip enough. So my problem in this context was that this was a show written about two very young people, twenty years of age who had gotten married very, very young. And it was about their very young marriage. I was, by ten years, the oldest person in the room, and there was a guy in the room that just didn't respect my ability to write about a relationship like that. And his personality was *too big for the room*. And it was a miserable room that accomplished nothing as a result of the fact that there were no clear lines of authority drawn, work was constantly being thrown out, and there was no real feeling that we could ever accomplish anything.

So when assembling a staff, I will look for people I know, and I know these people by now. It's not like I have to interview them, I've worked with them before. I've been on a dozen first-season shows in the last dozen years; no one has ever returned. It's always been different staffs. I've worked with ninety different people in the last ten years, and I can pick and choose people from those staffs when I have the opportunity to assemble the staff. I can pick people from those staffs that I know are creative, but will be symbiotic with the other people on the staff.

PD: You said you've also worked with a partner. How was that?

BM: In half-hour [series], it was very frustrating for me. Not because of him. He's great. And I actually recruited him as a partner out of college because we made each other laugh a lot and had a great time, so let's take our show on the road. We were stand-up comics for a while and then we started to write together. The problem for somebody like me is that half-hour comedy is always a very collaborative business. It's the kind of thing where if you have an idea, by the time it gets on-camera, it's gonna look a lot different. If you write a script, it's gonna look a lot different. And since I was hurrying to work and collaborating with ten other people anyway, then why was I splitting a salary? You know, it just didn't make sense to me.

> ## "The day I knew the partnership was over . . . an NBC executive came up to me . . . alone, and said, 'Hi, guys!'"

I was considered an individual writer, except when I was working on a script, but as we all know, a great deal of the writing, a great deal more than half, more than three-quarters, is done in the room. And you and your partner do not speak the same words at the same time. They're getting two opinions for the price of one. And that's just because you write scripts together. So I found that I was very stifled. I found that by virtue of the process, I'm a bad collaborator for my partner. I was becoming tyrannical. You know, it's got to be done my way, and I realized it was because of me. Like when you're in a relationship with a woman and you're trying to break up so you say, "It's not you, it's because of me." That was the case. It was because of me. I was not allowing him breathing room. And I couldn't stand not being an individual. And the day I knew the partnership was over, I was walking down the hall of our production offices alone when an NBC executive came up to me—meeting me in the hall alone—and said, "Hi, guys!" I said I won't be able to function anymore if this is the way I have to work.

PD: I'm curious: How do you know when something's funny? People who have done stand-up have developed a survival instinct because the situation is so immediate.

BM: People who play in front of an audience should always be funny. People will argue that because of that wonderful little laugh box, that anything can be funny in an audience situation comedy. That's not true. As a stand-up, you know that it's funny immediately. But that's only with that audience. We had an act once where the act got stale. We took two months off and rewrote the entire act. We go onstage, and for one weekend, our new act actually destroyed the audience. It was absolutely amazing. It was beyond anything we could have hoped for. We were so happy. From then on, it died. Doing it in that same venue, on the same night of the week, but it died. Why? Don't know. And why does a piece of material suddenly stop working for you that has worked for years for you? That also happened to us. It stopped working for us . . . you don't know. One audience differs from another. People who are writing without the illusion of a live audience, or for a laugh track, don't have to be that funny.

PD: So how do you know when something's funny when you write it?

"There can be a lot of reasons for why somebody laughs, or not. They could be sucking up."

BM: Well, when you're writing them, the first thing you rely on is whether or not anybody else laughed. There can be a lot of reasons why somebody laughs, or not. They could be sucking up. Depends on who you are. If you're running the Room and they laugh, they could be sucking up. If you're the "omega dog" in the Room and everybody laughs, you're pretty sure it's funny; everybody in the Room is pretty sure it's funny if they all laughed at the omega in the Room. But there are other times, it's just a matter of why you're laughing, and were you laughing because it's a funny Room joke; does it really work for the show? And then you take a chance; you go down for a run-through, and you put that line in, and that's the one advantage that situation comedy has, is that you'll hear it right at the table on Monday, and Tuesday you'll see a run-through, and Wednesday, you'll see a run-through, and in each case, you'll have a crack at that joke. You'll be able to try it out in front of yourself as an audience in the context of what it's going to look like in a show, but even by your rewrite on Wednesday, you're still guessing.

PD: How about your instincts?

BM: Well, there are some things that you just feel have got to be funny.

PD: The *intervention* . . . you knew that was going to get a laugh.

BM: Well, I think that if I had pitched that—I appreciate that—but if I had pitched that in the Room, that would have been the reaction to that . . . at least the moment that she opens that door and sees, in her urgency, that they've chosen that moment to intervene on her, that's got to get a laugh. Whether it continues to get laughs through the scene, who knows?

PD: I remember in another interview, one of the writers said, "The telephone is always going to get a laugh—you make the guy busy enough when the phone rings, you've got a cheap laugh if you need it."

BM: Yeah. Comedy is timing. And it's true; it's just the juxtaposition of moments or events, when they're slammed up against each other. How do those moments interact with each other? The moment of her coming in in haste and urgency, against something that she looks at that everybody else is urgent about is going to take hours, and they're not going to let her go, immediately you know that those two things slamming up against each other . . . that's not going to work.

PD: Do you think those years of stand-up helped sharpen that instinct for you?

BM: I don't think it hurt. We weren't an ad-libbing act, so we didn't actually exist in the moment on stage. Everything we did was very, very set, and it was a good act. It was very media-oriented, and commercial parodies with music and stuff like that. It was very set. And I think that we grew out of a sketch school.

PD: A writer who I interviewed in the previous incarnation of this book wrote jokes for Bob Hope. He said that Hope had incredible instincts for detecting what was funny. He said, "If you gave him ten jokes, he would point out which six were funny, and which two would work for his character." He had that instinct that was so finely honed because he had stood in front of so many audiences.

BM: Well, all his life. I mean, even before he got into show business, he was making people laugh, and he knew what he could pull off. My partner and I are very different in appearance. I'm the short, Jewish guy, and he is a tall, thin, WASP-y looking guy from Tennessee, with a perfect American accent—the newsman accent. And we were doing an act for a while where all the lines were split up, and it was okay, because the act was clever. We were good together and the act was clever. And all my life I've been a mugger, short with the comic face and everything, and I had been a mugger all through my college years. I was in a performing organization, which is where he and I met, and I was the kind of guy who got laughs off of my face. One night we're performing, or we were going in to perform, and I had laryngitis, and I couldn't talk. So I said to him, "I've got to save my voice." There are parts of the act where I *must* talk, but there are parts of the act where we just split up the lines. "You know all the lines, so you just talk and I'll just mouth." It was an epiphany night for us. That night, the act literally kicked up a level and became what our act legendarily became in later years, which was, I just sat there and I was sort of the puppet, or the animated character, and he was the announcer. And we each got laughs off of our individual skills. I returned to something that I knew I could make funny. I wasn't getting the laughs when I was reading the joke. The joke would get the laugh, but I wasn't. Bob got laughs because he's an announcer.

"She's not going to say in front of an audience, 'I considered killing my baby . . . '"

. . . And going to the Bob Hope reference, Roseanne [Barr] had an idea that . . . we were doing a show about a Lamaze class, and the situation that we set up that we thought was funny is somebody in the Lamaze class asking her about whether or not—about what her birth experiences were like. And we felt that since the audience really knew her feeling about her kids, this would be kind of a novel take. Did she go through Lamaze? Did she go through natural childbirth? Were there drugs? And stuff like that. It was pretty funny, but the moment that she wanted to do was, "When I had my third child, I hadn't lost the weight from my second child, and they said, 'If we give you drugs, enough drugs to sedate you, it could kill the baby.'"

This is her exactly, "It could kill the baby. So I thought to myself . . ." and that's the Jack Benny "Your-money-or-your-life" moment. "So I thought to myself," she says, and we're watching a run-through—because she invented it on the spot—we watch it in a run-through and I'm like, "Oh my God, oh my God, she's not going to do this. She's not going to say in front of an audience, 'I considered killing my baby,'" so we wrote it out. We wrote around it, which is what we would do; we wrote kind of around it, where a sense of those words were kind of in it, but ultimately it was a

Gifted comedy writers are all funny in their own way. They are students of comedy and thieves. We mean that in the most positive sense of the word. Writers know all the old jokes and take what's come before them and make it their own. When Bob Myer refers to the Jack Benny joke, he's talking about the famous bit that featured the longest pause in the history of radio. It originated on Benny's radio program. A thief (played by Mel Blanc, who was the voice of Bugs Bunny and most of the voices on the classic *Looney Tunes* cartoons) holds Jack up at gunpoint and says, "Your money or your life." There's a long silence. The longest pause in the history of radio. Again, the thief repeats, "I said, your money or your life." Jack says, "I'm thinking . . . I'm thinking."

The joke has never been topped, which is why writers steal it. *Monk* and *The Big Bang Theory* have both used it. Bob's story about Roseanne Barr's creative reimagining of the bit is worth studying. It reminds us that as a writer you are always building on the work that has come before and making it your own.

different joke, and we got a call from the stage saying, "She wants to do this joke; she feels she can make it funny."

And I said, "Who am I to argue with a woman who is one of the biggest stars in comedy right now? If she doesn't know how to make this funny . . ." Biggest laugh in the show. Biggest laugh in the show. When it was over, she just looked at me. Biggest laugh in the show. The audience just went bananas. They just went crazy, because it's Roseanne, and our thought was, "She would have a take like that, but I never thought it would be *that* one."

JD: Did someone mentor you?

BM: No, no, my family was a big joke-telling family, and I learned early that they would laugh at my jokes, that I was an equal in the family, and that if I could tell a joke, they would laugh. I still have, thank goodness, a very funny uncle, after whom I allegedly took. But we were always telling jokes to each other, and they were always encouraging the youngsters to tell jokes, and I had a particularly good sense of humor for the jokes that they told, and I would get them before my siblings would. I would get the adult jokes earlier than they would. And they were very encouraging. And then if ever I was in a high school play, you couldn't keep my parents away. And then I was in the camp plays where the parents weren't allowed, but they drove up anyway and [they would] stand outside the rec halls looking inside—I had to say it was my family. And my parents were very, very supportive.

PD: Are they artistic types themselves?

BM: Not really. My mother played piano, my father worked at a plant that manufactured cloth for sweaters, stuff like that. He was in the rag trade. But it was just one of those warm, funny, loud Jewish families. And when the extended family got together, my mother's brothers, my uncle, when the extended family got together, it was all about jokes. At a certain part of the evening we would just start telling jokes to each other. It's still that way with him. There is nothing better than sex! When you're an eight-year-old, there is no sex. So better than anything is getting a laugh on a joke, or even a remark that you came up with, and I said, "Geez, this is cool."

"I was constantly singing and dancing around the bigger people . . ."

Then the other thing that honed my instincts was my size. I was always really small. And so in order not to get picked on, it's a very common story, in order not to get picked on you get very large friends, which I did. You recruit them because they think you're funny. When you make the bullies laugh, they won't beat up on you so much because you're funny. Funny people are likable people, you don't want to hurt somebody that you like. So I was constantly, especially in elementary school and junior high, where I was really short, I was constantly singing and dancing around the bigger people, in large venues, like trying to be on the stage if there was an eighth-grade play, or anything like that, or a smaller venue, just making them laugh in the classroom.

PD: Were you aware of this as it was happening?

BM: Yeah, I knew that I had to joke my way out of some very scary situations. But, you know, the truth is, with any individual, you only have to do that once, then they decide they like you and that sort of builds a fan base; in my case, a secret service to protect you.

JD: You mentored people, whether intentionally, or unintentionally. What does that entail?

BM: It's basically got to do with being in the Room, and you can have good Room runners who nurture you, and try to get the most out of you, or you can have Room runners who are there basically for their own glory and will pick you clean, not give you any credit, not take you farther along the road. I had mentored people, people who cite me as their mentor in *Written By* magazine [the Writers Guild of America West's magazine], who get cover stories, and I get cited as "The Mentor." Where is my cover story? That's what I want to know. But these are people who've become much more successful than I have.

I learned about mentoring because I was in a Room where nothing you could do was ever really recognized, that you were always second-guessing yourself, that you were worried about pitching anything. It was an environment of fear and dictatorship, as opposed to a nurturing environment. When I lived, struggled under that, and became a show runner after that, on that same show, I saw how everybody lightened up when they realized that I said, "Yeah, that's good." They were words they hadn't heard before. And when you do that, you get more out of a person, and ultimately your job is to make the show funnier, as funny as it can possibly be within the confines of the time that you have to make it funny. So it's just a matter of being efficient to nurture a person along. You're paying this person, you're not bringing him in and paying him so you can beat him up. You're bringing in and paying him so that he can make everybody's life easier and be funny.

After the interview, we remembered Bob saying that he has always had an animated face and mugged constantly. Being in a room with him, we both noticed that what he referred to as mugging was really an expression of the pleasure he gets out of the comedy creation process. For example, the closer he got to revealing the "intervention" line, the more animated he became.

An Interview with
Hank Nelken

A partial list of Hank Nelken's credits as a screenwriter includes: *Saving Silverman, Are We Done Yet?,* and *Mama's Boy.*

Hank Nelken is just another Jewish comedy writer from the Lower East Side—of Dallas. He went to school in the Lower East Side of Los Angeles, to the University of Southern California School of Cinema. When he was just a kid, he saw *E.T.* and knew he wanted to be a filmmaker. By eleventh grade, supported by his theatre arts teachers, he and a group of friends began writing and acting in comedy sketches broadcast live to his entire high school. Peter Desberg met him when Hank used his office to shoot a short video, *HOSTAGE: A Love Story,* for Will Ferrell's *Funny or Die* website. His direction shows his comedy skills and when we heard his writing credits, we knew we wanted to interview him.

PD (Peter Desberg): As we've explained in our Premise [see page 9], how would you go about developing the show's plot lines?

HN (Hank Nelken): Well, first of all, great job, guys. I really love it. I think it's great, I love the character. I love the setup of it. The world of it, you know. I've got a few notes, just a few thoughts and some questions. Overall, I feel like it's very situational, so it feels like a TV show. The big idea is that they were very well off, like the Madoffs, and he really didn't have what she thought he did, so now the mom is kind of screwed. It's such a strong situation.

"See, it's my natural instinct—I'm trying to please you guys like you're executives."

I like the idea that it's these two women who live together, mom and daughter. And I like the idea that the mom is the one who is this sex-crazed, fun-loving, man-loving woman, and the daughter is sort of the stick in the mud. To me, that's a fun dynamic. See, it's my natural instinct—I'm trying to please you guys like you're executives.

JD (Jeffrey Davis): Let's say you didn't have to please us.

HN: I like this process. I feel very empowered by this. Truly, what I would do is I would make it two guys. I don't write women as well as I do guys. I would make it that the dad moves back in with the son. Same exact characters, stick-in-the-mud son, and this really wild, fun, bachelor dad. And I would give the son a new wife. Basically, the parents get divorced or the mom dies, and the dad has lived this conservative life and he's always sort of provided, but when the mom dies, he doesn't know what to do. He's lost and he needs a place to crash.

He moves in with the son, who is this buttoned-down guy, and his new wife, and he never leaves. It's got the *Odd Couple* dynamic, but with trying to fit in a new wife and, at some point, a baby. And Dad will always be there in the way. I've always loved Rodney Dangerfield's *Back to School,* and I love that dynamic between the two of them [the father and son in *Back to School*]. It's a classic pairing of characters, and I just loved that he was the wild and crazy dad and the kid was the stick in the mud. It makes this kid the butt of the jokes, and then it's sort of a Ben Stiller type of character who plays the kid, and then you have any fun, great, older comedic actor, maybe [Jack] Nicholson, playing the dad.

There is another way to go, where he's a younger guy and he's not married. He's got a girlfriend. In some ways, maybe for a sitcom, that's better. The son has just finally gotten out of a roommate situation, he's moved into his own place, he's kind of ready to face the world, and he's got a good job. He's sort of getting his stuff together, and here comes Dad needing a place to crash. And so they become roommates. In some ways, maybe that's better, because then they can fight over the same girl at some point. Dad can cockblock him. Just when he's decided he's growing up, here comes Dad. I think this is a rich situation. You can launch it from here and really mine that material for years and years. You would watch the son fall in love and the real question is, "When is Dad going to move out?"

"... to make it into a feature, it needs an *engine*."

JD: In your heart of hearts, movies are what you love most?

HN: Yes, although I just wrote a TV pilot. And I'm going to go pitch another one. I've sold one pilot in my career. Features are where I've been for my whole life. I want to branch out and be directing TV and film. I think for this Premise, to make it into a feature, it needs an *engine.*

An engine is a drive. A thing that happens that is going to spin this character in a direction where he's got a mission he's got to accomplish. It's going to be difficult and full of obstacles. These two characters are going to go on the road together, like in *Rain Man*. It's a classic two-hander. Maybe it's as simple as, "All I've got to do is get from A to B and then I get my money." They need a goal and it would probably relate to the death of the other parent. Maybe it's getting the funeral together. And you're also looking for a high concept. There is something in here that really feels like the Madoff thing.

PD: How would you take it in that direction?

HN: I actually have some friends who thought they had all this money their dad left them. They had been spending all the money they made working, and then they found out the dad was tied into Bernie Madoff and all that money was fake. That changed their lives. But for a movie version of that, maybe their mission is actually to get the money back, or take down the Bernie Madoff character. If you can include the Madoff character, it might give them a goal, a drive.

Wait, let me go back to the female version for a minute. What if the husband died and Molly expects to get all this money, but then realizes there is nothing there when she goes to collect it? This could be the inciting incident or page-10 event that gets the ball rolling. I think it works better from the female perspective, because you feel like the men are dealing with the money. She could team up with her daughter to bring down Madoff. I definitely feel like that's where it gives it the high concept and gives it the drive of the movie. So now, this unlikely pair, who don't have a great relationship, have this need to bring down this guy to get their money back.

And then there also needs to be some kind of ticking clock working. Maybe once they find out the guy is packing up shop and wants to go to the Caymans, they've got a week to infiltrate his company, figure out what's going on, and bring him down. There is something kind of fun there, and in some ways, that is actually more fun for the two women. You get that great *Working Girl* or *Legally Blonde* feeling of female empowerment while bringing down this Madoff-type guy.

PD: Now the two of them have a mutual dependency. How do they get along?

HN: This relationship is the heart of the movie. They are forced to work together. I guess you could keep it a mother and daughter. But in this version, I don't know what Sarah's personal stakes are. Why did she have to get in on this journey? I'm not sure yet. But it definitely feels like the two of them are similar. I love the idea that the mom is still the fun-loving one and the daughter is the stick in the mud. So when Molly says, "Honey, we have to go do this thing. We have to get this money back,"

Sarah says, "No way!" The second act of the movie becomes all about their relationship. Neither of them wants to work together.

They've written each other off in some way. Maybe Molly says, "Look, we are going to do this. I know you don't like me. I don't like you. But do this. Get the money we deserve so we can keep financing our separate lives. And get justice and then go our separate ways." And they end up coming together. To me, that's the one that always ends up working the best when you have this push-pull like *Midnight Run,* a classic two-hander. One of them is trying to take the other one in, and the other one is trying to convince him that he's morally innocent. So they're at odds the entire time, but they come to develop this great friendship and come to love and trust each other. All great two-hander movies have that, "I don't like you, I don't want to be here" element in them. That's the engine that drives them together.

PD: How would you develop these two characters?

HN: It depends where you start. I either start with a character I've got in mind and then a story comes out of that character, or I start with a concept and then work backwards to fit the characters into the concept. Sometimes it's a back-and-forth process, like a crossword puzzle. You're just filling in different parts until you figure it out.

PD: Do you have an actual person you know in mind and start using their traits? Or do you start making trait lists?

"It's either the bravest guy in the world or it's the most cowardly guy you've ever met."

HN: It's a combination of both. I use real people because that's a great place to start. You get those real traits. One thing I've been thinking about lately is that in reality, people are very complicated, but in a movie, to have a great character, you have to strip away some of that complication. You want to depend on them being a certain way all the time. So I always take traits from real people, but then the process is also about heightening them, because great characters tend to be extremes. They are either incredibly cowardly, because you never write a character like, "Eh, he's kind of a coward." "He's a little nervous, he's scared, but he's kind of brave at the same time." You can't do that. It's either the bravest guy in the world or it's the most cowardly guy you've ever met. You have to take those extremes. Another way I come up with ideas is by taking that extreme character and figuring out what's the worst situation that character could be in. A great example is the cowardly lion in [*The Wizard of*] *Oz.* That's where you get the fireworks.

PD: So if you have a button-down, stick-in-the-mud character like Sarah, what is she going to be like?

HN: You would want to put that character into a situation where she's got to be a free spirit. She's got to use her heart. She has to use her imagination and really be uncomfortable. She's sort of an anal organizer, but somehow she's got to go into a world where she can't use her computer. It's just all kind of gut, and she's really bad at using her gut. If she doesn't have the protractor and the computer and the cell phone, then she's not good. So I'm not quite sure about her yet in this movie. Because she's trying to take down Bernie Madoff, she'd probably be pretty good at that. It would probably be a good thing for her.

JD: What about the mother?

HN: Molly is really fun for this story because she's been this woman who was a wife for her whole adult life. Maybe she was free-spirited in some ways, but she never had the responsibility and she was never taken seriously. She is the great character in the movie. She's been this wife who has had one kind of life, a life of leisure, and the big moment is when the husband dies on page 10 [of the screenplay]. Molly is reeling from that and doesn't know her place in the world. She has no money. And when she finds out it's Madoff, she decides she's going to get her money back. On page 30, she puts on her business suit and goes into his office to infiltrate and bring down this guy.

So this woman, who has never worked a day in her life, is now going to bring down the most powerful guy on Wall Street. That starts to feel kind of good. That wouldn't be Meryl Streep. You wouldn't do that these days, she's too old to be the lead. You'd bring the age down. Make it Reese Witherspoon or Jennifer Aniston and roll Molly and Sarah into one character. Now you've got the same movie, but the lead is thirty-five. So let's say it's Reese Witherspoon. She's been a mom, she's been this total little housewife and she's got this husband. He takes care of everything and he's got lots of money. It's great. Then he dies. She doesn't know what to do with herself. Then suddenly, she finds out all the money he had was with this guy who scammed him. There's no money. The lawyers and everybody say, "Honey, there is nothing you can do. It's over." And she says, "No way. It's not over. I'm taking this guy down." She takes the kids to their grandma, and she puts on a business suit. Actually, this is a great idea because it's zeitgeist-y.

Right now, everyone is reeling from this feeling of being scammed. And then you have this great female character at the heart of the movie who thought she knew her place in the world. But she's never really had anyone's respect. Now she has a week to get her money back. Say on page 30 she is working at the Madoff character's firm. She's in a low-level position. She has used her smarts to fake everybody out and get enough of a résumé together to fake an entry-level job. She thinks she's got plenty of time and that she's going to work her way up. But on page 45, she hears that Madoff is shutting down the whole shop in one week, or one month, and it's all over. He's going to the Cayman Islands and there will be no way to retrieve the money. Then suddenly she has to do what any normal person would take twenty years to do—but she's got to do it in one month. She's got to rise up through the ranks and win his confidence. And the only way to win his confidence is to be really savvy. Somehow, she's actually going to help him close up shop and get him safely to the Caymans, but in fact she's double-crossing him.

JD: Would you have Molly's husband die in a funny way, as in *Private Benjamin*?

HN: It's a comedy. In this pitch we are going with now, maybe it's a divorce that sends her off into the movie. The husband dumps her. But then again, he can't just leave her, because then he'll still be in the movie. So I guess it could be a comedic death. Death by blowfish. He's been on this exotic trip and she's told him not to go. He's an adrenaline junkie and in a bungee-jumping activity gone wrong. Molly says, "Of course he died, he shouldn't have been jumping out of helicopters to ski." So, some comedic death like that, and she's left out in the cold. It really is like *Private Benjamin*. That is a great model.

This movie is *not* a two-hander. It's a vehicle for one of those great women. And then you populate it with fun ensemble actors. The other great role is the Bernie Madoff roll. Then you pair up Reese Witherspoon with a great older actor. Nicholson or [Robert] De Niro. Or go younger and make the Madoff character Hugh Jackman. If you play it a little younger, you could potentially develop a love story between them that could be really interesting. She could be falling for him, despite herself. Or he's falling for her. But he's still the guy she's trying to bring down.

PD: Those guys are very charismatic, or they couldn't do what they do.

HN: Oh, of course. It's a great part.

PD: And that's an interesting conflict. On one hand, she knows how this guy swindled everybody, but he is kind of cute . . . in his own way.

HN: Right. You talk about starting from complete opposites. Not only does she despise him, and not only did he personally screw her out of all this money, but she is on a mission to bring him down. But she can't help that she's falling for this guy. And he sees something in her, but he thinks she's very green and he's exploiting her.

PD: Do you also use this as misdirection? The audience thinks, "Uh-oh, now she's falling in love with him. Is she going to cave in?"

HN: Yes, I think you tease it all the way. I guess what you're getting to in the end of the second act is that she's become conflicted, and in the key moment in which she could squeeze him, she lets him off. Somehow, that's the kiss. That's the moment where she's fallen for him. And in the next moment, he has completely screwed her. He was playing her. The business is shut down. He's off to the Cayman Islands. She's completely humiliated and horrified. Now in the third act, she has to become determined to bring him down. She has the goods on him. She kept the incriminating data.

PD: Everybody's expectations of her are so low that there's a lot of room to surprise them.

HN: Right. That's the thing. Her husband's lawyer buddy, who is taking care of the will, keeps telling her, "Look, there is nothing you can do." She's a housewife who is now thrust into this alien world, and she has this specific mission she has to accomplish. I actually *really* like it.

JD: You mentioned there would be some subordinate characters that would be fun?

HN: I think those characters are in the world she goes into in New York. Maybe Molly and her husband are from St. Louis or Milwaukee. People invested with Bernie Madoff from all over. It wasn't like they had to live in New York. So Molly's husband could have been investing with him for years and years. She's this very suburban housewife and she packs up and moves to New York City. She's a fish out of water in Manhattan. A fish out of water in this Madoff-like guy's firm. She doesn't know what she's doing, and the people she befriends, the fun characters, are all in their twenties. That's who she ends up connecting with because everybody else is so beyond her skill set. The female intern and the mailroom guy. She could potentially end up living with them.

> ## "The lesson I took from USC was when you go shoot on location, always leave it cleaner than when you found it."

PD: All the USC film graduates we've interviewed have had a strong sense of story construction. Did you get your sense of story from there?

HN: No! The lesson I took from USC was when you go shoot on location, always leave it cleaner than when you found it. The other thing I learned from USC was networking. I had this meeting with a legendary producer. I was going to bring my résumé and he was going to take me by the hand and lead me. He was supposed to be my mentor. I sat down across from him. In my memory, it's a giant office with a long table where you do the "pass the salt" joke. I'm clutching my résumé. He said, "One word, kid . . . networking." And the next thing I remember, the doors shut and I walked out and I didn't know what the hell I was going to do. Life was beginning.

So I have to say, I learned story construction and everything *after* film school. My experience there was very lean on writing and much more heavy on production. It was about directing. For every writing class, there were five directing classes. There was editing and cinematography. Actually, when I came out of school, I felt like I really didn't understand writing at all. I still had not written a feature screenplay and that is one of the things I feel like they should do. You should have a feature script. I guess you do if you're in the writing program. I was in production. But I think even production students should have a feature script coming out of there. You need to have written a feature and know what that feels like. I had only written shorts, so I didn't have the experience. A short film is just not enough.

My sense of story construction came from doing it over and over and over again. I hooked up with a writing partner who had come to L.A. from New York. He'd gone to graduate school in playwriting, and he really had the story construction side of it down. I had all the other stuff . . . all the gold, all the comedy. No, I'm kidding. He was really funny and I learned a lot from him. And after we split up, that was about eight years ago, that was when I had to do it on my own. That was when I really internalized this feeling for structure, which has become an internal part of me.

"When people aren't laughing it's like, 'Oh, I've written drama. How nice.'"

PD: Have you done dramatic writing as well as comedy?

HN: Sometimes my comedy feels dramatic. When people aren't laughing it's like, "Oh, I've written drama. How nice." The closest I've come is writing a dramedy. Like a Cameron Crowe movie.

PD: Did you grow up a funny kid? Were you a class clown kind of guy?

HN: When I look back at videos and things, I was very serious. I remember I always loved directing. I loved film and I especially loved Steven Spielberg. When I went to USC film school, I thought my Spielberg story was really unique. I saw *E.T.* when I was nine or ten and it just changed everything. Even in that moment, I knew I'd make movies. I got to USC and found out everybody had the same story. Earlier, I was into filmmaking and made a very serious movie about drinking and driving and it won a big national award. I was very serious about the film and its message, and that next year I just somehow dropped all that and got into comedy.

My dad's side of the family was always into jokes. Not only the actual telling of jokes, but other forms of humor. They just had an appreciation for humor. My dad also loved movies. It was clear that being funny meant something. And making him laugh meant something. I always grew up laughing at him.

PD: When did you realize you could do it?

HN: Junior and senior year of high school, I got into a great group. I went to this amazing high school in Dallas under the auspices of two theatre teachers, Lynn Zednick and Craig Wurgo. It was under their tutelage that this great group of kids who were creative acted and did videos. We did school announcements in the morning, and instead of blaring over the loudspeaker, they would have a TV in every classroom and broadcast the announcements. They were just straight news broadcasts. But then we decided, "Let's make them funny." On Fridays, we would do the announcements, and it was basically our *Saturday Night Live.* Once a week, we did an *SNL* kind of a show for the entire school. It was such a great experience. It would be ten or twelve minutes of material that we would *create* and everyone would see it. That was where I really started having fun with comedy.

PD: Have you ever tried your hand at stand-up?

HN: I never have. I've always been a huge fan of it, but I never wanted to do it. You've got to focus in this business. Even when I loved acting in high school, being a filmmaker was my passion and my heart. I love to act in my films. I had a small part in one of the movies I wrote. *Mama's Boy.* Diane Keaton was in the movie. It had a great cast. Jon Heder from *Napoleon Dynamite,* Jeff Daniels, and Anna Faris.

PD: Can you tell when something you've written is funny?

HN: Yeah, it's learned over time, and you get more confident over what is or isn't funny. You have to put it in front of an audience, too. You think something is funny on the page or you think you shot it funny, and then you watch an audience and there's nothing. They're just stone-faced.

". . . I wasn't even developing it to move forward. I was developing it to get the job."

PD: How much interference do you end up getting with what you write?

HN: Development? In this last year I've gotten very tired of pursuing writing jobs. I've gotten tired of developing things and then not going the next step with them. It's gotten to be such a cattle call of writers coming in that I wasn't even developing it to move forward. I was developing it to get the job. I don't mind developing something if I'm getting paid for it and we're all working together to make a movie. The trick is finding a way to interpret the notes, figure out what the underlying issue is, do it, and still keep the integrity of your piece.

PD: Did they make a lot of changes in *Saving Silverman*?

HN: We [Hank and Greg DePaul] were actually the only writers on that movie from beginning to end. And that was kind of the first experience I had. It was a big movie and we never got fired. In fact, the director brought us to the set, so we were there for the entire shoot.

PD: Just before we started the interview, you said that what we are doing with these interviews is what development executives hear all the time when writers are pitching to them.

HN: Yes. I wish I could be one of those development executives, just to hear what they hear. I've gone out for so many projects, and basically you hear just a one-liner idea they want you to develop. There was one book I really loved called *The Retired Kid*. It was about a little boy who decides to retire and moves into a retirement home. It's a great idea. But how do you know where that goes? You could do that in a number of different ways. I know they heard a lot of different takes, and I wanted to hear what people came up with. So you're giving people a really cool way to experience that. I'm dying to read what other writers came up with here using the same Premise.

When Hank finished reading the Premise, he didn't launch into developing it like the other writers did. He said our task reminded him of a situation he frequently found himself in when he was given an idea and asked to work it up for development executives sitting in their office. He said when he finished, they nodded their heads and said, "Thanks," which really meant, "Next." He was one of many writers asked to do this on a regular basis. He always wondered what the other writers came up with. He told us he would love to hear what the execs got to hear. Reading this book will be as close as he'll get.

An Interview with
Tracy Newman
and Jonathan Stark

Tracy Newman and Jonathan Stark's credits as creators, show runners, and writers include: *According to Jim, Ellen, The Drew Carey Show, The Nanny,* and *Cheers.*

Tracy and **Jon** often break each other up as they work. They met doing improv. We're not talking about some obscure club in Duluth. It was at The Groundlings—L.A.'s premier improv theater group. The key to improv is the ability to take any idea that is fed to you and go with it, rather than stop the flow and question it. No hesitation—just pure acceptance and then take it further. This background shows up in how they work together to this day. When either of them throws out an idea, the other grabs it and runs. Ironically, while improv is all about fluidity and dealing with surprise, Tracy embraces structure. Her songwriting background gives her a strong sense of story structure. She makes it a point to figure out where a story is going before writing a word of script. Then Jon steps in and develops character and dialogue. This combination has a lot to do with the success of this Peabody and Emmy Award-winning team's amazing success.

PD (Peter Desberg): As we've explained in our Premise [see page 9], how would you go about developing the show's plot lines?

TN (Tracy Newman): Well, right away I want to go dark with this premise. So I'm thinking, what if Molly is the kind of mother who comes on to her daughter's boyfriends?

JS (Jonathan Stark): I think that's a great idea.

TN: I think I've seen it before, but I'm playing with the idea that Sarah understands that's what her mother is trying to do. It's usually done where it comes as a surprise to the daughter.

JS: Well, you can turn that whole thing into a competition.

TN: Yeah, and she could be an attractive, young fifty.

JS: You can do an episode where she does that, and the boyfriend likes her. Is she too old for that? Fifty? Come on! Fifty's nothing. I mean, to us, it's nothing.

TN: I know of a real situation where it went this far. Listen to this. The mother wrote a letter to the guy her daughter was going with, offering to take him to Europe. It was devastating for the daughter, but the thing that was great was, the young woman, the daughter, was so resilient and strong. And she knew her mother was like this. It wasn't so much that she forgave her mother, but they had a playful relationship even as this was happening. Now I wonder, how that can happen? That's the part I'm not sure about.

JS: What if we take that idea and go to the fact that they become roommates. Roommates in the sense that they are both in the same boat. Molly is nuts about guys. Sarah isn't nuts about guys. It drives her crazy that her mother has now become her roommate and girlfriend. Molly gets all her dates and her mother is living a wild lifestyle. Maybe even make Sarah a little more conservative than she is in the Premise. Develop that a little.

TN: Sarah's attitude is probably, "Well, I know in my early twenties, I was with a lot of guys." I know I was.

JS: That's an understatement.

TN: Don't you see that the only reason we had a career is because I'm so good-looking?

JS: I was good-looking before I started smoking.

TN: You're still pretty handsome. Come on. The thing is, at Sarah's age, my career was the main thing that troubled me. Not so much guys. So what if Sarah's in a situation where she thinks, "Oh, my God, I have to make it." Because probably, she doesn't have a lot of money. I'd make another change. What do you think of this? Molly isn't broke. Molly has some money, and she's ready to live the carefree life. Maybe her husband was quite a bit older.

JS: Forget all that stuff about losing the money? Great. And maybe let's go back and say that Molly never actually did live the life she wanted to live. I mean, she loved her husband, but . . .

TN: . . . she got married young and had kids . . .

JS: . . . and that stopped her.

TN: Sarah doesn't want to do that. She wants to have a career and is concentrating on that. They've done this sort of thing before. But I'm not sure they've done the whole story. The whole story is that the mother wants to be the girlfriend, and the daughter . . . does the daughter want mothering? Maybe Sarah does.

JS: I'm going to say we go even a little darker. You set it up where Molly never really loved Sarah's father. She always wanted to cheat on him. She tells her daughter this. And this is news to her. Sarah is floored.

TN: And did she cheat on him?

JS: No, I don't think she did.

TN: She tried to cheat, to break up.

JS: I don't know, but if she's actually *not* done that, then that's what she now wants to do. She wants to do all the stuff she didn't do when she was married to this older guy. And maybe Molly never really gave Sarah the time she needed, and now Sarah wants mothering. But she's getting exactly the opposite. The daughter has to be the mother and this is really pissing her off. "I wanted you to mother me. Now that Dad has died, I want you to be my mother. You have time now."

TN: Sarah says, "You can cook. You can scrub."

JS: "No, I don't want to do that," Molly says. Now you have your conflict. I can even see the end of the first episode. They go through this argument, and they finally come to some kind of understanding about their relationship, and this new arrangement. Sarah says, "Fine. We'll just take it slow." Cut to the next morning. Sarah wakes up, and there's a guy coming out of her mother's bedroom. "Okay, I meant a little slower than that."

"I was cheating on him with his best friend the night he died.'"

TN: I think it's good. Wait, though. Back up a minute. Is there any way we can do it that Molly really did cheat on the father? Is this too hateful? Because I think it's funny. Molly says, "Honey, your father wouldn't leave me. I even cheated on him with his best friend, and he found out about it, and he still wouldn't leave me."

JS: "I was cheating on him with his best friend the night he died. I feel really guilty. You have no idea how bad I feel."

TN: You know, I think there are more people cheating now. Television has treated it like it's just a hateful thing. You just don't do that.

JS: I don't know. I think your world is really f–cked up.

TN: Maybe Sarah is going out with somebody. She wants to break up with him, and Molly says, "Here's what you do. You sleep with his best friend. He'll never get over it."

"For network, she's too hateful."

JS: That's a great first episode. "I've been going out with this guy, Tom, for two years, and I really can't stand him." Maybe the mother takes it upon herself to break up the relationship by seducing him. You can take it further if you're doing it on cable. For network, she's too hateful.

TN: But really, it's not hateful if what Molly is doing is showing her daughter that he's not a good guy for her: "You see, he slept with me!"

JS: "See, honey, I helped you." "You banged my boyfriend!"

TN: It's a noble seduction. That's a couple of episodes, actually. One episode is where Molly convinces Sarah to let her sleep with the boyfriend. What if the mother is dating someone who is getting clingy and wants to get married? And she's not interested, but she can't break up with him. So the daughter sleeps with him.

JS: Okay, that's way too creepy.

TN: I wasn't actually going there. Well, you know what I mean, though. You've got an episode where the mother sleeps with the daughter's boyfriend, seduces him, and makes him break up with her.

JS: But I think what you want to do in this thing is have them be opposites. The daughter is the mother; the mother is the daughter. That's what the basic premise is. If I were going in to pitch it, I'd say they've switched roles.

TN: Once you're the person who takes care of other people, that's what you do. It's not like, all of a sudden, your daughter takes care of you. If you took care of your mother, then you're taking care of your daughter, too. Nobody is ever going to take care of you. That's what you do. As long as you are a caretaker, the people around you will be letting you take care of them.

JS: But Molly never wanted to be a caretaker. So she is now living the life she really wants to live.

TN: So you add this element. When Sarah was really little and Molly was a young mom, the daughter took care of her mother. Her mother would say things like, "Look how much she likes to clean. She *loves* to clean the bathroom. Look at her! Just give her a rag." That would be a good quality for the daughter, because she's always been a caretaker and the mother has never been a caretaker.

JS: And she's expecting that when her mother moves in, things will be different. "Now I'm going to have the relationship I never had."

TN: "Now I'll be able to go look for jobs, and come home and have a hot meal waiting for me," Sarah says. "And you'll read to me." "I'm not going to read to you," Molly says. "Tickle my feet before bed?" And then you cut to Sarah tickling her mother's feet.

JS: That is a great conflict right there.

TN: I don't think I've seen that. Where the caretaker continues to be the caretaker. Sarah took care of her mom when she was little, and now she's still doing it. They can't reverse roles.

JS: And I'm thinking of that woman on *Two and a Half Men* who plays the mother. She's really kind of brash and she's, you know . . .

TN: . . . drunk.

JS: Well, I don't know if she needs to be a drunk. But she's brash and she's living the life she wants to live now. This is it. This is the way it is. But Sarah is pissed off about it.

TN: I think in isolated incidents, the daughter is all for it. "You should be out there doing what you want." But as each little thing happens, Sarah disapproves more and more of her mother. She becomes the mother. A mother tries to subtly guide, the daughter becomes that, so that you don't have constant bickering, like on *Curb Your Enthusiasm*.

PD: At the beginning, you said Molly seduces Sarah's boyfriend. That's a funny conflict, but what does that do to their relationship?

TN: Well, I think it wouldn't quite work.

JS: What I think we came up with later works better. Sarah wasn't happy to be with the boyfriend. It wasn't working out.

TN: Yeah, the noble seduction is how it works.

"Your job, as a writer, is to make it so that maybe 50 percent of the audience understands why he did it, and that they would possibly do the same thing."

TN: I don't know. We dealt with this on *According to Jim* all the time. [Jim] Belushi would do something that was completely not okay. And the audience is sitting there going, "No, no! He's not going to do that!" And then he has to explain to his wife at the end why he did it. Your job, as a writer, is to make it so that maybe 50 percent of the audience understands why he did it, and that they would possibly do the same thing. We had a situation where Belushi's character wouldn't apologize. That was the rule at the beginning. He said, "I won't apologize. I don't want to apologize." So that gave us an interesting problem on every show, because in the pilot, he takes one of the kids out of her school and changes schools and doesn't tell his wife. Think about that. I mean, in reality, nobody would really do that. Your wife would kill you. And when he explains it in the end, you're actually moved at his reason. So if Sarah is saying, "Maybe I do want to date this guy now," that worries Molly, so she seduces him.

JS: Maybe *seducing* is the wrong way to go. Maybe Molly brings him to the point where she knows she could seduce him, and tells her daughter to get out of the relationship. She proves to Sarah this guy isn't faithful to her. So she doesn't actually sleep with him. That's probably too much.

"You'll go down a road sometimes, and you'll go down it for two days, and then you say, 'Nope, got to go down another road. This one is taking us nowhere.'"

TN: But I think that's your job, as a writer. You have to come up with something where it seems like, "My God, how can these people do this to each other?" And then, when you hear their reasons, you bring a lot of the audience with you. There are still going to be a certain amount of people who say, "No, that's wrong. Just wrong." But there's going to be enough people being affected by it and think, "Yeah, I might do that myself."

JS: But also, a lot of times, when we work, we'll come up with this idea and we'll say, "Well, this is crazy," but then you just try and go down different roads. You're trying to make it not just palatable for the audience, but actually somehow find a reality in it. You're not just doing something ridiculous. You'll go down a road sometimes, and you'll go down it for two days, and then you say, "Nope, got to go down another road. This one is taking us nowhere." So you just keep going down all these roads, and still there's no guarantee that you're going to come out with anything.

PD: You started with the idea of an actual seduction. It makes me think of a pool player. You don't think about the shot you're making, but where it leaves you for the next shot. You started with an actual seduction, but then pulled it back to make it *look* like a seduction. But there was no consummation. Molly is trying to show Sarah something. And it turns into Sarah saying, "Gee, I had this all wrong."

JS: Sometimes, you realize all you've got on the table is the 8 ball, and then you have to go back and rack them up again. It is a lot of just going back, and going back again, until you feel like you've found a path. And that path can change when you write the script. The details change a lot.

TN: The interesting thing about the core of this Premise, as it's developing—and maybe this is because of my own life—is the idea of a caretaker. Once a caretaker, always a caretaker. That's the premise of it. What would you call the opposite of caretaking?

JD (Jeffrey Davis): Narcissism?

TN: Yes, the mother is a narcissist. And the daughter's the caretaker. The daughter is an enabler.

But what ends up happening is when you're the caretaker, you infantilize the other person. It also makes it easier to come up with stories. We know the daughter is always going to end up the caretaker and the mother is always going to be the narcissist, and behave like a narcissist. And yet, they are both lovable.

JS: I can see episodes. Molly wants to go skydiving. And Sarah says, "No, we could die!" "We're not going to die. We'll be fine." So Molly takes life by the horns and Sarah is right behind her going, "I don't know about this. I don't know about this."

And then maybe actually we do an episode where the daughter decides to do something a little bit risky. You see the "Molly" in her come out. You can do episodes where they're not always the same. Sometimes you see sitcoms where the characters are always like this, and you say, "But nobody is always like this."

TN: We knew someone on *The Drew Carey Show* who told us about her skydiving experience. She decided to do it, and her chute didn't open. And, you know, you're supposed to wait ten seconds and then pull another cord for the second chute. So during that ten seconds, of course, your whole life apparently really does flash before you. She was positive she was going to die, but she said to herself, "I'm going to do exactly what I was taught to do, but I'm sure I'm dying."

I was talking to her about it, and she said, "That has totally changed my life." Her whole direction changed. She left the show shortly after that. She ended up getting married to an artist. She has a lot of kids. She has pets. Her life just drastically changed from that one incident. That's an interesting thing to have happen to somebody, and especially in the case of this Premise of Molly and Sarah. Somebody goes through that, Sarah maybe, and she thinks her life is going to change. But that's an interesting episode for Sarah. Because skydiving is just something she'd never have thought of doing on her own.

JS: What about Sarah's work?

TN: Are you thinking of a bank job? Or do you want her to be potentially creative, like a painter? Somebody who actually has the ability and is afraid to go for it.

JS: It could be anything. It could be a bank, an ad agency. The point is that she wants to move ahead. She'll do anything to move ahead. She's the one who does all the work at the agency.

TN: Well, she's a caretaker. So maybe whatever she does, she is so overworked because everyone knows she is the go-to girl.

JS: Right. So in the first episodes she's like, "I take care of everybody at work, how can I do this with you, Mom? I will not do it!" "Can you get me a soda?" "Sure." But the idea is that her whole life is taking care of people. That even makes it stronger.

TN: Oh, my God. What if Sarah became the director of a nursery school? She's been teaching at this nursery school and she's in line to become the director.

JS: And she's like, "If they find out about you, that you go out with all these guys." Her mother is screwing all these guys, and she's not going to get the job. There's that thing hanging over her. "The lid has to be kept on this."

TN: Molly comes to the school and says, "And you think I'm going to ruin your chances of running this? You actually *want* to run this? What a horrible job."

JS: "And Mom, next time, don't wear hot pants."

TN: We've got a lot of rules for this fifty-year-old woman. She's got to have great legs.

JS: Oh yeah, I think she's got to look great. She's got to look really good. I'd even make her fifty-five. I'd go just a hair older.

TN: The mom could be forty. We could even do that, if we wanted. Forty-five and twenty-five. That could be interesting. Because as a forty-five-year-old woman, having been there myself, you think your life's over in a way, and then you realize it isn't. You just want to dress up, and look great, and go out.

JS: I just thought of a funny episode. The one we always wanted to write. Molly uses hormone cream.

TN: Oh, my God! You know that testosterone cream for women? I'm not going to go into detail about what you do with the cream, but you become like The Terminator. You start scanning the horizon, and you realize, "I'm actually looking for a man for sex." I just think it's funny that . . .

JS: . . . Sarah literally has to lock Molly in a room until the stuff wears off. "I'm taking it away from you. That's it."

TN: Physically, it's like the woman's opportunity to see what it's like, a little tiny bit, to be a man.

JS: Sarah can't go to work. She's babysitting.

TN: They're in line at the bank and the mother is perking up her chest.

"Tracy's room was on one side, my room was on the other side, and the assistant's room was in the middle. And we'd have these screaming fights and she'd just sit there quietly. One time, I went out to her and said, 'Just because Mommy and Daddy fight doesn't mean we don't love you.'"

JS: The thing that's so great about working with Tracy is that we just laugh all the time. We certainly had our fights. We had an assistant. Tracy's room was on one side, my room was on the other side, and the assistant's room was in the middle. And we'd have these screaming fights and she'd just sit there quietly. One time, I went out to her and said, "Just because Mommy and Daddy fight doesn't mean we don't love you."

TN: People always asked, "Well, how do you and Jon work?" When we were in development, we would meet at 8 o'clock in the morning at Disney. Nobody was there, and we would work until 12. We would work four straight hours because we had nothing else to talk about. We didn't like each other very much as people. That's exaggerating. But really, I had no interest in what he was doing with his life, and he had no interest in mine. So it was really laughter for four hours. But then we would go to lunch, and then we'd see other guys in development out there on Mickey or Goofy Avenue. They were sitting on the benches smoking cigars. They'd get there when we were leaving, and I don't know what they did. But we wrote a lot of pilots.

JS: At Disney, they'd always try and screw us with money. We were eating quite well, and all of a sudden one day we got the menus and all this stuff was blacked out. You couldn't have this, and you couldn't have this, and you couldn't have that. I went nuts. I threw a hissy fit and I said, "You get them on the phone and you tell them I'm not even doing a show until they stop this petty, ridiculous nickel-and-diming."

TN: And they did. They stopped.

JS: So, let's continue with this. I would just like to figure out who the other characters are. We certainly want to write something for Tim Bagley. [Noted character actor, *Monk* and *Will & Grace*.]

TN: Yes, Tim could be officious, but I'm thinking back to the caretaker and the person who gets taken care of. If Sarah's boss is someone who needs to be taken care of, then that's sort of funny, too.

JS: I think you want to keep that separate. These are the satellites that go around Sarah and Molly. So I wouldn't put as much into them at this point. But how does a supporting character affect Sarah's life? That's what you want to know. Other than having to take care of him, how does he make her life more complicated? He could be the mail boy who has a crush on her.

TN: He could also be her assistant who she has to give orders to. And she has trouble giving orders.

JS: But how do you get into the place where that character is in the show? How is he there every week? Because of work? Or do you go back and forth from work to the house?

TN: Maybe he's her assistant and he lives next door.

JS: Or he's Sarah's brother who lives with her, who is just so messed up that maybe he lives across the hall and he's over all the time. Is he the brother that is not a care-taker and isn't particularly taken care of? He's just kind of floating out there. He never really had all that stuff, but he's now trying to bond with the family that he got left out of.

TN: Or maybe he's just someone who sees exactly what's going on between the mother and daughter.

JS: Maybe he's the moral compass. Maybe he's the voice of the audience.

TN: Maybe he just turns to the audience and says, "What would you do?"

JS: That old fourth-wall break. It always works, doesn't it? That's an interesting idea to have somebody like that, because neither Molly nor Sarah are the eyes of the audience. At the end of an episode, he makes his long speech to Molly: "And you, you never took care of either of us." Then he turns to Sarah: "And look at you, you're taking care of everyone." They both look at him and say, "Shut up!"

TN: He's the one that keeps saying the truth, and then they go right back to their lies.

JS: And he's the one that always gets sucked into the mother's schemes.

TN: He's got to do something for each of them all the time.

JS: Well, maybe the daughter has a suspicion that the guy she is going out with might be gay. So they ask Tim to try and seduce him first, and that doesn't work.

TN: Or it does!

JS: Or maybe the mother tries to seduce the boyfriend and he doesn't go for it. And the mom's like, "Wow, he really is a good man. He didn't even go for me, and there's no man that doesn't go for me."

TN: And then Tim says, "Let me try something."

JS: You talk about the main characters for a day or two and then something always pops up, and you go, "That's what we can do with an older man, or a younger man."

Four characters is plenty. Because I remember on [*According to*] *Jim*, we had trouble finding stuff for four characters. I don't know how people can do six characters.

"Aren't you guys going to ask us any standard-type interview questions?"

TN: Aren't you guys going to ask us any standard-type interview questions?

JD: Here's one. Who mentored you?

JS: Bill and Cheri Steinkellner.

TN: The Steinkellners gave us our first job. They did mentor us.

JS: I was in an improv class and Bill came in to substitute teach it. They didn't end up using him at that place, but I followed him out and said, "If you ever end up teaching an improv class of your own, here's my number." He called me six months later, and I've been working with him pretty much ever since. And he is totally my mentor.

PD: Did you two meet in The Groundlings? [An L.A.-based sketch comedy group]

TN: Yes, in The Groundlings.

PD: And were each of you actors first?

TN: Jon was definitely an actor. He's a really funny performer. Really, he still performs. He still does shows every Saturday night. I was always singing and playing guitar. I was in The Groundlings for fifteen years, but before that, I was singing and playing guitar and writing songs. I'm just back to that now.

JS: When I really got to know Tracy in The Groundlings, I did this show called *Casual Sex*. It was before the movie came out. I did a part in it, and I had to sing and dance. I was like, "Oh, my God, I can't do this." So Tracy, thank God, helped me through a lot of that. But in the show, I played this Armenian—or French Algerian or something—guy, and I was always in my big wig and swimsuit.

PD: Do you come from show business families?

TN: In a sense. My real father—my mom divorced when I was five—was an actor. My mother was a singing, dancing kind of person in her late teens in New York. But when they moved out here to L.A., whatever year that was, it was hard times and he started drinking. So I never really saw show business back then.

JS: So you were more from a drinking family, then?

TN: That's the part that I remember.

JS: I knew her whole family. I liked your stepdad. One time, her stepdad said, "Hey, we're going to get barbecue. Bring Jon."

TN: Remember, it's a Jewish family and he couldn't be more Gentile. I don't know why, but that somehow says volumes about this story.

JS: So we go to this place downtown, and I get the barbecued turkey sandwich.

TN: He gets a barbecued turkey sandwich on white bread. And there's ribs and these other things, and not only did he get one of them, he got two of them. And my stepdad couldn't get over it. He kept saying, "You're ordering a turkey sandwich here?" He thought it was so funny.

JD: What about your family, Jon?

JS: I'm from Erie, Pennsylvania. My parents were in local theatre. They used to do shows and sometimes I'd go, too. They did *The Rose Tattoo*. There was a scene on stage where the little kids have to start the show off, where they're running off stage. I did little things, you know.

TN: He's really very funny on stage. He's one of those people who are not afraid.

PD: When you were in high school, were you already singing and writing music?

TN: I actually was. I started when I was about fourteen.

PD: You were both pretty early starters? You knew you had the calling?

TN: Yeah, I was doing comedy, but I really was more of a folk singer. When I say I was doing comedy, I mean patter and stuff like that, between songs. It got funnier and funnier, just because it just does.

JS: I told her I wanted her to write a folk song for me about how she's made millions of dollars. But apparently, with folk songs, they don't like that kind of stuff. She has an excellent sense of story, and sometimes I don't quite have that sense, so it's always good to have that.

TN: But you developed it, made it better and better. It's amazing. I think improv training, that thing of not denying, is probably the main thing in television right now.

JS: Keeping the story going.

TN: Just saying, "Okay, well, if we do that, then what about if we do this, too?" Rather than saying, "No, I don't want to do that."

JS: We would also write twenty-page outlines when we did a script because we didn't want anything to be left to chance. Because when you're writing a fifty-page script, you don't want to have to throw it away. We were very specific.

TN: Sometimes our biggest fights were over the fact that I can't even move forward if I don't know how it begins. If they walk in the room, what are they doing? And sometimes he would say, "Let's get past that and go to the second scene." Each scene, really, I need to know where it starts, but especially the whole thing, because things fall into place. It's really true with a song. If you understand what you want to say, how you begin it is a major thing. We spent a lot of time on that.

JS: We spent a lot of time on the "coming out" episode of *Ellen* because we wrote the first half of it. So we had to come up with the characters and what they did.

TN: It was a one-hour special event. The first half-hour ends with her saying she's gay. So we had the responsibility of doing that part.

JS: So we had to set up everything. And we were lucky because we were only working two days a week on the show, so we didn't have to be there all the time. But you have to really figure out, how are these characters going to be honest and real to ground this huge thing Ellen is going to do? And so we had to come up with pretty much what they did. That took us a long time to do, to get it right.

TN: We had the whole season, practically. I mean, we worked on every show that season, but I remember you were reluctant because you thought that it would be under a microscope.

JS: I thought they'd kill us. Everyone talked about what a great show *Ellen* was, but when it was on, people just nailed it all the time.

TN: But I said to him, "Jon, we have the whole season to write the first half-hour. You think we can't get it so that *we* think it's great? Yeah, it will probably be smashed by some critics and they'll think it's terrible, but there will be people who will feel like we do." We had the whole season to do it.

JS: And that goes back again to rewriting. Rewriting is really the most important part of the writing process.

TN: And the thing is, you really don't want to turn anything in that you don't think is the way to go. And so the only way to know that is to keep rehashing and keep really, really, really getting the details right. That's why our outlines made it pretty easy to go to script.

PD: Having been grounded in improv, you get feedback all the time. Your instincts must be incredibly honed.

TN: Well, you know, he's very funny, so I figure that if I'm laughing at him, maybe at least 50 percent of the people are going to be laughing at him. And every time he would do something, if he read it or said it, it would make me laugh. This is standing the test of time, really. And if I said something funny and he laughed, we *knew* that was funny, because that was really rare.

". . . if you don't trust your gut, you're going to be all over the place."

JS: I think you have to develop this attitude. It's a survival attitude, where you go, "This is what I find funny and interesting." And if somebody says, "Well, I didn't," then you go, "Well, then you're wrong!" You have to, because if you don't trust your gut, you're going to be all over the place. And these people behind the desks, they don't know. They don't know what's funny.

TN: I don't think it's that they don't know what's funny. I think they laugh when things are funny like anybody else does, but their job, in their mind, really is something else.

JS: Their job is analyzing. Our job is just putting it out there. You have to ask, "Is this funny for me?" Because as soon as you start trying to please everyone, you're just going to be rewriting all the time, and then it just isn't going to be funny anymore. It's especially easy to write just what you like after you've had a successful series on TV for eight years. It's a little easier to say, "Well, I don't want to write that. I want to write this." The characters and a story are always what are going to sell a show, and are going to keep it working.

PD: Were you funny kids?

JS: No. I don't think so. I was pretty quiet.

TN: I don't think I was. I'm older than Lorraine, my sister, and she's a twin. So it's

Lorraine and Paul. They were so funny and I appreciated that. I was a bit older, but I was always in the house laughing at Lorraine and Paul and the things they were doing. So I think more than being funny, I've been an appreciator of what's funny. I think I know what's funny, let's put it that way.

JS: It's kind of the same with me. In junior high school I had a red book bag, so I was like, "Loser!" But my brother and sister, who are much older than me, would get together and they would just start riffing and making me laugh. I was the guy saying, "Yeah, yeah, and what if the guy does this?" And they'd look at me funny. So I knew if I wanted to survive, and be part of that group, I really had to hone my skills. Also, you realize at some point in your life, "So, this is how I can get chicks. If I'm funny."

TN: It doesn't work with women, though. Although, if you appreciate humor, you'll go out with funny guys, which is what I did.

An Interview with
Dan O'Shannon

A partial list of Dan O'Shannon's credits as a creator, show runner, and writer includes: *Modern Family, Back to You, Frasier, Cheers, Suddenly Susan, Newhart,* and *The Odd Couple* (2015 revival).

We met **Dan O'Shannon** at an International Humor Conference. For those of you who've never attended one, they're events where academics from all over the world come to study humor. In other words, they try to make sense out of why something is funny—until it *isn't.* What's a nice, professional comedy writer doing in a place like this, especially one with Dan's credits?

After spending the afternoon with him, we discovered that he straddles the fence between both worlds. He was writing a book about humor.* It is based on a mixture of many years of experience in situation comedy coupled with many hours of deep thought, some insights that came from therapy, and thinking about how he does what he does for a living. This combination of strengths forms the basis of the way he tackles the mother/daughter Premise. It's heartening to learn that you can be analytic, neurotic, and funny all at the same time—and get paid for it.

PD (Peter Desberg): As we've explained in our Premise [see page 9], how would you go about developing the show's plot lines?

DO (Dan O'Shannon): My first question is, "Who came up with this and what were they looking for?" I want to get as close to the original idea from the person who presented this to me as I can.

I'm happy to lead with women. I tend to enjoy writing women just a little more than men. I think you can get away with more with women, emotionally. I did a show once where a woman was married and considered having an affair with a guy. She is very sympathetic and very sweet. She is falling in love with her boss, even though her marriage isn't particularly bad. If this would've happened with a man,

---

*O'Shannon, D. (2012) *What Are You Laughing At?: A Comprehensive Guide to the Comedic Event.* Bloomsbury: London.

Many of the writers in this book have pointed out that if they cast their work with an eye toward the marketplace by making choices studios or networks will favor, it maximizes their chances of getting paid. Getting paid, after all, is the goal of all professionals. Dan goes a step further. He believes that if he understands the intentions of the people who came up with the idea he's assigned to, it's easier to give them what they want. But Dan often likes to go deeper into character and story than many executives are comfortable with. Later in this interview, he tells a story about a *Frasier* episode he pitched in which we see alternate realities of Frasier's life—two ways it might go. Some people were worried that the audience would become confused. In the end, it worked, and it is a story Dan is rightfully proud of. Give network executives what they want, and they give you a bit more latitude.

everyone would've just called him a hound and nobody would watch the show. As it happened, a hundred people watched the show.

I think that parents are getting younger and younger all the time. People used to get old faster, and now they're getting old slower. When a new crop of adults comes up, their parents aren't that much older than they are. It's easier to reverse roles and have parents almost as peers. But you still have the dynamic of being embarrassed by your parents or wanting to assert individuality.

I'd start thinking about casting now. But I wouldn't go too far. I'd want to know what's underneath. I'd start thinking, if this woman is stuck with her mother in her life, what is it that she wants and needs out of this relationship? She cannot like it, but there must be something underneath it that she needs. Maybe there's something she's trying to get that she never got out of her relationship. I think about Molly's relationship with her husband. Did she feel betrayed about the way things ended up? Or did she feel like, "Oh, well, it was good while it lasted, and now I've got this whole new chapter of my life?" Or is she just putting a good face on despair? That is something I would find out in the pilot episode.

I'm going to start her like Auntie Mame. This is the beginning of a new life now. "I'm gonna do this now . . . I feel young." Underneath, there's a little bit of desperation. You can't just let go of who you've been and grab on to this new kind of vision of yourself without mourning the loss of who you were. And then you've got Sarah mourning the loss of who her mother was, and who she thought her mother was and who she thought her father was. I don't know about the grandparents yet.

PD: Are you seeing this as a sitcom or a movie?

DO: It's a situation . . . a long, ongoing situation. It could be either. A movie is closed and I think in terms of a sitcom first, because that's what I've been presented with for twenty-five years. So I start with, what's the arc of this thing? What can we come to so that the hundredth episode isn't exactly like the first episode? Where do they grow, where do you go from here?

If I started thinking in terms of a pilot, I would look for a scene that made me feel something. I don't mean made me feel something like, "Oh, isn't that nice." I'm not looking for the "big hug" scene. I'm looking for a scene that makes me understand something differently. From the big scene, you can always get to comedy. I just want that comedy to fill in something for me. Also, the big challenge is to say something that I haven't heard before. I'm groping for something that's universal and unique at the same time. I don't like to go into big hugs directly unless the scene calls for it.

"You can't actually complete the arc in a series without destroying the thing that made it funny."

I'm beginning to think it might be more appealing to me as a movie than a series. A series has to promise further high jinks. You can't complete the arc in a series without destroying the thing that made it funny. The resolve in a comedy generally ends up destroying all the funny circumstances that made you laugh. You can't really resolve a pilot that way.

In a movie, I can tell a whole journey. In a TV show, my problem is laying out the kinks in this woman's life when the mother comes back. Now they have to forge a new version of their old relationship. But it isn't entirely new, because there're always pieces of the baggage that they both carry with them. When you're setting up a series, you have to stop there and spend a hundred episodes on that. You have a little bit of growth, a little bit of growth, but you've got to keep stepping back so you don't evolve away from the stuff that made it funny.

With a movie, you can take it to whatever extreme you want. Then, you can come back and get to someplace where there's a new reality you've created based on everything that's happened so far. You can resolve it and look back at the journey. You can say, "This is who I am now at the end of the movie, versus who I was at the beginning."

Now, I have a closed-end story about Sarah, whose mother comes back. I still want to know a lot about who Molly was in this girl's life. I would probably start designing flashbacks, not that I would necessarily see them in the movie, but in my head. What are key elements that happened in these two people's lives?

You may have some scene where Sarah's out having a cappuccino with her friends and they're complaining about the sex with their husbands. And she would probably tell stories about things that happened with her mother. "Oh, there was a time that I wanted to have a birthday party and she did X and then she brought somebody over and she was drunk, and then she did Y, and I never forgave her for that." Toward the end of the movie there would be a really sweet thing where it was Sarah's birthday and Molly gave her this thing that she wanted when she was a kid and you'd close the circle that way. And she does this in a very sweet, unexpected way.

"When a writer reintroduces a character back into someone's life, it helps creatively to go backwards in order to go forwards."

Another way to go is to have something that has been a black spot on Sarah's life that she always blamed her mother for. Or, she screwed things up in a different way, but it can still lead to this new understanding. Sarah could say, "She's always been a screw-up. It wasn't me. It was her. And the fact is, in some crazy way, this particular screw-up is a part of who I am and I do screw up at work sometimes. I come by it honestly and, God bless her, at least I have a story to tell that nobody else has. I know who this person is in my life. She's not particularly a nurturer, but she's somebody who provides me with a lot of insane stories and probably makes me insane in a way that one day my daughter will want to kill me."

When a writer reintroduces a character back into someone's life, it helps creatively to go backwards in order to go forwards. What were they? What are they? How can who they are now make you look differently at what was in the past? And I tend to look at the whole timeline. The grandparents, right now, are still a blank.

The grandparents are more in line with Sarah's sensibilities. Maybe they all see Molly as this crazy black sheep. Maybe the grandparents are in a facility and Molly actually visits them and takes care of them in a way that we would not expect. Maybe she's more affected by the frailty of her parents than she ever lets on. So her desperation to embrace this new life, this new lifestyle of being pals with her kid, is a desire to regress. It stops the clock from moving forward. In some crazy, psychological way, it stops her parents from becoming more and more feeble and dying. Because she has to deal with the reality of her parents' aging, it sends her into her desperate need to stay young.

"I'm kind of a fan of the audience knowing more than the characters."

PD: It seems like you're making Molly the focus of the movie.

DO: I think that Sarah would actually be the focus of the movie, but Molly's influence is crucial. She's trying to take charge of her own life. Her mother is an asteroid knocking her out of orbit. Sarah's wobbling and I want to see the effect on her.

I'm kind of a fan of the audience knowing more than the characters. I like writing shows that flash fifty years into the future, showing us things that the characters will never ever know. I like the idea of Molly visiting her parents in the facility and taking care of them, and being a different person with them and seeing how their life affects her. I wouldn't mind if that was something the audience saw that Sarah never saw. And we have this extra understanding. So now we're watching this film on two levels. Whenever we see Sarah bristle at Molly, the audience now has sympathy for Molly. "If you knew this, you would act differently." We're always acting towards people based on what they present us and not based on a fuller picture of who they are. This mother and daughter never really get the full picture of each other that the audience gets.

First impressions are hard to break. Your first impression of your kid is this little needy being who is very malleable. And maybe Molly never really got past that. I do this with my daughter. My daughter is fourteen and sometimes I resent her for swallowing up my seven-year-old daughter, who used to follow me around and be my best friend. Of course I still love her, but why can't she be seven for a day? We'll just go off and do fun things that I like to do. She'll think they're fun because I think they're fun, instead of having her own ideas of what's fun, which don't include me at all.

Although I'm fascinated by Molly, I want Sarah to be the main character. And I want to find those things that are interesting in her. I want to find the arc through the movie. What is it that she wants? What is she trying to get that Molly is getting in the way of? Who are her friends? What is her life? I want the audience to feel as she does. Molly's an imposition. She is a crazy person. And then they get a deeper understanding of her. But I think the understanding that Sarah comes to about Molly is good and serviceable for Sarah and for their relationship and, hopefully, satisfying.

I want a fuller, more empathic picture of Molly, but start in a place where she's annoying. If she comes from this place of sympathy right off the bat, then you're not

A "saver" is a joke or a bit stand-ups use to distract an audience when a joke bombs. Their biggest fear is that the audience will say to themselves, "Oh, that poor guy, he must feel so awful. Nobody is laughing at his joke." Once an audience feels sorry for them, nothing they come up with will get a laugh. The two emotions are incompatible. Dan makes use of this idea of incompatible emotions, constructing his story in a way that ensures that the viewer doesn't sympathize with Molly too early. She has to be able to evoke laughter—and annoy Sarah and the audience—long enough to distract them before she can become likable.

laughing at her or feeling the annoyance you need to feel while you're identifying with Sarah. So I would have the husband leaving, maybe she drove him away, like she drives a lot of people away, but that's okay, because she's going to re-bond with her daughter.

> ## "I haven't pitched one joke, I haven't found one funny situation at all. But I'm supremely confident that a couple of other writers and I would come up with things that are absolutely funny."

Now that the audience knows that Molly is taking care of her parents, I would have to figure out Sarah's relationship with her grandparents. I haven't pitched one joke, I haven't found one funny situation at all. But I'm supremely confident that a couple of other writers and I would come up with things that are absolutely funny.

PD: How much of Sarah will Molly see?

DS: It's the theme of the movie. First impressions. The first impression that Sarah had of her mother is, "This is my mother, and she's crazy." Molly's first impression is "This is my child, so I know best." Even as you grow up, it's about trying to break free of first impressions. It may be Molly's inability to see more of Sarah. My parents visited me when I was on *Cheers*. I'd been there for a few years. My parents came to a show. I think their whole attitude toward my being able to exist in this industry is that they think, "For some reason, people in Hollywood are being nice to Dan and we don't know why, but we appreciate it."

My parents also came to a filming of *Frasier*, a pretty good episode. It was one I'd written with another guy, and it did really well. We got big applause. The audience loved it. On our way to our cars one of the writers said to my mom, "You must be very proud of Dan." Without missing a beat, my mother said, "My other son's a lawyer." And then when I started doing stand-up, I said to my father, "I want to do stand-up. I want to do jokes." And he said, "You're not funny!" My dad had known me since I was a little kid, and kids are not particularly funny when they're trying to be funny. To this day, my parents are a little flummoxed by the fact that people pay me money to be funny. In their memory of me is me as a teenager, trying to be funny. I was not at all funny.

"Without missing a beat, my mother said, 'My other son's a lawyer.'"

So I've got parents who can't really see past their early impressions of me, and maybe in some ways, that's something that both of these characters deal with. In order for them to function in a new relationship, they must break the molds they each have. And it's something that one, or both, of them can't ever get past. Or, maybe they do, and what they realize in the end is they need people playing those roles. Maybe they do break through and it turns out to be a disaster in an entirely different way. Maybe there's something to be said for having that person out there you can blame for all your problems. Maybe one side is to impress them, and the other side is to say, "Ha, ha, look what I did without you."

My biological father left when I was three and I didn't see him again until I was thirty-nine. I met him—or first, I talked to him on the phone. I was filling him in on my life, and I was saying, "Well, I did this and I did that and I did that . . ." and I realized as I was saying it that I had two feelings about this. The first one was, "Hey, look what I did, be proud of me," and the other one was, "Hey, look what I did without you, you bastard." So I wanted him both to be proud and suffer for it. And these two feelings did not negate each other. They did not contradict each other in any way. They both basically fed to the same action, and so . . . I keep talking about me when I'm talking about the writing, but I think that's where my head keeps going.

I think you guys want some comedy here, but I always assume the comedy will come. I would start breaking out the story. I'd start going into what is it that's funny here. What is it that Molly interrupts or shows up during? What's her attitude that starts to make things funny? Maybe Sarah is starting to crack up in other parts of her life. Maybe she's found someone else to start blaming. I don't know if I'm painting a picture of a particularly healthy person here.

Around this stage is where I would probably go online and play Scrabble for a while. And then, probably around dinnertime, I would start talking about it. I'd be ready to jump in when I felt I had enough psychological underpinnings or I had a place to go to that I felt was interesting and would fool the audience.

I was going to settle on the idea that we need this dysfunctional relationship in our life on some level, and without it, we're actually less healthy. Now I have a place to go to and I've got a way to fool the audience into thinking that I'm aiming these people toward a healthier understanding, only to find that the healthy understanding isn't healthy at all and that we need the unhealthy thing.

I would spend the next couple days going, "Okay, what are the funny scenes?" I want to identify what's funny for these types of people—not just what's funny, period. How does someone react when their mother comes back into their life? Like mothers and daughters as adults falling into old patterns, old ways of arguing; do we see back-to-back scenes of these two bickering twenty years ago and juxtapose it with bickering now? Do we see that, psychologically, each is trapped there? Do you do a scene where the mother is arguing with the daughter and from the mother's point of view, her grown daughter is actually still fourteen? So, in her mind, that's the argument, and then we cut to the other point of view and it's the daughter, grown up, talking to her mother as though her mother is who she was back then.

You could borrow a device from theatre. You could have all the different versions of these two people on stage at all their different ages. You would have today's Sarah, Sarah as a teen, Sarah as a little kid, Sarah as a toddler. And then you'd have Molly, who seems unchanging. And Molly is trying to be a mother. And she only talks to the child, but won't recognize the adult. I think I would end up turning this piece into a ninety-minute therapy session. A meditation on relationships.

JD (Jeffrey Davis): That's a very fresh approach.

DO: I heard a story from my therapist, who called it "the red dress example." It was about a patient whose father wouldn't allow her to wear anything red in the house. When she became an adult, she only wore red because she could. She didn't realize that her father was still controlling her. Sarah has grown up and is now forced into this informal reexamination of herself. She looks at how she was with her mother and who she is with her mother now, overlapping past and present.

I know I'm not talking about comedy really, but let's take a look at this scene. You've got the mother and you've got the multiple Sarahs from different points in her life trying to have a discussion with Molly. If Molly's always talking to the teenager, then you've got cross-talk between them. This is going to get very funny. I don't have to write jokes for it, it's going to be funny, especially the frustration of the adult Sarah. She not only can't get this person to see her, but can't stop herself, in the form of these younger selves. She keeps engaging like a child. This pisses Sarah off, because she's telling her younger self, "Don't do this! Don't do this!"

This becomes funny and has nothing to do with jokes. The joke itself is small, but all the thoughts and feelings it brings up in the audience are so familiar that they'll laugh. It's enhanced by their identification. It's giving voice to what happens to Sarah when she tries to talk to her mother. She'll have a discussion about something now and realize that in some way, she's having a discussion about something that she was trying to do when she was eleven when she wanted to go to the circus instead of school. She never let go.

PD: How often does Sarah "wear red"?

DO: I think she has to find that she's been wearing red without realizing it. I would have people point that out to her. She would think, "All those people are crazy." Maybe you can do a scene later in the movie, when she's at home and she realizes that there's some red running through every piece of clothing she has in her closet.

PD: Would you have the audience discover it before Sarah?

DO: I don't know on that one. As I said, there are some things I want the audience to be ahead of the characters on, or know things the characters never figure out, but in this case, I would let them find out with her. Then the audience says, "I've been watching this person wearing a little bit of red and a little bit of red and a little bit of red throughout the whole movie, and I didn't see it, just like she didn't." To me, that would be a satisfying way to do that part of it. This is why no one asks me to write a movie.

PD: Are you still trying to prove to your parents that you're funny?

DO: I don't try to prove to them that I'm funny by being funny around them. Sometimes, I'll crack a joke if it's too good to pass up. But I'm not as needy as I was because I'm getting approval from strangers. There's a part of me, especially with my stepfather, the one who said, "You'll never be funny," that is an unattractive part of me. But, there's a part of me that feels a little vindication. I think there's a little animosity there. My father was someone who constantly told me I'd never make it because I spent too much time daydreaming and trying to be funny.

My stepfather, the one who raised me from the age of nine to twenty-two, thought that I was going to come to naught by trying to be funny. He really tried to discourage me from pursuing anything in the realm of being funny. "What do you think, you're Woody Allen?" I'll tell you one quick story. He and I were walking in downtown Cleveland. I thought he was in a better mood than he was. A nice car drove by and my father said, "Boy, that's a really nice car, but those are really expensive." Without thinking, I was probably seventeen or so, I said, "Well, when I'm rich I'll buy you one." He got angry. He whirled around and pointed at me, screaming, "You're never going to be rich because you're never going to make anything of yourself, because all you do is daydream and goof off, and you'll never be anything." Then he just snapped back into the walk, and I had to follow with tears in my eyes. But I remember thinking, "You just f–cked yourself out of a car!"

PD: To what extent is this in Sarah's character? Is she learning that she *does* want her mom to say, "Okay, you are an adult now, you are functional," which Sarah doesn't get?

DO: Well, maybe she never gets it. And her journey is to be okay never getting that. In fact, to realize that if she got it, then she'd have to lose some other things.

I tend to want to find all the underneath first. In my twenties, I started going to therapy, and I was actually very nervous about doing it. I was funny, and I could write jokes. I was just starting *Cheers.* I was afraid that through therapy, I might get rid of the quirks that made me funny. What I didn't realize was that the more I understood myself, the more I understood my characters, and then I could find these richer veins of humor. I could find ways for Cliff or Norm to tell jokes that were not just funny, but gave us little insights into who they were. And I understood why they were moving around the way they did. Even if it's a stupid reason, just give me a reason that the character moved from here to here.

I think conflicts themselves are rich and funny and unmined. So much writing is surface, unless we're aiming to tell that underneath story. I did a few episodes of *Frasier* that were really psychology-heavy. I had Frasier locked in a cabin, and the actions we saw were his mental images. We had his very first wife from when he was nineteen, a flower child. Then Lilith, and then Diane from *Cheers,* and his mother. All the main women in his life were in this cabin with him. They were all parts of his mind, but we had the actresses come in and play the parts. And as he dealt with these people, asked questions and was trying to figure out why he couldn't succeed with women, what he came to was the realization that all women were competing with these four women. He could not move on because he could not get rid of them.

The character for years and years was a failure with women. He managed to get married to Lilith, but then he's on date after date, all going badly. At some point in the series, you've got to say, "Why can't this guy get a woman?" I provided a psychological answer in a way that was dramatically interesting. You're seeing Diane and Lilith and Frasier's mother. It's them, but not them. It's Frasier's version, and it becomes a very engaging couple of scenes. And I did one where there was a therapy session, which I did with another writer, John Sherman. It was a therapy session between Frasier and his mentor. Frasier was feeling unsatisfied as a psychiatrist. And again, the questions I wanted to ask were, "What drove Frasier to become a psychiatrist? What is it that's lacking in him?" It came down to the fact that his mother was in the field and he was trying to emulate her, but he also wanted to understand other kids. He was eight years old, trying to understand, and his mentor is yelling, "There's no such thing as an eight-year-old psychiatrist!"

> **"If something changes, you need to explain the change, but if something stays the same long enough, you have to explain why something stays the same."**

Those episodes don't sound particularly funny, but I find them fascinating, and the funny comes along as these characters unfold. I like to answer these questions in a series. Series need to have repeating patterns to keep them long-running. Frasier always has to keep striking out with women because you don't want him to get married and add a new character to the cast. That would change the tenor of the show. If something changes, you need to explain the change, but if something stays the same long enough, you have to explain why something stays the same. That's when you start going inside the character, and that's fascinating to me. There are a few episodes of *Frasier* that got psychological, and we did our special effects and digitally put in this person, and that place, to explain what I was saying. I like writing symbolic scenes as though they're physical.

JD: Would you have Molly see Sarah at different ages? Or would it just be Sarah seeing the different parts?

DO: The more I talk about this, the more it does feel like Sarah's journey. When I started talking about the scene with the different versions of Sarah and the one version of Molly, what I realized is that all the different versions of Sarah always see Molly as "the mother . . . the mother who gets in the way . . . the mother who's overbearing." The definition of "mother" has never changed for Sarah.

Sarah's definition of herself is always very different. "I was this. I was that. I was this. I was that." She never really sees how her mother has changed, how she's been different from the age of twenty-five to fifty. She is always just the force that controls things. Sarah's journey is to redefine her mother, and to understand what their relationship is now. I would try to approach it as Sarah's journey and have the mother not work so hard at it. If Sarah's working to figure out, "Why is this always happening? Why can't I be more like . . . ?" then I don't need two characters really trying to do that with each other, unless it comes to a scene where they have a summit. They say, "We've got to change this." Maybe the two of them go on a retreat together and decide to let go and they are going to start anew. That's the grand experiment of this movie. Maybe they do and they realize they miss the old roles, or they keep falling back.

PD: Will a lot of the comedy come out of Sarah's frustration to change the perception?

DO: I think so. People trying to change can be funny, because you're uncomfortable with the new version of this relationship. "We're now just two grown women who know each other, and I never knew this about you." It's a surface-y change that you think is going to be a universal change. But, there's a lot of stress in that because you're trying not to access all these feelings that have been overpowering you for years and years. But, they manifest themselves elsewhere: "Now I'm snapping at my boss at work all the time. I've turned my boss into my mother. The fact is that when I turned my mother into my friend, I always turn somebody else into my mother. Oh, my God, I've just turned my sister into my mother. I've turned the milkman into my mother."

I'd probably start putting the whole thing together piecemeal. I've got this little section here and I know I'd want a sequence where the two of them make the conscious decision to let go of who they've been. Maybe there's a guru that they talk to, or there's some TV psychiatrist. They could go on a show and talk about it. Well, that might be a bit big, but maybe they go on a retreat. It's this mother's wish: "Can we go on this retreat? Please, please!" "Whatever. Yes. Fine."

Or maybe it's because Sarah realizes that she's so controlled by this image that they get to a scene where the two of them are literally rolling on the floor, trying to choke each other, before someone pulls them apart and says, "All right. You two have to do something! Either you never see each other again, or you work it out!" Or maybe they realize, "Oh, my God . . ." and maybe even as they're rolling around, choking each other on the floor, you do these quick cuts as it's happening, where sometimes it's a little girl choking her mother, and sometimes it's Sarah as an adult. The psychology of that would be a fascinating scene visually, where all these versions of this person are choking the one that's getting in the way.

Maybe later in the movie, there's something Sarah needs and she ends up running to her mom. It might be a little too corny, but I'd find a way to make it less so. She runs and throws her arms around her mom, and you do the same thing with the cuts. You see the little girl doing it. You see the different parts. They all need their mom at this point. So now you've got something emotional that's been built on this very funny thing. Without this person, you turn to other people . . . you need her . . . and that's the first nice time that you've intercut. I also like what these images say. They will stick out more than the jokes. I mean, the jokes I'll find. Okay, now I've got something to play with. I can start to build a story that goes to that. That's how I do it.

PD: Would you be willing to take one of these areas and go for some comedy to show us how you do it?

DO: I can describe it more than I can actually do it.

PD: Whether it's something extreme like the guru experience, or going off to the retreat, or something as simple as Sarah needing something immediate from her mom, goes to get it, and doesn't. It would just be interesting to see how you set it up. I know it's putting you on the spot.

DO: It's funny, I don't actually think of those as jokes until I'm writing, and then I find the funny in the dialogue. I think so much of this would come out of the behavior and the psychology. If I were writing a scene that got into a choking match between the two of them, I'd have to figure out what was that last straw that led to this. Are they both pissed at each other, and why? I'm starting to describe the scenes rather than write the comedy of them. I would save the comedy for the dialogue.

Let's say that I was doing a scene where all the different versions of Sarah at different ages, like a high school student, maybe a preteen, a nine-year-old, and her now. You get to a point where they're arguing with their mother. Let's say that in this argument, the mother mentions sleeping with some guy that Sarah had a crush on when she was seventeen. Now we've got the preteen Sarah going, "Oh, my God, Mother, you slept with Billy?" And the nine-year-old saying, "What's so bad about sleeping with someone?" And then it becomes a thing between the two of them. So the younger versions are surprised to find out about it. So now you've got the woman who's trying to fight with her mother and you've got younger versions of her disappointed in who she became, and so she's trying to shut them up, but not say anything inappropriate. So then it's back and forth, back and forth.

Also, you might get comedy out of how these people argued then. I think there's something funny when you go back and meet yourself and see how you look and the ways you argued and the things that you believed passionately. You see all the things that made you want to kill yourself. Maybe the fourteen-year-old version of Sarah always went to, "Well, then I'll kill myself!" You cringe at the fact that that's what you used to be.

As they're rolling around on the floor and doing this, you have the camera following and just different cuts. Sometimes these little hands, the little girl just choking this woman who's trying to choke the little girl. If I've got a few things to go for like that, I could stretch a movie across and get to a realization, taking the viewers on a trip. Sometimes they're ahead of things, sometimes they're discovering with the characters, but they come out to a place they didn't expect to go when they were going in. Now I'm happy.

PD: When somebody flips out and gets incredibly angry, sometimes it's the immediate event that happens, but it's always more interesting when it's a series of little things that have built up and it's the last straw, and what you've done is shown a really interesting way to show the straw through the flashbacks.

DO: That's exactly right. You're not fighting over the thing you just said right now, "I'm fighting because when I was fifteen you wouldn't let me do this, and I'm fighting because when I was seven you showed up at my school and did this . . ."

I want to pull back the camera as far back as I can. I did a show, a series called *Maggie.* I used a device where at some point in the episode, a guy comes in and says one line and leaves. A day player. Then I'd ask, "What are the events that made that day player come in at *just* that moment and collide with this person?" In the second act, I'd have a process server come in and hand papers to some guy. I would set up the process server in the first act as a bad waiter, and one of our characters yelling at him. The guy says, "I don't care, tomorrow I start my new job as a process server. Who knows what kind of lives I'll step into and change." Way later in the second act, when things are going bad . . . *knock, knock, knock.* The process server comes in. There are all these marbles in the universe and we set them on the course to collide at exactly the right moment.

JD: You have a novelist's sensibility.

DO: What's frustrating is that you can have that sensibility in a form like a sitcom if people will have the kind of confidence to air those kinds of shows. We're so used to a sitcom being what we think of as a sitcom. This has to happen, and that and that, and the funny things, and then we've realized something in the end. Executives get a little skittish when they think, "People won't understand. It doesn't make any sense. How do the characters know?" The characters can know and not know at the same time. "How do you do an 'alternate reality' show?" I did a "sliding doors" episode of *Frasier* [referring to the Gwyneth Paltrow movie *Sliding Doors*], and some people thought it was great, and other people were nervous when I started pitching it, and then it turned out fine. But you can have that novelist sensibility; you can apply that to the form of a sitcom if you have confident people behind you who are willing to put that on the air. And we were really lucky on shows like *Frasier*, where we could.

"I learn in little flashes, and sometimes I unlearn and I have to learn again . . ."

PD: Did you do stand-up?

DO: I did it from late '82 until about mid-'84, then I eventually wanted to come out here.

PD: And did that experience have a big effect on your writing?

DO: Yeah. Actually, I'll tell you a quick story about that. I learn in little flashes, and sometimes I unlearn and I have to learn again, but I have these intuitive leaps that are few and far between. I had one when I first started doing stand-up. I would do jokes about pretty much anything. I did different kinds of jokes, I used props, and I would have everything grouped by topic. And that's the way I think everyone starts. I was very hit-and-miss. I would go up one week and I'd win the Amateur Night prize, fifty dollars, which was big to me. And then other times I would do the same material and I would die. And I couldn't figure it out.

Then one day, I'm in the backyard cutting grass thinking about it, and all of a sudden, like a lightning bolt, the answer hit me. I was standing there with the lawnmower vibrating in my hands and I realized what the problem was. I turned off the lawnmower, went into the house, and I looked in the mirror. I was nineteen at the time. I had a very young-looking face. I looked like I was fifteen. I looked like I was nine really, back then. And I remember thinking that *this* is who the audience is looking at. And from the moment they say my name, from the moment I walk out on stage and take the mic and start talking, they're already deciding who I am. So if this person, who they've decided is this clean-cut, fresh-faced nine-year-old kid, starts talking about sex, politics, and current events, I've got no credibility. It is actually going against what they've decided about me. I'm cutting across the grain.

I immediately cut out everything in my act that was worldly and the next time I went onstage, I wore a sweater that was two or three sizes too big, as if it was my dad's sweater. And I pitched my voice up a little higher and had frenetic energy. And it wasn't cute. I hate things that are cute. But I had more energy and enthusiasm and I told jokes about my girlfriends or school or different things I saw on TV. I talked about people I knew. And all the jokes I had worked out big. Jokes that were already big became huge. I suddenly realized, in that moment with the lawnmower, that I had thought of myself as merely the delivery system for jokes. It should've been, "Every joke is telling you more about me." You're not laughing at jokes. You're laughing at the guy.

PD: You found your voice.

DO: I found my voice, and I understood that that's the difference between comedy and character comedy. And literally, I killed for two nights doing that, and then I got an offer to do something in Pittsburgh, and then New York, and then I started working. So that was a huge learning experience for me. Also, I was pretty good at writing jokes; I would sell jokes to comics coming in and out of town. I sold a lot of jokes to people back then.

PD: Some of the writers we've interviewed have had stand-up backgrounds and feel that it gave them an edge in terms of deciding what's funny. It was a survival mechanism.

DO: I think that it did give me an edge in joke writing. I've always been analytic. I think I learned from the outside in. I decided to be funny when I was eight. I had another one of those big flash moments. I was sitting on the gymnasium floor with a bunch of other kids from my Catholic school and we were watching some sort of a presentation at an assembly. There was a guy on the stage who was very funny. I cannot, to this day, remember what he was doing, except that we were all out of breath, laughing at this guy. At one point while he was waiting for us to catch our breath, he leaned against the mic stand and said, "There's nothing like the feeling of making people laugh." And a lightning bolt hit me. I remember looking around to see if anyone else had heard that. The idea that you could make someone else laugh when you decided to was fantastic. I remember looking around, astonished that it seemed to gloss over everyone else. Nobody seemed to catch that like I did.

In a way, everyone else had changed because I suddenly saw them all as a potential audience. And so I decided to be funny and had no idea how to go about it because I was eight. I started the way any kid would. "So what makes me laugh? Well, I'll do that." Jerry Lewis makes me laugh, so I will be Jerry Lewis [*Dan says this imitating Jerry Lewis*]. That gets a laugh now, but when I was eight, it didn't. I was far too young to appreciate the difference between comedy that was enacted on a screen with a script and trying to put that out in real life. And so I went for years not being funny. At the time, there was no Internet. There was no way to study it formally, but I watched all the comedies I could and I really tried to figure out jokes.

Thank God for sitcoms being so prevalent. I started hearing joke patterns, and I could start to make jokes. Somebody might say, "Oh, someone's been in the fridge . . . he must have been very small." Or, "Oh, I hear there is a pie in the fridge. Do you know what kind it is?" "It's a Frigidaire." I could start to hear it in the way people talk. There were alternate ways to interpret the line so I could come up with something. But it was slow going. And so I feel like I was not innately funny, but I sort of figured it out along the way.

"I was somebody who figured it out more than having been born funny."

PD: By high-school age, were you funny?

DO: By the time I was in eleventh grade, I finally had a batting average that was high enough that people didn't want to slug me all the time. I went through different phases of what I thought was funny. I went through a teenage rebellious phase against the rules of comedy. I thought sheer incongruity would be funny in and of itself. It's not funny; it's just baffling. Or the kind of ironic phase, where I would tell jokes like "What time is it when an elephant sits on your fence? Time to get a new fence." I would tell them in an ironic way, and then really look down on the people who weren't hip enough to understand why that was so funny. I was just obnoxious. I thank God every day for the people who did not kill me back then.

I was just trying to understand what the rules were and how far you could go. I wanted to know what worked and what didn't. I was somebody who figured it out more than having been born funny. I know people who were funny as a defense mechanism, and they were just naturally funny. I was very jealous of those people as a kid. "How are you so funny all the time? I try that and I just . . . I don't . . ." Because I had to always think my way to it. But those people, I think, are the ones who might have more of the edge doing stand-up than I did.

PD: As a writer, were you mentored?

DO: No. There were people who impressed me and I would emulate them.

PD: But you weren't really taken under anybody's wing?

DO: Not particularly. I mean, for brief periods of time. On my first show, there was a team of writers who shepherded me through my first script and taught me a lot. And then people who looked at my stuff early on and gave me notes that were extremely valuable. I was fortunate enough to work with both good and bad writers, so I got to see what really worked and then what didn't. I would pick and choose who I wanted to be. I can't think of any one person who showed me the ropes. I kind of, like, figured it out as I went along.

An Interview with
Cinco Paul and Ken Daurio

A partial list of Cinco Paul and Ken Daurio's credits as screenwriters includes: *Despicable Me* (and sequels), *The Secret Life of Pets, The Lorax, Bubble Boy, The Santa Clause 2, College Road Trip*, and *Horton Hears a Who!*

One of them works on visual humor, the other on verbal. Throw in a bathtub, and you have the writing team of **Cinco Paul** and **Ken Daurio**. They feed off each other's ideas and often become very animated as they develop characters, conflicts, and stories. Their process goes from brainstorming together, to writing apart, coming back together to try and make each other laugh, to improvising dialogue, to getting stuck until Cinco takes a bath to figure out the solution to a problem. (Thankfully, they didn't demonstrate this part of their process during our interview.)

PD (Peter Desberg): As we've explained in our Premise [see page 9], how would you go about developing the show's plot lines?

CP (Cinco Paul): I would make it father/son, that's what I would do.

KD (Ken Daurio): Right. Who knows what women are thinking?

CP: So almost everything we've done, we just do "guy" stuff. And it's easier to be funny with guys, I think. So that would be my first suggestion.

PD: Just the idea of a guy named Molly makes me laugh.

KD: Can we just make it Wally?

CP: And father/son . . . both Ken and I have . . .

KD: . . . and we're both sons.

CP: And we both have complicated relationships with our fathers.

KD: Yes, we do!

CP: I think of the dad who's like . . . the wife took care of him his whole life. He never had to do anything and now she's gone.

KD: I get the Molly character more as a woman. It makes more sense to me that she would come. This is like her time to sort of be a kid. I don't know, does the dad do that?

CP: Yeah, but I think it would be . . . yeah. Maybe.

KD: Does the dad do that, does he just say . . .

CP: I think he hated this woman that he was married to. He hated the mom, and now he's like . . . now it's his chance to be free and freewheeling, right? He wants to be a single guy again.

KD: Yeah, that whole dating thing with the son, I see that. To me, that's easier to see with the two guys.

CP: Especially if you're thinking of a movie. What's the hook? It seems like it would need some sort of bigger hook than this.

KD: Right, this is like the setting, and that's what sitcom is.

CP: Right, right, it's the setting. So for a movie, you're going to want something that pushes it. It's like the second bump, and it would be trying to find that . . . which is, obviously, the guy is Ben Stiller. Right? And then the dad is . . .

KD: Jerry Stiller.

". . . it's like the thorn-in-the-side movie."

CP: Yes, yes. And the opening scene is, Anne Meara's dead and they're burying her, and then . . . it's sort of like something we have done at least two or three times, it's like the thorn-in-the-side movie. We love that sort of movie, which is *Planes, Trains, and Automobiles*, and it's *The In-Laws*. And [Ben] Stiller was made to live in those movies. And this is it. The dad is a thorn in the side. He cannot get rid of his dad. His dad has now moved in with him and wants to be part of his life.

JD (Jeffrey Davis): Is that the second bump you were talking about?

CP: I don't know if that's the second bump yet. The second bump might be trying to fix up his dad with somebody. What is the hero's goal? And [what are] all of the obstacles that are going to come into the story?

It's similar to *Dinner for Schmucks*, a project we worked on which is a French movie, and we did the American version. A guy who's very much like Stiller has a boss who has a group of friends who get together, and each try to invite the schmuck-iest guy to dinner. It's sort of a competition—by the end of the night, who has invited the biggest schmuck to dinner? And so, the boss's schmuck drops out, so he gets Stiller, his VP guy, and says, "You've got to find me a new schmuck by tomorrow night." And so Stiller finds this schmuck, but then ends up not being able to get rid of this schmuck for twenty-four hours. So the schmuck is with him for twenty-four hours, and ends up totally destroying his life in the process. And then it leads to a nice moment where he also sort of becomes friends with the schmuck, and so at the end he's got to choose: "Do I . . . ?"

KD: ". . . send him into the game?"

CP: "Do I feed him to the lions? Or do I let him know what's really going on?" And all this is happening during the biggest week of Stiller's life.

KD: Right.

CP: Whatever he ends up doing, in this Premise, he's like a VP somewhere. But it's got to be like the biggest week of his life, and unfortunately, his dad is there with him. It could be a business trip. Maybe his dad wants to come with him. He's going somewhere and his dad's coming along.

KD: Wanting to help out.

CP: Right. Like if he were in advertising. Stiller is in advertising, and his dad was like an old jingle guy, back in the days when they still wrote jingles. He's got his big presentation he's going to make. But his dad is like, "I'm going to help."

KD: But where's the jingle?

CP: Right, there's no jingle.

KD: You can't sell pharmaceuticals without a catchy song. Write one of the—like one of the old songs. Like "Plop, plop, fizz, fizz," how easy is that?

CP: Yeah, yeah, that's it! And it'd be great if his dad has written at least three or four classic jingles that we all know. Like "Plop, plop, fizz, fizz," or . . .

KD: "I'm a Pepper, you're a Pepper . . ."

CP: Right, he wrote, "I'm a Pepper . . ." or "Look for the Union label." And so if you put his dad in a room with people and a piano, he's like the life of the party. I think that's what is key to these movies. Everybody else loves his dad.

KD: And Dad doesn't understand why Ben hates him.

CP: Right. "Your dad is the greatest guy. He wrote 'Plop, plop, fizz, fizz.' How could you not love this guy?"

KD: And Ben says, "Yeah, I know. He wrote 'Plop, plop, fizz, fizz,' I get it!"

CP: Yeah, so a key scene would be: We're at the bar, and there's a piano, and his dad sits down and starts to play, "Here's another one I wrote," and everyone's gathered around the piano, and they're like, "Plop, plop, fizz, fizz."

KD: It's the big business dinner and Dad's there to sit in with everybody, and Ben says, "Dad, just go wait in the bar."

CP: "Oh, I see I'm not wanted."

KD: And it's like somehow he gets the whole group meeting to the bar . . .

CP: They're all at the piano [*clicking fingers and singing*], "You! You're the one!"

KD: His dad's going to help him work on the presentation, whatever it is he's doing, whatever he's there for, and Ben is going to reject it, let's say. So it's going to be the breakup.

CP: Yes, what this creates is a conversation between the new methods of advertising and old school. And what's great is advertising right now at this moment is just . . . they don't know what they're doing, right? They're freaked out because everybody is TiVo-ing past their commercials. They have no idea what they're doing or how to handle the media. Maybe what he needs to learn is the sort of spirit that his dad had. I guess his dad would say, "It was all about people . . . and connections . . ." it wasn't about your clever . . . paying people to tattoo the logo on their face, or whatever it is they do. His dad would be disparaging.

KD: Unless you have a song that people want to sing.

CP: Right, they're singing in the shower . . . yeah. He's all about the jingles. Then ultimately . . .

KD: . . . it is going to be about the jingle. And Dad's going to have to save the . . .

CP: . . . yes, he's going to have to save the company . . .

KD: . . . save the day.

CP: They check into the hotel room and his dad has ordered the keyboard and the whole setup and says, "Alright, let's get to work." And it should—whatever client it is—a jingle is completely inappropriate.

KD: It's like Vagisil.

PD: Singing the side effects . . .

KD: [*Singing*] "May cause nausea . . ."

CP: "Dad, please!"

KD: We've got to twist it.

CP: It would work in the classic way where it's just like, every time he thinks he's gotten his dad out of the picture, his dad keeps popping back up. Wherever he is, he thinks, "Oh, I'm rid of Dad," and Dad just keeps on showing up and he's never done.

KD: There's also the beat where . . . [*Cinco accidentally kicks the microphone*]. Now I've lost where I was.

CP: Well, yours probably wasn't that good, I guess, if you could lose it in five seconds. I was saying you want to set up as many things for his dad to ruin, so I think he's got to have some sort of office romance, if this is a business trip that he's on. He should have some sort of office romance, and she's with him there, and Dad's going to screw that up as well. I don't know how it is. It could be something along the lines of . . . years ago, in his dad's opinion, years ago he should've asked this girl to marry him. Right? Because his dad is more traditional, and so his dad is sort of pushing him in that direction. Maybe trying to orchestrate a proposal, or something against Stiller's will.

KD: "Here's how we proposed in my day!"

CP: Against his will, right? It's like, "How long . . . it's three years now with this girl and you haven't asked her to marry you . . . and she wants . . ." and Stiller: "We've discussed this, we don't want to get married. We don't need that. That was your world. That's not ours." But his dad would be pushing him, and ultimately, it's going to be good. Stiller needs to ask her, and probably she's secretly wishing he would, but . . . so something along those lines. But at the end of Act Two, it's got to be that his dad has completely destroyed everything, right? The girl has left him. He's lost the account. He's fired.

KD: I'm thinking about the end . . . the scene where Dad overhears his son ridiculing him in front of everybody. "That old coot, he doesn't know what he's talking about." It's that moment when Dad's heart just breaks, and he walks away.

CP: It's not the funniest moment.

KD: No, no, no . . .

CP: But it's the one that kills you . . . you see his dad overhear . . . yeah, I like that.

KD: And then in the end . . . I think it's Ben's choice to use his dad's method, even though his dad isn't even in the room.

CP: Right, so that he's not doing it at all to make his dad happy.

KD: Yeah, I think he does it because he's still guilty about what he'd said about this great, old guy, and maybe they do sort of think he's a joke now. And I think it's just Ben realizing, "You know what, my dad is right and this is all wrong." You know, there's the big presentation and he's got to do what we don't expect him to do, which is use his dad's approach.

And in the end, Ben does the jingle and he's fired. And they hate it. He's fired. But, the relationship with his father is much better, and he's marrying the girl, and everything is fine. Maybe.

CP: I'm trying to think of what else . . . we would want a rival for Ben at the agency, who's there trying to sabotage him.

KD: Or he's the guy who . . . he's nine steps ahead of everybody, like in Japan, how they have those bus stop ads. There's all these advertising techniques, where it's like on the buses, as you pass certain points, there's computer sensors that trigger screens to come on in the bus for the stores that are outside. He's way ahead of the game, and he's like putting out these . . .

CP: . . . he wants cookies . . . People have cookies, so as you walk by the sign it'll know what stores you've been in in the mall. But it should be . . . you want some sort of rival there, who is someone that his dad can help him take down at the end, because otherwise, there really is no bad guy in this. He thinks his dad's the bad guy, but then his dad can help uncover this smarmy guy.

KD: Or it's the other agency that's up for . . .

CP: . . . yeah, it would be the other agency, not someone within his agency. There's another agency, it's highly competitive. "Can we get this huge account?" And that guy is really trying to screw over Stiller and make him look bad, and nail him, and then his dad maybe comes to the rescue . . . somehow. I don't have the exact details of how he does it . . .

JD: Meanwhile, how's the dad feeling about himself?

CP: Maybe there's a moment where his dad does need to realize . . .

KD: "I need to let it go."

CP: He needs to let it go. But it is that classic John Candy: "I like me. My wife likes me. I talk too much. Well, I also listen, too," you know, it's that moment where he says, "Yeah, I know I'm a joke, but, you know . . ."

KD: Well, going where you were saying, you know, maybe if Ben does the jingle at the end, and it flops, it's like Dad can swoop in with whatever Ben was doing and fixes Ben's techniques . . .

CP: Right, right, right, yeah.

KD: And together, that's more of your feel-good, happy . . .

CP: . . . yeah. That's what everybody wants.

KD: It is what everybody wants.

CP: "We've got to get the account," Ken . . . What are you saying, they're not going to get the account? But you know, it's also . . . I don't know how long ago we would have the mom . . . how long ago she died. Because you don't want that pall hanging over the whole . . .

KD: . . . it's been a while. But Dad . . .

CP: . . . but Dad's going to sort of suddenly show up. He's lonely. Somehow he's gotten a kick in the pants, which made him decide, "I need to . . ."

KD: Maybe he's gone through the other kids and now it's . . .

CP: . . . no, no, maybe it would be nice. See, Stiller has to bring it upon himself, for instance, like, "Dad, you've got to get out. You've got to do something. You've got to experience life."

"He brought his father on himself" is the smarter way to do it. Instead of his dad just showing up. It's like, "Dad, this is sad, you know, Mom died, it's been a year, you need to get out, you need to do something, and . . ." But he means, "far away from me . . ." "No, I meant!!!" "Well, you told me Florida."

KD: "You miss your dad, don't you?" "I got the message, you don't have to say it!"

CP: It's like, "Oh, no, I was thinking more of going on a cruise, or something." "No, but this is so much better." And what we would usually create is the incident, right?

It's like, in the past, a moment when his dad completely humiliated him as a child, which is great, to go to a flashback of that. I don't know exactly what it would be. Did he make his son sing in front of people?

KD: I was thinking . . . you know how they used to do the live sort of ads in between the . . . like, the live commercial in between the show? In-studio commercial. He was supposed to sing the song.

CP: Right.

KD: And he just couldn't do it.

CP: He was going to have his kid do it and he froze . . . and it was just totally humiliating, how far back would that be? It's like the Texaco Hour.

KD: So maybe it wasn't that.

CP: It probably wasn't that because I'm thinking . . . our main guy . . .

KD: Or maybe he wanted to do a commercial, or something. Like he was the original Oscar Mayer Wiener Kid, but he couldn't pull it off. He choked.

CP: Like, "My bologna has a first name."

KD: Yeah, my bologna . . . with the fishing rod . . . that was supposed to be Mikey . . .

CP: Right, yeah. He was the original Mikey but he just blew it, and then he blew his chance to be on cereal boxes and everything. Something along those lines. And it's great . . . the advertising world, and his dad was part of this, because everybody knows these ads and these songs, and it's good to meet the king. The jingle king.

PD: Has the Mikey thing haunted Ben?

CP: Yeah, it must've, yeah, something that he's always resented his dad [for], and maybe going into the same business is a way of proving he's better than his dad, right? "I'm going to be more successful than him. I'm going to do the same exact thing he did. I'm going to end up more successful." Because he can't see himself doing it out of love, or emulating his dad. Well, maybe deep down inside.

KD: Although it's nice if it's one like the Oscar Mayer Wiener Kid . . . the bologna . . . whatever it is, where he was supposed to sing a song, so that at the end, when he has to sing the song in the meeting, it's sort of like he gets his shot again. And his dad's in the back of the room, just crying. That used to be his lullaby, he would sing to him to sleep with it.

CP: But he wanted Stiller to sing the song in a commercial when he was a kid, and Stiller wouldn't sing the song, "I hate that. I'm never going to sing that song." And then at the end, he sings the song in the middle of the presentation.

KD: Yeah, and then a bunch of funny stuff happens. In the middle . . .

CP: There'd be set pieces . . . I don't want to get too technical . . .

KD: Those take months to create. We would start there, and go with the scenes, and start to figure out what makes it funny.

CP: Yeah, that's what we would do.

JD: When you work, do you talk it out for a long time?

CP/KD: Uh-huh.

JD: Do you do a scene list?

KD: We do an outline, and then we'll . . .

CP: . . . then we do a scene list. We take the first act, "Here are all the scenes, you do this one and I'll do this one." And so we just separate. And then we go off and write our scenes, and then come back, and then—the goal is you try to make the other guy laugh with what you wrote. And if it doesn't make us laugh, then we . . .

KD: . . . we try again. That's when we'll go in together and look at a scene. After that pass, if something's not working, we usually go at it more together.

CP: Yeah, yeah. We've gone apart, then as we're reading through it—well, we just read through everything first, and try to make the other guy laugh, and then we'll go back . . .

KD: . . . and then we together sort of try and roundtable it.

CP: We have found things that were better, one of us is better at it than the other, so we'll divide scenes up.

KD: We can look at the scenes now and we know, basically . . .

CP: . . . like any scene with emotion in it is mine. So I handle emotion.

KD: I don't know what you're getting at.

CP: I'm not getting at anything. I'm just . . . for the people that are interested in how we work, I just said that . . .

KD: . . . I guess I save them for me. I don't like to give them away . . .

CP: . . . but in general, Ken is more visual—he gets the visual stuff—I get the more verbal stuff. I think structure-wise, sometimes it's like I will go off on my own a little, and figure out structural things.

KD: Yes, he probably is the structure man.

CP: And then I'll sort of . . . I'll say, "I got it!" And then I'll pitch it to him, and then he'll make it better.

"He goes and takes his bath . . . comes out . . . *'I got it!'*"

KD: And generally, that's done in the bath, so I'm not part of that process.

CP: Ken, do we have to do that?

KD: He goes and takes his bath . . . comes out . . . *"I got it!"*

CP: I thought we talked about the fact that we weren't going to . . .

KD: . . . what? It's a very creative environment for you.

CP: It is. Well, since he's brought it up, a lot of times I'll just say, "I need to take a bath to figure things out." Because really, it's not worth starting until you know where those big beats are, especially at the end. Like, *Dinner for Schmucks* led to a really nice ending where it's a moment of truth. You want it to lead to a moment of truth. This guy is a schmuck, this guy has destroyed his life, but he only did it because he wanted a friend. It's like, do I deliver him up to the lions? Or, what do I do? And you want it to lead to that moment, and I don't think in this discussion we've found that moment yet here.

KD: Do you have a bathtub? Twenty minutes and he'll be out, wet, and writing things down.

CP: I think that's it. Then you just populate it with the characters. This is basically a "two-hander," which is a two-star movie, like *Planes, Trains, and Automobiles.*

JD: How do you know if you're funny?

KD: Having two people automatically helps that whole thing, knowing whether you're funny or not.

PD: How good is your intuition? Before you go in and pitch something, do you have a pretty good idea of what's funny?

KD: I think we have a pretty good idea. Every once in a while you get, "Wow, you didn't get that one, did you?" Or, "I missed that one," or you know you're going to kill, then he reads it and there's nothing. Every once in a while that happens, but for the most part . . .

CP: . . . we know where the big laughs are going to be. We've gotten a feel for them. I think the main reason we do it this way is it's faster. I once tried writing something else in collaboration, where we were writing the scene at the computer together, and it was like pulling teeth. It was just a nightmare. This is much better. We just go off, write, and then we'll come back, and then we combine it. Yeah, we try to make each other laugh. That's what it's all about. I mean, it's totally unpredictable what people are going to find funny.

"The reason I'm in movies right now is because when I was in the fourth grade I saw a Marx Brothers movie on TV."

PD: How did each of you get your background in comedy?

CP: The reason I'm in movies right now is because when I was in the fourth grade I saw a Marx Brothers movie on TV. And that was it for me. And I'm a huge Marx Brothers fan now. But I just became really obsessed with that, and I'd go to the library and rent Super 8 [films] . . . they had Super 8 [Charlie] Chaplin and [Buster] Keaton, and I just really sort of watched it all set in . . . and we had this little Super 8 camera, and I just started making movies. There's the Marx Brothers, Woody Allen, Monty Python, there's the old revival house, I'd go all the time to watch them. And that was it. I was schooled by that sort of stuff. But you kind of have to be born funny in a way, because I was always able to make people laugh.

KD: Well, I think to some degree, we both have that same sad experience in that we weren't the cool kids, so for me, a lot of it was the defense, you know, I could always make people laugh. Maybe I wasn't as good at sports, but that was my thing. So that was sort of what I had, and I used it a lot when I was a kid, and as far as just movies . . . always the escape. When you wanted to get away from realizing the fact that you weren't the cool kid.

". . . you get a lot of comedians who are very depressed . . . that's not us."

CP: I don't think, for either of us, that it came out of, like, suffering or pain. Plus, you know, you get a lot of comedians who are very depressed . . . that's not us. We're both very optimistic, easygoing guys. So it didn't come out of there. I don't know where else.

PD: Your work shows a lot of craft. Did you just pick it up, or were you mentored by people?

CP: I really didn't know anything about structure until USC [University of Southern California]. That's where they really teach you structure. David Howard ran the program there. And Frank Daniel was sort of the guru of the structure that was taught there—three-act structure, but eight sequences. So that's where I learned structures.

JD: [*To Ken*] Did you go to USC, too?

KD: No, I did nothing. Right out of high school, I started making music videos with a friend of mine, and we just kind of figured out a way to get a connection with a band. Once we got one, we got another one. I did that for about ten years. I made over a hundred music videos. So that was great experience, just holding the camera, and editing, and all that. But making music videos isn't really storytelling. You try to get a little story in there, but the goal was ultimately to go onto features, and so during that time, I'd written a couple of little things. And I've always wanted to make movies, and be in movies, and I just loved everything about it. And so . . . Cinco and I just met sort of at the end of my ten-year music video run, and we just met as friends, and started talking about things. It was the sense of humor that clicked immediately, and we were on the same page with that. And Cinco said, "We should write something together."

CP: Yeah, because I'd been writing on my own for . . . I was at USC from '91 to '93. And then I got out of that two-year program, and then I wrote a script, and that script sold as a spec. So then that sort of gave me a career, and from then on, I'd work product to product to product, but nothing was getting made. It was a little stagnant and so then, Ken revitalized me and helped me find the funny again.

KD: I think, ultimately, and especially after being on the set and watching a movie get made and watching the control slip right out of your hands, things happen where you can't do anything about it. Ultimately, we want to write and direct our own thing, and we tried that. We did a little test run of that. We made a short film together and it was great, because you never know. We know we can write together, but we didn't know if we would actually be able to make a film together, but it was great.

"'Oh, we could get a rewrite from them for really cheap if we attach them to direct.'"

CP: It was just a short film. It sort of demonstrates the talent to the town, that we can write and direct. So now we get offers to rewrite and direct stuff. It's for people who couldn't afford whatever our rewrite number is . . . our fee. "Oh, we could get a rewrite from them for really cheap if we attach them to direct."

JD: If you didn't have to worry about any constraints from studios or executives, would you change anything you've come up with in this Premise? What effect would it have?

CP: I wouldn't change anything, but I'd be relieved that we wouldn't get any dumb notes from executives.

JD: What's the dumbest note you've ever gotten?

CP: Well, *Bubble Boy*, this is the dumbest note, which was from a senior VP at Disney. And he bought the project and it's there, but he said, "We've got to get him out of that bubble as soon as possible . . ." He was like, at the act break from Act I to Act II, he wanted him out of the bubble. We're like, "The movie's called *Bubble Boy*. He cannot spend like only the first act in the bubble. Like, the whole idea is . . . Act II he's in the bubble suit, and that's what makes him the 'Bubble Boy.'"

KD: He's just a guy in a room . . .

CP: So anyway, he says, "By the midpoint, he has to be out of the bubble." We didn't have any choice, we did a draft with him getting out of the bubble halfway, and it was . . .

KD: . . . crazy.

CP: It was horrible, horrible. That was the craziest note. You should've seen our faces when he said, "You've got to get him out of the bubble."

KD: Like, are we changing the name of the movie to *Boy*?

CP: Right, it's just like, "the Boy." The boy who used to be in a bubble, but now is just sort of out. And we're like, "Well, what does he do?" "Well, he's all germaphobic and . . ."

"Like, are we changing the name of the movie to *Boy*?"

KD: "He's going to taste . . . It'll be like his first time feeling things, and tasting spicy foods" . . . Spicy foods!

CP: Like, he could eat spicy foods when he was in the bubble. Being out of the bubble doesn't, like, suddenly give him the freedom to eat spicy foods. We reference the "spicy food" thing quite a bit. But we love the executives. We do. Everyone just wants the movie to be the best it can be.

JD: Were you guys mentored, either separately or together?

KD: Cinco has mentored me.

CP: Yeah, from USC . . . two years there. My thesis instructor was Dave Bower, but other than that, that's like a very official mentor, and really we didn't have much of a connection once I was out of school.

PD: If you're writing sitcoms, you start out in a Writers' Room as a young guy and the older guys . . .

CP: . . . right. Features? No. I mean, Frank [Wuliger], I would consider kind of a mentor, he helped to show me the ropes and sort of figure out how this business works.

KD: Yeah, I didn't know anything like structure.

CP: I did mentor Ken. I did!

"'Let's write something together.' He said, 'I can work with this kid.'"

KD: The script that I showed Cinco, right, it had all this funny stuff in it, but there was like, nothing. It was, like, one act. But, hey, that's what made you say, "Let's write something together." He said, "I can work with this kid."

CP: I remember liking the scene with the camel.

"... as far as structure goes, and all that stuff, thanks for going to school, Cinco."

KD: Yes. I knew. But yeah, as far as structure goes, and all that stuff, thanks for going to school, Cinco.

CP: You're welcome, Ken, you'll get my bill.

JD: Were there people in your families who were funny?

CP: My parents aren't funny. I mean, I love them so much. They're really not very funny. And I don't know anyone . . . No one on either my mom or my dad's side of the family is what I would consider funny, really funny. How about you? [*Cinco asks Ken*] Nothing?

KD: No. Nothing.

CP: So isn't that weird? Where does that come from? I don't know. It's a mystery.

PD: Were they artistic at all?

KD: No.

PD: Interested in the arts?

CP: My mom's musical. After a while, I thought I was going to be a pop musician or something. That was like a big focus in my career. But as far as anyone making a living from something artistic, it's so foreign to either side of my family. My dad's a life insurance salesman. But they're very supportive.

KD: I don't know where it comes from.

CP: And we've talked about that, too. What's interesting is Ken and I . . . we just sort of met at a very late point in our lives but who knows when the end is . . . we had very similar upbringings and family situations, and . . . does that situation create a certain sense of humor because it's very similar? Like with our dads, our parents divorced, and we each have one sister and that's it . . . very similar and maybe that . . . little petri dish.

JD: Were you the original writers on *The Santa Clause 2*? Or were you brought in to rewrite?

CP: We were brought in to rewrite, but here's the story on *The Santa Clause 2*. Every scene in the script was our scene, but they changed almost all the dialogue. Then they brought in guys after us, Ed Decter [*also interviewed in this book; see page 67*] and John Strauss, who changed almost all of the dialogue except for a couple of scenes.

KD: It was surreal to watch because it's exactly what we wrote, but no, nobody says the words we wrote.

CP: So it's like the scene . . . like the beginning, middle, and end of each scene was sort of created by us. Some scenes were there from the script before. A couple, maybe three or four scenes, stayed from the other script. It was like a big rewrite.

JD: From the way you worked on the Premise, it seems like you brought a lot of yourselves in, and also that you started from character. Is that how you typically work?

CP: I think maybe in this case, it was easier to do it. This Premise is character-driven. Although I've never been accused of being a character guy before. Usually, we get a little criticized for that. We're more story-driven. I know that's how my brain works.

When you go to see a movie, you often have no idea who actually wrote it. That's because additional writers are often brought in to polish or completely rewrite the script. Charlie Peters, who is interviewed in this book (see page 222), often earns vast sums of money for his rewrites, but you don't always see his name on the screen. The Writers Guild has a rule that only seven writers can have writing credit on a film. The second *Charlie's Angels* film is rumored to have had thirty-five different writers who worked on the script. Often, writers including Cinco and Ken get brought in to rewrite comedies that studios think are not quite working, and both sets of writers will receive writing credit.

Cinco and Ken mention situations where budgets become an issue. They have been offered directorial credit to lower their writing fees. They also lamentably say that they are asked to fix broken scripts by adding more jokes because that's quicker than fixing the structure of a bad script. Cinco and Paul also talked about a situation in *The Santa Clause 2* in which they rewrote the script, but then had their dialogue rewritten by other writers. They saw their scripts without their words, which they described as "surreal."

KD: I would agree.

CP: So this is probably more of an exception. But you saw us sort of clinging to what is the story.

KD: What are the moments? We need those moments.

CP: Right, you create . . . oh, make it a business trip, so you've got a ticking clock. I cling to that sort of stuff, because it helps. It makes everything else easier.

PD: So a lot of your humor comes out of events, as opposed to character?

CP: Yeah, and if we had more time, the next thing we would do would be very carefully plot out the twists and turns, and the bumps along the way.

PD: You are good at getting situations that have a lot of conflict in them, and a lot of them are human conflicts that are character-oriented. I like the way you bring the conflict together. They seem to be very situational.

CP: When we pitch, we have a lot of fun pitching, because we'll take the character and we'll just do the little dialogue things, which we did a little bit of here, but that's generally pretty effective. We become the character and just like . . . work off of each other, back and forth.

KD: Trying to figure out what that guy would say. And we can kind of hear it. When we get into the story, and we kind of get into the character, we just sort of react.

CP: You kind of riff on that character, yeah. Kind of like improv.

PD: Do both of you guys do the dialogue?

KD: Uh-huh, we do.

PD: Because you work so closely together, do you get to a point where each of you could write similar dialogue for a character, so that it just meshes nicely?

Many of the writers we interviewed in this book worked as actors and comedians. Cinco and Ken did not. During their interview, they assumed character roles and created dialogue through those characters as they were developing the Premise. They described their creative process as improv. As they get into their development, they quickly sense which of them relates more to one character than another. Then, they decide on which of them will write the dialogue for a character based on this initial improv.

CP: Yeah, I think so.

KD: Sometimes. It depends on the character.

CP: Yeah.

KD: There are certain types that are more you, Cinco.

CP: Yeah, Ken'll usually say, "You write that stuff. That's you. This is a Cinco speech."

KD: Our lead character, we go back and forth because they're in the whole movie. We decide on who this guy is, and we can both usually do it.

"The more real you make it, the funnier it gets."

CP: Like the thing that we pitched today, what we like about it is that it's real. The more real you make it, the funnier it gets. We try to resist stuff that's too crazy and broad.

KD: Like *Bubble Boy*. But there's reality within that.

JD: Jokes are great and you've got to have them, but they can get in the way of a story. Do executives ever ask you to funny it up?

"But they don't realize that the reason it's not funny is because it's broken in a lot of other ways . . ."

CP: We do hear that. The sad thing is we'll get a lot of scripts to rewrite because we do comedy and they want us just to make it funnier. But they don't realize that the reason it's not funny is because it's broken in a lot of other ways, and usually they're not willing to fix that other stuff. They just want icing jokes.

An Interview with
Charlie Peters

A partial list of Charlie Peters's credits as a screenwriter, director, and television show creator includes: *Three Men and a Little Lady, Blame It on Rio, Her Alibi, Paternity, Hot to Trot, My One and Only, Music from Another Room, Passed Away, Krippendorf's Tribe,* and *CBS Summer Playhouse: Tickets, Please.*

By the time you finish reading this interview, you will feel like you have earned the equivalent of three credits in a university writing class. **Charlie Peters** is the college professor you would have loved to have a beer with after class. His interview blends premise development, comedy theory, and story construction, with personal industry stories woven in. He explains the rationale for each decision as he makes it, often using classic films to make his point. Charlie's working style is a rare blend of technical virtuosity and creativity. Or, as we describe it, "he's real smart." He makes the point that in a good script, the characters want the story to end, but as you're reading this interview, you will hope it never does.

PD (Peter Desberg): As we've explained in our Premise [see page 9], how would you go about developing the show's plot lines?

CP (Charlie Peters): My inclination would be to develop this Premise as a movie. The difference between television and movies is that a television premise is more situational. It has to promise much more story. You pitch a pilot and you have to come in with fifteen plots. A movie can be about a single day or a single hour. So a movie is much more event-driven in terms of the comedic. If I refer to movies, I refer to classic movies that most people have seen. Like *Tootsie*. The situation is a man pretending to be a woman, but the event is essentially romantic. In a TV pilot like this mother/daughter Premise, you're talking entirely about situation and not event. When I'm thinking about stories in a comedy, it is essentially that you want the worst possible thing to happen at the worst possible time.

Unfortunately, some writers create a whole movie, and I will read it, and very often I will find very little conflict in it. Because with the amateur, no conflict actually exists in the movie. The thing about writing movies is that it's a very unnatural thing to do. Because the whole point of everyone's life, even my dog's life, is to make life easier. And what you're asking a writer to do is to sit there for hours on end and figure out how to make someone's life harder. And, you know, in the morning, you get up, you take a leak, you go downstairs, you get the coffee, you get dressed, you get the keys, you get in the car, and you go to work. In a movie, everything has to go wrong. You go downstairs and the coffee pot doesn't work. You can't find the car keys.

"The motivation for every character in a movie should be to stop the movie right now. It should be to get out of the movie."

Look at Woody Allen's really good films. There are no scenes in which people are *not* arguing. Every single scene is about an argument. And it's what we all, by nature, try to avoid. So we're being asked to be incredibly *un-human*, because drama is all about conflict. The times I have directed, in theatre and a couple of times in film, actors have asked me, what's the goal of this character? You have to know the motivation. The motivation for every character in a movie should be to stop the movie right now. It should be to get out of the movie. Once a character is in the movie and enjoying the movie, the movie is over. If they had their choice, they would get *The Guns of Navarone* on page 2. No one should want to be in a movie for exactly the reasons I told you. It sucks to be in a movie. You want to watch the movie, not be in it.

You start to fall in love with your characters and you don't want them to have problems. But you to get to page 120 and you have this whole problem-less life for them and it's a really boring movie. It's very hard to actually do. Given a Premise like this one, with Sarah and Molly . . . it's a television premise . . . it's a movie premise, too. If it were a feature premise, it would read like an ensemble movie with a young woman looking for love. People looking for love is obviously the stuff of 50 percent or more of movies.

I have done some TV, but less successfully than my movies. I did create a pilot. It was like *Cheers*, only on a train. It took place in the bar car of the New York Central Railroad in the morning, taking these people to work, and the second half of the show was them coming home. Eventually it would have moved off, in the 100th or 200th episode. But it was a situational thing. But when you pitch it, you have to come up with an event you can throw these people at and see how they bounce off this particular thing.

So here you have a story which could be a tri-generational story. Sarah is a young-ish woman living with her parents, and then there's the influence of her grandparents, who are Molly's mother and father. The feature people responding to this would be looking for an event. They would say, "Kill the grandparents. No one wants to see old people in movies."

"The story is only important as bait to an element."

It's shocking, you know. The business has changed so much just in the last few years. The first thing they would do is cast it. The story now is not really important to a movie. The story is only important as bait to an element. An element is either an actor or a director. And there are very few director-elements anymore. More and more directors are less and less elements. In movies, actors are now the only elements that matter. The studios would say, "Who would be in this?" Now, it is a negative to the studios that it revolves around a woman. Women, notoriously, do not open films as strongly as men. There are a few that do. But, generally, they prefer to open a film around a man.

"He looks at me very seriously and he says, 'What do you think the opening weekend will be?' I said, 'How do I know? Probably be cloudy, maybe like 60, 65 degrees.'"

CP: They would ask, "Who is the guy?" You have Sarah's father, basically middle-aged, my age, which means he's ready to be shipped off to Siberia because he's useless and incompetent. All they think about now when you tell them a story is the opening weekend. They mention one word. *Poster.* They want to see the poster. I actually worked with a man once who was the head of Paramount Pictures, and I was told he was a genius. I pitched him an idea he really liked. And maybe he had too much to drink, or maybe he didn't have enough to drink, because he looks at me very seriously and he said, "'What do you think the opening weekend will be?' I said, 'How do I know? Probably be cloudy, maybe like 60, 65 degrees.'"

I mean, what kind of a stupid question is that? But it wasn't a stupid question. That was ten, twelve years ago. It's become more and more the *only* question. Anybody can tell you this about the business. It's been totally corporatized. But what's sad is the lack of producers. There are development producers and there are people that open the movie. But there is no producer with the balls who could say, "Mr. Spielberg, I think you should cut twenty minutes from this movie. It put me to sleep." Because that producer would just be sent to another nation. There's no more producers like Sam Cohn [famous Hollywood producer of the Golden Age], saying, you know, "My ass fell asleep. Cut the shit."

". . . the actors, the director, the craft services will change the dialogue."

Anyway, my sense of a story like Sarah and Molly's story is, what are the worst things that can happen? What are the problems? You can look at this in any sitcom. Some of the better ones just find a more clever way of doing it. But it's all about the worst situation. Having made my living at this for a while, it seems sort of hypocritical to say that dialogue is sort of irrelevant. But I think dialogue is just supportive of the action in the scene. And I think when you write a scene in a movie, if you make it rely entirely upon dialogue, I think you're really creating problems for yourself. Because the actors, the director, the craft services will change the dialogue.

Take one of many great scenes. Al Pacino, going to shoot the police chief in *The Godfather*. There are a couple of funny lines in it, but who cares what they say? It's him nervously going to kill his first human being. He's in a restaurant in the Bronx. He has to go find a gun stuck behind a toilet. And for a second, he almost doesn't find it. You can't do anything to that scene. I'm not knocking actors and directors, because they come up with great stuff. But it is sort of director-proof, actor-proof, and it's sort of writer-proof as well. And that's essentially what you want to do when you write. And so with Molly and Sarah, each episode has to be driven by an event, although television sitcoms are essentially more verbal. They hire comics nowadays. A hundred years from now, they'll look back at this society: Schlubby, overweight, funny men were married to very attractive women who put up with a lot. Or lots of kooky friends lived in apartments in New York. They had no jobs, but the apartments cost $12,000 a month.

Meanwhile, I think it's patronizing the way people look at the 1950s. Trust me, this was an era that was coming from the Depression and World War II. There wasn't a person in America who thought they lived like *Leave It to Beaver*, okay? That's not what people believed. We tend to think that, but it's not true. These were people who starved when they were children, got their asses shot off in war. And now they're doing TV shows? We look back and kind of go, "Look at the people who made these shows. Oh, they were so naïve." My parents watched those shows. They were not naïve. They looked at the shows as a way to leave their problems for a little while. As opposed to shows today, which are the opposite. Which is like going into a neurosis of a situation like this.

A lot of times, young people do live with their parents. Sarah could live with Molly and her father. So what are the problems of living with your parents? I mean, it's pretty evident on one level. What's good about this is that you have three levels, but first we're going to kill the grandparents off. There's an event. The death of the grandparents. The funeral. Funerals are always good. Big laughs. Funerals and weddings. Weddings are in movies a lot because they are a much more used device. I don't think you find it that much in Europe or South America, but because it is really the only place where we are, in this culture, allowed to openly show our emotions. The event is orchestrated to allow us to show emotion. It opens a sort of wound. People behave at weddings like they behave nowhere else. And I think that's part of it. As opposed to cultures where people run up to each other, kiss, and stand really close. So there's another episode, the wedding. And a funeral at the same time. Saves money.

We have to be invited to weddings, but we're expected to go to funerals. What does that say? We're very cheap with our emotional joy, but we're very generous with our grief. But I'm only going to invite people to my funeral. This is how I'm going to be different. If you're not invited, don't come. And come with a gift.

"In fact, if the mother were younger than her, it would probably appeal to the studios."

So anyway, let's think in terms of relationships. The idea is . . . and this has happened . . . Sarah and her boyfriend, her love interest, decide to move in with Sarah's mother and within a month, they're looking for assisted-living housing for themselves. So the living situation, as it is in the Premise, clearly can't work. Molly is a charming socialite. What she does is . . . she's usurping or hijacking the role of the younger woman, which can be funny as long as the mother is cleverly cast to be two years older than Sarah. In fact, if the mother were younger than her, it would probably appeal to the studios.

That's a whole different episode. It never occurred to Sarah why her mother is younger than her. Like in Episode 4. If Sarah is twenty, the mother could be fifty or forty-five. We can make them both attractive. One is essentially Lolita and the other is a slightly older Lolita. So I would look for episodes in which Sarah is attracted to some guy who's attracted to Molly, although I'm sure he doesn't want to bed the mother, although there's another episode.

There's a sophistication and grace to older women that younger men find comfortable. When I was in my twenties and thirties, my girlfriends' parents and I often got along far better than my girlfriends and I. There's an ease that's there, so you have that element between Molly and Sarah. You could also have the dead grandmother come back to life, and there would be the guys that she would be attracted to.

Probably being a TV series, they would want one who's attracted to the grandmother, that she's not attracted to. A romance is about two people who don't get together. The classic thing is that if they're going to be together at the end, they have to be as far apart as possible at the end of Act II. And if they're not together at the end, they have to make love at the end of Act II. In most romances, the couple is together at the end, but it's finding the obstacles. I think that's why *Brokeback Mountain* is such a successful movie. The obstacles to their love are so profound. It's not only just scary. They have obstacles in and of themselves. Today in romance, the obstacles are essentially neurotic, which makes for good psychiatric visits but not for very good films. When I say neurotic, I mean the guy who's saying, "Well, I really want to marry her, but I still want to f–ck a lot people, too." And then the woman saying, "Well, he's really cute and everything, but maybe he still wants to f–ck other people and maybe he doesn't make enough money." I mean, it's all about your interior problem, which means there are really not that many obstacles.

Conflict and *obstacle*. Obstacle is sort of like a physical obstacle, you know. Conflict is what you feel emotionally. Again, you have to have that obstacle. You have to have that conflict. If there's an argument against independent films versus Hollywood movies, the one thing that Hollywood movies do better is they alternate the emotion. Not to knock independent films, because some of them are great, but they tend to be monotonous. Each scene may have a certain feeling. But each of those scenes tends to be pretty similar. Whereas in Hollywood movies, the one thing they tend to do pretty well is bring you way up and then let you down.

PD: So Sarah's love interest problems end up being neurotic problems? How would you find the obstacles?

CP: In romance, they tend to be very tragic. In the story of Molly and Sarah, I suppose illness, you know, classic things . . . falling in love with someone you find out is married. Falling in love with someone you find out is a Republican? I used to write the romantic comedy things. I wrote so many of those things in film and I just find them uninteresting now. I want to see people in a romantic comedy sit down and say, "Yeah, I want to have sex with you, but what do you think about the death penalty?"

"How do you want to bring the children up?" Clearly, it's a fantasy, as is most love anyway. And then you put it in a movie and then it becomes fantasy to the nth degree.

JD (Jeffrey Davis): What would make this Premise more interesting to you?

CP: What would save it for me is putting them in a situation they can't get out of emotionally or physically, and then having them find their way out of it emotionally or physically. To create an obstacle. Right now the obstacle in the Premise—the mother moving in with Sarah—is annoying, but it's not really an obstacle. It's not the German army arriving just when you're about to blow up *The Guns of Navarone*. A lot of times I'm given things that are high-concept. In a high-concept story, the attraction of it is that you go into these studio cretins and you're able to, in the shortest period of time, get them to see it. However, it's a very difficult thing because when you have a high concept and you give it to them for any length of time before you start dealing with it, they can start coming up with ideas of their own. But it's an easy sell for the studio executive to go to his or her boss, because the person you pitch it to is never the person who says, "Yes," unless you're a major filmmaker. So what you have to do is wrap the idea in a way that they can take it to their person and make it seem palatable. And very often, by human nature, we do know what makes a good story. You have to give them an event . . . an obstacle.

But it's a dangerous thing, because the concept sometimes overwhelms the story. I mean, you look at the really good stories; again, I'll mention *Tootsie*. It's a perfect balance of high concept and story because of the brilliance of the writing and the acting and the direction. But the high concept is the sort of booster rocket, the conduit that exists all the way through the story, until the second-to-last scene. But the writing of the obstacles of the romance is so good that it's always seen as a means. Once the high concept becomes the most basic, the most interesting part of the movie, you're really dead. Which is true for a lot of these pilots. The morning after they're aired, they're cancelled. Because they're about people in their thirties, because most of the executives are in their thirties, looking to have sex or love or sometimes both.

Now that's a high concept, that sex life. But it doesn't work because it's just the notion of wanting to find sex or love, but it's not enough to carry something unless it's well-written. Which is why *Sex and the City* was successful, despite what I think was its rather archaic view of femininity.

PD: You say this Premise needs conflict in it. If you were talking about it with a producer, and he said, "Give me some examples of conflict that you would put in here. Give me four or five and then we'll choose." How would you go about choosing?

CP: Well, we see the conflict between characters. If you have conflict, you can separate it. Mother vs. daughter. Mother vs. husband. Daughter vs. father. Parents vs. daughter. You can see it that way. But the father's dead, isn't he? I think he should be dead. He and the grandmother run off together, *dead.* There's a high concept.

So you can have the father as a ghost. But episodes could also be about jobs. Sarah's job. What does she do? Does she have a job? She could be let go and Molly tries to find her a new job. She goes in with Sarah and maybe meets someone. And the person wants to hire Molly and not Sarah. And then there's the conflict of jealousy—I think much more so with mother-and-daughter jealousy than there is between fathers and sons. Or a son and his mother. That's a whole different kind of jealousy. Like, "Who's wearing that red lamè dress tonight? Now that my mother's dead, I don't have those problems anymore. I've got all her clothes."

Molly and Sarah could be evicted from their apartment. There could be episodes where . . . you know, the *Seinfeld* episode where everything is on the subway. That's a high concept. *Seinfeld* worked, too. That was pretty much a high-concept show. The New York subway is such a wealth of characters that the concept is kind of fun, as long as there is stuff to bolster it. To fill it.

PD: When I asked you for those examples, you said, "Okay. I can take conflict A to B, B to A, A to C, C to A." It was really logical and then you started going out from there. Is that sort of the way you work?

CP: I guess so. Sometimes it's good, in a scene or a sequence, to do a writing exercise. I'll rewrite the scene, saying, "Okay, what if the person were a dog?" I mean, something just totally outrageous. Just to stretch it and to see it in a new way. It's very difficult to rewrite your own stuff.

JD: Why do you think that is?

CP: Well, because you've been through the process of doing it. When I was acting, I'd write myself things to play, and the hardest thing to do for me as an actor was to memorize my own lines. Because I knew the process. I knew the first line that I thought of. And I could recognize the final line, which may have been ten or fifteen reincarnations along the way. But when another actor threw a cue at me, my first instinct was to go to the first line I wrote, almost to go back to the process. So it was just weird. Hard to avoid.

JD: If you could do one thing to this story that would reflect your sensibility, what would it be?

CP: It's probably a story, to be honest, that I wouldn't be that interested in doing. It's just not dark enough for me.

JD: Make it dark.

CP: There's a Quentin Tarantino movie. *Dark for Fun.* My instinct now, after twenty-five years of writing romantic comedies, after *Three Men and a Little Lady* and all the rest, is to do very dark stuff. And I'm having fun doing it. I'm trying to think of the things I'm doing now, and how they would relate to this. They're very personal. This is essentially a simple and clear domestic emotional connection between mother and daughter. I think it would be wrapped around a mystery. All parent/child relationships are about what's unspoken. It's about the mystery you find when one parent is gone, and maybe Molly is not gone, but Sarah is discovering mysteries. My parents got a 16-millimeter camera when my brother was born and so, of course, they took home movies. And my brother put together a little video of those home movies and the most fascinating thing is . . . home movies are, in a sense, the opposite of life. They're the simple moments of these short reels at the party. Or Fourth of July. Christmas. And when there was blackness, when there was a piece of black between the shots, that's when my life really happened.

So this blackness between the home movie idea would be when Sarah's father died. This is when their house burned down. This is when they all got sick. They didn't have home movies of these moments. Home movies are such a small part of what the relationship might be between Molly and Sarah. And finding goals for each of them that not only don't match, but goals that collide, which I think is the stuff of sitcom. You have mother and daughter stories in which the mother and the daughter are criminals. And they're cons. And they work together as cons, and then

Charlie talks at length about what is missing from the inexperienced writer's work: conflict. Life is the opposite of drama. In life, we are always trying to avoid conflict, whereas the writer's job is to create it. One device that can heighten a scene is borrowed from Charlie's background in theatre. A *third object* is used when the conflict between two characters is flat. Charlie likes to bring in another person or thing.

Charlie uses an example from Jean Cocteau's classic 1946 film, *Beauty and the Beast.* Out walking after their first dinner together, just as Belle is beginning to think that the Beast may not be such a bad guy, they see a deer. The deer is the third object. She notices its loveliness, while the Beast sees supper. The audience understands, without having to be told why this relationship is already in trouble. The animal's presence in the scene, along with the Beast's gnarling and drooling, externalizes the conflict without having the characters tell each other, or the audience, some necessary information or explain their feelings in "soap opera" fashion.

of course something happens where one of them falls in love with somebody. And they can't do it. That could work.

You can—if you have two characters like this, a mother and a daughter—bring in what I call the third object. If you can't find a clash between the two characters in a scene, there is the third element or the third character. The best example is in [Jean] Cocteau's *Beauty and the Beast*. I remember seeing this as a kid. It's their first dinner together and they're at this long table. He's at one end and she's at the other end. She's kind of like, "Well, he's not such a bad guy. He's a beast, but he's very gracious and actually quite wonderful." And at the end of the meal they go for a walk on his property. And suddenly they're walking and they're talking and he points and there's this beautiful fawn grazing in the field. And they do this two-shot of the two people. And they don't see each other. Only you see them. And she looks and she goes, "Oh." And he looks and he gnarls his teeth and the drool comes down. That's the third object, the deer. That tells you exactly why this marriage is not going to be great.

Without the third object, there is no movie. Often in a seemingly emotional or a comic thing, the third object is very clear. I call it the third object because if there is only one character and an object, you need someone to bounce off one's feelings to another during the movie. It saves you from writing voiceover. But finding a third object in a situation like this—the mother and daughter could be quite happy together. To make it a little edgy, in walks a guy they both find attractive, like *Lolita*, which is my favorite book.

Back to the notion of the high concept. I could see people pitching *Lolita* today. But it's like . . . it's actually quite tragic. Obviously, it's about the middle-aged guy and the young girl. But I mean, she [Lolita] dies in childbirth and it's very, very sad. But that's an example of a mother and a daughter. The daughter doesn't kill the mother, but in certain ways she sort of drives her to the madness of this car crash. So you can find that third element. I guess taking what we said earlier, the third element should be the least comfortable thing to deal with. It's the thing that causes the most conflict.

PD: So one way to really make this dark is your choice of the third object?

CP: I think so. It could be this attractive person coming between Molly and Sarah. Whatever creates jealousy. Movies are about people being less than good. There aren't many movies about Mother Teresa.

"I said, 'What's the difference between a device and a trick?' He said, 'A device is a trick that works.'"

PD: Do you think, "I've got this sort of dial. How dark do I want this conflict to be?"

CP: Generally, I do that within scenes. What ratchets up the tension? I had a scene last night in which a guy is dealing with the woman who was his son's teacher. It was kind of okay, but I needed a call from somebody outside the scene to call the guy and tell him really bad news. To get into a conflict with him. Which hopefully ratcheted up the whole thing. I mean, there are devices or tricks that are pretty obvious to the audience. Which reminds me of what Brian Friel [famous Irish playwright] once told me. I went to school in England as a kid and I spent some time in Ireland. And he was talking. He said, "Make sure it is a device and not a trick." "Well," I said, "What's the difference between a device and a trick?" He said, "A device is a trick that works."

JD: Do you always know where your ending is?

CP: Most of the time, I know the ending before I know much of anything else. People talk about characters driving their stuff. I think that's true, but I think characters are essentially plot anyway. What are you but what you do? I think it was Graham Greene who said, "Plot is character and character is plot.'" 'Cause you've only got so many pages before you've got to get there.

"My director's cut would be eleven minutes."

JD: What do your second, third, and fourth drafts look like?

CP: I just go through and say, "This is terrible." I'm very, very easily bored. I'm sorry, what's your name? When I directed my own movies, it was depressing. Writer/directors are notorious. They love everything. My director's cut would be eleven minutes. I go, "Oh my God, I'm dying here. Cut this. Cut this. Cut this." Literally, if it was more than ninety-two minutes, I mean, it was just shocking. I hired famous actors to do specific scenes, then I had to call them up and say I cut it out of the movie. I think a lot of that had to do with the fact that I'm not a good director. I'm the only person in Hollywood who says I can't direct a movie. I mean, I've seen the movies, so I can admit it. It's really interesting about directors. I've met a lot of them and I've worked with amazing directors. I've worked with Robert Mulligan and Bruce Beresford and Stanley Donen and, you know, I've worked with some of the greatest directors in the last half of the twentieth century. And they're really boring a lot. And I mean this in the sense that, who else can put up with spending an entire day filming a car driving up to a door? I just wanted to throw myself in front of the car.

Maybe I have some sort of ADD, but it just drove me nuts. I just didn't have the patience, which is why I think digital filmmaking is probably a good thing for someone like me. You don't have to light it for nineteen hours. What I always compare film writing to—well, not my writing in terms of quality—but the sonnet, the Shakespearean sonnet. Arguably, the Shakespearean sonnet is the greatest love poetry of all time. And it is also the most formulaic. You have love, which is so huge; it is almost an indefinable thing. But if you put it in fourteen lines, you give it a power. If you let it go all over the place, it loses its power. And the form of the movie or the television situation comedy, which is great, is that it is compressed to a form, which is why I think, very often, the worst cuts of movies are the director's cuts. When they're forced to confine themselves to a certain amount of time, they're much better. They don't believe that, of course. The cut of a movie shown on airplanes, the clean version, is almost inevitably a better performance than the four-letter version. It is really shocking, when you watch an actor, because they've done it, they know the emotion, but they're confined by their language. It is almost always a better performance.

Yeah, but then you have the outline. Some people go, "Oh, it's all so formulaic." But that's my point. Within the formula, you're free to be. You know, it's like why my house is so spare. Because there's so much that's not spare in the other part of my life. So, you know, spareness on spareness is like frosting on frosting. You've gotta have the cake, somewhere in there.

"The problem with writing a screenplay that's funny is that it has to be funny to the executives."

JD: After you've written a couple of drafts, are you able to tell if it's funny, or do you have to go to someone else?

CP: The problem with writing a screenplay that's funny is that it has to be funny to the executives. I used, for the first ten years, the same twenty-five jokes in the first thirty pages of the screenplay to get them to know it was a comedy. Those jokes never made it into a movie. If they made it into a movie, well, then I couldn't use them again. Well, actually, I could a few years later. But you have to tell the guys it is funny, because very often what's funny in the screenplay is not funny in the movie. The difference between a screenplay and a movie is such a huge difference. And the ability of those in the business to make that jump is virtually nonexistent anymore.

PD: What if somebody says to you, "Punch it up"?

CP: Well, they don't say that to me anymore. They used to. I don't want to do that work anymore. The last thing I did was a romantic comedy at Warner Brothers. It was a very good premise. A sort of a Cinderella story. We had a good producer on it. I did probably one of the best romantic comedies I've done because it was a good premise. And Warner Brothers just didn't make it. But they gave the project to an actor who said he wanted to make it funnier. The problem is that what they see as making it funny isn't just making it funny. You do have to change things structurally because comedy in good, successful movies comes out of the structure. And so you have to create scenes in which those third elements, those conflicts, those obstacles are heightened. That's what makes it funny.

It was a classic situation. Two twins. Girls. Very competitive. There was a scene in the movie. It was the bait scene, basically, where I thought it would get the actor interested, and it did. I got an actress, but I got the wrong actress. It's a twin movie, and so what happens is at one point each twin has to pretend to be the other one, and they meet at the same restaurant since they're both in love with the same guy at the same table. But they're both being the other person. So they're essentially playing four roles. So I did that and the executive said, "Oh, wow, that's really original. I'm glad we paid you, and now we'll pay you some more to come up with more stuff. You come up with stuff that sort of kicks it in." But I'm not, like, a gag man. I've been to those tables where fifteen people sit around and they show the script right there on the wall and the director sits there with the assistant and people just start throwing, spitballing ideas.

I did it for the movie *Snow Dogs*. There were a lot of TV writers in the room. They were fun. They were cool guys. But I stopped because I said this was the film moment. Because they were just going on about the gags and I said, "No." They built

There have been many changes in the movie industry since Charlie started in the early 1980s, many of which he laments. The business has become more and more corporatized. Charlie refers to directors, producers, and stars as *elements*. They were necessary to interest a studio in making the movie. Today there is only one necessary element— the star. Because of this, he's had to write what he calls a *bait scene* into every script. A bait scene is designed to show off the star actor's talents. It's worth studying the example Charlie gives from the Disney twins movie he worked on.

The bait scene is not a new concept. When we interviewed Edmund Hartmann in the first incarnation of this book, he told us the requirements for writing an Abbott and Costello movie. The writer was given one of their classic burlesque routines, like *Slowly I Turned* or *Who's on First?*, and they had to write the movie around it.

up this one moment and the producer said that was what they paid me for, just to show some sort of sense of what the story was about. And they cut it out of the movie anyway.

"I was twelve years old and I was writing advice for young women."

JD: How did you end up in the arts?

CP: My mother was sort of a journalist and I used to ghostwrite for her sometimes. She had several jobs after my father died. So I would help her, and we were paid three cents a word. So it's odd that I was introduced to writing as a job and only later, when I became a boring, self-absorbed adolescent, that it occurred to me that it was artistic. It is usually the other way around. It is usually, "Well, this is my love. Poetry. Poetry is what I want to write." And then finally, Dad says, "Who's going to pay the rent?" But it literally was three cents a word. My mother would write a story and send it in to the editor, and it would come back with red pencil marks through words. This meant there was three cents less for everything we needed. So we had to learn to write. She wrote some wacky stuff. She wrote an advice column for teenagers, which I ghosted for her sometimes. I was twelve years old and I was writing advice for young women. Now there's a story. Molly could be a famous columnist and she's starting to get early senility and Sarah has to take over.

But the other thing is, I went to school in England when I was a kid, and I just got involved with the theatre over there. The way they teach it, it's more like a subject. It's not like an after-school club to sort of keep kids from doing crime or jerking off. In fact, theatre is probably a way to make them jerk off even more. But it was really funny. It was just one of those things where you had just one teacher who was a catalyst and several of my roommates and classmates became really famous. I mean world-famous: Charles Sturridge, who directed *Brideshead Revisited;* Edward Duke, an actor who did the P.G. Wodehouse shows. There were about ten of us, and we're all sort of in theatre and film. And I just always liked to tell stories. I was always a liar.

PD: You said you had done some acting?

CP: I did acting when I was in England as a kid—in school, when we took shows on the road. I was very dark when I was young, and I was kind of odd. I was a foreigner. I was American. There weren't any other Americans at this school. So I milked it.

And then as I got older, I realized that people were getting just as dark and as angry as I was. And then I did a couple of shows professionally, which was really boring. I mean, saying the same lines over and over, night after night. I mean, no offense to actors, I think they're extraordinary, but I just couldn't.

"I actually have the power of someone laughing at me when I'm having sex."

PD: Have you ever done any stand-up?

CP: I did a little bit of stand-up, because I wrote a play about a stand-up comedian, so I tried some stand-up. And then the actor who was the lead in the play dropped out, so I had to do the play. Even though it was a play, we sort of did stand-up every night. It's very interesting, there's no fourth wall; it's the most brutal thing. It's also like the most successful thing. I mean, I'm not a comic, but comics will tell you it's better than sex or drugs. When you actually have the power of someone laughing at you. I actually have the power of someone laughing at me when I'm having sex. No, I wasn't going to be a stand-up comic. I wasn't good enough. I mean, I really wasn't. I at least had the structure of a play to fall back on. I did work on a script with Robin Williams and went around with him to clubs in San Francisco. So I got to see it really from the top level.

PD: Did that experience influence your writing?

CP: I guess every experience influences your writing. My stuff is more situational in the sense that it's sort of like an uncomfortable comedy. Sometimes in movies, comedies really don't get that much laughter. I remember going to see *Working Girl*, which was directed by Mike Nichols and was quite a brilliant comedy, and the audience laughed once during that movie. They laughed when one of the executives says, "Let's have some coffee." And the main character is a secretary pretending to be an executive and she says, "I'll get it." It wasn't even a particularly funny moment, but the audience was given a *cookie line*. In a cookie line, you keep all the tension going, and then at the end of the scene, or somewhere in the scene, you have to burst it. You ask people coming out of the movie, was that funny? "Oh, God, that was the damn funniest movie." But there wasn't a lot of laughter in it.

JD: You've probably written yourself into corners. What do you do when that happens?

CP: I usually just keep going. I just finish it. I have, you know, dozens and dozens of scripts on the bookshelf and the bottom drawer.

JD: That's what's so hateful about you. You're so prolific. How many scripts do you work on simultaneously?

CP: Well, I've worked on as many as two or three at the same time. Right now, I'm just doing one, but I've got two or three in my mind. I've realized that I have really good plots. A lot of my friends who write books say they're jealous of me because I have so many plots. And they have so much they want to say. You know, character and emotion and all this, but I have to distill the emotion into moments. And they can go on for pages and pages, so I hope that when I'm tapped out in film writing, I might try to write something a little longer in prose.

"Most people say they don't walk their dog enough. I walk mine fifteen, twenty times a day. I have a very short attention span."

PD: Do you always write alone or do you work with partners?

CP: I tried working with someone once. I just can't do it. I have a very bad attention span. I work for very short periods of time. I mean, no more than twenty minutes at a time. That's where the dog comes in handy. Most people say they don't walk their dog enough. I walk mine fifteen, twenty times a day. I have a very short attention span. I write in short periods of time. I write no more than a couple of hours a day. I mean, but it gets done.

PD: Does your attention span differ when you're editing?

CP: Yeah, when I'm editing it's actually a lot easier to stay with it because it's all there. I can sit in front of the screen and spend a half an hour editing, and I look up and it's three-and-a-half hours later. But it's a little indulgent. People spend hours and months and years changing things, and it's irrelevant to the reader unless you change something in a movie that is, you know, dramatic. *He dies. She kills him.* To change a line here, a location there? It's all a little bit . . . it's all indulgence.

JD: But that goes with your view that movies are more event-driven than character-driven.

CP: Yeah, exactly. To really change something is to change the event.

> ## "Having been brought up on three cents a word, you can't exactly sit around and wait for inspiration."

JD: What do you do when you aren't feeling inspired?

CP: Having been brought up on three cents a word, you can't exactly sit around and wait for inspiration. As Samuel Johnson said, "Anyone who writes for any other reason other than money is insane."

JD: Who mentored you?

CP: I had some really great teachers. They weren't writers, they just let me do what I wanted to do. I think part of my mentoring was really just from . . . I mean, I am a voracious reader and seer of movies. I'm always going to movies. It's actually depressing to read so much, because there's just so much better out there than the nonsense that I do. You know, which is fine. I make so much more money than they do. No, I could buy and sell those schmucks.

PD: When you go to the movies, are you analytic?

CP: No, not at all. When I go to movies, I am the best audience. I know this director who doesn't like any movies. I always go, "Oh, you've got to see *Capote,* oh, it's great." And he'll say, "Oh, I hated it." "See this?" "Oh, I hated it." It's like, there are so many people who make movies who don't like movies. I really like movies. Except for really, really bad movies. They all amuse me. And I see everything. I mean, with video, how can you not? When I see a movie, I really want to be seduced. So you really have to see it a couple of times to really study it.

PD: It sounds like some of your mentors were flesh and blood and some were celluloid and paper.

CP: Oh, yeah, yeah, some of them were flesh and blood.

PD: And that you look at stuff and say, "Wow, I like how he did that. I can use that."

> ## "I think the hardest thing about teaching is being just as good with the students who you aren't impressed by as you are with students you are impressed by."

CP: Yeah, what I usually say is, "I can steal it." I think I learn somewhat subconsciously from watching what I like. I like a certain kind of British humor. I think that's because I came into my adulthood in Britain.

PD: Did you enjoy teaching?

CP: I did enjoy teaching. I think the hardest thing about teaching is being just as good with the students who you aren't impressed by as you are with students you are impressed by. As with my stuff, I get bored very easily. I did a graduate screenwriting course at USC. They actually came to my house and had dinner. Five or six people. Once a week. And the first year I did it, I had this hugely successful movie come out of my class, which was the second-biggest movie of the following year, *The Hand That Rocks the Cradle*. After that, everyone in the United States wanted to be in my screenwriting class. But it wasn't me.

"He gives me his scripts to read, and I tell him to get out of the business."

JD: Who did you mentor?

CP: Amanda Silver, the writer of *The Hand That Rocks the Cradle*. She came up with the idea of the notion and originally the villainess was simply a woman who took the husband, came in as the maid, and took the husband away from the woman. But during the class, which lasted a year, Amanda became pregnant. Not during—she didn't get pregnant in the class. She was married. And she became pregnant. And her focus shifted, and she changed it to the baby and the hand that rocks the cradle thingy. And reading the first draft . . . there was one of those film moments, when it comes together, and you're like, "Oh, my God, you're going to sell this for a million dollars." So I gave it to Robert Cord and Interscope when he was doing a string of amazingly successful movies, and that was one of his most successful. She would have been successful anyway. A close friend's son is at USC now. I kind of mentor him. He gives me his scripts to read and I tell him to get out of the business.

I do find that I'm steering people towards television more. Because I think cable television is the most interesting medium that there is now. Network TV is what it is. Feature films? I just don't see the chance of most people getting in there. The likelihood of winning the lottery is . . . you have to believe you can, but . . . yeah, but getting it done? I'd even work on network television, because you're in a room and you're writing and you see your stuff the next week. I have films I've been working on for eleven years, and I'm probably still not going to see them get made. You ask how you know when something is funny. Well, you learn by seeing your stuff done. And if you're a comic film writer, it's hard. And then by the time it's done . . . well, it's like learning archery by shooting the arrow and then going to Europe for six months and then coming back and seeing where it landed. You aren't going to become much better at archery.

". . . it's like learning archery by shooting the arrow and then going to Europe for six months and then coming back and seeing where it landed."

That's why I would love to do something on TV. But something that takes a little bit more time, like HBO or Showtime or, you know, the countless cable outlets. Oxygen and FX. American Movie Classics [AMC] is starting to create its own shows. A friend of mine just made a huge deal with Turner Network [TNT] to get away from Westerns and start doing really intelligent drama-driven TV shows. It's fun because it's getting done. Most of my feature friends are just like me. We're sitting around writing, getting paid, and nothing's getting done. If I get a job this year, rewriting something or writing something for a studio, it won't get done, it just won't. [Since 2005, Charlie's screenplay *My One and Only*, starring Renée Zellweger, has gone into production. It was released to theatres in 2009.]

There are some great stories. They're getting deluged with stories. That's why I tell these kids, "Think TV." All of them go, initially, "Oh, television. I don't want to do television." But they all come back to it. Because their friends who graduated a few years ago, none of them are selling anything. There's a large industry of developing movies for studios. I get a lot of those jobs, but I am quite aware that they will never make them. Because the producer has to develop a certain amount of projects to justify her discretionary fund and her salary. It's alright. It's like I said, it's not the way I generally work, or most people. If they were on TV with a table full of writers, the producer might come in and say, "Okay, Joe's going to do this week's show." But that's the fun.

I'm so jealous of the kids today. Growing up, I only saw what movies were in the movie theatres. There was a place in New York where you could go and see old [François] Truffaut movies. But I mean, every movie ever made is virtually on DVD now.

An Interview with
Heide Perlman

A partial list of Heide Perlman's credits as a creator, show runner, and writer includes: *Frasier, Cheers, The Tracey Ullman Show, Stacked,* and *Sibs.*

A warm and open person, **Heide Perlman** nevertheless embodies what we'd describe as a sweet cynicism about television. It's a love/hate relationship. Heide says that too often, situation comedies try to cram "happy" stories into half-hour, neatly wrapped packages. For the most part, network television is afraid of the meaner side of life. She suggests that not every character has to be likable. She points out that by broadening a situation, by using parody and satire, skills developed as a writer on *The Tracey Ull-man Show,* life's absurdities are revealed.

Heide Perlman trusts that great comedy can stem from deep-rooted scars left by unresolved relationships between people who are related but may not necessarily love each other.

We think it's interesting to compare Leonard Stern's interview (see page 361) with Heide's. In a way, they are opposite sides of the same coin. Leonard makes conflict that springs from love. You will see that there are as many ways of looking at character and conflict as there are writers, and where their work springs from.

PD (Peter Desberg): As we've explained in our Premise [see page 9], how would you go about developing the show's plot lines?

HP (Heide Perlman): Okay, I would make it that the daughter and the mom's relationship was never good and the daughter is, in fact, extremely jealous of her mother. What I would do, I'm sure, would never sell.

All the sympathetic relationships are so sickening, so I would have it that Sarah, to spite her mother, has made something of herself, and she's focused. And Molly has always undermined her in backhanded ways. So now the dad's dead. The dad was really the only constant real connection in the family because Sarah and her mom, from Sarah's perspective, never got along. Although Molly may not be aware of this. Molly sees herself as the good mother. And she's an extremely self-centered person who took the gravy train by marrying the wealthy guy and never had to work, or was like a lot of other women, kind of the hostess.

Okay, so now Molly finds out she doesn't have any money. Her parents aren't going to give her any because she somehow burned her bridges with them, so she needs her daughter. Her daughter is only compelled by guilt to take her mother in and she can't actually refuse her. And she takes her in, even though it's at great emotional expense, but her mother is totally unaware of this. Molly thinks that she's "to the manor born." She's more like, "Of course this is going to be great."

So I guess the arc of the series would be to have their relationship be more of a real, honest relationship than it has been. Yeah, I'd like it to be more torturous than anything else. With the mother/daughter thing, it's really hard for a mother to change her role. Maybe when the grandparents are starting to go mentally, and that's kind of changed them a bit, so that could actually be good for Molly. If her parents were really uptight and disapproved of her, now—like, I find my mother has mellowed a bit. She's just not as feisty as she was. So there's something perverse—something about Molly celebrating that her mom, Sarah's grandmother, is losing her mind.

I once saw a documentary about this daughter and her mother, who had Alzheimer's. The mother had always been the kind of character who was very contained. The Alzheimer's, in a way, made her go back to her youth. The daughter saw parts of her that she never saw before. She would sing, for example, and she never did that before. So in a way, the Alzheimer's enabled her to have fun, like the kind of fun that she repressed and contained her whole life. For the daughter, it was a revelation. But that would be the nice side of it. What if it was Sarah instead, seeing it in Molly? Not the grandparents. What if Sarah saw ways to take advantage of her mother as her mind is going? And at the same time, she sees things in her she never saw before. You could have that moment. I'm just not in the mood for nice moments.

I guess you could have situations, like, Molly finds some guy to hook up with and is obviously going to exploit him. And she should really still have all her stuff. Although she starts worrying about her age, she's still good, and knows how to work it. Rather than being, "Oh, I've been protected by this man my whole life and now he's gone, and what am I going to do, I don't know how to get out there in the world," she has all those qualities that can make her survive, because she's so self-centered.

PD: She's also really calculating.

HP: Sarah's kind of torn between getting rid of the mom, 'cause she went off with this rich guy, and she's going to take him for a ride, that kind of thing. And obviously, it could be someone that she works with, to make it more complicated and sitcom-y.

JD (Jeffrey Davis): If you had your way, would you just dump Sarah and make it about the grandmother and Molly? Sarah doesn't seem to interest you that much.

HP: Well, I am interested in Molly's relationship with her mom. I'm interested in that perspective of the daughter, who's a little bit in the *Ab Fab* [the British sitcom *Absolutely Fabulous*, which was the basis for the American sitcom *Cybill*] mold where it's just totally frustrating for the daughter. But I wouldn't . . . I don't know if . . . obviously, they tried to make that character as nerdy as possible. The grandmother was really ditsy. I think you need the younger character. It would be the total frustration, right? That would be the frustration of the child, the daughter, who in her own world is okay. She's an autonomous person, but when her mom is there, her mom pinches her butt . . . unconsciously, to such an extent that she just reverts to all of her childhood behaviors. I think that could be funny.

JD: Can you think of something that makes you revert?

HP: My mother has a habit of saying, "Right?" after a statement, forcing you to agree with her even if you don't. "Oh, you love tuna fish, right?" "No, I don't." "Yeah, you love it, right?" And then even if you try to move on, if you don't say, "Yeah," it's like, "Whatever." "Right? Right?" Like just forcing the issue, and you're thinking, "What does it matter if I say 'right'?" I know I don't like tuna fish, but it's just like . . . the fact of being forced into agreement is frustrating.

JD: That could be an interesting conflict.

PD: Network-based sitcoms have a lot of rules and structure, is it much easier writing for cable?

HP: Yeah? You'd be surprised. First of all, the cable outlets are very, very specific as to what they want, and they all say, "If it can be done on network, we don't want it." But then, that's not necessarily true, because every character has to be sympathetic down to their core, really, and they have to really love each other after all. I guess people get upset if they feel like people really don't like each other. *Seinfeld* was none of that. Okay, *Curb Your Enthusiasm* is a good example of the funny sitcom that has the improv aspect, even though it could be written. It basically is written by Larry David. I think that's a good example of what could be done. Okay, a show like *The Office*, I don't think it would've been made without the British version. I think there's British versions of shows that kind of give permission for the American version to be made.

If the network has deemed that it worked somewhere else, then it's okay. But if someone comes in and pitches that, it's like, "No, no, no, that's way too dark," or, "We'll never like that character." And then it turned out, no one cared.

PD: You made the Molly character unsympathetic at this point. She's opportunistic and calculating.

"You're still having to learn a lesson from a sitcom that's twenty-one minutes, and four acts, and the credits over the last moments of the show?"

HP: To me, as a writer, who's written so many of these shows, and been in so many Rooms where someone asks, "Well, what's the takeaway from this?" You're still having to learn a lesson from a sitcom that's twenty-one minutes, and four acts, and the credits over the last moments of the show? It's insane. How can you feel that this is any kind of reality when, like, the last moment of the show is this print running over it . . . things popping up in the corner, "Hey, we're the crazy guys from the next show!"

PD: Does Molly have any sort of maternal instincts? It's that, since Sarah seems to have relationship problems, Molly is skilled, does she manipulate that problem, or does she . . . ?

HP: . . . you mean, like help her out?

PD: Does she actually do something for her daughter, or does she say, "How can I use this?"

HP: I think Molly would feel like, how can Sarah be so inept? Like, anything she teaches her would have to go . . . she would teach her the hard way. You know, when she's like, "Oh, my darling daughter, let me help you. This is how you get a man. Here, dear, put on this wig." As long as it was something that hurt her daughter's feelings. And you can make her daughter overly sensitive to that kind of stuff, because she's traumatized.

PD: Can you make up an example where that would happen?

HP: Molly would say, "You're going to wear that?" I'm now thinking of the funny thing, so she would dress her, and she'd look horrible; it would be not Sarah anymore. It would be not the daughter. And the mom would kind of be forcing her to go out like that, and it wouldn't work with her. And then she would have to change outside. Like whatever she does makes it even worse. The mom, in helping her, screws things up worse for her.

PD: So Molly would actually be frustrated by the fact that her daughter was inept.

HP: Yeah! "You had the best teacher in the world growing up, and you didn't even take notes." "You went away, no wonder you're in the state you are. You don't have to have a job." The daughter comes home complaining about her work and how hard it is: "You don't have to have a job. You can use your resources, get way more money than you're making now." Maybe the mom doesn't really understand that kind of self-worth.

PD: When Sarah says, "That's not the way I'm doing my life, I've got plans and ambitions," how does Molly react to her?

HP: Well, she would think that's ridiculous. "Fine, live your stupid way!" I think every daughter wants to throttle her mom, even the ones with the good relationships. I don't know, there's something very special about that relationship in terms of frustration.

JD: I liked what you were setting up with the three generations, using the grand-mother, who is just diagnosed with Alzheimer's, and Molly enjoying the fact that she can manipulate both of them. What is the arc of the series for the three of them?

HP: Well, obviously, if the grandmother has Alzheimer's, it's not going to be funny. My mother's sister has Alzheimer's. When we talk on the phone, she sounds fine. You can talk about stuff in the past. Then it's like, "So, did your sister have Thanks-giving at her house?" "Yeah, everyone was there, blah, blah, blah," and then it's like, "So, where was Thanksgiving?" It's hard to make that funny.

JD: During your time on *Frasier*, there were always these dark and light moments. Just the whole fact of the father living with the son was done differently. This guy that never understood his son.

HP: That's true. And it's also true that the cast, who were really wonderful actors and people, they had been together so long that toward the end, they didn't want as much conflict as they had in the past. They would say things like, "But they love each other . . ."

JD: Worst thing you can say to a writer is, "We don't want conflict."

HP: Yeah. The whole thing is bizarre. When you conceive something, just from a writing point of view, it changes completely once they're an actor, because they have all their stuff. Whenever an actress would play the Molly part, she might not want to be . . .

PD: . . . quite that unsympathetic.

HP: Yeah, yeah. People can't help that. A writer is a puppet master. You can get out all your hate and all your bad thoughts, and your manipulations: This is how I would get back at my mother! I'm going to put every bad trait of every person I've ever met and had to deal with into this character, but you know, that actress won't do this unless she's British.

"In my experience it is harder to get actors to do some of the meaner things."

That's true, yeah. I keep coming back to *Ab Fab* because that's the basic self-centered mom with the frustrated daughter, but yeah, just that she was such a buffoon, that she was so pathetic. And that's another example of the writer playing the unsympathetic part. So maybe that's what you need. You need a bunch of Larry Davids being willing to be the unsympathetic character that people relate to—relate to, and like to laugh at and enjoy. In my experience, it is harder to get actors to do some of the meaner things.

In this show I did, *Sibs,* it was about three sisters and they were going to see their dead mother, who they feared and hated. So I wanted it to be the scene from *The Wizard of Oz,* where they were walking down the hall to see Oz, and they were really scared, you know that scene? They were walking really slowly, and then at the end of the scene, the lion runs out and jumps through the window? I wanted to do that scene. Because I thought . . . it's broad, it's very broad . . . to have someone knock on your door . . . it was like, they're walking down the hallway in the apartment building, they knock on the door. The stepmother opens it, and one of the sisters runs down the hall and dives through a window. And the actress didn't want to do it because she couldn't motivate that cartoon of an action, where she would actually dive through a window.

JD: They ended up not doing it?

HP: Well, she did it, but it was a big fight and of course it didn't come out exactly how I wanted it because I wanted it . . . knock on the door, door opens—it was actually Tracey Ullman who was playing the stepmother, in makeup—and I wanted that like, [*Heide screams*] run and jump through the window.

JD: Would you add any of that cartoon-y element to this Premise?

HP: Probably, but that's the kind of thing where when you get down to it . . . like in Rooms, I tend to pitch the most cartoon-y ideas just because it's hard for me at this point to think of these shows as reality. Because once you've done a lot of them, you have to play with it to stay interested.

"... I tend to pitch the most cartoon-y ideas just because it's hard for me at this point to think of these shows as reality."

JD: So that'll be your way of staying interested?

HP: Yeah, because I find it amusing.

PD: You keep things moving by introducing conflict right away.

HP: I'd be interested to hear some of the other takes on this Premise. Does anyone have a really mushy take on it?

PD: Leonard Stern had a really interesting idea. He said, "I don't like mean comedy," and what he came down to is he said he likes to create conflict by having two people that care about each other, and through their acts of caring, get in each other's face, frustrate them, and so it's a comedy of good intentions gone really, really wrong.

HP: Wow. There are a lot of people who say, "Oh, TV's so mean." And actually, I guess I don't feel like a lot of people. I don't see TV being that funny. What's funny on TV now?

JD: *The Tracey Ullman Show,* which you were an important part of, had a cartoon-ish element, but it took risks.

HP: Yeah.

PD: If you take what you started here and said, "Okay, I've got no constraints, I can make it as dark as I want, as intense as I want," where would you go with it?

HP: I still like the small story. I think that the stuff I said would be just like what it was made out of. It's like the daily hell of everybody's lives that I find interesting. Basically like being stuck in [the Jean-Paul Sartre play] *No Exit.* It's just things don't really change that much, especially in familial relationships. And I think that was like the great thing about *Everybody Loves Raymond.* That it was exactly the same every time.

"It's like the daily hell of everybody's lives that I find interesting."

JD: And no "B" stories, ever.

HP: Yeah, well, who needs a "B" story? I know that networks and studios still want you to do "B" stories, or even three stories. Three ten-minute stories. Yeah. Take a show like *Green Acres.* It's just a cartoon, but that show was great. I saw one recently where everyone in the town was on the party line. It was just hysterical because it was so lame. I like that lameness that's funny.

JD: Heide, you're the one who did the most thorough development using all three generations in the Premise.

HP: Yeah, well, you could do that kind of cross-ages thing that the networks accept, but ultimately, it has to be about the young people. I don't want to do that to this story.

PD: A number of writers started by saying, "These days, if I can't produce or direct, I don't want to be part of the writing team anymore. I want some control. I'm tired of having my stuff just shredded and twisted."

". . . if it's not yours, you're not getting your heart ripped out."

HP: I agree with that, except there's so many outside forces that you're going to have your stuff shredded and twisted. I'm kind of feeling that way right now . . . sitting in that Room and doing stuff that just seems false and ridiculous. It's not appealing, but in a way, if it's not yours, you're not getting your heart ripped out.

Oh, my God, can I just tell you one experience? I did this pilot years ago. It was a mother/daughter, but like a mother and a four-year-old. And it had a scene where the mother is trying to go out, and the four-year-old is like, "Mommy, don't go, don't go," like four-year-olds do, "Don't leave me," and she throws a fit, and then as soon as she goes, [the daughter is] fine! The babysitter says, "You can have ice cream, whatever you want." And then as soon as her mom walks out the door, she says, "So, can I have the ice cream?" So we got the kid to cry and even though that was the scene where you know the kid's fine, and it's on film, the executives said, "You have to take this scene out. It's too sad. We won't show the pilot unless you take this out." And I did. I took it out. And the pilot, I'm not saying it was only because of this, there were a lot of other problems with the pilot. But that was really a knife in my heart.

"The changes you make that hurt you usually turn out to hurt the whole project, anyway."

... I was just trying to do something that was real, that happens to people every day and that I think every family, every mother can relate to, having a little kid . . . it's just common. It's just like every little kid using emotional blackmail, and then they're fine. Yeah, it's like, move on. It just kills you. I shouldn't have done it. The changes you make that hurt you usually turn out to hurt the whole project, anyway. So you might as well just die. You might as well say, "No, this is how I want it," and they'll say, "Okay, f–ck you, go away anyway," and then at least you have your dignity. But there's really little dignity right now.

JD: Jerry Belson [Emmy Award-winning writer and director] was your mentor.

"He always said on his gravestone would be written, 'I did it their way.'"

HP: My first job was *Cheers,* and he did one day a week. And I saw immediately that this guy is different. You know, he was always a curmudgeon, but had the most original mind. Just funny, funny, funny. And the things that he would say, that everyone would laugh at, would go in the script, but usually only worked if he said it. And sometimes they were just so outside, like he pitched this joke for Coach, where Coach goes into Sam's office saying, "There's a small, black man asking for you," and then

---

There's an old saying: "Experience is a lousy teacher . . . it gives the exams before the lessons." Heide says that if she had the experience of *Sibs* to do over again, she would have followed her instincts and not conceded. Elliot Shoenman (see page 317) tells a story about an episode of *Home Improvement* they wrote about a cancer scare. He got Tim Allen to champion it and the network backed down and let them shoot and air it. It got huge ratings, and the network asked for more "disease" episodes. Bob Myer (see page 141) talks about how *Roseanne* wanted to do an episode where her character contemplated an abortion. It also received strong ratings.

he says, "Oh, wait, it's the phone." Talk about bizarre. He always said on his grave-stone would be written, "I did it their way."

JD: Did he encourage you?

HP: Yes, he really did. He always recommended me for jobs, different kinds of things, a rewrite thing, or this or that. He had a good, good heart, even though he could be really biting, but such a good person.

JD: He had a very dark sense of humor.

HP: Very, very dark.

PD: How did you get into this? You didn't major in comedy writing.

HP: Nepotism! When my sister [actress Rhea Perlman] moved out here, I was kind of just doing this and that.

PD: Did you always write, even as a kid? Were you a good writer?

HP: Yes, I won the literary award in high school.

PD: You had a feel for the language? You had a sense of how to structure things?

HP: I always wanted to be a writer. When I dropped out of college, I went off to be a writer, but of course that didn't work out.

PD: What kind of writer were you trying to be?

HP: Oh, something very deep, like [Samuel] Beckett. By that time my sister was married, Danny [DeVito, Heide's brother-in-law] was out here doing *Taxi*. They also were trying to do their own projects, and I would just write little things to send them. That was one of the things I did to entertain myself and my friends. At one point, they said, "You could write as good as these guys out here," which I think a lot of people say to themselves. They watch something on TV and say, "I could write that." So I just came out here for a while and I read all the *Taxi* scripts because Rhea had them. And I also hung around *Taxi*, but mostly it was from reading the scripts. I learned, "Okay, here's the dumb guy, here's the selfish guy." I basically had learned sitcom from reading *Taxi*.

PD: As well as always being good at writing, you always had a good sense of humor.

HP: I don't think there's a lot of people like me anymore. Everyone now went to good schools. They know that it's a profession, that's what I mean. There's all the Harvards and the Ivy Leaguers.

PD: Did you learn sitcom writing by reading those *Taxi* scripts?

HP: Yeah, they had their own structure. They used the same basic structure on both *Taxi* and *Cheers*. *Cheers* was my first spec script, so after I read all the *Taxi*s and I hung around there and I think it was . . . I guess Len and Les Charles were developing *Cheers*. So I read that pilot they wrote. It wasn't on the air yet, but I thought, "Oh, well, I'll try this." I was relieved because maybe I could get a job. So I wrote a *Cheers* spec script and because I had my way in, I knew them, not very well. I had met Len and Les and my sister was on the show, so I gave them the spec script, and they didn't have a staff like they had later. There was only [David] Isaacs and [Ken] Levine on staff, and then they had Jerry Belson one day a week, and David Lloyd one or two days a week.

So they liked the spec in terms of how I wrote the characters. They thought I got them, so they gave me an assignment, right, which was bizarre. I had no idea of what it was at all. I wasn't like a production assistant. I never came up. I didn't work in a mailroom. I just was *there* all of a sudden. I think it was extremely helpful to me, because I probably would've sunk myself somehow if I thought, "People write spec after spec before they get a job," and all that kind of thing. So I wrote one spec and they gave me an assignment on *Cheers*. I wrote the outline and they hired me on staff from the outline because they needed stories. It was really right place, right time.

PD: The nepotism gets your script read. It doesn't get you hired.

HP: I also read the outlines that they had. They gave me a bunch of outlines, and so I thought, "Okay." They were substantial outlines, where each scene and jokes in the outline were laid out. Although they changed a lot, you put a lot in those outlines, which now you have to battle over everything, you have to go to the studio. It's insane.

Yeah, and the joke that I think they really liked was the one where Diane's cat dies and Sam takes advantage of her emotional distress to try to hook up with her. The joke I wrote in my outline that they loved, and I think got me the job, was that Carla comes up to Diane and says, "Oh, I'm so sorry about your cat. I've been through it all with the kids . . . the turtle, the fish," and Diane says, "Yeah, but cats are different," and Carla says, "Yeah, you can't flush a cat." And I think that was the joke that got me the job.

An Interview with
Phil Rosenthal

A partial list of Phil Rosenthal's credits as creator, show runner, and writer includes: *Everybody Loves Raymond, Coach, Down the Shore, Baby Talk,* and *Man in the Family.*

Only two things in this interview did not surprise us: One, that we were interviewing another comedy writer who was Jewish; and two, that **Phil Rosenthal** turned out to be as nice as many of the other writers in this book, as well as several of our friends told us he was. Co-creator of *Everybody Loves Raymond,* Phil could be called a professional nice guy. Along with all those Emmys, he has earned an industry-wide reputation for being as old-school gracious as he is creative and shrewd. It shows in the way he chose writers and managed the Writers' Room on *Raymond.* Almost everyone on the staff stayed with him throughout the nine years it was the number-one comedy on television. Even when they had lucrative offers to go to other series, they stayed. In all that time, Phil had one rule: If something didn't ring true, it didn't make it into a script.

As you watch him develop this Premise, you'll notice a deep understanding of human idiosyncrasies. Phil values believability and humanity over jokes. He makes certain his stories are universal. He does this without devices or tricks. He's as universal as he can be by being as personal as he can be.

PD (Peter Desberg): As we've explained in our Premise [see page 9], how would you go about developing the show's plot lines?

PR (Phil Rosenthal): If I was in charge, if suddenly you proved incompetent and brought me in, I'm not going to help. The first rule to everybody is, you can never win that way. But if I was to be given this rough Premise, the first thing I would do is to make Sarah a guy. That is how I approached my show. I don't know if I would have written *Everybody Loves Deborah* as well as *Raymond.* I can identify with Raymond because I feel I *am* Raymond. I know what it's like to be that guy. I don't think it hurts your Premise. It may even be more commercial. Everyone always tells me that shows with a male center sell better. It would be foolish not to address the business, yes?

I've seen the mother/daughter show before. That's another reason it's more interesting to change Sarah to Sam. We haven't seen the mother/son show, whereas there was that show that ran for years where the mother wanted to be more like a sister to her daughter. *Gilmore Girls.* I never watched it, only because I didn't relate to it. It's not for me.

What if I was suddenly in this situation? What if I had to live with my mom when maybe I'm closer with my dad and he's dead, and now what Mom wants is to be my buddy and I don't want to be buddies with my mom. I want a mom. I think it's even better making Sarah into Sam. Sam has a boss who's a woman, and he's trying to do the typical male thing and advance. And while he's trying to advance, this woman is keeping him down. I think that's a better dynamic. Ideally, I think you want a Tom Hanks-Shirley MacLaine dynamic between Sam and Molly. Of course, it could still be more different.

JD (Jeffrey Davis): What would you do to make it more different?

PR: I would make it as Jewish as possible, but call it Italian. It seems to have worked before. Write Yiddish, cast British. I would make a pilot that served this purpose. Otherwise, I would make a pilot that served this Premise. "Where do you go from here?" is the question.

This is a perfectly valid Premise here, where you see him at work, he's going for the vice president, but he has a female boss who's not going to allow it. He's not going to get the promotion, and to make his day worse, his father dies. You always want to raise the stakes, so you've done that. I made a big change here in making Sarah into Sam. So now, I think you put a funeral at the beginning where you are seeing and introducing your characters, and maybe it's a one-camera show, which seems to be in favor these days. And maybe during the father's funeral, we are doing flashbacks of Sam's relationships with his dad. And maybe forget what I said earlier about how Sam was close to him. Maybe he was an absent father, so that Sam's not devastated by the loss. To do that right away in the pilot, it's such a downer. Of course, I'm just spitballing.

Here's the thing. You don't want something that you can't recover from. "Oh, my God, he lost his beloved father, now he's depressed for the rest of the show." I think it's better if he didn't really know his father. Sam says, "I haven't seen my father in fifteen years, let alone loved him." Maybe the dad skipped out on him and Molly. Now it's the funeral and he's obligated to go. Everyone else is going. Maybe there's money, but he gets there and the bad news is, maybe there is no money. But Sam gets his mother instead. So maybe that's the act break.

Now his mom is moving in, and suddenly this is not the upwardly mobile track he thought he was on. Women are ruining it. Bubby and Zayde, the grandparents, have always been close by, and their daughter Molly is not as close with them. In fact, maybe that's the comfy distant relationship. Instead of the way you had it here where the mother and daughter had a comfortable, but distant relationship. What if it's Molly who has one with her parents? And maybe it's Sam who enjoys having the grandparents nearby and likes to check on them once in awhile. So maybe he moves them closer. Now he's at the center of a fight between his own mother and her parents. What often happens is you become the parent of your parent. Maybe that's the relationship between Sam and Molly. If you flesh that out a little bit, you see that he's between his mother and his grandparents. He identifies more with his grandparents than his own mother. Maybe she's kind of a hippie. Maybe? But absolutely, she must be a pain in his ass. That's very important.

That's kind of where I would head in the pilot, and it's what you always want to do. You head down the road until you see it doesn't work. You start writing with this in mind until somebody throws you a question. "What about this?" "Oh, I didn't think about that. You're right, that's terrible." I find in writing, you have these decisions and you make the decision and you run as if that's the best decision. You run toward it until you fall. Now you say, "Maybe that's not the best decision." That's what happens in the Room. That's what's so great about the Writers' Room. You get to have these different, hopefully brilliant heads, challenging your ideas and coming up with their ideas of what's good and what's not, and then debating it, discussing it. Many people hate the writing-by-committee approach. I only loved it because if you had bright, funny people in the Room, they only made you better. Yes, you should have a strong sense of what you think the show is.

If this was my Premise, I would be protective of it. I would have a feeling of ownership of it, but that's not to say I would be close-minded to other opinions, even from the network. A good idea can come from anywhere, even from the network or the studio. At the end of the day, they're actually people too. You want your show to come across to them, too. The people you are writing it for. They may ask a question that someone in the audience may very well ask, but if they are only coming from purely commercial terms and you smell that, you say, "I will take a look at that." And then you do what you want.

"'Do the show you want to do because in the end, they are going to cancel you anyway.'"

JD: It helps if the show is a hit, right?

PR: Even if it's not. You say, "That's very interesting. I'll take a look at that." But you must do what you want. The best advice I ever got from anybody was from Ed. Weinberger [writer/producer, *The Mary Tyler Moore Show, Cosby, Taxi*]. He said, "Do the show you want to do because in the end, they are going to cancel you anyway." You can't go to them when they are canceling your show and say, "But I took all your notes." They don't care.

PD: You started with a great conflict with the boss.

PR: In the pilot, your last scene would probably be back at work, if that's where you started. However, once we got into developing episodes, we might find the strength of this show is at home. We'd see very little at the office. Or, we might discover the strength is at the office. You don't know until you get going. I always like to use the example of *The Mary Tyler Moore Show*, where the strength of the show is at the office. As the show went on, more lives of the characters at that TV station is where the series lived. It could very easily have gone the other way, where we are only concerned with Mary in her apartment and her dating and all about how her friends at the office were going to take it and interfere.

I do believe it always tips to one side. Raymond was a sportswriter. Who cares what he did? The money was in the living room, when the parents came over and bothered him. What he did for a living, it didn't matter. We picked sportswriter in 1996 because the job of comedian was already taken by Jerry Seinfeld. That's what Ray would have been most comfortable doing, since that's who he is, but we made it sportswriter because that's a male-obsessed thing. We wanted him to be the typical male, obsessed with sports. Ray certainly wasn't the first sportswriter on TV. Oscar Madison . . . my favorite.

JD: You rarely saw Jack Klugman and Tony Randall's characters at work on *The Odd Couple*.

PR: Very rarely. Who cares?

JD: In *The Odd Couple*, you saw the relationship of those two characters. They stayed very true to the play.

PR: Very true to the play, and expanded it in a beautiful way. I think it is, to this day, the most successful adaptation of a play, to a movie, to a situation comedy show in the history of the business.

"I'm ten years old watching the show.
Gay never enters into it for me."

JD: I remember my father [Jerry Davis, producer of *The Odd Couple*] saying the network was worried about two guys living together. The show lasted five years.

PR: I'm ten years old watching the show. Gay never enters into it for me. Of course two guys live together. Why wouldn't they? They are friends. It's a perfectly reasonable premise. It was funny to me at ten. I remember thinking, "Look at that guy. He acts like the wife. Felix is bothering Oscar the way my mother bothers my father when he's late for dinner. That's funny because he's a man."

JD: Do you think it could get on now?

PR: No, because it's good. I loved it so much. I just thought they were both fantastic.

JD: If you could just throw the network out the door . . .

PR: . . . Okay, sounds good. Keep going.

JD: If there was something you always wanted to try in TV and you could put it in here, what would it be?

PR: Honestly, I would love to unashamedly make them Jewish. If that was allowed. Only because that's what I know. Not because they need to be Jewish. Last year, I pitched a show where the characters were decidedly Jewish. The wife wants to have Friday nights at home. I wasn't stupid enough to say the word "Shabbos." The wife wants Friday nights at home, and she wants to light the candles. I think that when you are true to what you know and who you are, that's when you hit other people. Take *My Big Fat Greek Wedding*. I'm not Greek, but I identified with the specifics in her life because they matched some of the specifics in my life.

PD: Where would you take this if you made the pilot?

PR: It's a tone. It's the specifics things they do. Maybe Sam's not religious and Molly is. That's funny to me. Not only is she going to impose on him by being in his apartment, she's going to impose religious rituals there that he doesn't like. Or, what if he's religious—not Molly. Switch it. Sam identifies with his grandparents, who are more religious. Maybe Orthodox. That may be interesting. Molly comes in and she's not at all a religious Jew. She's a hippie. She's still stuck in the 1960s or '70s. Sam is actually shocked she's like this. I mean, it shocks and embarrasses him.

PD: How far would you take this?

PR: The networks would be deeply afraid of Jews on TV. They are. I couldn't get a pilot shot of the show we were pitching because the characters were Jewish.

PD: What if you had the freedom to make a movie out of it?

PR: Why not? Larry David addresses it all the time. Sometimes in a really ugly way.

"We only had one rule on our show: Could this happen?"

PD: How extreme would you make it?

PR: As extreme as need be. If I found it was working that way, I would go as far as I can go with it, keeping it believable. That's the other thing. You want to keep it on planet Earth. I always find the moment you do something that is not believable, the audience won't buy it, and you've broken that covenant with them. Now they are just waiting for the next hilarious joke. You are only as good as the last joke. We only had one rule on our show: Could this happen? Not what definitely happened the way it would in real life. Just, could we believe it was plausible that it could happen?

JD: I think of the Thanksgiving episode of *Everybody Loves Raymond.*

PR: With the tofu turkey. We were experimenting with healthy alternatives because we were all getting fat on the show. You know, in sitcoms, the only sunshine coming in the Room is the menu for lunch or dinner, when you order whatever you want. You get fat. We were all talking. Tofu was discussed, so I think that's where that came from. So yes, it could happen. Somebody goes all the way with that and makes a tofu turkey.

Food is always important in a show. It's such an obsession with everybody. We do it three times a day. It's what we look forward to. It's the best break in our day sometimes. It's what we love. Look at The Food Network.

PD: It's part of every cultural ritual.

PR: Every culture. We identify. In this show we're developing, there might be an obsession with Jewish foods. Maybe Molly's parents or Sam are obsessed with it. Just like there was an obsession with Greek food in *My Big Fat Greek Wedding* or Italian food in *Raymond.*

JD: How would you work that into this show where you want to make it Jewish, but not phony—not *Abie's Irish Rose?*

PR: Maybe Sam's tie with his grandparents is, his grandmother's a wonderful cook. It was essential in *Everybody Loves Raymond.* It was essential that his wife was a terrible cook and his mother was a great cook. Why would Raymond put up with that mother? Why would he continue to live across the street from that mother? You had to give him a very damn good reason. The reason there was, nobody cooks better than her. You're willing, I think, to put up with a lot. You have this conflict. We had several episodes where that was a thing.

PD: Where are some other places in the Molly/Sam Premise you would heighten conflict?

PR: It looks like four main characters. Sam, his mother, his grandparents. We could throw in a girlfriend for him to create tension. He could get involved with his boss, this woman who won't allow him to rise in the company. Maybe he decides that the way to defeat her is to date her. That gives you two areas of conflict to play with. The office, where maybe it's a secret they're dating. And then home, where the grandparents and Molly are. Once he bridges the personal with his boss, now she can come over. Now she can come into the house.

PD: Is she Jewish?

PR: Probably not. My gut reaction is you always want an outsider.

PD: How does she react to the Jewish-ness?

PR: Do what all Gentiles do. She reports it to the authorities. She's a stranger in a strange land. It's *Bridget Loves Bernie.* Don't hold me to any of this because it's all spitballing off the top of my head. Why not? You go down the road until you can't.

PD: You jumped right in and created the conflicts and dimensionalized the characters.

PR: It's important, I think, to jump right in . . . better than if you fret, worry, and think. Why not start running and see where that goes without pressure? Let's assume your first idea stinks, and let's get that over with. Then you have something on the wall you can address. It's not nothing. You want to start from a believable, real place. You do it, hopefully, with a sense of humor, thinking of comic possibilities there.

So many things you read that couldn't happen. I don't buy it. I'm out. They are from space. I'm sorry.

". . . I don't feel I am good enough yet to write what I don't know."

PR: I get movie scripts to rewrite and I just don't like where they are going, or I don't believe it. I think it's a lack of self-confidence, if we are going to be honest. At this point, I don't feel I am good enough yet to write what I don't know. I feel to do my best work, I have to be inside the characters' heads. That doesn't mean I can't do a lot of research and get inside. So far, I really haven't had the opportunity to do that. This thing in Russia I am doing, what do I know about Russia? The documentary I'm making, about making *Everybody Loves Raymond* into a Russian TV show, is actually about finding out. So I'm bringing what I know to this new experience, and we are all finding out together. But I'm still me. I'm not playing something that's not me or pretending to be something I'm not. I think we need to bring ourselves into whatever we do to do our best work. That's why my immediate idea was to change it to Sam instead of Sarah, so I can have a way in.

Of course, on any given day as a writer, you're not going to do it the same way. It's about making a strong, hard choice and following through and really committing to it. That may be a terrible choice, and may be destined to fail. I think once you make your choice, you live with it and go with it.

PD: With your approach of keeping it plausible and having conflicts that everyone can relate to, it's hard to be way off.

PR: That's right, unless it's such a cartoon, and that cartoon is hysterically funny, you live by the sword and die by the sword. You will only be as good as your last joke because the audience won't have the realism and identification to latch onto when it's not supposed to be hysterically funny. I think some drama, a little emotional moment now and then, not only centers your show, it also does something commercially and sets you up for a huge laugh right after.

PD: It was really funny when we interviewed Sherwood Schwartz [see page 280].

PR: Love him. Nice man.

PD: On one of his shows, a writer had such-and-such an idea. Sherwood would say, "No, we saw that on *My Three Sons*. It was done, so we threw it out, and today you can't get it done unless it was already done by somebody else."

PR: That's a good point. I have no idea what they want and neither do they. I don't know if movies are better than TV. At least on TV, once you get rolling, you are king. In movies, not so.

"I have no idea what they want and neither do they."

PD: Movies get rewritten.

PR: Which could be the day after you hand it in.

"That's maybe the number one reason television is lousy. People get through on false credits."

PD: You have an excellent reputation for the Room you ran on *Raymond*. How did you structure it to keep the dynamics working?

PR: Well, first, you read a ton of scripts. Once your show gets picked up, your home becomes a fire hazard with all the paper that comes to the door. You get tons of scripts. I was stupid enough to say to every agent who called, "Send me your top three people." Oh, my God. I should have said *one* person. Scripts were piling up in my house. You read the first ten pages of everything and beyond that, you read all the way through the ones you like—maybe. Then you meet with some people. You never know what they are going to be like, really, until you work with them. I was going to call my book *Everybody's Nice in the Meeting*. [The actual title of Phil's book is *You're Lucky You're Funny*.] You don't really know until you work with them that they are an axe murderer. We've had that situation. "Oh, you were totally different when I met you. You never really wrote this spec script. I was stupid enough to believe you." That's happened. That's maybe the number-one reason television is lousy. People get through on false credits. It's a dirty secret of show business. No, I think it's known.

So you find your people. Usually you're going to take people you worked with before because you know them and you like being in a Room—no small thing, that you like being with them in that Room, you gotta be in that Room, you need to be in that Room more than your own home—welcome to your family, for good or bad . . . I pick very, very well, I think. The proof is that 90 percent of the writers on *Raymond* stayed all nine years. It was disgusting. We became sickeningly sweet in that we are bound together forever. What can I say? I'll never have that again. You hope and pray you get to work at what you love, and then to have people that you love doing it with you.

"I learned from my experiences being on terrible shows what not to do, which is just as important as learning what to do."

PD: After you picked the people, you had to do more than that to manage them.

PR: Yes. I never ran a show before. I never ran a shoe store before I was a writer. You can be this nebbish in your room, who never comes out into the sunshine and never has to talk to people, until your show is picked up. Now, suddenly, you're the head of a giant corporation. That's literally what it's like. You have to make executive decisions. You suddenly have to understand budgets. You have to understand personalities and manage personalities. If you're not used to doing such a thing, it can be troubling to say the least. You can stay up all night worrying.

PD: You were in Rooms before *Raymond*. You knew a lot of the dynamics.

PR: You know the dynamics, but you're not in charge of the dynamics, and that's a very different thing. You can leave your worries there when you go home. If you're in charge, you can't. I learned from my experiences being on terrible shows what not to do, which is just as important as learning what to do.

"I remember distinctly thinking when I got this memo, 'If I'm ever lucky enough to have a show, we are going to have milk on the cereal.' That's how I ran my show."

"Yes, I would not like to run my place this way." I talk about it in my book. Before *Raymond*, I was lucky enough to be on another hit show. One day we got this memo: "We noticed that some of you are putting milk on your cereal when you come in in the morning. The milk is for coffee. The cereal is for snacks. Please do not put milk on your cereal." I remember distinctly thinking when I got this memo, "If I'm ever lucky enough to have a show, we are going to have milk on the cereal." That's how I ran my show. An army travels on its stomach. The food is the most important thing. If you are working hard, it could be the only nice break in your day. It should be nice. It should be important. That's how you make a family.

Armies may travel on their stomachs and, as we learned, so do Writers' Rooms. The memo that said, "The milk is for coffee. The cereal is for snacks. Please do not put milk on your cereal" had a profound impact on Phil. We often learn a more powerful lesson from an unpleasant experience than from a positive one. Phil not only gave his writers the freedom to use condiments as they saw fit, but more importantly, food became one of the ways that Phil showed his team how much respect he had for them. On *Raymond*, food did more than fuel the writers—it also fueled the stories. Raymond's mother was a better cook than his wife—way better—which created many conflicts. A discussion in the Room about the writers all gaining weight led to an episode about having a tofu turkey for Thanksgiving.

Peter Casey's development followed a similar path (see page 51). The phrase, "I ate more dinners at *Cheers* my first year than I ate in six years at *The Jeffersons*" jumped out at us. The Charles brothers used food as a way to express appreciation and respect for their writers. It is more than coincidence that Peter and Phil ran outstanding Rooms with devoted writers who they were careful to nurture and feed . . . not necessarily in that order. This gives us a different way of looking at the phrase "food for thought."

JD: You come from the theatre.

PR: I was an actor in New York, which is an even tougher life than being a writer in Los Angeles.

PD: You studied theatre in college?

PR: I did. That's all I ever wanted to do. That's all I knew. When you are a kid and watch *The Honeymooners*, you don't think that there is writing and directing and producing. In my case, I saw Art Carney, and started imitating Ed Norton. I wanted to be Ed Norton. That's who I loved. You start seeing other shows and you try out for the school play because that's all you know.

PD: Always as a comedic actor?

PR: Always. Never interested in being serious. My parents were kind of funny. My dad did a little tummling [a Jewish tradition of a funny hotel social director mixing with people] in the Catskills. He hosted in the evenings. I never saw it. I remember one time seeing him in the city. He got up for a relative and did something. I was so proud of him. I remember thinking I wanted to be up there with him.

PD: Was it prized in the house?

PR: Currency of conversation. It was the way we communicated. We communicated through making jokes—by being funny when we weren't yelling at each other.

PD: You learned early on you had the ability to do that.

PR: I was encouraged by my parents laughing. If they didn't laugh, I wouldn't be here. My little brother, if I didn't make him laugh, I wouldn't be here. These are the people, first and foremost. Then you try out for the school play, and holy cow, other people are laughing. So you think, "Wow, I'm famous. I'm a star." And you think, "Wow, this is what I'm supposed to do." Then you graduate from college and realize, "Oh, there's others."

PD: How did you get into writing?

PR: Failing as an actor.

PD: Was there a place you learned the structure?

PR: Alan Kirschenbaum. He's also from New York City where I grew up. Alan already came out here and he was working on a sitcom. I came out because an agent saw me on a show in New York and said, "If you come to Los Angeles, you will never stop working as an actor." Like a schmuck, I packed a bag and came out here and never started working as an actor. Someone else asked me if I would like to write a spec comedy script with them. Albert Goldstein. I was in his plays as an actor in New York. He was a writer in New York. Columbia Grad School. Albert came out a year before me and tried to make it in sitcoms. Albert says, "Do you want to write a spec script?" I say, "Sure, what's a spec script?" I asked Alan in fifteen minutes at a terrible seafood restaurant up on Melrose. He told me about structure in that time. My real school was the years, years, and thousands of hours of childhood, adolescence, young adulthood I wasted in front of the television.

It becomes a part of you. You understand it. It's in your makeup, how you think. I can't explain it better than that. I would have liked to have gone out with girls more. Who's to say I would be in the nice house. I did get a nice girl.

"I had been the Monkey in the Rooms I had been in before. You can't do that and pretend to be in charge and be the captain of the ship."

Lew Schneider [also interviewed in this book; see page 265] is maybe the funniest person I know. In the Room, there are different roles for different people. It naturally

Most of the writers in this book have weighed in on what makes a Writers' Room healthy or dysfunctional. Phil offers an insightful view of the dynamics inside the Room and how it puts sitcoms together. According to Phil, there are key roles for writers on a series. One of Phil's talents is recognizing each writer's gifts and making sure that the key roles in the Room are matched up with the right people to achieve balance.

Our favorite is the Room Monkey. Quite the opposite of the way it sounds, the Room Monkey is a coveted position. Pure energy, creativity, and inventiveness, the Room Monkey provides necessary spontaneity and enthusiasm. He's the spark plug that ignites an entire room of tired writers. On *Everybody Loves Raymond,* Lew Schneider played this part with distinction. Phil is quick to point out that it was the role *he* usually assumed on previous shows. As far as Phil is concerned, nobody was ever better at it than Lew.

comes to the surface for each individual. Lew's role on *Raymond* was Room Monkey. He'll admit this. When you needed to jumpstart something funny, a comic spirit in the Room, he would pretend to have sex with the thermostat.

It's essential to have that Monkey. Now, I had been the Monkey in the Rooms I had been in before. You can't do that and pretend to be in charge and be the captain of the ship. Thank God for Lew. He was a better Monkey than I ever was. He's absolutely hysterical to the point where you are working now and you have to say, "You must stop. Please put your pants back on and come back to the table because we need you."

An Interview with
Lew Schneider

A partial list of Lew Schneider's credits as a producer and writer includes: *The Goldbergs, The New Adventures of Old Christine, Everybody Loves Raymond, Less than Perfect, The John Larroquette Show,* and *Men of a Certain Age.*

Lew Schneider got his start in comedy because he was a good boy . . . he listened to his mother. Following in her footsteps, he attended the University of Pennsylvania. During his sophomore year, his mother suggested that he join Mask and Wig, the campus comedy group. Once he began writing with them, he gave up the idea of going to law school. He knew he was going to become a comedy writer. Along the way, he did some acting and a lot of stand-up comedy, which strengthened his writing skills. Throughout the interview, his stand-up skills are evident as he used them to express the original ideas he kept coming up with.

PD (Peter Desberg): As we've explained in our Premise [see page 9], how would you go about developing the show's plot lines?

LS (Lew Schneider): Everything's coming through the filter of what I'm working on right now. I'm currently working on this show about my mother. And as I have a blast writing, I'm getting, "I'm sure everyone's anxious to watch your show about a sixty-eight-year-old licensed clinical social worker." So, I feel like you're heading down the same road: "Hey, what great old lady characters." Alright, but never mind that, how funny is it? These characters . . . obviously you've given me a generic sort of Premise. These characters are no better or worse than any other characters, to my mind. It's how you fill them out.

I get freaked out by the high-concept show. So I would hate it if you'd have given me a thing that said, "Now Sarah's an albino welder. She's the best welder in the world, but the proximity to sparks makes her skin glow abnormally, worse than usual." Then I'm like, "Oh, we can only do four shows." So this is okay. In order for me to jump on this and write this properly, I would have to cast these people in my head and start writing.

" 'Now Sarah's an albino welder. She's the best welder in the world, but the proximity to sparks makes her skin glow abnormally . . . ' "

. . . So I always do it by name. So you have the name, Sarah. The Sarah I know in this case is [my friend] Sarah Cabbot. You have a couple of character traits, but nothing that you would go, "I know this voice right now." We'd really have to figure out how to get the grandmother and grandfather into the same location with Sarah and her mother, because I think you want to catch Sarah—I think she's your hero—I think you want to catch her in the middle. And I think if you put her in the middle, you've got plenty of stuff with the grandparents. If she's like these old people, first of all, it makes a young person crazy to find out that they're not like their parents, but like their grandparents. Oh, my God, that's even worse. And to have the mother . . . plus, then it would highlight how immature her own mom is. So I think to have those people there, maybe I would have the mother be flat broke and the only place she can live . . . maybe the grandparents are on this Coast and everything has been fine. And if Sarah's out here with her grandparents. . . .

Yeah, what I'm thinking is maybe they are out here all together and—I know a guy who's going through this; he realizes that his dad never had anything. His dad gave his brother a car for his graduation, and he wondered why he didn't get one . . . because there was no money that time. You know what I mean? There sometimes was money, and then you got a car. And he got lucky enough to graduate and got the car. His poor wife has her mother-in-law working for her. I would probably steal that idea. I think maybe I'll have the grandparents out here.

I think Sarah's so dutiful. I could buy that she's so efficient, and so composed, and so steady at her job, and probably responsible . . . though I'm not finding how any of these things are funny. All these are un-funny characteristics . . . unless she's really obsessive. She's living with her grandparents, or helping her grandparents because she thinks that's what the dutiful daughter should be doing, and that's what her mother *would* be doing if she lived here. Then, when the father dies and the mother moves here, she realizes, "My mother wouldn't be doing any of this. She's a big screw-up." That would be a funny thing maybe, if what happens is Molly doesn't move in with Sarah, Molly moves in with her own parents, and Sarah's then having to raise her mother . . . manage that relationship, the mother and grandparent relationship. And she's probably upset because maybe she thinks . . . no, her mother's always saying, "You should get out with guys." Now that she's here, she'll take care of her parents. "I don't have to babysit Nana and Papa as much. Put out all those stovetop fires." Sarah says, "I can start having as much sex as I want, even though it'll be responsible sex, 'cause that's the way I am."

"I will have some responsible sex." And then the mother comes out here and doesn't want to deal with the parents, wants to deal with her. That might be a funny episode, where "I've got an idea about our living situation. I'm going to downsize Nana and Papa, and you and I . . . we're going to switch. You're going to go live in your apartment, that's perfect, and then you and I can live together." I wouldn't do that as a pilot, necessarily. There's always that question of "Premise Pilots."

JD (Jeffrey Davis): What's a Premise Pilot?

LS: If we're going to do this as a Premise Pilot, we're going to introduce our characters, and this is how the situation came to be. In other words, Dad has just died, and we're moving Molly to the Coast. Molly's coming out here and she's going to live with Sarah. That's the Premise Pilot. They don't love those. When we say "they" . . . I'm hearing now that a lot of time, 70 percent of the time, you don't write a Premise Pilot, you write a show where Molly and Sarah are living together, or Molly living with her parents, and Sarah has to come and . . .

JD: So the Premise is in the backstory.

> ## "The only thing worse than that is taking care of a parent who's supposed to be taking care of *her* parents."

LS: Yes, the Premise is the backstory. For example—funny episode—if you had Molly living with her, like, ninety-nine-year-old parents. They call Sarah, complaining: "She's playing her music too loud, she's entertaining men here . . . she used all our Mrs. Dash, our low-salt . . . do you have any Mrs. Dash? Ours is gone. She used our toothpowder . . . she doesn't have her toothpowder . . . my stimu-dents are gone . . ." and all the old people jokes. "How do you know?" "I count them." "Why do you count them?" "What else am I doing today?" These are old people. I love stimu-dents and always used to look for a place to put them in. "Where's the Sanka?" "Postum!" "She won't drink Postum, we all like Postum, we put it on the list; she doesn't buy it. She buys something called Crystal Light. We don't even know who Crystal Light is."

Alright, so maybe it is bad enough. This may be a workable show. In an age when many of us are caught taking care . . . caught in the generation where we have to take care of our parents, the only thing worse than that is taking care of a parent who's supposed to be taking care of *her* parents. So there may be the show. That might be the show, where Sarah, this poor woman, has everything to take care of at work, is then taking care of someone who she thought had been taking care of her own father, and never really was. Her parents never had to be parents because she was always so good raising herself, and Molly can say, "You practically raised yourself." I think I could wrap my head around that a little bit. Of course, the grandfather character has to be a virulent racist. Of course, I think that all old people are Jewish. I guess there are some old people who aren't Jewish. Some of them are Italian, but Jews are the funniest old people. No one ever says, "I saw the funniest old Gentile . . ."

JD: You did stand-up, didn't you?

LS: A lot. Yeah, that's how I come to this. So that's where I go. I'm locking in my answer. It's a young person whose life taking care of her grandparents got worse when she has to find that she has to take care of her mother, who she thought was going to take care of her own parents . . . finally. Her mother's supposed to take responsibility and all, and in the end it should become clear: "Oh, my God, my mother was never a suitable mother, and now she's not a suitable daughter." And the grandparents: "We could've told you that. We did everything we could with her. But she married well, that's all, and made a beautiful dollar." "No, he didn't." And things should come clear to her: "You were so smart"—went to college on a scholarship—and the mother says, "It's a good thing, too, we didn't have any money." "You didn't? I never would've gotten the scholarship if I'd known the pressure was on." Now that, I think I can write a funny Episode One of that. I don't see this as a series . . .

JD: Everybody has stayed away from the grandparents. I think it's so interesting that you integrated them in.

LS: Oh, because I have an eye for failure. I know exactly what America wants to see. Plus, I'm sure there's a lot of planning for funerals . . . there should be a constant mention—please don't steal this—I'm dealing with this in a script. Three brothers in my show argue about, "When Dad passed away . . ." "Don't say 'passed away' . . . the mortician is allowed to say 'passed away' . . . gone to his heavenly reward . . . you can't say it . . . die!" People say, don't say it like that, that makes it too big of a deal, just [say] "die." So then you have to have . . .

PD: I had that conversation with my doctor today. His father died a week ago. I said, "Sorry to hear about your father." He said, "He was senile for about ten years . . . it was time for him to go."

LS: Did you use an awkward term? Did you say, "I'm sorry to hear about your father?" That's perfect. They cannot make the condolence card small enough.

Go back to, "Sorry to hear about your father." Stop! It's always like, get to the obligatory . . . this much left, just enough room for, "I hope that the warm feelings of the relationships you have will sustain you . . . I hope you duly note that I wrote you this letter and next time you see me, you won't think what a putz I am."

I'm going to go off-story for a second. My favorite moment in the last ten years was something that happened when my father died. In the week that my father died, we were at the Shiva. My parents have a friend named Doris who . . . she's the last invite for family occasions. She has teeth that click. "Lewis Schnaia, I can't believe how wonderful you are. Let's go out and have some, let's go to Applebee's . . . get your brother, we'll go out for a little bite to eat . . . you'll like the chicken Caesar." [*Lew clicks his teeth throughout this section as he tells the story about Doris.*] And my father was so great to her his whole life. "Oh, Doris means well, of course we have to include Doris."

Alright, so I'm home. My dad's died. We just had the funeral. We go back to the house. And it's really a good time. It wasn't a sudden thing, and there are eighty to 100 people, mostly social workers, so everybody's worried about everybody's feelings, they're all great, everyone laughing and telling great Herb stories. We're having just a wonderful time. The phone rings—and I don't live in this house anymore, I haven't lived there for years, been out here [in Los Angeles]. But the phone rings, and you're back now, so you pick up the phone. "Hello, Lewis." *Click.* "Oh, hey, Doris." "What are you doing home?" She has no idea that my dad has died . . . somehow in the shuffle, she doesn't know. And she's the kind of woman who would make a big deal, like, "How come you don't call?" But perfect, I'm the victim here . . . I get to play it. "Oh, Doris, I'm home because my father died." [*Lew makes a loud screaming sound to imitate Doris's reaction.*] "I know it, Doris, isn't it awful." [*Lew screams again.*] My wife says I'm a horrible bastard. Too bad! And Doris couldn't yell at me. It was fantastic, she couldn't go, "Why didn't you call me?" "I'm sorry, I was overcome with grief . . . I couldn't call you . . . right after my dad died, I was busy holding my mother's hand. There, Doris! There!"

Alright, so I f–ck off for those fifteen minutes, now I'm back to the story. I'm good for ten-minute bursts of incredible activity, and then I've got to tell a "Doris" story.

JD: That's what made *Everybody Loves Raymond* great, were the Doris stories.

LS: The old people are always worried about when they go. There's got to be that sense of . . . they want to make sure all their affairs are in order. So they have their daughter, Molly, help organize their stuff. Good luck! So you see Molly. She's an organizer. She puts all the money they have into a boat, or into a restaurant . . . a floating restaurant. Sarah comes and, "No, no, no, no, no, no, no, we're not buying a timeshare in Darfur." Maybe Molly's redecorating the house. Somebody should break a hip. Got to figure someone breaks a hip. You know what I also like? The old people. I know we've seen this a lot, but there's this funny relationship. Very, very old people don't get along. I know we did it on *Raymond,* but they weren't very, very old, but I had some grandparents . . . their marriage was iffy for, like, sixty-five years. Who knows if they'll even be together . . . everybody knew! In a world where soup can't possibly be hot enough . . . trying to think of other stories.

I guess Sarah—and this I'm stealing from my show—when Sarah does date men, people can't believe how great Molly is. They just think she's great. "Everyone thinks my mom is great. I want to kill her." "Your mother's so great."

"I know, I know, on paper she's great. I know when you meet her, and you talk to her, and you spend time with her, and you eat with her, she's great, but then when you leave . . . You know, I'm her son and it bothers me."

You know, your parents always bother you. And I think it's funny that Molly would confide in Sarah like an adolescent: "Look at Dad, you know, my parents are impossible." "You're fifty, your parents can't be impossible." "Do you find me impossible?" "Yes, because you're impossible."

"The key for any sitcom is it has to go bad for your hero . . ."

I'm just trying to . . . all these are bits. The question is, what are stories? I'm having trouble coming up with stories in this. I guess it would be nice to make Sarah beholden to Molly in some ways, that she's not just her responsibility. For example . . . *maybe* the boss has a soft spot for Sarah, when she sees her dealing with Molly. So she decides that because she's so fantastic at managing *that* situation with Molly and her parents that Sarah *will* get her position as vice president, which only adds more work for Sarah. Maybe the whole reason the boss was unwilling to move Sarah up was that her boss believed, "No one can do this as well as I can." Now Sarah has proven what she can do . . . that she really is Superwoman and can do all this. It should always go bad for Sarah. The key for any sitcom is it has to go bad for your hero, and you have to be able to root for your hero. I don't think Sarah can be particularly gorgeous. She should be cute. You know, that's what I loved about *Less than Perfect*. I worked on *Less than Perfect*, and I just loved that our actress, at least when the show started, she was heavy, and plucky, and optimistic, and those things are all not cool traits, especially in New York. But then the actress got thin and beautiful, and pessimistic.

It would be good to fill her out a little bit. I do think that the grandparents . . . I think they were very competent in something; they should come from competence, so they would blanch at every attempt of Molly's to fix things. For example, Sarah said, "You should take care of them, they're your parents; they're here now." And she tries to do things, and the grandparents know better, they were doing just fine. But they have a sense of obligation, so they want to do what's right, so they have Molly move in with them. The only reason why I don't want everybody in together is that just feels *too* sitcom. Only with sitcom worlds do three generations live together. The closer to real life, the more the people can identify. *Raymond* . . . the only high-concept thing about *Raymond* was that the guy lived across the street from his parents. But that's not so crazy these days.

It comes from Ray's life. And in my neighborhood, my brother just moved into my mom's old house. My mom moved into a condo, not across town, but three miles away, so she's too close. She arrives in a bathing suit a lot. She doesn't have a pool. She arrives in a bathing suit on her way to the JCC [Jewish Community Center]. And the Jews don't care that there's no robe, or anything, it's just ass on a car seat. "Come on, Mom!" "Oh, what do they care? I'm just driving over to the J!" "Please cover yourself." I guess Molly would have to drive around . . . she'd have to show up—oh, by the way, that's funny, if these grandparents still drive. They're eighty, and they still drive.

Molly thinks that she's trying to do the responsible thing, and she takes her parents to the motor vehicle place to get them re-tested . . . or there can be a big fight. She thinks they should be retiring. *"We drive great. You drive poorly."* She tries to get them surreptitiously tested, or she tries to videotape their bad driving. So she thinks they're bad. The funny thing is that . . . no, I want them to be good. I guess the funny thing is if Molly's a shitty driver. And then you have an eighty-year-old person saying, "Let me drive."

Yeah, Molly's from New York. That's funny. She has to get her license, because I know people who—I know a guy who can't move here because his wife is such a shitty driver, and beyond the age at which she can be trained. He would be a millionaire, instead of being whatever he makes in New York, which is fine, but he doesn't make what he'd make out here, and they would move, but she can't drive. She keeps failing the driver's test. So I think Molly has to get a license, that's in there. Molly has to move to California and get a license, because in that eventuality, she's saying, "Someday, you won't be able to drive," and the grandfather says, "I'm going to drive my car 'til the day I die." I think they have to complain to Sarah, "She's got to move out. She's taking care of us, and it's awful." Sarah says, "I don't want her." "But she's your mother; you live with your parents, that's what you do." "You take care of your parents. We took care of our parents."

PD: Who teaches Molly to drive?

LS: That's an interesting question. Oh, the funny part is Molly's father, of course . . . that's a much funnier scene. The father . . . because there's always that problem—it's always funny to watch a father teach a daughter to drive. It's funny when the father's forty and the daughter's sixteen. It's got to be funnier when the father's eighty and neither can see! Molly's near-sighted. Neither is seeing very well. And the grandmother, she's along for a ride in the back. She's backseat driving on two people. That's a funny show. We got one.

One. We've got one story, maybe . . . we've got half a pilot and one story. We're screwed. I wouldn't try to sell it. So what else?

Molly's the fly in the ointment. If she decides she's going to start her new life, and her new life may be, "I'm going to get a master's." "Don't you need a bachelor's?" Combine bachelor's . . . "I'm going to get a machelor's!" I don't know. She needs a work-study job; she appeals to Sarah to give her a work-study job. The more complicated you can make Sarah's life . . . and I think refereeing the fights between . . . The thing with *Raymond,* and what I'm remembering most, was that Ray was a man caught between his wife and his mother. That was the core relationship in the series. Sarah's a woman caught between her mother and her grandparents. I think that's where I would go with it.

PD: What was it like working in a Room?

"The Room's a great break from the writing, and the writing's a great break from the Room."

LS: That's why I do it. I initially thought I would never enjoy the writing. And when I started on *Raymond,* I couldn't wait to not be out on a draft, and to get back to the Room. I love the Room so much. That was the most fun for me. Let me get my hands on somebody else's crap, and get a few jokes in, and screw around, and that was always great. Then, I found myself dancing down the hallway, after getting notes, going, "I can start writing the script, I don't have to go in that stupid Room!" And that's how it was. So the answer is, I like both. But the Room's a great break from the writing, and the writing's a great break from the Room. The two sides serve each other. But the Room was amazing. I've been part of a lot of good Rooms.

It can also be bad, there can be some comic intimidators. There can be one sort of guy who sits there, looking for reasons to hate your stuff. I begged off a job last year because I heard they get a lot of nodding and tapping of heads, and they pitch whole ideas . . . What if character A opened the door, but left it halfway open? . . . They were fully formed, all the scenes and images. That's not how I work. I'll pitch a million things and somebody goes, "How can you have both?" I go, "You can't have both, I just thought they were both funny; pick the one you like. I don't care. Just pick the one you like." Sometimes I'll pitch a bunch of stuff, and someone will say, it'll be the fifth thing, and someone will say, "That was great, why didn't you pitch that first?" "I don't know. I just like to talk."

JD: You work on instinct.

"... if people are laughing, I'll keep pitching 'til they say it's very funny."

LS: Yeah, I'm very impulsive, and if people are laughing, I'll keep pitching 'til they say it's very funny. "That's very funny, where do I put it?" "I don't care about that." Then we can't put it in. That's why I had to become a much better outliner, because there's a tendency . . . I used to not do outlines as thoroughly, and I'm having this problem . . . this script I'm working on now.

"Funny dialogue, that's really the last part of the icing, and before that, it's funny behavior that might get comic, and before *that*, it's all the story."

I would get a decent spine for the story, and then I would start writing dialogue, and bits of action, and I would write scenes, and then I realized I would be rewriting that stuff too many times. I was replacing funny things, what I hoped were funny things, with other things that I thought were funny. And then I realized it wasn't serving me. You have to know the story so well first, and know what each character needs in that scene first, and then the funny stuff will naturally fall on top . . . you'll be able to layer . . . it's like putting icing on the cake. That comedy stuff is all icing. You don't start with the comedy; you certainly don't start with the dialogue. Funny dialogue, that's really the last part of the icing, and before that, it's funny behavior that might get comic, and before *that*, it's all the story. It's what each character needs in the scene, and that's where I had to come up with a better outline, because you can start just talking and then you realize you're not getting anywhere.

PD: Do you have a good sense of what's funny?

"As soon as you start analyzing comedy, it becomes very dry and unfunny."

LS: I think so. I really try to be accommodating in my real life. I really try to give other people the benefit of the doubt. Even when I feel judgmental, I try to . . . "Wait a minute, I'm being judgmental here, let's listen to this guy, or woman, and hear what they have to say." I try to see it from their angle. And I find myself not doing it as well in comedy. I sound so cocky, but I'm more sure about me thinking I know the comedy answer, and I would get called on it. A friend of mine would say, "Oh, it's funny, why, because you say it is?" "Yes." "Why?" "Because I'm the arbiter! Because I know what funny is, and everybody else should line up behind me." And then he would yell at me, and you know what, he's right. I mean, I don't know, but there are certain times that I'd go, "That's just real funny." And you hate to analyze. As soon as you start analyzing comedy, it becomes very dry and unfunny.

PD: You've done some stand-up. A lot of writers didn't come from that background. Do you think that makes a difference?

LS: I used to think that stand-up guys were going to be the funniest. But that's wrong, because most stand-ups stink.

PD: But we're not talking about *being* funny, it's *knowing* what's funny.

LS: But then I found that the stand-up guys were just as funny on the page, so it was, "Oh, you know what, there's no right or wrong answer." Anybody can be funny. The quietest person . . . often that quietest person, you pick up that script, you go, "Holy smokes, this is hilarious. Who wrote that?" And it's the guy who's not talking. Everybody has a different process.

One of my favorite things in the [Writers'] Room is sitting next to the quiet people. First of all, I'm proud of myself when I don't interrupt and can keep myself quiet for a few minutes. I'm thrilled and I can hear somebody else, and there's a good joke, I love it. I also love it when someone pitches something, almost under their breath. This has happened a couple of times when someone pitched something, and I just think it's hilarious, but the Room didn't hear it. So I'll say, "Pitch that again." And he would ask me to pitch it for him. And I would pitch it and they would laugh, and I'd say, "That's great, it was his." Then they would tell me to shut up. What's so gratifying about that experience is, first of all, that means someone thinks enough of your skills to have you pitch something of theirs that they consider dear to them. If the idea tanks, they know you'll fight for it, because you already were a champion of the idea. You'll go, "I thought it was funny. Okay, you guys don't want to use it, that's fine." So they feel trusting, and anytime someone trusts you, on an interpersonal level, it's a great thing.

If someone says, "Pitch this for me." "Okay, I'm going to go pitch this for you." And you do the standard comedian thing—when it tanks, you get to go [*Lew points to an imaginary writer sitting next to him and holds up one hand to shield the fact that he's pointing at him, indicating that "It's him, not me!"*]. If you can get them to trust you, then you can shit on them, then it's funny! The idea of spending eight hours a day in a room with these people. It's the most gratifying experience. You're screwing around so much. Everyone's looking to laugh, whether it's about the script, or somebody else, because you're just trying to break the monotony until lunch comes. Then that's one good break, and then a couple of phone calls, you're done for the day.

"That Room, that felt like camp."

My dad taught a course called "Task-Oriented Groups." He was a social worker, and said that those are the strongest connections you make in your life. They are the people you work with, and the people you go mountain climbing with. All of these groups are task-oriented, and the *Raymond* Room was the greatest task-oriented group I've ever come in contact with. I always compare it to summer camp. That Room, that felt like camp. We kept our group together for nine years. Four or five of us were there from the beginning, but a couple came and went, but we're still sort of friendly with everybody, even the people who left.

PD: What did you study at Penn?

LS: I was a history major. But I really majored in a group called Mask and Wig, which Bob Myer [see interview on page 141] was in. My mother went to Penn, and she said these guys are the funniest guys on campus, and my mother is so not funny. She's the most literal person in the world, and we consider her like hemophilia, we consider her a carrier, because my brother's funny, I'm funny, my grandparents are funny . . . she's not funny. So it skipped a generation, she just carries the gene.

So she encouraged me to join this group, and I steadfastly refused, and then I met a few of these guys by chance my sophomore year, and said, "I've got to join this!" So I joined right away my junior year and got heavily involved my junior and senior year. It was a great experience. You wrote a show that was done thirty or forty times, and in college that's rare to do a show every weekend, because it felt like a professional job. You had exams? That's too bad, you have to do this show. My grades went up during that time because, the more you're doing, the more you get done. So after college, I knew I was not going to become a lawyer, I was going to do comedy.

PD: Where did you learn to create comedy?

"We never cut a joke."

LS: In Mask and Wig, you had to write two different shows a year, and one of them was done thirty or forty times, the other one was done twelve times. But you had to write the material, and that was like a Room, too. You wrote it with other guys in the show. It was mostly scenes and there was a lot of editing. You could've learned a little more about writing for character and about writing, about not doing all of the jokes. We never cut a joke. We did all of the jokes every time. It's like, "Less is more, guys." They still do that. Anyway, the shows were a good experience.

Then I went to Chicago. I had a director who said, "You should go with Second City." [A Chicago-based improv group.] And so I went out there to take classes and I never auditioned for the group because it was in 1985, and they needed stand-up comedians. It was like the Army. They needed you as soon as you didn't have flat feet, and could do five minutes. You got to go on a mission. So I worked with some great guys in Chicago, and they took me out on the road as their opening act. Pretty quickly after, I started doing stand-up. And then I was an actor and I got a couple of shows, and that's what got me out here. I went to New York first and did a lot of stand-up there, and then came out here. And when the acting part dried up a little . . . if you're an actor, you can only act when they need you. If you're a writer, you can write all day long by yourself, if you want. My writing staff buddies, guys who'd been on shows that I was an actor on, said, "You should write. If I get a show, I would hire you." I didn't realize what a magnanimous thing that was.

PD: What was your first writing gig here?

LS: My first writing gig was actually with Peter Tolan. He had been a writer in Hungary on a show called *Wish You Were Here,* about a young man who went around Europe with a video camera, and I got to write a lot of that show in post-production. We'd have a lot of second-unit stuff shot, and I just would make up jokes about that stuff. And Peter wrote on the show there, and then when we got together out here, he was already writing on *Murphy Brown,* and he had a deal. And I was doing an impression of the *Car Talk* guys, and he's from Massachusetts, and he really got it. And he said, "Oh, that's a great idea for a show . . . we should do that show." And I thought he meant "we," like his production company. And he said, "Shake my hand, we're partners." He could've stolen that idea and I wouldn't have even known he was stealing it. This is what a great guy he is. I would've said later on, "Let's do a show about *Car Talk,* that's a good idea." But he didn't do that.

JD: So he mentored you.

LS: He really did. I've had a bunch of mentors. I knew Alan Kirschenbaum from college; he went to Penn, and my wife Liz was in a play with him, and he knew Phil Rosenthal from high school. [See Phil Rosenthal's interview on page 252.] So after *Wish You Were Here,* I got a job as an actor on *Down on the Shore,* that's where I met Phil Rosenthal. So, Phil Rosenthal, of course, became my rabbi . . . nine years of *Raymond,* he is a singular talent. This guy is as good as they get, and every time I give him something to read, he'll give me a note, or something, and it's one of these "Why didn't I . . . and it's so easy." And it's so hard because Phil sometimes says, "Oh, I don't know . . ." "YES YOU DO, YOU KNOW EVERYTHING! Don't say that, because I've been basing all my behavior on you! So don't say you don't know, because then you pull the rug out from my being." But then, Tolan was great, and guys like Leo Benvenuti and Steve Rudnick, who wrote *The Santa Clause* and *Space Jam,* those were my first comedy guys. I would go out on the road and open for them, and they were the funniest guys I'd ever seen on stage. They were hilarious, and they took me around. And they introduced me to John Riggi, who wrote on *The Larry Sanders Show* for a long time, and John and I are good friends. So I worked for Mitch Hurwitz, I worked for him on *The John Larroquette Show,* so that was sort of between the Tolan show, and before *Raymond.* I worked for Mitch on *Larroquette,* and he was great.

JD: Who have you mentored?

LS: I didn't mentor anybody. I'm still early in the going. I don't feel comfortable in that role yet. Until I've gotten a show on the air and been successful. All my notes are given this way: "I just had a pilot done, so I don't know anything, but maybe you might want to try this." I'll give that note. And the best note that I can give—or get from someone—is, "I'm confused by . . ."

> ## ". . . the best note that I can give—or get from someone—is, 'I'm confused by . . .'"

But you know, when the network gives you notes, that's the note you want to hear, "We weren't sure . . ." What I don't want to hear is, "We don't know a lot about what kind of company Sarah works for." No one gives a shit about that, I can assure you. It's a company that has offices, and she's really good, I mean, believe me, nothing's more boring than, "I want to see that she's competent" . . . that's going to be a boring part of this show.

JD: How do you write *competent?*

LS: How do you say things like, ". . . our third-quarter profits . . . since I took over the . . ." Horrible!

PD: Why was this interview different from all other interviews?

LS: I'm always nervous about being interviewed. There's something about them that makes you feel stupid. As soon as they put it out: "Oh, is that how I sounded? They laughed when I said it, why does it feel so stupid now?" First of all, I feel like I'm making these declarations . . . I don't really speak in declarations, not usually. Usually I speak in complaints.

You know who's great? Jon Stewart always seems so self-effacing. That's how I want to sound. I want to sound like Jon. He's a friend of mine. And people have said, "You remind me of him." And I'm like, "Except he's really smart and cool and . . ." Ray [Romano] is also self-deprecating in such a great way. I don't mean to be intentionally self-deprecating. I really do feel terrible.

You know why developing this Premise was hard for me? Because it's something I would never do. This is imposed from the outside. And I know some successful writers who like doing that. They think, "Just give me the Premise. That's a great idea." It's so antithetical to me. I have to have something bothering me to start writing. There has to be some big fight with the wife, or some big relationship I can't stand.

I would have to find the things that are annoying in my relationship and try to transpose them onto these characters. And that's why I think I had to make more of a big deal out of the grandparents—to put people at odds. I needed more people to be at odds.

"I would have to find the things that are annoying in my relationship and try to transpose them onto these characters."

PD: We've had writers switch Sarah and Molly to men. Nobody has ever noticed the grandparents.

LS: And I told you it's a terrible idea, because no one wants to watch old people on television. Can they be circus folk? Circus folk are interesting.

PD: Even though there was a lot about the old folks . . . the fact that you have Molly's reaction to the old folks, and Sarah's reaction to Molly, made it interesting.

LS: You're trying to put people at odds.

PD: But you did it intergenerationally, so it wasn't just about old people; it was more like, how do old people affect . . . ?

LS: I was really working on how to give Sarah a temper. She would have to be very upset with these people, and that would be the fun part to watch. Watching her lose her temper . . . that was the fun part of watching Ralph Kramden [on *The Honeymooners*], watching him explode. So watching Sarah's anger would have to be funny, or her sadness would have to be really funny. So that's what would have to be funny about her, and so that's where you have to go to the nightclubs and find your Sarah. I'm being facetious. You have to find a Mary Tyler Moore out there to play this. Casting is everything. We can talk about this all day long, but you have to find the right funny people to do this, and then if they're super funny, characters that people love . . . some of this writing doesn't have to be so great.

An Interview with
Sherwood and Lloyd Schwartz

A partial list of Sherwood and Lloyd Schwartz's credits as creators
and writers includes: *Gilligan's Island; The Brady Bunch; The Adventures of
Ozzie and Harriet; Love, American Style; Alice;* and *The Munsters.*

Sherwood and **Lloyd Schwartz** are one of the rare father-and-son comedy writing teams. Watching them work together and seeing their mutual respect was very uplifting for us, as the parents of teenagers ourselves. Then, when you realize that this is where *The Brady Bunch* and *Gilligan's Island* came from . . . most teenagers have no idea, or interest, in what their parents do, and are totally clueless about their grandparents. So what made the interview even more interesting to us is that Lloyd's sixteen-year-old son sat through the entire interview in the background, clearly impressed by what his father and grandfather were able to create within a very short time.

Lloyd and Sherwood evolved a successful system of working together in a way that enhanced both their personal and professional lives. Sherwood passed away in 2011, leaving behind a legacy of beloved classic television.

PD (Peter Desberg): As we've explained in our Premise [see page 9], how would you go about developing the show's plot lines?

LS (Lloyd Schwartz): When we were doing our shows, people would come in with a premise, and we'd listen to it and then we'd say, "You know, we saw something like that on *My Three Sons,*" and we'd say "no" to it. Now creativity is limited by television, where somebody comes in with an idea and the network says, "Yes, that's perfect because we saw that on another show." We were always trying to be unique, and now the standard is, you want to be *like* something.

SS (Sherwood Schwartz): Frankly, if I have any fame or glory, it's the fact that two outstanding shows that I did had nothing to do with anything that had ever been on before.

LS: That is right. If you look in *Variety* or the [*Hollywood*] *Reporter,* it always says,

One of the best parts about doing these interviews is dealing with icons who forged the direction that comedy took in the twentieth century. Sherwood and Lloyd looked at innovation as one of the main ways to decide whether writing was acceptable or not. It makes them sad that in today's network television marketplace, something has to be *proven by precedent* before it will be used. To them, that means *unoriginal*. In their view, innovation has been replaced by safety. Being *first* is no longer a plus—it is now a liability.

"This is a *Brady Bunch*-type show." Or, "This is a *Gilligan's Island* show set on the moon."

SS: I didn't write two shows, I wrote two type shows that now everybody compares. If you want disassociated people brought together, that's *Gilligan's Island*.

"I'm sure we've even been a verb sometimes; I'm sure somebody said, 'We *Gilligan*-ized this script.'"

PD: You can't get much higher praise than becoming an adjective.

SS: I guess that's true. I'm sure we've even been a verb sometimes; I'm sure somebody said, "We *Gilligan*-ized this script."

LS: Somebody actually told me about a thing called "A Sherwood." They teach this in a New York Film School. It's an outline format using the way that he developed an episode. It's the plot, the subplot, and the act break. They hand this out as a form that you fill in. It was named after him, and he didn't even know about it.

SS: I didn't know it because that was just a form that I used to give to writers to discuss their story, and tell them to fit it into that plot line.

LS: So it's A-Plot, A-Plot, B-Plot, and they come together; and you see that to the extreme in a *Seinfeld* episode, where things are so outlandish and then they always come together somehow. But we always managed to do that, and it always ends up with everybody at a square dance, or something. Now the Premise you've just given us is mostly a verbal show. One-camera shows are much more physical, and I find this is so character-driven that you would make it a three-camera show.

SS: It strikes me as a three-camera show, too.

LS: I think that the thing that is missing from this is the specificity of the nature of what . . .

SS: Say that three times fast [*Laughter*].

LS: I think what Sarah does is very important, because we're going to travel with her. And then you have a busybody mother who's going to get involved in messing up not only her social life, but her business life as well. And we would see her meddling. You'd have subplots of the mother somehow getting involved in the business Sarah's involved in, as we travel with her. [*Turns toward Sherwood*] You see what I'm talking about, Dad?

SS: Yeah, I agree with you so far.

LS: What I would probably want to do is figure out an ethnic thing here, either in terms of whether she's Jewish, or not Jewish, or Black, or not Black . . .

SS: I think that's good.

LS: You want the mother Black, and the daughter . . .

SS: No, I don't want it to be *that* good! No, I think they should be whatever they are, which is mostly whites and Blacks separately, for the moment.

LS: Okay, Molly's mother and father both have a strong work ethic, "and find their free-spirited daughter baffling," so if Molly's in her fifties, then these grandparents have got to be . . .

SS: Seventy-five.

LS: Yeah, seventy-five, and they have a strong work ethic.

"But ghosts don't have strong work ethics."

SS: Let's decide whether they're working, or . . . one of them could be dead, but we don't want to deal with a dead character.

LS: Ghosts . . . we'd have ghosts of the grandmother and grandfather.

SS: We could do that, don't pass it up.

LS: But ghosts don't have strong work ethics.

SS: They go through walls. They're terrific people. We could have a father who just appears as a spirit. There's been no show like that, which means nobody will want to do it.

LS: The father suddenly dies. Sarah's mother Molly finds that her financial situation is a disaster . . . maybe her husband didn't have such a strong work ethic after all. You know that work ethic thing can sometimes skip a generation. It's like talent . . . sometimes we skip a generation. [*Lloyd turns to Sherwood, smiling*] I don't mean personally [*Laughter*].

So here's what we've got. Molly's parents had a strong work ethic, and Molly's husband who died had a lot of money and spent it, right? So now you have Sarah, who's also got a strong work ethic.

SS: And Molly apparently didn't have such a strong work ethic.

LS: So she was a spendthrift.

SS: That's right. Probably she was a big spendthrift, while he was out there trying to make good money.

LS: So, they're both responsible for the financial situation. They were obsessed with appearances. He made it, and they spent it.

SS: They spent it. And she was as guilty of spending it as he was. Lloyd, this reminds me of your mother and me [*Laughter*].

LS: You write what you know.

SS: Yeah, we should find out what business Sarah's in.

LS: Okay, now, this is today, and I think that one of the neat things is that so many people who are parents of young people starting off have no concept of some of the kinds of businesses their children are in. If Sarah was to get involved in some kind of high-tech business, which Molly would not understand . . . you know, it's like you and the computer. You know how you can't even scroll up or down.

SS: Yeah.

LS: So you have to print everything out.

SS: Look, I still work with a pencil. I need to graduate to a fountain pen.

LS: So Sarah is doing very well. I see a scene where Molly's totally intrusive into Sarah's life, "I'm not going to be any problem," and the doorbell rings and the moving men move all of her things in. So you have some physical humor right at the top.

"'I'm not going to be any problem,' and the doorbell rings and the moving men move all of her things in."

SS: I think that's a great idea for an opening scene because she arrives unexpectedly with a change in the dates, or something, and the daughter isn't even expecting her that day, and all her stuff starts to arrive with the moving man.

LS: That's right, and Molly's directing everything. When kids go to college, they gain an independence, and then when college is over, if they move back, it's not like what they want it to be. They move back and the parents now resume telling them what to do. But they've already tasted independence when they went off to school. Sarah's at the stage where she's done with her parents. She's got her own life; she's got her own boyfriend. The boyfriend stays over sometimes. Well, my God, he has to stay over when the mother is there. So in the first episode, it would probably deal with all that stuff coming back, and then hiding the fact that the boyfriend sometimes stays over.

SS: Well, if her mother's furniture arrives, that's one element of the story. The other element is her boyfriend arriving. So you've got these two clashes. An A-story and a B-story.

LS: This is like your Uncle Bob.

SS: Yeah.

LS: We always write from our own lives. His uncle married a non-Jewish girl.

SS: This was seventy years ago.

LS: Yeah, worst thing you could ever do. "Oh, my God . . ." And they kept it from this woman. So you would live at home for a while, and Bob's sister still didn't know that they were married; then, finally, their kid was about to be bar mitzvah'd.

SS: And they had to invite their families, and they didn't even know he was married. I wanted to write that as a play.

LS: And they finally told her. What was her response?

SS: Oh, that was so funny. One of the sisters was very Jewish. The other brothers and sisters, and the mother and father had to keep the news from her. And I happened to be in New Jersey on a visit, when they had to break the news to this woman. They knew she was going to either collapse, or grab a knife and commit suicide. And I was there when they said, "Look, a lot of things happened here and I'm just going to tell you everything right now. Bob is married . . . to a non-Jewish girl and their son is about to have a bar mitzvah."

And she said, "Oh, is that right?" and went on with her conversation. For thirteen years, they've been hiding the fact. And I'll never forget that day when she said, "Oh," and went right on with her conversation.

LS: So what I'm thinking about how this story applies here is that after the furniture's in there and Molly's telling everyone what to do, and Sarah goes to the grandparents and says, "What do I do about my mother?" They say, "That's not your biggest problem. Your biggest problem is that your boyfriend stays over" . . . and eventually, at the end, we find out that Molly did the exact same thing with her boyfriend. She was a little bit ahead of her time. So I think that's kind of the overall shape.

SS: Yeah, the only thing missing so far is what Sarah does for a living.

LS: Whatever it is, it ought to be what Molly is not used to. So I'm saying it's more of a high-tech area.

SS: Or—the ad agency business is a foreign business to most people. We do have to explain . . . somebody pays not only to put this ad in the magazines or on TV, but somebody has to advise them how to do it. There's a chain of command in these things, which most older people don't understand. They don't know that comics are saying things that somebody has to go in a room and write.

LS: One of the practical things in TV now is that it promotes ageism, not just behind the camera, but obviously, in front of the camera. They don't want any leads who are over a certain age. And it's very unfortunate.

I don't think it's a mother/daughter relationship show. I think it's Sarah's show, with the influence of the mother. Television is based on the idea that you don't change brands over the age of thirty-five or forty-five. So all television has to be skewed to the people that are under that age. The truth of the matter is that people over forty-five are the Baby Boom generation, who change brands in a second. That's the age that has all the money and that watches television. So they're actually devoted to this core audience. So just looking at selling this Premise to network television, I would have it all focus on Sarah, with the influence of the Molly character. At Sarah's job, there is a guy who is running the business who could develop some kind of relationship with Molly. He could be some kind of a possible suitor who she finds attractive.

SS: So he's an older gentleman.

LS: Maybe he founded the agency, and there's a similarity between him and Molly. We have Sarah's boyfriend, maybe as a continuing bit, where Molly never knows that he's there. He's in, he's out . . . sneaking him in, sneaking him out. And I think that's funny; I think that's very today. So the people she would explain that to are her grandparents, who are simpatico. It's that skip generation thing with Sarah. They're the people she can confide that in.

SS: Yeah, I think it's good, so far. I'm just searching, as I always do, for stories. The magic of *The Brady Bunch*, which made it different from all other shows and made the writing easier, is you not only had sibling rivalry—which other shows had—since it's two different families, and there are children from each family, you had *cross-sibling rivalry*. And the two youngest kids are rivals, so there were sixty ways to go for stories, instead of the traditional twenty. So that kept it alive and made it an icon for new shows that came along with different family relationships that weren't traditional.

JD (Jeffrey Davis): So you were always looking down the road to see how many stories can we get?

SS: Yes, absolutely.

JD: If you could do anything to this that the two of you wanted to—to Sherwood and Lloyd-ize it—what would you do?

LS: I'm fascinated by history. One of the things networks don't like are dream sequences, and I love those. And I would love to have a parallel universe using skipping generations, and with the grandparents at a young age, and we could go into sepia tones, whereas we have this story and then maybe have a parallel story in the grandparents' earlier age. And this is something that people are always advised not to do, and I always try to do it.

We have been surprised to see how many successful comedy writers have a science/math background. Mitch Klebanoff (see page 109) and Elliot Shoenman (see page 317) credit their attention to story structure to their science backgrounds. Sherwood, who has a master's degree in biology, is analytic about structure. He points out that a large part of the success of *The Brady Bunch* was due to his creation of a "cross-sibling rivalry" on the show. All sitcoms are concerned with creating enough stories to sustain the show over several seasons. He points out that there were sixty ways to go for stories on *The Brady Bunch*, compared to twenty for most other shows.

"So it wouldn't be a ghost. This would make him a real person, but only in sepia."

LS: Molly would be the same age as Sarah would be at that point.

SS: I love the idea . . . sepia tone . . . with Molly and Sarah shown in a previous generation.

LS: Yeah, I'd do that. Also what that does is that makes the father alive for those sequences.

SS: So it wouldn't be a ghost. This would make him a real person, but only in sepia.

LS: Does he get less? Do we have to pay him less? When we had the family show, Dad would give me mostly the parent point of view, and then I would be there, *au contraire*, the kid. So both sides were expressed in that. So even in what we're talking about here, I'm appealing to him.

SS: Not very [*Laughter*]. One of the biggest laughs I ever got was a joke on *The Bob Hope Show*. He was a rogue with women. This woman in the scene said, "I appeal to you on bended knee . . ." He said, "You appeal to me in any position." That was a big laugh.

LS: In this Premise, those kinds of jokes will be represented by Sarah's dad. One of the most fun parts of the show for me is the boyfriend. Molly never knows that he's living there is really something. If they were able to have John Ritter pretend that he's gay as a premise for a hundred episodes in *Three's Company*, we can get away with this for a while.

SS: Let me just say a very important word. The word is "impact." Why is this show different from all other shows? And that's impact. If you tune into a show, you should know instantly what that show's about, even if you don't like it. When you see seven castaways on an island, you can't not know that that's *Gilligan's Island*. That's the show. Nobody's in an office; nobody's dressed in normal clothes; that's the show. Now, like it or hate it, you know what that show is, and most people liked it, fortunately.

LS: You know what's funny is that the show was just raked over the coals when it first came out. Now we read articles, they talk about the "acclaimed *Gilligan's Island*." This has to do with the identity he's talking about, where just, boom, you know what it is.

If you see most of the shows that we're talking about, with the heavyset father and the beautiful wife, you don't know what show that is.

"You know how often the kids came down that staircase?"

SS: Let me tell you what the impact was on *The Brady Bunch*. That staircase! Impact! When you see *that* staircase, you know that that's *The Brady Bunch*. It doesn't look like any other room, no other staircase with a thundering herd. You know how often the kids came down that staircase? Very, very seldom, because you couldn't use kids like that all the time because of the child labor laws.

LS: When we did *The Brady Bunch* movie in the White House for Fox, it was a satire. We had 'em fall down the stairs for the first time. You'd never have allowed that in the original series. It took me twenty, thirty-five years to get them to fall down those stairs.

JD: How involved were you in the two Shelley Long *Brady Bunch* feature films?

LS: I produced them. I wish there'd been some article somewhere that gave us a little bit of credit for being the first people to satirize their own work.

PD: How did you work on that?

"Excuse me . . . you couldn't just string a bunch of episodes . . . together and call it a movie. That's stupid."

LS: It was a brutal experience because we originally had sold it. Paramount said they wanted to do a *The Brady Bunch* movie, and we wanted to do a *The Brady Bunch* movie, and then we came back and we had a long talk about that right in this room . . . how there was no movie; there were six kids and a house—unless we did it as a satire. And we went back to Paramount and we said we have to do it.

SS: Excuse me . . . you couldn't just string a bunch of episodes from *The Brady Bunch* together and call it a movie. That's stupid.

LS: We went back to Paramount and we said we'll do the movie, but it has to be a satire. And Paramount said, "We don't care," because they just thought *The Brady Bunch* would be enough.

SS: They didn't understand that a name is not a show.

"Three girls . . . my three girls . . . all prostitutes."

LS: So we wrote a movie and it got a green light. Brandon Tartikoff was president of the studio, and gave us a green light. We were ready to make the movie, and excited about it. And then he's deposed as president of the studio. The new president comes in, refuses to read our script. I said, "Could they at least read the coverage? It says how funny it is." We'd seen the coverage, which explained how funny it was. Alright, so they bring in two other writers, they rewrite it, and they do a brutal satire. We wrote an affectionate satire for people who loved *The Brady Bunch*. They would laugh at it, and people who didn't like *The Brady Bunch*, they'd laugh at it, too. These writers had all the girls as prostitutes.

SS: Three girls . . . my three girls . . . all prostitutes.

LS: Then they green-light *that* movie.

SS: And they're not living in that house; they're living in a slum part of Hollywood . . . as prostitutes.

LS: So we said, "Okay, we recognize you own the copyright, you could do this movie. However, we, as individuals . . ."

SS: This is a direct threat from me to Paramount.

LS: "However, we, as individuals, have the right to go on every talk show advising people not to see . . ."

SS: "Not to go see that show."

LS: Which we were going to do immediately. So then, all the notes we'd given to those people were accepted, switching it all back to what you saw, which was this affectionate satire. We don't do that very often. But, the line was in the sand and we had to do it. We made a lot more money for Paramount than we got out of it. We had a meeting yesterday . . . we have certain guidelines for that, and we've had to take stands against people who want to do it in a certain way.

". . . they're just trying to get their way, and if you let them do it their way, it's going to fail."

SS: It's hard to take stands, because studios promise you things. "If you'll do it our way, we'll somehow inject your ideas into future episodes, you'll get what you want" . . . future film, whatever. And it's all bullshit. Because they're just trying to get their way, and if you let them do it their way, it's going to fail.

JD: If you had to do it with this particular Premise that we gave you, what comes off the top of your head?

SS: I'll tell you what just came to the top of my head. The recognition factor of this show will be the word "sepia." It will be on no other show. The word "sepia" indicates two different generations. It will be the same as the kids running down the stairs.

LS: We have often been the first people to do something. We were the first people to do a movie on videotape. The first ones to have the kids sing the title song, all these things. None of those things, including this "sepia" thing, is done for the purpose of being different. It is all done for the purpose of what's right for the show.

SS: Sepia, don't forget, will just be—out of twenty-two minutes, which is all a show is—will be maybe a minute and twenty, thirty seconds. But that will be an identification factor.

JD: How do the two of you work together?

SS: Well, Lloyd is a writer who writes first drafts quickly, right off the top of his head. I don't do that. I write much more slowly.

LS: More carefully, too.

SS: More carefully. And so we adopted a technique between us . . . we didn't adopt it, it just developed as we were writing alone. He does a first draft. But first, we agree on a whole outline.

LS: If we were talking like this . . . we would spend a couple of days . . .

SS: Yellow sheet, with the stripes . . .

LS: Broad stroke outline. And then we would agree on it. And then I would go away.

SS: Yeah, and he would write his first draft. He believes in first drafts, and I don't like the words, even, because until I'm into the seventh draft, I haven't even started to write the script. So he gives me that . . .

LS: That's my draft. Then he does a draft.

SS: I do a draft, which is not too careful, but it's a lot more careful than his, because his is just the thought process, and mine was more a considered thought process. And then we just go back and forth several times.

LS: And then we would usually take his, and then we would sit down and agree, and then that would be our quote-unquote first draft. We started one time—I think it was when we were doing the movie called *Rough Draft*—and we started to write it together and I don't think we lasted a day. We stopped speaking. It was awful.

SS: We'll never do it that way again.

LS: There's no right way. I write with my sister [Hope Juber]; we've written several things together, and we can sit in the same room. All I can say is, this is what works for me. I've had this discussion with Neil Simon, about outlines and things. Some people say every meticulous comma . . . outline it. Simon hates outlines; I hate outlines because there're no specifics.

JD: Sherwood, do you like outlines?

SS: I like outlines.

JD: You think it's partly the process you grew up on? How you started?

SS: I grew up trying to become a doctor.

JD: I mean when you started in the industry.

SS: I just wrote jokes for Bob Hope on the radio.

PD: How did you get into joke writing?

SS: Well, I needed money, and I was here taking a master's degree in biology . . . let me see . . . my master's thesis is here . . . it's right here.

LS: It's not a big seller.

SS: Only two copies were made . . . and one of them didn't sell.

LS: The musical rights are available.

PD: Did you always have a great sense of humor?

SS: I guess I did.

PD: How did you discover you could write jokes?

SS: I grew up loving a book called *Microbe Hunters*. That's really what influenced my life. It was about the great humanitarian doctors who were guys, like Dr. Banting, who discovered the islands of Langerhans . . . it's hard to put it into layman's terms. He was the one who discovered the islands of Langerhans's relationship to diabetes, and the effect it has on your body. The book starts way back, with doctors like Pasteur. That's the kind of doctor I wanted to be. And for some reason, I was convinced that the secret to all this was in—and that was part of Dr. Banting's idea, too—was in a ductless gland. So I wanted to become an endocrinologist. And instead, I wrote for Bob Hope.

"I wanted to become an endocrinologist. And instead, I wrote for Bob Hope."

LS: His brother was a Hope writer.

SS: My brother, Al.

PD: Would he show you stuff?

"'If I write some jokes and if you give them to Bob, maybe I can get five or ten dollars a joke.'"

SS: Nothing, no. I came out with a master's degree in biological sciences at USC [University of Southern California]. At that time, I stayed with my brother, Al, who had gotten a job writing *The Bob Hope Radio Show* in 1938. It's a long time ago. And so, I was in the house, hearing Al and the other writers from time to time, and it didn't seem to me to be very hard to write jokes. So one week I said to my brother, Al, who was a really wonderful man and he's no longer with us, but he was a really nice man, great guy. I said to him, "If I write some jokes and if you give them to Bob, maybe I can get five or ten dollars a joke," which now sounds like a joke, but in those years, for ten dollars you could eat like a king for a whole week. And I was taking advantage of my brother, in a sense, because I was living in his place. And anyway, I wrote some jokes and he gave them to Bob and they got big laughs, and after two or three weeks of that, Bob said, "Why don't you come on the show as a regular writer, because you write very funny jokes." So I said, "Well, I'm supposed to be going into a medical school . . . this new degree helps me get into the school." He said, "Well . . ." He was a really nice man, Bob; you hear a lot of stories about famous people, but to me he was really nice. He said, "Why don't we draw up a contract and . . ." In those years you'd draw up a contract for seven years, and he said, "If you don't get into a medical school, you'll have a job as a writer." And that's what happened.

Yeah, now most of the time a comedian, if you leave him, he will hate you. If he fires you, he will hire you back any time. It's traditional. It was with Henny Youngman, or Ed Gardner, or any of the old comics. They love you and they will hire you back if you love them; but if you don't love them, which is indicated by the fact that you have left them in the lurch, then you are . . .

But I left Bob, and it was the most difficult meeting I ever had in my life. When I left him, because I was drafted from *The Bob Hope Show* into the Army, and I spent four years in the Army writing *Command Performance* and *Mail Call,* a lot of comedy shows for the Army, during which time I used Bob on some of these shows. So we remained friends, in that sense. But after the war was over, I didn't want to go back to writing those same kinds of jokes again. I wanted to do what I did. I went to work for *Ozzie and Harriet* after the war because I wanted to do story shows, which I didn't with Bob. So I had to explain that to him and not have him hate me. And I said, "I just . . ." It was awkward, it was in his dressing room at NBC, and I said, "I know you expect me to come back," and he said, "Of course." I said, "Well, that's what makes this tough," I said, "because I really don't want to go back to writing the same kind of material," because in the Army I did a lot of story shows with important stars like Clark Gable, and other stars of that magnitude, and they were good; they were comedy, but they were stories. So I said, "I hope I can explain it so you understand it, Bob," and he was very nice and he remained my friend.

I think it was his ninetieth birthday . . . some big hotel, it was on Sunset . . . at that time, they had big events there. Anyway . . . and it was a combined event: It was Bob and George Burns, and one of them was ninety-six, and Bob was only ninety. The two of them were up on the stage at the same time, at this point, and they hugged each other—it was a moment I'll never forget. These two men . . . giants. They hugged each other, and one of them said, "Do you realize we have 186 years of comedy between us?"

PD: When you were first writing for Bob Hope in those early years with all these other writers, was it like going to school, just learning all these tricks and all this craft?

> ## "And Bob was a master of knowing what he could do, and he would take these different scripts and put them together somehow . . ."

SS: I wrote a script. Everybody wrote a script. And Bob was a master of knowing what he could do, and he would take these different scripts and put them together somehow, so he had a choice every week of six scripts. He worked just as hard as we did on the scripts in those years.

JD: You mentored your son in the beginning. How did you get into this with him, if you don't mind sharing in front of your son?

SS: Well, he started at the bottom. He was on the stage with *The Brady Bunch*. He read scripts with them.

LS: I had done a summer job on the show he did . . . *It's About Time*, with Imogene Coca and Joe E. Ross, but that was just brief, as a dialogue coach. And then he created *The Brady Bunch*, and I was going to UCLA, and then I went to graduate school at UCLA, and he said he wanted me to be a dialogue coach for the show with these six kids, and I said, "No, I don't think so." I was a comedian at the time, my partner was a Black Panther. I was doing stuff . . . I wrote for *Love, American Style*, and I said, "You're just giving me that job because I'm your son, and I don't want that." And he said, "Well, who should be a dialogue coach for this show? I've got these six kids on there." I said, "Well, you should get somebody who works with kids." And he said, "Well, you ran a summer camp," and I go, "Well, yeah, I did that, okay." And I said, "You should get somebody with an English degree." "Well, you've got a bachelor's in English."

SS: I was describing you.

LS: And I said, "Alright, I'll do it!"

JD: You let him think it was his idea!

SS: Yeah . . . I always do that, I truly do.

". . . as an associate producer, I could bring him into editing rooms so he'd learn about editing, and cutting from scene to scene . . ."

LS: So what happened was I said I'd be dialogue coach, so I did that in my own way, and he let me do it in my own way, it was treated somewhat like summer camp for the kids. I was given complete freedom, I didn't know what I was doing. By the end of the first season, I said, "I'm done with this 'dialogue coach for kids' thing." I was getting a reputation as being a very good dialogue coach for children, which is not what I wanted to do with my life, and they sent me out to do pilots and things like that with kids in them. And so he said, "What can you do?" And I said, "I can be an associate producer." And he said, "Well, no you can't . . . only if you keep doing the dialogue coach." I said, "Okay." "But we can't make you an associate producer." So they made me a thing called "production associate." I said, "What was the difference?" "Well, about eight hundred dollars a week." So in about six weeks, I realized there was no associate producer and I was doing that job.

SS: That was very important, because as an associate producer, I could bring him into editing rooms so he'd learn about editing, and cutting from scene to scene, stuff like that, which he couldn't do as dialogue coach. So he gradually filled new positions as he grew older and got more experience.

LS: That's right, and then he gave me more and more, and we never talked about it, really. Yeah, but I didn't know if he had to take anybody on to say, "Hey, no, he's doing it," we never discussed that. And then by the end of the third year, I was directing episodes. And then I produced, and then since that time we have been executive producer on just about everything together.

"I find that writers/directors fall in love with what they've written and find ways to direct it . . ."

SS: I never directed anything. I think it's wonderful to write and produce. I don't think it's wonderful to write and direct. I think you need a different kind of guiding influence after the script, and it's not producing, it's directing, and that's a separate form.

LS: Most of the time, I don't direct; most of the time, I do produce.

SS: I find that writers/directors fall in love with what they've written and find ways to direct it, instead of saying, "Let's not do that, let's do something else."

LS: I'll give you an example: An episode of *The Brady Bunch* I directed . . . it got very good notices, in terms of the network, and as associate producer I had to dub, which means to add the laugh track and music. If you watch it on the air, the laughs are way too big. I was just trying to prove it was funny.

SS: And you can't prove it that way.

LS: I think it's different in movies, though. We're talking television. In movies, I think the writer/directors are a very valuable animal, but on TV, I think it's better being a producer.

JD: Who did you give a start to in the industry?

LS: We started David and Jerry Zucker, and Peter Casey. That was a very interesting one because he was selling sandwiches at Paramount; he came onto our set, he gave me a sandwich, we talked . . . "Can I give you a script I wrote?" I said, "Yeah." And we gave him a job as dialogue coach on one of the *Gilligan* movies. [See Peter Casey's interview on page 51.] And then it comes full circle, because a few years ago my older son [Andrew] was at UCLA, and Peter had won nine Emmys. I called him up: "Peter, you got these shows on, I've got this kid looking for a summer job." "Let me call you back in ten minutes." He called me back, "Andrew starts work on June 14 on *Frasier.*" [*To Sherwood*] You've started a lot more writers.

SS: I don't even know how many I started. Because every writer who came in was staff . . . all writers would come in with ideas . . . turned into first drafts, final drafts, it was a learning experience for them. I guess it was mentoring in a way . . . I never heard the word. I was just the producer, but nobody left that office without input from me as to why this scene should go here . . . so it was mentoring, but not with that word. So I don't know how many writers I started.

"... people are expanding the script with bad jokes just to stay alive."

JD: How do you feel about staff writers?

SS: I never used them. The danger is that a show can go to hell because everybody wants to get his joke in, whether it fits or doesn't fit, or else he'll be fired. So people are expanding the script with bad jokes just to stay alive.

LS: And Dad says, "A show is really only good if you can take out the character line, the name of the character, erase all those, and you can look at it and know who says what."

JD: So you would say a joke is expendable?

LS/SS: Absolutely.

LS: There's actually nothing valuable about a joke.

SS: Unless it fits the occasion exactly. That was my test of every joke—erase the name of who said it.

JD: You knew what Ann B. Davis [Alice on *The Brady Bunch*] was going to say, and you knew it was going to come from her character.

SS: No one else could say that. Same with *Gilligan's Island.* There was no line where you had to say the Professor had to be the one who said it, or Gilligan, or the Skipper. All had such identifiable styles; that's why the show has lived as long as it has lived.

An Interview with
Paul Chitlik and Marc Sheffler

A partial list of Paul Chitlik and Marc Sheffler's credits as writers includes:
Who's the Boss?, *Perfect Strangers*, *The Happy Days Reunion Show*,
The Twilight Zone (1985 series revival), *Harry and the Hendersons*,
Charles in Charge, and *Small Wonder*.

Our role changes from interview to interview. In this interview, our biggest challenge was to realize we weren't necessary. The creativity that flowed between **Marc** and **Paul** made us want to jump in and contribute; we wanted to play along with them. They made it look so easy. This team proves that a mark of professionals is economy of motion. They are playful, innovative, and free, yet they always pay attention to structure. They jump freely from content to process issues without missing a beat. The results are original and funny. A few weeks after this interview, Paul called and said they were going to use some of the material they dreamed up in their future work.

PD (Peter Desberg): As we've explained in our Premise [see page 9], how would you go about developing the show's plot lines?

PC (Paul Chitlik): Sarah's parents live on the East Coast? Okay, we just moved them to Palm Springs.

MS (Marc Sheffler): Sarah's parents are swingers.

PC: Big swingers. They go to square dances. Square dancers are among the biggest swingers in the country. They square dance and after the square dance, they pair off and they f–ck their brains out. There is more venereal disease in square dancers than there is in punk rock. My ex-girlfriend's mother, when her husband dropped dead, started to square dance and she just became a nymphomaniac.

MS: Because we all know how erotic it is.

PC: Well, have you ever heard of it? No. So it might be interesting to do for this show.

MS: *Dance of the Seven Veils and the Three Barn Doors?*

PC: Well, they've got plenty of places to go, the barns, with all the animal smells.

MS: The animals would be like, "Look at these idiots."

PC: "What are they doing?" You don't see a lot of Latinos square dancing.

MS: No, it's a very white thing. You don't see a lot of Jews doing it, either. You know what they say when they're asked to square dance? "What?"

"One thing I learned when I was a producer is that you always have to have an answer. It doesn't have to be good."

PC: One thing I learned when I was a producer is that you always have to have an answer. It doesn't have to be good. So, the protagonist is Sarah and she's got a work place and a home place.

MS: Are you asking or telling?

PC: I'm discussing . . . I'm disgusting . . . do you need longer arms?

MS: No, you need shorter words.

PC: She's got confidants at the workplace, at the water cooler.

MS: There don't seem to be enough complications for her. What if Sarah's at a point in her life when everything is settled and all hell breaks loose? Just when you think you have it figured out, the world throws you a curveball.

PC: She thought she was going to be the vice president of this company, but she doesn't get it. What kind of company is it? Let's figure that out, too. Let's not set it in Los Angeles. Let's set it in Phoenix. It's hot, they've got a lot of retirement . . .

MS: . . . a hundred thousand miles of kitty litter . . . I don't know Phoenix.

PC: My brother lives in Phoenix. That's where he goes to Harley Davidson Mechanics School. Maybe she works for Harley Davidson . . .

MS: . . . or a motorcycle repair shop.

PC: Why would Sarah work at a motorcycle repair shop?

MS: Not a repair shop. A manufacturing company.

PC: Okay, it's a manufacturing company. So she's dealing with a lot of macho types.

MS: She's the only woman.

PC: She's the only woman in the place. Okay, there's the conflict right there.

MS: Run by a former Hells Angels.

PC: Okay, that's good, we're on track here.

MS: Sarah's the only one in the room who never killed anyone.

PC: She's the only one who doesn't know a thing about engines.

MS: The only one that doesn't have to report to a parole officer.

PC: Molly lives with her. Does she ride a bike? Some of these older people buy Harleys and they ride them. But I don't think so. Molly's against her daughter working there. How did Sarah get this job?

MS: Ex-boyfriend. A bad boy.

PC: Right, every woman loves a bad boy. So, she got the bad boy and then the bad boy got arrested and then that was the end of him. But she likes the job because she likes the hum of the Harley.

MS: Right. She's the financial brains behind the company. She's turned it around . . .

PC: . . . because it was floundering . . .

MS: . . . it existed only to transport meth.

PC: It was a front for the drugs, because outside of Phoenix is like outside of San Bernardino. You know what? Let's set it outside San Bernardino, because that's where they have the best meth labs in the country.

MS: And you know this how?

PC: I just told you, my brother is a Harley Davidson motorcycle mechanic.

MS: And they have a class in meth-making?

PC: It's big, it's huge. It doesn't really matter. San Bernardino or Phoenix.

MS: It matters because you're close to Los Angeles, closer to things we're familiar with.

PC: So San Bernardino's good. It started off as meth running with a bunch of motorcycles. All those guys got arrested, and they ended up with a bunch of motorcycles.

MS: There's a concept. Make motorcycles and sell them. Wait a second. What if she's a court-appointed receiver?

PC: That's interesting. All right, go on.

MS: So she shows up on orders from the court.

PC: With orders to sell everything. She goes through the books and realizes . . .

MS: . . . that this thing could turn a profit. This could actually be a business.

PC: Okay, so she talks the guy into it and he says, "Okay, you run it." So she's running this business with nothing but Hells Angels and former meth runners and mechanics.

MS: And these are all macho guys, you know, "Women are objects used to sitting in the back seat of the motorcycle, getting the second hit on the pipe."

PC: So how does she control these guys? How does she whip them into shape? Withholds drugs?

"If they're all straightened out, they're not funny anymore."

MS: No, they're all recovering. If they're all straightened out, they're not funny anymore. That's rule number one. If we do this normally, they're not funny.

PC: So they're not normal? So let's create some of the characters. So we've got one mechanic.

MS: Blind.

PC: He can tune it by the sound.

MS: A blind mechanic.

PC: He can feel it when the piston is rough.

MS: Totally by feel.

PC: Totally by feel. Okay, that's funny. He can't see himself in the mirror.

MS: He needs other people to dress him.

PC: For sport . . . he's got a wife.

MS: Every morning she dresses him like an idiot and tells him how good he looks.

PC: "You look so handsome today, honey."

MS: In fact, it could be funny if somebody gets a phone call and all you hear are, "Uh-huh, khaki pants, blue shirt, brown shoes, uh-huh. Got it." The guy walks in and he's dressed like Bozo the Clown. And the wife cheats on him in front of him.

PC: She likes the danger of almost getting caught. Okay, but what challenges does he present to Sarah at work?

MS: Nothing, but I think there's an antagonist who opposes her.

PC: The owner?

MS: I don't think so. Let's take the legal side of it. She came up with the idea that it could actually make money and she petitioned the court. She said, "Give me a year to turn it around."

PC: "Just don't shut it down."

MS: "A lot of people work here, it's not good for the community. There are some real reasons why it should stay open."

PC: Okay, it makes sense now. Who is against that?

MS: There would be somebody who wants the space.

PC: A landlord. The landlord doesn't get his full rent.

MS: Yeah, and it's either somebody on the outside paying somebody on the inside to f–ck things up.

PC: Well, let's do both. Let's make the landlord's son be a mechanic there.

MS: I think this is a place that employs parolees. Let's get a little dark with it. Everybody's got a dark criminal background of some sort.

PC: I was just thinking the criminals sit around asking, "What are you in for?" "Murder." "What are you in for?" "I slit the throats of three guys that I robbed." "What are you in for?" "Tax evasion." Something that's like, "I didn't pay the fine on my . . ."

MS: You don't get paroled for spitting. You can pay a fine. I think these are hard-ass guys that are in for drugs and . . .

PC: . . . gang-banging. This is a dark comedy.

MS: Sarah has to walk into hell. It's got to be primal. And she's got to be the opposite.

PC: She wears the suit. She wears high heels. She goes into this place. Everybody's dressed like . . . you know, they're all wearing their . . .

MS: . . . they don't work, they just hang out. It's like a big warehouse . . .

PC: . . . with a bunch of parts and motorcycles all over the place. There's a frame over here. There's a couple of wheels. There's a tank. There's probably about thirty motorcycles there if you assembled them. How does she motivate these guys to get them to work? And who's paying them?

MS: That's the thing. If there was money in the bank from the meth business . . .

PC: . . . which they can't use.

MS: Sarah talks the court into releasing the funds so she can disperse them, but only for the business. How does she motivate these guys? I don't think she knows.

PC: She has to find out. That's her power, to figure out how to get these guys to do stuff.

MS: I think that she's maybe one of those people that goes along in life and kind of copes and doesn't ever do anything spectacular or ever do anything other than maintain. And without even realizing it, she's put herself into a situation where in a very short amount of time, she has to succeed or fail. It's a new feeling for her.

PC: So why does Sarah take a chance for the first time in her life?

MS: Why does she take a chance? She has to. Bringing that personal thing in, that thing with her mother, you know.

PC: On her salary, Sarah can't afford to keep Molly in her own place.

MS: On her salary, she's stuck with her mother.

PC: But if she makes more money, she can get away from her mother. Is that enough?

MS: No. Okay, let's go back to basics. Sarah's brother is successful. She has a successful sister. She's the one in her family who's never done anything. And her mother is up her ass about that.

PC: Yeah, but her mother wouldn't be staying with her if that was the case.

MS: Yeah, but she's the only one who her mother can control. The other ones are successful and don't give a shit.

PC: But her mother could go live with the siblings.

MS: No. They have the money and the money gives them the power and Sarah has no money and no power. They always go after the weakest one.

PC: Like in the wild.

MS: The mother is a predator.

PC: Another issue is that the father died suddenly and he had a false front and he left them with a lot of debt . . .

MS: . . . which Molly tries to put on Sarah because she's a predator. She's got three children and Sarah's the weakest of the three.

PC: It could also be that maybe the father owned the condo that the daughter lived in and had borrowed up to the hilt.

MS: Yeah, that could be. I'm just trying to come up with the reason why she takes the chance and has to succeed.

PC: She's a court-appointed . . .

MS: . . . yeah, she's an accountant . . . number cruncher, a bean counter.

PC: She's only, what . . . twenty-eight?

MS: Twenty-eight, twenty-nine. Master's degree in business administration. Accountant.

PC: CPA.

MS: CPA. Boring. Has no life except simple math.

PC: So was there a fiancé, a boyfriend? What?

MS: Nothing. Zero.

PC: The first guy she ever falls in love with is one of the guys in the shop.

MS: Bad boy. She finds herself strangely attracted to a bad boy. Clearly a man who never had a bar mitzvah.

PC: He was one of the chief runners. And maybe he's on parole or maybe he's the only one *not* on parole. Maybe he never got caught. Maybe he was always smart enough to get out of whatever it was. I don't want to make him too bad. Maybe he's the opposite.

MS: She has to do this to prove to Molly and herself that she's more than a bean counter.

PC: Well, that she's also an individual. That she's separated from her mother.

MS: The thing is, we're searching for the emotional through line of this story. One of the things you learn about good situation comedy, and I learned from the masters, it's got to be somebody's story. And that journey has got to be that person's journey. And they have to go from here to there.

PC: Instead of a court-appointed receiver, Sarah's father ran a motorcycle factory, that's what everybody thought. But as it turned out, her father was the meth-runner. And the motorcycle factory was nothing. And when her father dies, she goes to close down the factory and finds there's nothing to sell off.

MS: No, I don't like it and I'll tell you why. I like her. If her father ran a factory, there's some pre-existing knowledge. It's too much of a blind for her *not* to know something.

I like her walking into a strange environment. I like that fish-out-of-water thing. She comes into something that she thinks is one thing and then . . . surprise. Let's look at the structure of a story. You got this factory and all these whack-jobs running around. A blind guy who dresses funny and whose wife cheats in front of him. So you do a couple of minutes of that, just to establish where we are. They're all sitting around doing nothing. Sarah comes in and, you know, they're dressed like Hells Angels and she's dressed like a bean counter and she announces to everyone who she is. "I'm here from the court. I'm not going to be here long. I'm just here to liquidate."

PC: What if the guys go into the office and say, "You can't do this. I'll lose my job. I have a family to support. They'll put me back into prison if I don't have a job." And the next person comes in and says, "I have a family to support . . ." It's the exact same speech.

MS: Exactly. No, and he does this. He says, "I've got a family to support. I've got three . . ."

PC: " . . . four children."

MS: "And I will go back to doing hard drugs." Then a parole officer . . .

PC: The parole officer comes in and . . .

MS: . . . he's the romantic interest. He's the guy. So that's who becomes her love interest.

PC: So she's got to keep him happy. She wants to keep him coming back.

MS: You remember that episode of *Seinfeld* where George was collecting unemployment and the woman had a daughter. And in order to be friends with this woman, George went out with her daughter. Well, this girl should be a hidden beauty. This parole officer hits on her and she's so unused to guys hitting on her she has no idea what it is, okay?

PC: Sarah knows she feels pretty good after he leaves. So who does she call to tell that to?

MS: She's got to have a friend.

PC: I don't want it to be the "gay" best friend. Let's have another best friend. Is she a single woman or is she married or does she have a boyfriend? I'm thinking she would like a parole officer.

MS: Maybe it's a girl who is the opposite of her. A party girl? A flight attendant?

PC: How would they get along?

MS: A flight attendant who's in and out of town.

PC: That might be how they get along. She's in town for just a little bit.

MS: A friend from college. An old college roommate, just somebody she hangs with. Somebody she talks to. We'll worry about that later because we know we're going to do that.

MS: Okay, so the crisis is . . .

PC: . . . that's what makes us want to stay there. It's not about fixing the factory. It's the guy. Is that enough?

MS: It's enough for the beginning. So what happens is she's in this thing and she's got all these rough characters and he's the wrangler for these guys.

PC: And when do we see Molly? Only when Sarah goes home?

MS: The mom is . . .

PC: . . . Molly's gone. We don't need no stinking mom. Now we've got the basic emotional incident.

JD (Jeffrey Davis): How long have you two been working together?

PC: We met twenty years ago, but we only started working about two years ago. We hadn't seen each other for many years. I pitched to Marc at *Charles in Charge* with another partner. Not long ago, I was sitting at a local coffee hangout and Marc walked in and I said, "Hey, I know you." And he said, "Paul?" And for months we'd come in the morning and we'd talk and we'd throw ideas around. And one day he said, "You know, I have this great idea and I just don't know what to do with it." And he told it to me and I said, "You know what, it is a great idea and you ought to write it." And he said, "No, *we* ought to write it." And we did, and after that we wrote several other things.

MS: We have different skill sets. Some are the same, but our strengths are in different areas.

PD: It was interesting watching you guys start. It was like watching musicians warming up by playing scales. You were fooling around, making jokes.

MS: Oh yeah, that gets you warm.

PC: You just have to completely open it up to let it flow all in and around.

MS: We all knew kids when we were younger who were funny at parties. It's a whole different ballgame when you have to do it on a button, do it on command, and you develop over the years a mechanism for beginning that process. When I first started writing on shows, I had to learn, "Okay, they're paying me a lot of money, they expect me to perform, and I can't say I don't feel it right now. I have to find that place inside of me where it exists and develop a system to access it at will." There have been times in my life when I've overdeveloped it.

PC: But you develop as you work more and more in comedy. You develop a certain way of approaching things and you know what's important in a comedy. The number-one thing is the conflict. And the number-two thing is the emotional through line.

MS: Every writing team has a different process because it's so out of the box just to do that thinking about what you do, but you have an ultimate goal. Sam Denoff (*The Dick Van Dyke Show* and co-creator of *That Girl*) taught me this a long time ago. When any comedy writing team is doing it right, if somebody else reads the script, it looks as if one person wrote it. It's not schizophrenic. You could put one name on it and it could be plausible that it was written by one person. When you have two strong personalities, two adults with a tremendous amount of experience, that's a lofty goal. So we worked out quickly how to do that. And if this were a project that Paul and I were really doing, at this point I'd leave and Paul would get at the computer.

PC: I'd write up the first draft the roughest possible way. Just to get the tone of the story. And then I'd send it to Marc.

MS: Email it to me.

PC: And then he would rewrite it and we would go back and forth fifteen or twenty times until we got it to where we wanted it to be.

"On my writing days, I go to sleep really early and I'll get up at 12:30, 1:00, and I'll write until daylight."

JD: When do you actually sit in a room together?

MS: We meet at Priscilla's Coffee Shop because he writes in the daytime and I write at night. I write in the middle of the night. On my writing days, I go to sleep really early and I'll get up at 12:30, 1:00, and I'll write until daylight.

PC: Whereas I get up at 6 and I start writing at 8.

MS: So we find a time in the daytime when I've completed my work and he's seen it. He prints it out. I have a copy of it. We meet. We go over the notes. And then I go to sleep and then he does his draft. He emails it to me. I get up. I pull it off the computer. I do mine and we continue that process back and forth and back and forth, until there's nothing about what I send him he wants to correct and there's nothing about what he sent me I want to correct. And that's how we know we're finished.

"We went through the whole alphabet twice up to Q. So it's *Whitley Grove*, Draft I, QQ."

PC: About how many times did we do that with *Whitley Grove*?

MS: Thirty times, maybe.

PC: This was just a pilot. For the pilot, we gave each draft a letter. We went through the whole alphabet twice, up to Q. So it's *Whitley Grove*, Draft I, QQ. Sometimes that's just proofreading. I have thirty or forty drafts of *Whitley Grove* on my computer. And that's our process.

PD: How would you guys describe yourselves?

MS: I'm shorter.

PC: I'm more of a structural guy and I'm always looking for the emotional content. Marc is very quick with a joke and very good with character.

"... we're like two kids flying a balloon ... we're both there to have fun, but we need each other to make the experience work."

MS: I think that we're like two kids flying a balloon ... a helium balloon. Paul is the kid holding the string and I'm the balloon. You know, we're both there to have fun, but we need each other to make the experience work. Paul provides grounding and a rooting for whatever it is we're doing, and I provide the opposite.

PC: I'll just say to Marc sometimes, "You know, we need a joke here." And he'll go, "Uh-huh," and then he'll deliver the joke.

MS: I see things in images and pictures and Paul sees things in structures and words. I see things completely, especially now that I'm directing. I'll see everything in images and pictures. And then we kind of meld together and make it words.

PD: Paul came up with structural ideas in several places and Marc came up with jokes.

MS: Mostly that's my area. I have a background in stand-up comedy, and so being funny instantly on my feet is just a reflex reaction for me.

PC: One that's gotten you into a bit of trouble from time to time.

"'Now that you're out of the closet, could you still be in the hallway?'"

MS: Oh, yeah. At the nadir of my first marriage, my wife decided she was a lesbian. She announced it one day in a marriage counseling session where she began to volcanically explain what she was feeling. So we get back home and our marriage is over and she couldn't even look at me. So I turned to her and I said, "Hey, I got a question for you. Now that you're out of the closet, could you still be in the hallway?" And she looked at me, and she said, "This is all a big joke for you, isn't it?" And I said, "Well, I'm a comedy writer and this is a horrible event, I mean, what do you expect?"

And then I went off and did like twenty lines. I said, "Hey, now that you're like this, when you go shopping in West Hollywood, do they give you a discount?" It was like line after line after line. Clearly, it was pain and anxiety that was producing this. And it was the pain and the anxiety that was being filtered through the prism of my personality. And it was coming out as jokes. Where some men would have screamed at them—or worse-case scenario, smacked them around—I pummeled her with jokes. She didn't laugh much. She got upset that I wasn't respecting her. She said, "You better behave yourself because I've already been to the Gay and Lesbian Legal Defense Fund and I've got a lawyer." And I said, "Hold on, I'm just a regular guy heterosexual."

JD: You've both been in Writing Rooms.

PC: Oh, God, I hate Writing Rooms. The problem is there are two kinds of Writing Rooms. There's the smart Writing Room and the stupid Writing Room. The smart Writing Room is run by an executive producer who is smart enough to understand that he's not the smartest guy in the Room and not necessarily the funniest guy in the Room. He's open to listening to other ideas. Then there's the guy who thinks he's the king of the world and if he thinks he's the king of the world, the politics of the Room are going to be terrible. You've heard the saying the fish rots from the head down? It's awful when the king of the Room is like that, because you can't be funny in a Room like that.

"... you don't always have to be right; you just have to know what right *is*."

MS: The thing about running a Room is that if you're running the Room, you don't always have to be right; you just have to know what right *is*. Many, many years ago, I was a young staff writer. We'd sit around the room and any time anyone had a suggestion the show runner didn't like, he would scream at them, even if it was better than his. "You don't know what you're doing. I'm the boss." And we went on for five, six, seven episodes, and it was horrendous. We just feared going in there. I knew the guy socially and had hung with him and so he didn't bother me, but there were a couple of writers who were in tears. This guy was a tyrant.

So, one night we're doing a rewrite. The guy on the right makes a suggestion that I knew was correct. And the guy on the left shrugged. And so what happens was the executive producer is taking us through the script. "Page 12 is great, nobody has any notes. Great. Page 20. Great. We're out." The next day, we went to do the show and the executive producer was fired between the dress show and the air show, and I looked at him and said, "How could you shoot that? It was the worst piece of shit we've ever seen." And we got rid of him. Because we knew this couldn't go on. So that's an example of what Paul meant when he said the fish rots from the head down. The tone of the Writing Room is always who's running it. And if the person who is running it is open and available and generous, you get a better show.

"'I don't care what you have on tape,' he said. 'I wouldn't have ever said that.'"

PC: Like on *Who's the Boss?*. Those guys were terrific. Garry Marshall was terrific. But we also wrote freelance episodes for a creepy producer, and we wrote several in the first season. The first one, he said, "This is the best script that's ever been done for this show. It's fantastic." The second script he said, "Guys, guys, you call yourselves professional writers? I don't accept this shit. What's the matter with you?" And we go, "Oh, my God, how could we have screwed up so badly?" We walk out of the Room and two of the other producers said, "Don't worry, this is his thing. This is what he does. Every other script he's going to tell you this to keep you in your place." We got a three-script commitment from him after that. Obviously, we were professionals. He was that same guy who said, "Where did you get such a stupid idea?" And we said, "You gave it to us." And he said, "I would never have said that." We said, "We have it on tape." We taped all of our sessions. "We have our notes on tape." "I don't care what you have on tape," he said. "I wouldn't have ever said that."

MS: I'll tell you a great story about shows and Writers' Rooms. I had a deal at Columbia a while ago. I get a call from my agent saying they want to see me on a certain show, and it was one of these shows where the central character was an African-American woman who had spun off from another show. She was the star of this show and they were backlogged. They had stories, but they didn't have scripts. They were in trouble because they couldn't get drafts out. So my agent set a meeting for me to go over there and meet with the executive producers. I go into their office and it's like a mausoleum that hasn't been opened up. There's one writer lying on a couch. One producer is sitting in a chair and the other is sitting on a chair behind a desk. He's pale. He's got no color in his face. He's like a Jabba the Hutt character, and I said, "Hi, I'm Marc Sheffler." And Jabba said, "Yeah, alright, you write fast?" And I said I got it done pretty fast. "We need some help. We have stories. We don't have many drafts, but we have stories. Do you write fast?" "Yeah, I just said, I get it done pretty fast." He said, "We'll pay you lots of money."

I'm looking around; it's like an opium den. And one of the executive producers is high. And then a little voice went off in my head and I asked them, "Is there anything you're not telling me? Is there any fact you haven't disclosed?" And he looks at me and says, "The star has creative control of the show." Once I heard this, I said, "No, I don't think so. I'm outta here." And it was like there was oxygen again.

JD: What do you view as the difference between writing drama versus writing comedy?

PC: I was on *The Twilight Zone* [1985 revivial]. It was a lot less stress. It's a lot easier to write a dramatic program. First of all, there's no late night rewriting. You have your dramatic ending and you move on. So you don't have to sit for fifteen minutes trying to think of that joke. I can write drama completely on my own. Comedy? I feel that I write much better if I have a partner because I need somebody to work off, to see if it's funny. Stuff that I think is funny might not necessarily be funny, as Marc will tell you.

PD: How did you learn the craft of comedy writing?

PC: I was totally thrown into it. I was with my former partner writing dramatic stuff and our agent said, "I think I can get you an interview on this show if you have a spec script." I had no idea how to do it. And we did one and we pitched it and they liked it, and suddenly I was on staff. I just learned it from being there. I had no mentor. I was already in my second career. I was an ESL college instructor up to that time and had been a journalist before that, but I had never done that kind of writing. I had thought I was going to be a novelist, so writing comedy was totally foreign to me. And then I wrote tons of comedy scripts after that.

PD: What were you doing before stand-up?

MS: I had no life. I came to Los Angeles having sold a "Movie of the Week" to NBC. So I came here surfing on that wave. Suddenly, I had a ton of cash and I was living in Los Angeles with a credit. And then I got an agent and I did stand-up, not because I wanted to be a comedian, but to perfect my ability to pick up women.

So I hung out. The guys I know that I started with are Jay Leno and David Letterman and Tom Dreesen, Robin Williams, Billy Crystal. These are all guys I hung with and still know. I had an agent who was working for me getting me writing jobs, and I was doing stand-up, and I never had any formal training in writing other than watching a zillion shows and understanding the structure on an unconscious level. I didn't know what anything was called, but I knew that I could bullshit my way through a story because I knew how the stories evolved. And I learned the names for everything. I just knew it belonged here, or you had to do this here, because this is how this worked. I kept my mouth shut long enough and pretended that I knew what I was talking about until I actually knew what I was talking about.

PD: Was that the same with stand-up?

MS: The stand-up I just did naturally. I could walk onto the stage and pick a subject and just start talking. And it would just come out funny because that's how I see the world.

It's not even a reach. Sometimes I have to stop myself from being funny because it's inappropriate. You know, when you have children and you have to go to school and do what parents do. My natural tendency sitting in a principal's office is to be a smart-ass. Sometimes I would call the school and say, "My son has an appointment with Dr. Ginsburg," and that meant, "I'm getting you out of school and we're going to a movie." Being in comedy means that you have to be an iconoclast. You have to look at the world the way it is and then look at it how it *really* is. It's perception.

PD: Do you think people have a tendency to start writing too soon?

MS: It's an interesting process, because getting to a point where you're good at this is a series of steps and missteps. And I don't believe you can make the steps without the missteps. Many years ago, my agent put me together with Bud Austin, who ran Paramount Television, and then went off on his own. I had an idea for a half-hour comedy. Bud and I developed the show together and I was hot to pitch it. I wanted to get it out there. And he said, "You're not ready yet, it's not ready yet." But I forced the issue.

> **". . . you should never be asked a question you can't answer about your show. That's like somebody asking you a question about your children."**

So we went to a meeting at CBS and the executive asked me a question about the show that I couldn't answer and I fell flat on my ass. I had flop sweat. And Bud just sat there. Needless to say, they don't buy the show. And we're walking out of CBS and he was just the sweetest man, and I had just fallen on my ass and he knew it and I knew it, and he knew that I knew it and he knew that I knew that he knew it. And we get to his car and I said, "So, I f–cked up." And he said, "It's not that you f–cked up, it's that you weren't ready. Now we'll get you ready and you'll be fine." And we spent another month and a half, and I ended up selling it to NBC. But the point is, I didn't know I wasn't ready. It had nothing to do with my ability to pitch it or sell it. It had to do with the fact that I didn't allow the process to go forward enough to the point where I was comfortable answering those questions. And the thing about pitching and selling is that you should never be asked a question you can't answer about your show. That's like somebody asking you a question about your children.

"If you don't get intimate with your work, you end up writing very thin material."

Writing is a developmental process. You have an idea and it grows. It is a life form that gestates. And often the energy of a young, inexperienced writer makes them sit down and stare at the page and say, "I've got this great idea, why can't I write it?" Well, because you're not ready to write it. You have to know your material and you have to know when it's ready to write. And I always know when it's ready to write when I've got so many non-linear notes about what it is that I have to *now* write. I can't make any more notes; I have to see what it looks like. And I don't rush that process. It's very intimate. If you don't get intimate with your work, you end up writing very thin material.

PC: You really have to think about who your characters are, what the conflicts are. Well, we do that in the projects that we've written together. We talk about who the people are.

MS: What I do is, I carry a notebook with me wherever I go. The creative process is *non-linear* and *astructural*. So what I do is this: I know movies are written in three

There is only one way to write comedy, and each of the writers in this book has discovered it: They don't just agree on whose "right" is right. Some of their methods are similar, and others vary quite a bit. Some want to know where their ending is before they start, insist on an outline, and start at the beginning, working through the first draft. While Marc believes in structure, he has a system of his own for developing characters and story. He believes that people start writing scripts too soon. Before he writes a word of screen or teleplay, he gets out a notebook and free-writes, jotting down ideas in any order they come. Next, he figures out where these beats go, assigning them to acts. When he has enough notes, he begins to write a script.

acts, so let's say it's a movie I'm working on. I think of moments that I think are in this story. And it doesn't matter to me how I think of them or in what order. I fill up a seventy-page spiral-bound notebook. And when that notebook is finished, I open my computer and I go, "This belongs in Act I . . . this belongs in Act II . . . this belongs in Act III." And then I put it into the computer. I put all the Act Is together, I put all the Act IIs, I put all the Act IIIs. And then I say, "This comes before this, this goes here, I don't need this." And suddenly, without thinking about it, without forcing myself, without pressuring myself, I have an outline.

> **"I put myself in a movie seat, in a theatre watching a screen, and challenge myself to entertain myself."**

MS: And once I have that outline, it's a chip shot. Then I just get a draft. I put myself in a movie seat, in a theatre watching a screen, and challenge myself to entertain myself. How would I tell this story? What would make me really dig it?

PC: It's all about the story and the people. You just have to have a story to tell.

JD: Can you come up with stories like this on demand?

PC: In my early years, I wrote for Reuters. I had a 4 p.m. deadline. Not a 4:01 p.m. deadline. So if I didn't have my stuff ready by 4, that was the end of my job. Every day I just started writing about the subject, whatever it was I had to write. I just had to write about it until I found out where I was going.

MS: It's like lifting weights. You develop muscles. I wasn't even awake. You have to give yourself permission to explore.

PC: To go outside the structure.

MS: To be non-linear. Putting things in order is the easiest part of it. The hardest part is coming up with those moments of magic.

PC: And try to keep yourself structural and at the same time magical, because they work at opposite purposes. Let yourself go. Be free.

> **"The goal of any writing team is to create something that looks like it was written by one person."**

PD: You guys also have a real good sense of each other's strengths.

MS: That's why I'm directing now, because once it gets through the script stage, I'll take it from here.

PC: We have a movie we're doing together, and he'll be directing and I'll be producing, and that's the way it's going to be. But as for the writing, which is where it all starts, yeah, that's mutual respect and that's also because it's the product that's important.

MS: The goal of any writing team is to create something that looks like it was written by one person. Because whatever we finish up with is the best of Paul and the best of me. And Paul's the judge of what's the best of me and I'm the judge of him. So I give up control of certain things to him and he gives up control of certain things to me. And at the end of the day, we always have something finished that we both like.

An Interview with
Elliot Shoenman

A partial list of Elliot Shoenman's credits as a show runner and writer includes: *Home Improvement, The Cosby Show, Cheers,* and *Maude.*

Some young science types sit in a room and come out years later having proven math theorems or understanding the laws of thermodynamics. Young science guy **Elliot Shoenman** watched tons of sitcoms in his room and emerged with an understanding of how to write them. Shortly after leaving his room, he had the good fortune to begin his writing career working with the legendary Norman Lear on *Maude.* He says working with the Lear writers was like going to graduate school in comedy writing. It was certainly a long way from trigonometry.

There is a structure in the brain called the corpus callosum that connects the left and right hemispheres. Elliot's must be burning on all eight cylinders. His work is a wonderful balance of left-brain logic and right-brain creativity. As you'll see, as he develops the Premise, he brings tremendous discipline to story structure—while at the same time, he has an uncanny instinct for finding authentic humor in real-life, often dramatic situations, that makes his writing both moving and funny.

PD (Peter Desberg): As we've explained in our Premise [see page 9], how would you go about developing the show's plot lines?

ES (Elliot Shoenman): What I'm writing about now is the father/son relationship, because I have my book [*Nobody's Business*] about tracking down my father. My own instinct would be immediately to change the Premise to a father/son story.

I come out of the Norman Lear school, and I'm still influenced by that. I'm interested in some kind of social significance to anything, even if it's minor. The next play I'm writing is about ambition. So I would look for an undercurrent in this. My current form of writing would be to try and make it into a play. I would shy away from a screenplay totally, or from a sitcom, because it also seems like we've seen this a million times, when a parent moves in. The relationships . . . I always love the three-generation stuff, so that to me would be interesting. I'm not sure how you would do the frivolous spending of the money if it was a guy, although it would still work. He loses his wife, he's been frivolous . . . or a father/daughter thing, which I know less about.

The thing that interests me most is the father dying suddenly. My book, which is far from humorous, is about my father's suicide when I was eighteen. There is some interesting humor . . . more and more, I'm learning about how to mix the two. One of the things in my book is, my father was a stockbroker, and he left his office on 60th Street, took a cab, went to Riverside Drive to the Hudson River, and jumped in. We have never been to that site, my sister and I, and we duplicated it, and took the cab, and took that journey. And you know, I'm writing about it in my book and describing it—which, you can't get a heavier moment—and it suddenly occurred to me. My father's a German who was notoriously cheap. What did the guy tip a cab driver on the way to his suicide? And I wrote that in the book, and it really occurred to me, and I said, "Do I put that in? Does it break the moment?" But it's really what I thought about.

So what interests me too is finding out more about who Molly's husband was. I like the concept of the mother, and subsequently the daughter, finding out more about the father and this whole existence being disrupted. That's where I would take it, whether it was a mother and daughter, or father and son, or mixing the two.

I was twenty-six years old when I got a job writing on *Maude*. It was kind of, "Holy shit." I'd only watched the show twice, there were no tape machines to be had, so you couldn't get all their tapes. I read some scripts. But we were at CBS and we were across the hall from *All in the Family*. In those days there were only four writers on a show, so you did a ton of work. But the *All in the Family* staff and the *Maude* staff were all at least fifty-two years old, if I remember correctly, and I was only twenty-six. So I got this incredible thrown-in-the-water thing of how you write and what you're doing is sink or swim, and the guys who I worked with—Bob Schiller and Bob Weiskopf—were kind of my mentors.

Anyway, so, we were across the hall from *All in the Family*, and I noticed right away that we had much later nights than the *All in the Family* guys did, and I couldn't

Jeffrey was lucky enough to have Danny Simon (older brother and collaborator of Neil Simon and mentor of Woody Allen) as one of his mentors. Jeffrey's most indelible memory of Danny's teaching was the phrase, "Jokes are expendable." Elliot is a member of the same club. He stresses story and character over jokes. When you have a comic mind, jokes come from even the most dramatic—even tragic—moments; wondering how much his father tipped the cab driver is an example of this type of thinking. As you reflect on any topic, something funny will emerge if you stay with it.

figure it out. So, I asked Schiller and Weiskopf what it was, and they said because they [the *All in the Family* writers] have these outs, these dumb characters, where Archie could do a malaprop, Edith could do a dingbat thing back to him, or they can do a Meathead thing, and you know—because two in the morning, they could get out of there with sort of an old, cheap joke that would work for their audience. And it's also why, like on *Cheers*, they had Coach—I mean, I learned this as a trick.

On *Maude*, we realized there were no shortcuts. The audience was always oriented towards some great *Maude* high-end, clever line, and the only shortcut was, "God will get you for that," which she would say, but you could only use that four times a year.

But what I also learned, which was a sitcom trap, is everything was written for *her*. The other characters, although they were not untalented actors, they weren't really developed. You didn't tend to write scenes from other characters' points of view. And that's the real sitcom trap. When we did *Home Improvement*, we always wrote for each character. What I've been learning with the playwriting and screenplays is to see scenes from everybody's point of view.

If Sarah's father died suddenly, and you did it as a sitcom, there's no way in the world they're going to let Molly be the main character. It doesn't matter if it's a man or a woman, as a fifty-year-old. So it's going to be about the daughter. So you're restricted right away. Do I want the mother's life to be turned upside-down by finding out about the father's having an affair with one of her friends, or do I want Sarah to find out more about her father's affair herself? What's interesting and what ties into the broadest Premise?

The other thing I learned from those days with the *Maude* writers is to go for the character and go for the story, and not worry about the comedy. And, it was very hard in running shows, not so much on [*The*] *Cosby* [*Show*], but on *Home Improvement*, to get people comfortable with that. You've got to get the story right. A lot of writers fall in love with jokes and they'll bend a story to keep it in. Sitcom people tend to hold onto the joke at all costs, and one of the things that was interesting is we would have a reading on the Mondays of the script, and a lot of times it would read really well, really funny, really interesting halfway through, and then it would kind of take this tremendous dive. I would tell young writers that the comedy isn't that much worse in the second half; how is it possible that there's no laughs in the whole second half? It's because we lost the audience. So we fixed the story, and it took a lot to get used to it. Let's get the story right, and we're not going to go out of our way to make it funny, but get the story right, and during the week we'll find the humor, but get the story right.

That's the whole thing. The humor's coming out of the story. And that's really what I was trying to get young writers to do, you know, with the pressure to have comedy within the sitcoms. Nowadays, with something like this Premise, my instinct would be, forget the comedy. I can't personally write without comedy. You can go as far as going to your father's place where he committed suicide, and without forcing it, there is humor.

". . . killing himself is one thing . . . but not telling me about Mantle?"

And then I found out—it was in my book—I met my cousin, who's older than I am, who's a stunning blonde—getting back to baseball, we grew up in the Bronx near Yankee Stadium, and my father was a German immigrant, as was the whole family. We were very embarrassed by this part of the family who didn't know anything about baseball; the whole neighborhood was all Yankees. And I was telling this to my cousin, who I hadn't seen in years, and she said to me, "Well, my father had the furrier shop on the Grand Concourse." I said, "Yeah, that was the family hangout," where all these people spoke German and horrified my sister and myself and any American cousins. She said, "You know about my affair with Mickey Mantle?"

It turns out that my cousin Leona had a three-year affair with Mantle, from the triple-crown years, '56 through '58. There's a whole section in my book about this. And I said, "Do you want me to reveal this?" and she said, "Sure," and it turns out that they stayed at the Concourse Plaza Hotel, which was on the Grand Concourse a few blocks away, and my cousin, once she got involved with Mantle, became friendly with all the players, and she would invite them over on the off-days, which there were more of back then.

We had already moved to Queens, but my father still used to come there a couple of days a week, and on the weekends, and so I said, "My father was schmoozing with the Yankees?" She said, "Yeah," and I said, "And he knew about Mantle?" She said, "Absolutely, everybody knew." And she said, "I wish you knew. I would've taken you to the Clubhouse all the time." And my reaction literally was . . . you know, killing himself is one thing . . . but not telling me about Mantle?

That's my idea personally of good comedy because it's not a joke, I mean, that's your thought at the moment. So I would pursue something like this in our story, or almost anything from the standpoint of what's an interesting story, what can we relate to as an audience.

". . . it was the only way to get his jokes *not* in."

Yeah, the hardest thing on a sitcom was dealing with the punch-up guys, because they would drive you crazy: "Oh, it's funny, it's funny, it's funny!" And you have to really be very delicate about how you reject them. We had one guy who . . . the way I found out . . . he was pouting every time we didn't like one of his lines, and some of them were fabulous, and some of them were terrible, and I used to say, "It's fantastic, but I'm not sure it fits right." You know, it was the only way to get his jokes *not* in. And there was a guy on *Maude*, let's call him Bill. Bill could write brilliant jokes, but some were terrible jokes, so Schiller said to me, "Watch this," and Bill was a stutterer, he said, "If he says it like that [without stuttering], it's a great line; if he stutters, even though he thinks it's a great line, it isn't a great line." And there was some deep part of him that must've known . . . or he was unsure of it. And then he'd fight for it. Nobody wanted to insult him and say, "But you stuttered the line." It was unbelievable. It would happen most of the time. So to me, that was like graduate school in comedy with these guys, and I'm still involved with Schiller and Lear. It was an amazing time and place to work.

JD (Jeffrey Davis): Talk a little bit about Sarah discovering her father's death, and how that might play out.

ES: To me, the story is a puzzle. I need to put it into a form for myself, so I'm going to make it a play. Okay, so with a play, you're restricted scene-wise. I think it would be interesting to start in the past and see the relationship. If you had complete freedom of amounts of people and sets, I would say it'd be interesting to see the dynamic when Sarah was a teenager with her mother and dad. We'd see how her family acted around the dinner table, and what job he had. It says he was successful. Personally, I love color, so I would look for an unusual profession where somebody makes a lot of money—but I want to make the job more unique. I mean, a cousin of mine invented a new jar lid for mayonnaise that used a rubber thing. There was the person who invented Wite-Out. All these people made a lot of money. I'm tired of everyone using the same old professions. Every film you see is about a writer, is about an

Like the devil, good writing is in the details. For example, Vladimir Nabakov spent two months creating the names of Lolita's classmates. When Elliot read the Premise and saw that the father had earned a good living, he didn't gloss over it. He wanted to identify a specific occupation. Then, to find more possibilities for story and humor, he wanted to find an *unusual* occupation to generate more surprise in the viewers. This attention to details is found in many of the interviews throughout this book.

advertising executive. I've had a butcher as one character, another guy who worked for the sanitation department. I think you're better off with just regular old people. So I personally would look for an interesting background. I would establish them kind of on the way up.

PD: As you pick an occupation for him, would you link that to the character somehow?

ES: Yeah, I would try to. Going by my instinct, when you read something like this, you tend to go . . . the silver-haired, fancy executive. My own instincts take me more to a guy who made it, you know, in the garment center, or something—I think a self-made guy is a more interesting character. It's my own background from New York characters. So yeah, I would make it a guy who is self-made, and is proud of himself, and has his own characteristics. Again, I equate it always to real people. You might make it that this wife lives through her husband, but they have an understanding . . . she spends a lot of money.

And the other thing I would immediately go to is, are there siblings? Are there brothers and sisters? How does that affect the dynamic of this? Is there an age difference in the siblings? I would just look to more and more to fill it out. I also think that in the way it is, the daughter, who is Sarah, doesn't really have anybody to talk to. Yeah, I would tend to make it a sibling, and look for territory within that. What interests me also is the relocation city-wise, and how it would impact this obviously single woman.

Well, I think if it's a contemporary time, I think it sort of depends what you create. My wife could have her mother move in and deal with it. The last thing in the world I could do is have *my* mother move in, or my father, if he were alive. There's just no drama in somebody who has an easy time with it. So I'd make it . . . the financial circumstances . . . to me, you do everything in your power to keep her removed. But again, it feels like we've seen a lot of that, so I would look for some sort of uniqueness in it.

The other way would be to put Sarah in a relationship that has its own ups and downs, and have this mother come in as a disruption. That's actually where my instincts would take me, as I think about it, because if my wife and I were in a different financial situation, I wouldn't let my mother move in, even if I had to put her in a dog house. I just wouldn't do it. Linda [Elliot's wife] would want her mother to move in, and it would cause a tremendous amount of tension between us. And within that, obviously, is comedy, but I would look for the dramatic tension and find the comedy off of that. If these people are struggling, if I'm the husband, and let's say we go back to a wife—and again, I keep wavering—I wouldn't decide this early on, I would keep playing with it. If I'm the husband, and it's my wife moving the mother in, I'd probably give up almost anything to raise the money to get her somewhere else. So I think there's humor within that, and if they were struggling, or upwardly mobile—I mean, what would you be willing to do to get rid of your mother-in-law, and how much would you hide it? Would you take an extra job, which would give you more income and get you out of the house?

The emotion drives you to dramatic beats and comedy beats. How you harness all that is something I personally can't and don't do this fast nowadays. You know, in sitcoms, you have to do it fast. And one of the worst things I always found was at the beginning of the season, you're laying out story, and we were very organized, and as the staffs got bigger, which was horrible, you know, everybody wants to do something. On *Maude*, we had Bud Grossman, Schiller and Weiskopf, and me, so you only had to come up with three stories to start, and then there'd be another round. Nowadays, there are like ten writers, and you don't want people to do nothing, so I used to try and double people up, which they hated, and it was always a big fight; it was just easier to team them up. Plus, it's a collaborative medium anyway. People come up to you and say, "Well, in my story . . ." and you say, "Well, which story is that?" And you have to do it so fast that you come up with beats that sound okay at the time, and they may not be workable, and then the guy or woman turns in a draft, and they say, "But this is what we agreed upon." "Yeah, but when you got there, couldn't you realize that it wasn't working?" So I really became an advocate of trying to take my time on stories, and see the puzzle, and get the story right.

To me, it's the puzzle, and I'm constantly moving stuff around in this treatment, like, "This is too soon," or, "I've already said this, the audience already knows this." And the other thing, which I've learned through the playwriting, that is different than television, is the audience knows a lot more than you give them credit for, and there's nothing like watching the audience and saying, "Alright, they get it. The boat's sailed, keep moving." Somebody said it . . . I read a quote, I'm sure you know it: "The best writing's leaving out the part that people skip when they read it." And, to me, that's the key. What don't you need, and what do you need? So to me, the best process, and the best part of the process, and the most fun part of the process, is the laying out of the piece.

JD: Well, would you lay out a few of the pieces of the puzzle?

ES: First of all, I'm not that interested in Sarah's work situation, so I'd go right to . . . she has a great relationship with her parents. I would take "great" with a grain of salt. What would interest me is a starting point of some family dinner to establish the past and the dynamic. Let's keep it a girl for now, start with her at fifteen. So then I would go to another scene where she's, say, in a marriage—they're having some sort of problem, maybe about money. And she would get the call from her mother saying the father had died. I think it would be interesting to break it to the kid that there was more to the story and the mother knows it, which gives the mother a different kind of emotion. My instinct might be that they were a terrific couple at the beginning. Sarah's talking to her husband about whatever issue they're dealing with, she gets the call from her mother, "Dad died," and it's surprisingly unemotional, and she doesn't get it. It turns out there's more to the story and Molly's pissed at him. "Ma, the guy died, how could you be pissed at him?" Molly says, "Because he died doesn't mean he didn't do this," and I think it's an interesting scene.

What happened? He died two days ago—Molly got a call from the jewelry store. She figured it out somehow; or there was a piece from a jewelry store and he never came in to pick it up. She went in to pick it up and it's inscribed to somebody else. Maybe even with her eccentricity: "When did he die?" "Three days ago." "You didn't call me?" "Well, we have a lot going on."

Is there a brother? There's a lot going on . . . Molly says, "I realize we're broke . . ." And where he died, what the circumstances were, could lead to a delay. But mixing real stuff with color . . . "Am I coming back," say, to New York, "for a funeral?" She hangs up . . . the live-in boyfriend, young husband, "What happened?" "My father died." "You don't seem very shaken up." "I'm trying to process the whole thing." Now, does he know the mother? Has he met the mother? Maybe it's kind of interesting if he hasn't met the mother and he's magnanimous about it; maybe they've been together four months, and they're on the upswing. "You don't know my mother." "Let her come." Might be interesting that he talks her into it, not knowing what he's getting into, and then my instinct would take me to . . . she actually adjusts initially better than he does . . . the daughter thing.

The mother is okay when she first comes, and then she grows on Sarah negatively. But again, I like surprises; you expect her to have a tough time with her mother; maybe she doesn't at the first time, and it's the husband/boyfriend who has the tough time. That's the kind of beginnings I would take. Whether any of that is anything that's any good? Or, I would use what I used to say to the writers, and what I look for, and I'm sure you do too, is opportunities, and just openings, we used to call them. What gives you openings? What gives you possibilities? What haven't you quite seen? Again, how to make credible that it's been three days since he died. I like the concept of it. In reality, it's pretty unlikely, so to tackle an interesting idea or make it credible really pushes you as a writer. Maybe you can or maybe you can't. And you have to be open to not falling in love with that idea. If you can pull it off, it is interesting.

Then, I would go to questions as to, if the mother's coming, how big is the apartment? Is it an apartment? Is it a house? Is it a condo? Is it her apartment? Is he just moving in with her? Is it his place? All those things, to me, are the choices, and the kind of stuff I didn't think of when I was doing sitcoms . . . thinking from all the points of view. Now, how uptight is the mother moving in? Does the mother know that the boyfriend's living there? That stuff she has to deal with on the phone, you certainly wouldn't let her come without dealing with it. Is he really living there? Are they dating? Is he kind of living there? Does she not get their domestic situation? How conservative or liberal is she? All that stuff. Who are his parents? Is he a Republican? Is she an old hippie? All those things, without hitting it over the head, are their variations on those things? They are what I would look for . . . for opportunities. And what I would do is, I would just list shit: What's a plot point? Potentially, what's a character thing? What's a line you might use? And I tend to lay it out in sections and take the best guess I can, and then again, treat it literally like a puzzle. I don't know if you know this, I have a degree in math and physics, and I went to graduate school . . . in math. So I have this very unusual background of organization. People are always saying, "What a wasted background," but it's actually very good with plotting.

PD: So you approach writing like an engineer?

ES: Yeah, yeah, and I didn't know I did that, and I didn't know there was anything unusual. I actually didn't know that other people didn't do it, and I'm always kind of amazed by how disorganized some writers are.

I actually had this one writer who, we'd lay out a plot, and she'd walk in these insane tangents, and the only way I could get her to stop and think is I brought her— you know Brio trains, they're like little wooden train sets that the kids used to have? I got her a piece of Brio train track, where it's a straight track with a little curve that goes off, and I got a little Stop sign, and I put it on her desk, and I put the Stop sign half off/on the little curve part, and I said, "Every time you come up with a beat, whether we gave it to you or not, I want you to think, "Am I going this way [*Elliot indicates a straight line*], or am I going this way [*Elliot indicates a curved line*]? If you even *suspect* you're going this way [*Elliot indicates a curved line again*], look at that little Stop sign and come into my office."

And that's the kind of thing . . . you've gone the wrong way . . . maybe you're going the wrong way. To me, the biggest part is how do you go, what ultimately is your best guess, is the right way to tell a good story. And I was always astounded by how far people could go off. And I kept on telling people, "It doesn't matter how good a chunk you came up with . . ." and they'd be polishing, and polishing, and you

During the time that Elliot Shoenman ran *Home Improvement,* there was very little turnover in the writing staff. This is rare for a hit show because the writing staffs of popular shows get raided frequently. His staff liked the environment he created so much that, to quote from *Blazing Saddles,* "They stayed in droves." He frequently praised and supported the abilities of his staff while feeling comfortable enough to exhibit his own humility. At the same time, he was a very committed mentor.

The Brio train track example mentioned on page 325 shows the lengths to which Elliot went to get good story structure into the shows, and at the same time, to make sure that his staff developed. This can be traced back to his math/science background. He was able to create a *concrete* example of this abstract concept in a visual enough way that his writer, who clearly had serious structural problems, was able to *see* her structural problems, and then correct them.

can't get them to bring the f–cking script in, "I'm still polishing . . ." because you may be polishing stuff that's in the scene that we're not going to use.

PD: You closed the circle for me when you said you had a math/science background. A lot of the writers we've spoken to said, "You've got to get conflict." You used the word "puzzle," which I find very interesting. You really look at it like a problem-solving situation for the audience and you have to give them something to think about.

ES: To me, the story's everything, and how you tell a story is . . . the beginning and end are really easy, because the beginning is whatever you came up with as your premise, and the end is either a happy ending or a sad ending.

PD: You keep saying that the story's got to be logical; it's got to be credible, and yet there has to be something in there that's puzzling.

ES: Right, therein lies the problem, and therein lies, to me, the creativity. It's a very fine line. I think everybody has to relate to what you're saying, and yet within that, you have to surprise them. So what I discovered is that you need to have a good combination of the familiar and the surprising, and what that proportion is, who knows? But there's got to be some familiarity in a really good story.

Also, you can play up the self-involvement of the mother, because if she immediately discovered that they were not in great financial shape—"Holy shit, where does that leave me?"—it's an interesting dynamic between her and the daughter, who says, "It didn't occur to you to call me?"

What's so amazing about the stupidity of television is, it was my asset and my liability in the eyes of television, because I was known as a very good show runner who could do stories, but it became the mark against me in the networks: "Is the guy funny enough?"

"'Running a staff is like running a baseball team.'"

I certainly can write comedy, but it wasn't my priority. I know how to get it out of all the people, and I always used to say, "Running a staff is like running a baseball team." Some guys are good at something, you have to manage the whole thing, and when you're also around better comedy writers, your comedy becomes better. Just like I think and hope when comedy people are around somebody like me, their story writing gets better. If they're listening, it certainly does at the moment. And when Marley [*Sims, a writer on* Home Improvement *whose interview can be found on page 334*] and I wrote together, she learned a lot from my story sense. But when it comes to dialogue, holy shit, stuff comes out of her mouth that's just unbelievable. I can never write dialogue quite the way she does, but when I'm writing with her, my dialogue becomes better.

JD: So how would a Premise like this be limited by making it a sitcom?

ES: In sitcom, you have to service all these characters that have all these deals, so you can't really take things where they go, and you can't really take this Premise about Sarah and Molly in a sitcom where you want it to go. You have to get back to basically where you started. I would immediately take something like this and not want to go to a sitcom, unless you wanted to make money or get a deal. You can take it anywhere you want to take it; you can have the mother die.

JD: But you made it funny, which I thought was interesting, and I see what Peter's saying about how you use your background in math, but you made it funny.

ES: I can't *not* do that, because that's the way I see it. For my process, that comes later. I also think that this is the highest degree of difficulty in writing, which is to do drama with comedy, because a lot of the pieces that do that . . . some of the Woody Allen pieces integrate it, but a lot of other ones, they'll be funny to a point and then become dramatic, and they work. I think some of the Jim Brooks stuff is like that, and that's okay, but when you integrate it throughout, I think it's a very hard thing to do. I have the nerve to try it.

"... I said to Tim, 'This is one time you have to throw your weight around...'"

But you know, even on *Home Improvement*, we were the number-one show, and then, number three, number four, and I kept trying to integrate an occasional serious episode about the family, because I really felt like people could do it, and I got Tim [Allen] on board to try more acting stuff, so to speak, and Marley and I wrote a script. I pitched an idea to the network ... it was twenty-four hours in the life of a family where your kid has this serious medical testing and may have cancer, and what that twenty-four hours is like. And they just went crazy against it, even though we had the power to do it. And they said, "You can't do a cancer episode." And we said, "Well, Jonathan Taylor Thomas," who was a big star at the time, "... and Tim will do it." And the network just didn't want to do it. So I said to Tim, "This is one time you have to throw your weight around," and he was on board, and we did it, and it came in number one. It was the last time the show came in number one. And sure enough, ABC called and said, "What else do you have? What other serious things?" They were thinking of doing the *Tragedy of the Week*. It was unbelievable. But, even within the cancer thing, we found humor.

JD: Was this Norman Lear's influence?

ES: Absolutely, 100 percent. And again, what was tricky was the network's reluctance, and we had the power to just say, "We're doing it," and by that time, Tim had been won over. But they said, "Where's the humor?" I said, "I don't know yet, this is a tricky one. I understand that it's hard, but you just have to trust it. It may have to be found during the week, and the original table reading may have not much of it. But that's what we want to do." And there was enough in there of ... how you do it. I don't even remember how we did it, but we did it.

PD: But that kind of tension relief, when you get it, is huge.

ES: Absolutely. As a matter of fact, one of the things, which was really a crazy trick, at the beginning before they go up to the doctor's appointment, there's a lemon meringue pie, and Tim's wife says to Tim, "Don't eat that, no matter what, because we're taking it to my sister's." So she goes, and he looks around and he takes a spatula, and he cuts off the top, lifts it, and scoops out a whole chunk of the lemon, and then he puts it back. And we just left it. Then she comes back and they break this news about how they may have cancer and there's a really heavy scene between the two of them, and she's gone crazy, and we really distracted the audience. And at the

Freud wrote that humor comes from relieving tension. Elliot was constantly pushing the envelope on inserting drama into sitcoms so they would create more intense possibilities for humor. Although the network executives tried to prevent him from using an extreme dramatic device—a child who may have cancer—he fought them and won. The lemon meringue pie joke worked because of the huge comic relief that the cancer situation set up.

very end, she said, "I just, I don't know what I'm going to do with myself. I've got to have a piece of the pie." And he panicked. And she digs into the pie, and there's no bottom to it. And it got this tremendous laugh, but we found this gimmick where we really weren't cheating on cancer jokes, but the audience got it, and they forgot completely about the pie; it's just sitting there. You're worried about cancer. But once she went for that fork, there was a tremendous relief, and that really took some chicanery. And that came with building these two end-pieces to it. So it's all these little odds and ends, and that wasn't a dishonest moment. It's tough. It doesn't always work.

JD: Do you think the good situation comedy is, in a way, like a one-act play?

ES: I don't think there's any question about it, except that you don't have the time limitations [in a play], and you don't have the character limitations. People can die. You have limitations with sets and things, but you can take a story where it's meant to go. And for me, having done sitcoms, if it's serious, you could go serious as long as you want, I mean, if it's ten pages, fine, if it's a page, fine. But we're never under pressure to put jokes in, which on a sitcom you are, to a certain extent.

JD: A little bit about your history . . . were the people in your family funny?

". . . and I stole a line from *The Honeymooners* . . ."

ES: Not really. I think my humor developed as a defense. My father was a terrifying character. I locked myself in my room in Queens, and watched the sitcoms, and I had no idea that I'd learned this. When I got on *Maude* and I was so overwhelmed, Schiller and Weiskopf used to take me out to lunch. We used to go to the Brown Derby . . . farmers market . . . they would tell stories about [*I Love*] *Lucy* episodes. They had done a lot of the *Lucy* shows. And I used to say, "No, no, no, Fred Mertz was in the other room when that happened." And they kept saying, "Are you sure?"

And I'd say, "I'm pretty positive." "Yeah, I think you're right." And I kept correcting them, and I realized, and they realized, that I'd learned the craft without knowing it. I'd just watched so many shows that I really knew how to do this. I got in trouble with them once because I was desperate on a *Maude* show and I stole a line from *The Honeymooners*. I just didn't know what to do. And I gave them the script. Rod Parker was the producer and he said, "Boy, I really like what you did, especially that joke from *The Honeymooners*, which I originally wrote."

PD: You basically were locked in a room with sitcoms and because you're so analytic, you induced the rules of comedy writing on your own.

ES: Yeah, I think that's true. I think my sense of humor was a defense against my father, and obviously I had a sense of humor, which I think either you do or you don't. I do believe that dramatic writers trying to write comedy is usually a disaster; comedy writers often can write drama if they can get past their protection of the comedy.

PD: Good scientists have strong powers of induction and deduction. They don't just say, "That was good, and that was good." They come up with rules for how it worked and *why* it was good.

ES: That's exactly right. After college, I went to graduate school for only one term. I didn't finish, but then I worked for Lockheed as an associate scientist, so my background is exactly that. And the other thing, incidentally, which you'd be interested in, my wife is a psychologist. She's an MFT [marriage and family therapist]. And being with her all this time and her having no interest in show business, I learned a lot about thinking about people and why people do things, and their inconsistencies.

PD: So at twenty-six, you had figured out the rules for comedy writing by yourself, and all of a sudden you are thrown in with these comedy giants. Did you learn much from them?

ES: Yeah, it was like going to graduate school in comedy. And at that time, there were a handful of us, I think, who were very lucky. There were basically three schools of comedy working: There were the Lear shows, the MTM [Enterprises] shows, and the Garry Marshall shows. And they were all different kinds of levels of how you did things, but there was a lot of mentoring, and these guys really took it seriously about teaching you the craft.

"'Alright . . . just stick in a house number for now.'"

I once said to Schiller and Weiskopf, "How can I ever thank you guys for what you've taught me?" And Weiskopf said, "Just pass the craft on." And that's one of the reasons I love doing the theatre and nurturing young writers, because it's a very terrific situation. But they taught me everything; they taught me all the crazy terminology. It was so funny at the beginning; I was sitting there totally intimidated, and I'd be laying out my story with them, and they'd say, "Alright . . . just stick in a house number for now." And I'd go, "Great" . . . I had no idea what a house number was. And I'd be asking everybody, I'd go across the hall, "Can you do me a favor and tell me what a house number is." I don't know if you know what it is. A house number comes from the garment center and it's an example of the kind of thing you put in, the kind of joke you put in, *but it's not the joke.*

Early in his career on *Maude*, Elliot worked under the legendary comedy writing team of Bob Schiller and Bob Weiskopf. He credits them with giving him a graduate-level education in comedy writing. Among the lessons they taught him were constructing classic types of jokes including the house number, the malapropism, and the turn-around joke.

The *house number* comes from the retail shoe business: "We need a navy pump with a wedge heel in suede." It shows the characteristics of the shoe a customer wanted, but the store didn't have it in yet. As a joke, you put in what you are looking for, *but it's not the joke.* You keep it in until you find the right joke.

When Elliot worked on *Maude,* their Writers' Room was right across the hall from the *All In The Family* Writers' Room. Because *Maude* didn't have well-known comedic characters, every joke had to be written from scratch, and this could be very time-consuming. He said the writers often didn't finish until after 8 p.m. The *All in the Family* writers always got to leave at 5 p.m. If they had trouble finding a joke, they could always throw in a *malapropism* for Archie Bunker. Elliot included the great example, "Edith, I think I might have a hernia, I gotta see a Groinocologist."

The malapropisms come from a character named Mrs. Malaprop in Richard Brinsley Sheridan's 1775 play, *The Rivals*. Mrs. Malaprop frequently misspeaks (to great comic effect) by using words that don't have the meaning she intends, but sound similar to words that do.

At the Norman Lear school of comedy, Elliot also learned the *turnaround joke*. A character says, "A hundred percent, I'm not going for Chinese food." Cut to: A Chinese restaurant. They are guaranteed a laugh, even though it is often a cheap one. Elliot said that whenever you see a turnaround joke, you can bet that the writers wanted to leave the Room because they were getting hungry.

In the garment center, they used to say, "I've got a beautiful shoe for you, but I don't have it in stock, but it's the heel of this one, the sole of this one, and it'll have like this color," and they put together the kind of thing . . . a sample. And somehow it got into the comedy vernacular, and a house number is just the kind of joke you *would* put in, but it isn't a joke. And then we ran off it at *Home Improvement.* I came up with the offshoot, which was a "house laugh," which is something that we laugh at, but nobody else in the world is going to find funny. So we used to have some things that, in the light of day, were a house laugh. There were a bunch of them, but the biggest one for me was a house number. It's just kind of a perfect phrase for that thing. Those guys taught me just a ton of stuff.

JD: And who have you mentored?

ES: I ended up starting a lot of people in the business. Charlie Hauck. I started Neal Marlens, who created *The Wonder Years.* I gave him his first job. John Markus, who ended up running *The Cosby Show,* and I loved.

PD: How do you know when you write something funny?

ES: It's going to sound weird, but you just do. It's in your bones. I've told so many stories to people . . . such a big mouth. Somebody once said to me, "How come we're working together . . . you go to lunch and you have some unbelievable adventure every time you go to lunch? I go to lunch and *have a sandwich.*" "It's just the way I see it," and I learned that my descriptions were funny, and you just kind of have the confidence, and it is a crapshoot because sometimes you're right, and sometimes you're wrong. You're running a show and people pitch things, and it's your judgment to say, "This is funny, this isn't funny." Occasionally, somebody would fight hard enough, and [if] it didn't violate the character of the story, I'd go with it. And many times, I was wrong.

We feel also, you can always change it. You can always play with it. The one thing that I will not do and I hate, which you can get a laugh anytime, a cheap laugh, the old lady cursing, just stupid laughs, like, "This is f–cking bad news."

PD: In *All in the Family,* you had analyzed it to the point where this guy could always get a guaranteed laugh doing this. You had a good sense of the formulas.

ES: Right, and I'm not saying in the middle of the night I wouldn't go to that formula, because on *Home Improvement* we certainly had the ability to do a dumb joke, and when you're in trouble on a show like that, it's the handiest thing in the world, and I'll do it any time, but I wouldn't do it by choice.

PD: When you get to, "How much do you tip a guy on the way to commit suicide . . . "

ES: Right, those, to me, are highly intelligent jokes. A dumb joke is a malaprop. Tim using the wrong word, hitting himself over the head with something. Like the pie thing in the cancer episode, which is a physical thing, but that was a clever joke to me. That's an intelligent joke, because you've set it up and you don't see it coming. There's an intelligence to a certain kind of humor. I really tried over the years to learn how to do things where you don't see it coming. That's the other thing on a lot of sitcoms . . . you just see it coming a mile away.

The other terminology I learned from the Lear school is the turnaround joke, which is, "There's no way he's going to show up." *Ding-dong.* So it's that kind of thing. He also called it the ding-dong joke. Again, very cheap laughs, you see it all the time, cutaways to that. "A hundred percent, I'm not going for Chinese food." *Cut to the Chinese restaurant.* A hundred percent of the time it'll get you a laugh from the general audience. There's a million variations on the turnaround joke. I just hate them. You would have a hard time during my era to find a turnaround joke in *Home Improvement,* even when it was late at night, 'cause I hate that more than anything, because it's just so easy.

Elliot has written in almost every setting possible. He has written solo, with a partner, as part of a Room, and has been a show runner. This has given him a very broad perspective on the role of the writer. As we look at the direction of his writing, it may be summed up in an old sitcom industry joke: "How many network executives does it take to screw in a light bulb?" The network executive says, "Does it have to be a light bulb?"

One of the striking similarities we have discovered about people who write comedy is how painful it is to see their writing changed, rarely for the better. Several of them have said that they now only write if they can also get to produce or direct their work. Elliot has gone one giant step beyond. He now writes plays that he finances. He finally has some control over his writing.

An Interview with
Marley Sims

A partial list of Marley Sims's credits as a writer includes:
Home Improvement; Sabrina, the Teenage Witch; The Paper Chase; and *Soul Man.*

All of us have been stamped indelibly by the relationship we had with our parents. In this interview, **Marley Sims** calls up vivid images of interactions with her mother, using them as the basis for creating three-dimensional characters and compelling conflicts. Her Premise development is an inspiring example of writing from direct experience. Every element she creates blends a ring of truth with a touch of craft to make it uniquely funny. Marley's ability to recall interactions so clearly is responsible for her ability to write dialogue. Elliot Shoenman, her long-time writing partner on *Home Improvement,* praises this gift several times during his interview (see page 317). While most of us spend a great deal of our income and countless hours of our lives working through those critical recollections with our therapists, she earns a great deal of money by putting them into the mouths of her characters.

PD (Peter Desberg): As we've explained in our Premise [see page 9], how would you go about developing the show's plot lines?

MS (Marley Sims): They say "Write what you know," and I immediately relate to Sarah and Molly's story. My father died when I was a child and my relationship with my mother was very loaded. Given that, a mother and daughter forced to live together as grown-ups is what has the possibility of humor and heartache at the same time. I'm drawn to the long form. I think you can go deeper, and you can say anything you want to say. And I think the conflict would be deeper between the two women in a feature. It would be: Where did Molly come up short as a mother? Here's this woman who all of a sudden wants to move in with her daughter. To me, it's just so loaded. So I would have Sarah not want this . . . just not know how to say "No." And I think I would have the mother be strong, so that maybe it took Sarah a long time to move out on her own and get her footing. She's finally done it, she's finally broken away, and all of a sudden, here comes this mother who takes it all back.

I was talking with a friend last night who still lives near her mother and she's in her fifties, and they are very close, and I think that I would want to mull that relationship around in here. You meet her and she drives you insane, and it's great that far away, but on top of you, it's just not working. So I think the situation would be that Molly is here and Sarah says, "How long are you going to stay? Oh, boy, California's swell and I will help you find a condo, another husband, anything to get you out of here."

And maybe Sarah has friends who see a side of her mother that she never gets to see. You always like everybody's mother better than your own. I always thought a great idea for a movie, or a TV show, would be everybody's parents come to visit on the block, but they all stay one house over so that your mother's staying next door, and his mother's over here because everybody treats other people's kids better.

And I think it's funnier if Sarah's not a Type-A personality. If Molly is more Type-A and the daughter is scattered, and that the freedom that she got from being away from her mother was not [having] somebody on top of her telling her everything she was doing wrong. And here she is, back again. Having that critical presence. Something I think would be interesting is to make Sarah somebody who says things like, "I can't find my keys." It's ten times worse when somebody's around, standing there like this [*Marley stands with arms crossed, tapping one foot rapidly*]. "Are we going? Are we leaving?" "Well, in a minute." And in terms of guys, that's kind of interesting, maybe it's interesting to try and fix your mother up if that'll get her out of the house.

I'm trying to think what other things to bring into this. You know, if Sarah is an only child, that's also another pressure. I like the idea that she's an only child, because that would create much more pressure from her mother.

Molly is looking at every single detail, and she knows this child because that's all she's focused on. And I can create a disability for Sarah. Something neurotic. In my head she's scattered; just that kind of personality where she's always late . . . somebody who's just a step behind. It's such an effort to just make it on time. Maybe because she gets lost in noticing things that other people don't notice. She has an eye for detail that other people don't have. And she will stop and just stare at something, and take in the colors while the bus is leaving. "Shit, man, I'm going to be late." So in an odd way, I think their being together brings out the worst in each, because it forces Molly again to be in that critical position, and Sarah to be taken back to her childhood. Then maybe there's a guy. I think Sarah is feeling her oats in what may be the first real love relationship she's ever had, and she managed to keep a lot of her neuroses under wraps. That's an interesting character flaw to me. I think Sarah's job should be a challenge. She's not going to run an organization or business.

JD (Jeffrey Davis): What do you see her doing?

MS: Maybe she's here in Los Angeles, working as a personal assistant. Somebody who's constantly running somebody else's life, who can't get it together. And maybe the people that usually take those jobs are doing something else. Maybe she could be going to school, trying to go back to college, or get a master's degree, and this is a part-time job.

JD: You mentioned that there's something you always thought was a funny idea about other people's parents.

> "Everybody who used to meet my mother would say, 'What a sweet woman!' She was delightful in a room full of strangers."

MS: Well, I think everybody's parents are always on their best behavior with strangers. Everybody who used to meet my mother would say, "What a sweet woman!" She was delightful in a room full of strangers. They always say you should treat your neighbors like you treat your family, and treat your family like you treat your neighbors. I think there's something to that.

JD: Your preference would be more to do a movie than to do a sitcom?

MS: Because I think you can really dig in there.

JD: Where do you see it going?

MS: Well, the happy ending would be Molly moving out. She finds her own shtick and maybe she gets married.

PD: And there's a wedding scene?

MS: A wedding at the end? Sure. I think you want to do a happy ending, but it should be bittersweet. I don't think you can fix anything between Molly and Sarah. I think a relationship of a mother and daughter, you can work through some stuff. The mother's only fifty, she's a baby, for God's sakes. I'd make her seventy-five and a lot more set in her ways.

> "I have yet to see a guy say, 'I'm having a baby, I can't find a woman, I'm getting a surrogate.'"

JD: Who do you think isn't being served in the audience that we need to see stories about?

MS: My generation is missing the boat. You see all these stories now about women who are having babies without men. Clearly, we're taking a path where a whole generation of men is missing women and women are raising children alone. I have yet to see a guy say, "I'm having a baby, I can't find a woman, I'm getting a surrogate. I want this child. I don't want her to have anything to do with it." What was that story about that "Mister X 41" who fathered thirteen children? All the mothers brought the kids together. You don't see men doing that. You don't find men saying, "I must father. I must father." That, I think, is interesting. But I think my generation—I'm fifty-eight years old—where do we fit in? Where do we quite fit in? We're not a generation that's going down easy, I don't think. We're such a "Me, me, me, me, me!" generation.

I think I've got another twenty years of things that I could do. And I think, "What is it I want to do?" Great husband, we have a good marriage, we both took our retirement already; we can still write. But we've got some financial security. And I can't figure out what to do. I just can't. I'm volunteering. I'm doing some grief counseling and I love that, but I feel like, in terms of the business, I'm not going to work on staff on TV anymore unless a friend hires me. And most of them aren't working because they're in their late fifties.

"There's a part of me that thinks, 'I wonder if I'm too old to go to nursing school.'"

PD: Would you take some of those feelings you have and put them into this mother?

MS: Well, if I was going to do that and you made the mother sixty and Molly says, "Am I viable? Am I viable to do what?" And did she stay home? I don't understand the concept of a housewife. If your daughter's not been home, what have you been doing? I don't really have any friends who just do nothing. They either teach or they do something. There's a part of me that thinks, "I wonder if I'm too old to go to nursing school." I think I'd be a good nurse. Could somebody who is sixty say, "I'm going to go to nursing school?" I think it would be interesting to have Molly have a brand new career like that. To try and learn something brand new. I think that's something you can do in a movie. In television, unless you created the show, the characters already exist. You are handed their foibles and flaws.

While some writers give their characters pronounced quirks and flaws like drug abuse, Marley goes for more subtle ones. She keeps notes on interesting character traits for just this purpose. It's one of the reasons why her work has such a strong ring of authenticity. Her humor has universal appeal because we recognize ourselves, or someone close to us, in it. By asking Marley to develop this mother/daughter Premise, we sent her to Disneyland for the day.

PD: How do you go about developing characters?

MS: I keep little notes, personality quirks that are interesting, and I would have to think about the relationship between Molly and Sarah. Here are a mother and daughter who've been separated and now are going to come together again. I think they have to build to each other, build to their flaws. They're in conflict because of the past and I don't think you have anything without this conflict. I certainly can't write without creating that.

PD: How would you build these two characters, based around the conflict?

MS: Well, immediately I think maybe it's Molly moving into the space, literally entering the space of the daughter who has set up her life the way she finally feels comfortable. And where is this person going to go, this huge presence of a person? How does this fit into Sarah's space, having a mother walk in the door with way too many suitcases? Maybe Molly doesn't say, "This is going to be an extended visit." Maybe she just forgets to mention how long she's going to be staying. I'd go immediately to that conflict. "You can't stay. I've got to give you a time limit." That's what Sarah would like to say, but she can't.

PD: The mother is overbearing. She's dominant. She doesn't have to say it directly.

MS: "Can I have a key?" "Key? Why do you need a key?" Sarah asks. To have it unfold, I think I would have it that Molly knows her daughter. I would think she knows that her daughter is not going to want her presence forever here. I don't think parents are deluded in that way. So maybe that's why she piecemeals how much information she feeds her about how long she's staying. "Because once I'm here, what are you going to do? She hasn't got the balls to throw me out. She's a ditzy little thing. She'll make do. I lived with her for thirty years, she can live with me for a year, it won't kill her." "Wait, a year?" Sarah says. "You said a year? Where did a year come from? A year?"

To me, right away that's a conflict. Maybe Sarah's got an aggressive friend who says, "I can have her out in a couple days." I think I'd bring her in to try and get Molly out of the house. That seems like the start of a good premise.

PD: You started with a conflict and said, "Okay, Molly reacts by being subtly but manipulatively overbearing," and Sarah responds with passive-aggressive welcoming. Maybe she has a friend who says, "I can get her out." Then Molly reacts to somebody who's a little more aggressive.

MS: It's interesting, from my point of view. I hear you saying back what I laid out and I get another idea and it just reiterates to me how much I hate to write alone. I hate it. I always hated it. I've had some success with it. It got me *Home Improvement*, a spec script I wrote by myself, and I immediately got hooked up with a partner. Everybody got hooked up with other people on that show because they felt you can write faster. People were paired up who'd never written with anybody before and spent eight years doing that. That's how Elliot Shoenman and I got hooked up together. And I loved it. And if I never write another word alone, I'll be a happy puppy.

Yeah, as soon as I heard back, "the friend who's going to try and get the mother out of there," I thought, "No matter how many friends Sarah throws in front of this woman, *the mother just gets rid of them all.*" You know, just keeps them all away. I don't know that I would've had that thought if I hadn't heard you feed it back. And I think that is the brilliance of collaboration.

JD: You also said parents don't behave around their children the way they behave around other people's kids.

MS: Maybe that's the end of the movie; maybe that's where the movie goes. Molly's not going to change. Maybe Sarah gets to see what her friends see, and you just sort of have to buy what the garbage is. You have to buy it, you buy it with your spouse sometimes or with your children, and you say, "Well, this is what they do." But where does it weigh versus their goodness? So they live like a pig, *but* they come home. I think what Sarah is left with is lowered expectations.

Whenever my mother was coming out to California, I would say, "I'm *not* going to get into that same place we go every time she comes." Every time she came, we got into exactly the same place. Sure, she's dead seven years. The timing was perfect. We were getting along . . . and I even know what the trigger is. You know, we could be driving—my mother never drove, she lived in New York. I grew up in Brooklyn and I had a license, but I didn't have a car, so I never drove either until I moved out here. Every time my mother would come to visit, she used to love to go see the big, fancy houses because we had no money, we lived in horrible apartments in Brooklyn, and I'd take her through Beverly Hills. She used to love to go through Coldwater Canyon.

"To have this kind of money. Look how they live." And then she would always say, "I can't believe you can drive like this." And it would just piss me off. It was just . . . that was the beginning. And she'd always say it. Sometimes she'd say it three times a day.

PD: What did it trigger?

MS: That level of incompetence that I had growing up. "Why can't you do this? Why can't you do that?" And so it was a miracle to my mother that she had a child who could drive.

JD: Molly knows how to push those same buttons?

MS: Oh, yeah. Sarah is neurotic. The way I would make her neurotic, in terms of the incompetence . . . where does that come from? It comes from Molly saying, "Why don't you do it this way?" "What's wrong with the way I'm doing it?" "It's better this way." And Sarah thinks, "If it's better this way, then I'm doing it wrong and there's something wrong with me." When my mother had Alzheimer's—she had it for seven years—and by the end she oddly turned into a very nice person. She wasn't a nice person her entire life. But at the end, she really pissed me off. All of a sudden, this person . . . who was this? Who was this person?

PD: Your approach seems to be: "Let's start with what's really happening." Like the drive you describe. And then you find the humor in the situation. "Let's not go for the joke."

MS: Yeah, absolutely.

PD: You didn't take one of these two people and make them a comic book character, while the other one was three-dimensional. Both women have their strengths and weaknesses. You kept it much more real—and you were saying at the very beginning, when you write, it's going to have comedy in it, but the comedy comes out of your subconscious.

MS: For me, that's the best kind of thing to write, something that merges both things. I've never tackled drama. The only episode I ever wrote that was a drama was on *The Paper Chase,* and it was the same way I used to get my acting work. It was a show that had a comedy feeling sliding through it, and in my acting work I always got cast as some serious character with some goofy twist to it. So, I think it's just my nature if I sat down to write something; my mind goes to a place where I find the humor in everything.

PD: How did you learn to do that?

MS: I don't know. And I think that is part of my insecurity. Some people just sit down and really feel comfortable behind a keyboard. My husband, God love him, he could sit down in a room and just write all day long. Articles for the newspaper, even. He has a real good sense of his ability. I tell people all the time I think I suffer because I didn't study, and so I feel like they're going find out: "Oh, boy, geez, how'd you get away with that?" And I always knew I was funny and I always knew I could make people laugh. I just didn't know if I could do it on paper. When I found out I could do it on paper, I didn't ever really trust it. And I think that's why I like to write with somebody else. It makes me feel more confident.

PD: Are you comfortable working in a situation with a whole bunch of writers?

MS: Yeah. Yeah, I'm real good in that situation.

JD: What was that like? Were there a lot of women?

MS: The first year, there were four of us, and the second year they let everybody go, and then they brought me back the third year. I stayed the third year. There were never really more than two or three women around the table. I think you have to be a certain kind of woman to be able to get in that Room and be heard.

> **". . . it's a balancing act between finding that sort of feminine thing, and the 'Hey, hey, I got something to say, too, pay attention to me over here!'"**

JD: What kind of woman?

MS: I think you have to be a little pushy, and not a ball-buster, because there are a lot of men in there, and if you come off in a way that they see you as threatening I think you . . . it's a balancing act between finding that sort of feminine thing, and the "Hey, hey, I got something to say, too, pay attention to me over here!"

PD: Have you been in a lot of different Room situations?

MS: Not that many. *Home Improvement* was the longest, and I did *Sabrina, the Teenage Witch* and a show with Dan Aykroyd called *Soul Man*. I'm good at hearing little pieces of this . . . "Ooh, let's do this, and let's do that," and it's what I miss about the Room. I don't miss the hours. I don't miss the kitchen or the candy. I miss that kind of input when something wonderful happened on the news, some big story, and we would just come in there in the morning and get to it.

> **"Ten people worked on this thing, and they really believed whoever's name was on it, you did the bulk, and it was a real collaboration."**

PD: Did you do much improv?

MS: No, I didn't do much improv, but most of the people around the table don't have acting backgrounds. I never really worked with anybody like this. The people at *Home Improvement* were so supportive. Our script was on the table, and someone would say, "You got a better joke than that one, I'd love to have it." My name is the one on the screen. Even the actors, God love them, they'd come in and say, "Boy, that was a great script," like I did it by myself. Ten people worked on this thing, and they really believed whoever's name was on it, you did the bulk, and it was a real collaboration. I think that's maybe one of the places where collaboration was a good thing.

> **". . . the show was number one, agents were calling . . . 'You know, you're not making as much money as the guy across the table!'"**

I didn't have any political nightmares. They are still my closest friends. That would drive me nuts. I don't think I would've enjoyed it as much as I did. We had a very tight group. After the third year of *Home Improvement,* and the show was number one, agents were calling on the speed dial: "You know, you're not making as much money as the guy across the table!" There were a couple of people who just took development deals and split, but we stayed together a long time because—especially for me, I was also working as a consultant and had a little child at home, and they let me have the best schedule. I only worked three days a week. I worked the late rewrite nights and two other days until six. So I had a seven-year run that was fabulous. I was also writing with the boss, so who's going to complain?

> **"If I'm writing by myself and I'm not happy with what I did on Day One, I'll just do the laundry on Day Two."**

JD: Did Elliot Shoenman mentor you?

MS: I think he did. Elliot and I had different strengths. He had a much better sense of story than I have. I think that was something where I could run with the joke for two or three pages and just get lost. And I think I had a way with crispy dialogue, and so I think we brought to each other an amazing voice. He taught me a style which now I'm stuck with, that in some ways is a little crippling. On *Home Improvement,* we did twenty-three episodes together. We never had to rewrite. We would not move forward to Day Two if we were not happy with what we did on Day One. So by the end of eight days we had a really good finished script. Sometimes we'd wind up ripping up two pages, but we didn't move forward until we really were happy with what we had. If I'm writing by myself and I'm not happy with what I did on Day One, I'll just do the laundry on Day Two.

JD: Have you mentored anyone?

MS: On *Sabrina, the Teenage Witch* where there were some young writers, I read their stuff and gave notes. I'm very supportive of young writers. I turn them on to friends who have shows, and I came into the business at a time when you could get a part-time job if you were a woman. I don't think that stuff happens anymore. It's so hard to get a job, and you're up against Princeton graduates. The guy who was getting our coffee on *Sabrina* graduated from Princeton and he wanted to be a writer. I said, "Waste of time; don't get my coffee, let me get you some." You know, he's working.

JD: As a writer?

MS: Yeah. Gregory Thomas Garcia [creator of *My Name Is Earl*]. He's a great guy. He is just incredibly creative. Does it on his own. He's young, he's funny, and he's got a great family.

JD: You start with the humanity of a situation and then you build out from there. And it was really interesting to watch Elliot's process, because he's very analytical.

MS: On *Home Improvement,* we were doing a script on betting on football. Tim Allen was going to split season tickets with somebody. There was so much math involved I got a headache and Elliot is just doing his stuff [*Marley clicks her fingers*]. "You owe me thirty-seven dollars, fifty cents!" Yeah, we go to two other places, but we both are very emotional, so we both go to sort of what is at the heart of this, and what's the purpose of it.

An Interview with
Cheri and Bill Steinkellner

A partial list of Cheri and Bill Steinkellner's credits as show runners, writers, and creators includes: *Cheers, The Jeffersons, Who's the Boss?, The Pee Wee Herman Show, Teacher's Pet, America Tonight, Bob,* and *Hope & Gloria.*

Writers are usually most at ease behind a desk in their office. The **Steinkellners** are most comfortable around the antique oval table in their spacious kitchen. The setting is perfect, since Cheri and Bill Steinkellner are all about family. Picture Cheri seated behind the keyboard of her Mac, while Bill paces the length of the spacious room, offering us coffee and assorted treats. This multiple Emmy Award-winning team, whose marriage has been running almost as long as their partnership, start developing the Premise with a simple newspaper article and go directly to using what they know best—their family. They blend in some wonderfully funny stories about their kids and themselves and mix them together to create an imaginative and contemporary story.

As they work, the maid, the gardener, and a FedEx guy come and go. The Steinkellners never break stride. They work together with fondness and respect, with a little teasing mixed in. As you read this interview, you'll get the feeling that this is how they've always worked together. In fact, for us, the magic of this particular interview is that it's impossible to tell where the partnership ends and the marriage begins . . . or the other way around.

PD (Peter Desberg): As we've explained in our Premise [see page 9], how would you go about developing the show's plot lines?

CS (Cheri Steinkellner): Billy just cut out an article on helicopter moms, and gave it to me. I'm sending it to our son to show him, "Hey, see, I'm not that bad."

BS (Bill Steinkellner): You're a low-flying helicopter Mom.

CS: No, I'm high-flying. I'm not hovering.

BS: Oh, you're not hovering, no, no. That's an interesting idea. Let's go with that.

CS: It's a new phenomenon that hasn't yet been over-explored. So, here we have Molly coming in and Sarah being more of a helicopter daughter, looking to help Molly. I really do think that with baby boomers, this phenomenon of watching over our children well into adulthood in a very hands-on way is pretty interesting.

BS: It would be really difficult for you if your mom could just do everything. You're just starting out. Your friends adore her.

CS: It's like me!

BS: Yeah, like you. I was pitching you.

CS: I got that! I always have to stop myself because I'll just want to come in and sit and talk with my kids' friends because they're so interesting, fun, and lively. But it's the kids' friends. I have to remind myself to be age-appropriate, and developmentally appropriate.

BS: I wonder if this is too much. When we took our first kid to college, all the parents were supposed to leave at one point, leave the kids alone and say, "Goodbye, goodbye." So we say, "Goodbye," and then we go back just to fix a few things in the dorm room, and Cheri's lugging things in, and she's moved the bed out and is moving things out. All the other parents have already left.

CS: I'll explain that and you'll understand. Our son had a power strip with all the plugs right next to where his pillow was, and I just thought that the electromagnetic field was just not going to be healthful. I thought, "I really need to move it a little bit away from him."

BS: If Molly did that, it would be funny. She would just extend it just a little bit because some people might find it funny that he had an electromagnetic field near his head.

"I don't want them to get brain cancer, either."

CS: Yeah, unless he gets brain cancer. Then who's laughing? I request that our children speak on the speakerphone instead of holding it by their ear and getting brain cancer. They have good brains and I don't want them to get cancer.

BS: I don't want them to get brain cancer, either. Don't color me as the one who lets them have brain cancer, because that would be wrong.

CS: I'm trying to think. *Gilmore Girls* covered the whole, "We're mother and daughter, but we're really the same age, and we really have the same problems, and we're just like sisters, even though we're mother and daughter" thing. They did every possible permutation of that. But I think the idea of really over-parenting is usually something that's relegated to a side dish. It's usually someone like Holland Taylor [playing Charlie and Alan's mother on *Two and a Half Men*], over on the side making acerbic comments, and coming in all glam.

BS: I think I'd change the daughter to a son.

CS: I think maybe I'd give Molly two kids. Or three.

BS: I think there's really something about this, because it would take it away from *Gilmore Girls*. This way, the kids actually have the mother present where they have to deal with her. And maybe some kids see her as extremely valuable. And the thing is, when we were at Stanford, you really got the sense that these parents love their children, and these kids love their parents. You didn't get the feeling like, "Oh, thank God they're gone," from the kids or, "I couldn't wait to get away," from any of the parents. You know the parents work really hard, they just didn't check in on the kid every five years and go, "How're you doing?" And then they end up at a good university. I think there're a lot of people probably out there who would watch this.

CS: I think having Molly left alone . . . certainly it's a fun pilot, where the kids are so worried about Molly, and then she's basically Auntie Mame. She's so irrepressible that it's like, "Oh, my God, back off, Mom." I think it's probably a good idea to have a younger generation, just because for television you need to have young, pretty people and their funny friends.

BS: They'll be the hard ones to cast, but yeah.

CS: The question is, can you do a show from the mother's point of view? Certainly if it's *House*, if you write a compelling character and you find the female version of House, of Hugh Laurie, then you've got somebody who you just want to be with, and you can do it from her perspective, with a focus on her, rather than relegating her over to the Doris Roberts part. The funny side dish.

BS: You'd have to figure out how she was able to be there.

CS: Well, if she's left widowed or divorced. It's probably funnier if she's divorced.

BS: Because she's available.

CS: It's probably funnier. If her husband walks out on her, you can bring him back and have lots of good stories. Okay, so let's say her husband leaves her. Let's not do a younger woman. That's just so overdone. I think you have to have him dating a man. A senator, or something like that.

BS: Dating a senator he met during his travels?

CS: I think you need a really funny, outrageous gay character. I think it'd be really funny if it was the dad.

BS: Or the guy the dad's dating.

CS: Or the guy the dad's dating. Yeah, the dad could be just totally . . .

BS: . . . could be great. He's just, boring, boring, boring. So he's attracted to this guy's flamboyance.

CS: So Molly is starting life anew. The kids are on their own. *Mother Is a Freshman.* Have they done that since 1948?

BS: They may not have.

CS: But it's so common now. We know someone who was going to UCLA. She was going back for her MFA, but she was an acting student, so she was getting *all* the roles. She was sewing up all the age-appropriate roles. The kids were a little pissed. What if Molly's kids were already at UCLA, just because we know UCLA. She's got two or three children. It's a Bruin family, and the mom just sort of lands there, just because she's grief-stricken.

BS: There's your act break. The last kid is moving in . . .

CS: . . . her son?

BS: Yeah, her son. And he sits her down for the big talk. "You have to find your own life now. I know it's going to be difficult."

CS: Oh, she's helping him move into college?

BS: Yeah, yeah. "It's going to be difficult, but you go out there." And she says, "You're right, you're right! Thank you." And then you come back and she's enrolled.

CS: She's made friends in the dorm. She's going to be the housemother, something like that. Yes, it could work if he's the last one to leave, and Molly's just been left with an empty nest, and the kids are all really worried about her. She's just had this blow from Dad dropping her for a senator at the beginning of the summer, and now they've all been hovering around her all summer taking care of her. Now they've got to go back to school, and she's helping him move in, and it's like, "Hey, I'm not going back. I'm selling the house." You could definitely do it in an organic way because although she wouldn't be able to get into school right away, she could come in as a "winter admit." There are so many ways in. If she's really, really lively and friendly and funny.

BS: Like you.

CS: Does this mean I can go to Stanford with our son?

BS: You know what, it's actually possible to be permanently embarrassed. If your mother did that, you would have a flush on your face all day long.

CS: Kit [one of Cheri and Bill's children] would love it.

BS: She would have no problem at all.

CS: Kit would be fine because she's going to be twenty-one. She would love it. In fact, you could have the siblings at different levels of acceptance, and embarrassment, and control. Yeah, for Teddy, it would be the worst thing in the world.

BS: Oh, my God!

CS: I think you'd have to have it both ways.

BS: Yeah, that'd be fun.

CS: Then that would cause a lot of sibling disharmony. And there are certain things as a parent that you really shouldn't know about your children when they go away to school. You really aren't supposed to know if somebody's staying over in their dorm, or that they went to a frat party. And you don't want to know. That's why distance is a little bit nice. Like if our son Teddy was going to college near us, and he was right here, we might know too much. Or if he was living at home, there would just be certain things that . . . it wouldn't be okay.

BS: Yeah, sometimes when I go to the University, it's like they're still in high school, except now nobody limits them doing anything.

CS: That's what Teddy said. He has a roommate from the Midwest who's so cute, and so nice. They had their first dorm activity, a scavenger hunt in San Francisco, and they had sixty activities they could complete. One of the activities that only one person in the whole dorm completed was streaking Haight-Ashbury. That was Teddy's roommate. One of the first things he announced to me was, "I don't drink."

BS: "Occasionally, I take off my clothes and run in public."

CS: Then Teddy told me, the other night he stayed up all night playing ping-pong with the girl who lives in the room next door. They just played ping-pong all night long, and then he crashed on his bed, slept through his classes. He just got totally burned out on ping-pong. That's his whole idea of freedom. But you know what, if you had one kid . . . I don't know which one it is . . .

BS: . . . the roommate . . .

CS: But also if you have one kid who is, and I think this is Sarah, who's pretty conservative, pretty by-the-book, and Molly feels like, "This is your time to test the boundaries." Maybe it's something the mom never did either. Maybe she never tested her boundaries, and went wild. Although she would have, if she's in her fifties, she would have, because she would've grown up in the '60s.

PD: When I was at USC in the '60s, it was a very conservative school. There were girls from Orange County who had angora sweaters in their closets.

CS: So maybe that's her thing, that she missed the '60s. They flew right by her. She missed disco because she was so busy playing by the rules.

BS: "What happened? I kept meaning to, but never quite got around to it."

CS: She missed Reaganomics. She missed the whole "Gordon Gekko, money and power," thing. Now she's getting to catch up on all these things that she missed out on. Of course, none of this works if you don't cast it perfectly.

BS: That's true of almost every series. The weird thing about casting is—it used to kill me—all the people who won't do television. You think to yourself, "People who are in movies, and they're what, eighteen people, tops? They get to make a movie; that's about it, right? Everybody else is pretty much up for grabs, so get a job." There're hundreds of people who won't do television, and so you just cast the best you can, and sometimes it's tough. And sometimes you just don't get it.

CS: You want to cast this?

BS: It might be a little easier to cast.

CS: Who? It has to be somebody who's got so much . . .

BS: . . . maybe some British actors?

CS: Christine Baranski! It has to be somebody who's so truly fun that you can see where it's not going to be a huge drag for anybody except for her children. And an overpowering personality. I'm trying to think of who else. It's just anybody who could play Auntie Mame.

CS: Theatre personalities because they're comfortable being larger than life, and just a little bit more "out there." But there are other people. Kirstie Alley could do it. She would be fun, she'd be a blast. Who else is just so out there?

BS: I say go to England and you'll find somebody.

CS: Oh yeah, just bring Emma Thompson over, and call it a day. That'd be fantastic. But you wouldn't want her to be English.

BS: Oh, she wouldn't have to be English. Gregory House isn't English. Get rid of the accent. The Brits are very good at that.

CS: It seems like then you start the show in a campus setting. Is that a good thing? Do you want it to be a public university, like a big UCLA campus setting? Or do you want it to be Ivy League, or do you want it to be small?

BS: It seems traditionally that America's kind of scared of campus settings.

CS: So what do you do, then? Do you want to make it more a college town?

BS: Yeah, maybe . . . college town . . .

CS: . . . that's *Gilmore Girls*.

BS: Maybe make it a high-tech school like Austin.

CS: Yeah, but if the relationships are the heart of the series, if the people are the heart of it, then it really seems if she's coming into their world, invading their world, then you have to be in their world, right?

It just seems like she's got to be the fish out of water. She's got to be invasive. And so, if you're in a town where she's got outlets . . .

BS: . . . a college where you're not going to run into *Gilmore Girls*. It could be NYU.

CS: Oh, that's kind of cool.

BS: You're right in the urban area, but you're still in college.

CS: That's actually pretty neat, especially if they're from someplace like Indianapolis. If they're from someplace that's the opposite of downtown Manhattan. I like that. Alright, NYU. What else? In this article, they say the parents are like the Blackhawk.

It's a subset of the helicopter parent. With a Blackhawk parent, the children don't know what the parent is doing.

BS: The kids don't know?

CS: They don't know that someone like Molly is going in there and advocating for them. Checking their emails. Checking their Facebook, and all that.

BS: I wish I had parents like that.

CS: And you know what, I always tell our son, "Don't put anything on Facebook you don't want us to see." Because you know what, I Google his name, and somebody else will have something, a Facebook reference to him, and I can just link right to it. And then I can link to his Facebook from that. Not that I ever would. But I can.

BS: During a commercial, you've got to have something to do.

CS: So now all you have to do is start hitting on a senator so I can go back to college and live it. Then we'll get the story.

BS: I'm trying to think, are all the good-looking ones gone?

CS: He could be a governor; it doesn't have to be a senator. Although Barbara Boxer was pretty cute on *Curb Your Enthusiasm*.

BS: She's very cute.

". . . for the most part, I think critics like dark, but I don't think the general audience is like that."

JD (Jeffrey Davis): How do you feel about that "dark versus light" argument we hear a lot about?

BS: I'm not very dark. We appreciate people who do it. You know what, I think for the most part, I think critics like dark, but I don't think the general audience is like that. I mean, how many things that are dark fail?

CS: Is *House* dark? Is *The Office* dark? Is *Curb Your Enthusiasm* dark?

BS: Well, we did put a gay senator in here. So, I think we've definitely started in that direction. We sort of left that idea alone there, but that certainly started making it interesting.

CS: I really love *Curb Your Enthusiasm* and *House,* where it feels natural. It doesn't feel "sitcom-y." That's the one thing I'd be afraid of with the idea as we pitched it. It could go really *Two and a Half Men,* really standard three-camera, laugh track.

BS: The network will push you even further in that direction.

CS: Yeah, where you have to get really type-y, and you can't deviate from these molds that the characters are in. I think it's so interesting to have sort of complex, multifaceted, surprising characters, like on *The Office.* They behave out of character, but really just like human beings where they don't always react in the same way to the same stimuli. So I think I'd be interested in that.

"... we've been swayed toward higher concept and more of a hook. I think the hook can be a real trap."

PD: So how might you do some of that with Molly going to college?

CS: You'd want to build the surprises into the pilot, to let people know that these people aren't reacting in the standard ways. A lot of shows have done that, like *Arrested Development.* They did that in a really good, comedic way. Our best success has been just staying pretty low-concept. Low-concept, high-dialogue ... characters and relationships. I think after *Cheers,* and in all of the shows that we worked on, including the animation and everything we've done, we've been swayed toward higher concept and more of a hook. I think the hook can be a real trap.

BS: By the time you get to that second or third episode, the hook doesn't mean anything anymore.

CS: But when you establish a hook, I know as an audience member, I expect to see it. I expect an episode of *House* is going to start with just somebody seeming like they're going to have one kind of sickness, and then they have something completely different.

BS: "I would want to do what you want to do."
CS: "The secret of our partnership!"

CS: So you get into the rhythm as an audience member, you expect the show to fulfill your expectations, and then when it doesn't, are you delighted or are you annoyed?

And so I'd want to set up something where there's as few expectations as possible, so that we, as writers, could sort of feel our way through it, instead of having to retell the same story every week. That's what I would want to do. What would you want to do?

BS: I would want to do what you want to do.

CS: The secret of our partnership!

BS: I think it would be interesting to do a series that was so low-tech, sort of like a comedy version of *The Blair Witch Project,* only it would be a comedy. It'd be so low-tech, that would be the funny thing about it. You know, instead of like every other show.

CS: But that's what *The Office* is, isn't it? Yeah, *The Office* is low-tech. I mean, look at those sets. Could they be more beige?

BS: You go back and you look at the sets for *The Honeymooners.* Story lines in the drawer . . . see what's in the drawer today. Wow, off to the races!

"I would like the characters to be colorful so the sets don't have to be."

CS: I would really like that, and I really appreciate that. I would like the characters to be colorful so the sets don't have to be. It's like, oh my God, when you see these sitcom sets and this wall is lavender, and this wall is melon.

BS: Characters wear these light purple shirts. I can't think of Dr. House wearing a light purple shirt. But the costumer went, "Yeah, this would be good," but I don't see him wearing that.

CS: I'd like all the color to be in the character, and for the setting, and the costumes, and the hair to look real. That's what I really like about *The Office.* Pam's hair does not look like she just came out of a salon. It's real hair, and I love that.

BS: Now this is sort of true of us across the board. In theatre, we like . . .

CS: . . . minimal.

BS: Minimal, minimal. We like crummy little theatres. We like small theatres.

CS: Yes, cinder block, and posters, and Scotch tape. That's what's real. You know, we've been really tied in with The Blank Theatre Company because of our kids and the young playwrights' festival. It's a great company. We love them.

JD: How did you start working together?

BS: We wrote together in 1981 and then we married in '82.

CS: Billy was teaching improv, and he had a really good idea. In the classroom, we'd do these ongoing scenarios that we would write just to amuse ourselves. We did this in the second half of class each week. And he had an idea to do one that would be like, this was back in the '80s, a contemporary Los Angeles version of *Our Town*. And I said, "That's a really good idea, but I think you should write it, not me." At the time I was an actress, and Billy was a writer.

PD: Were you a student of his?

CS: I was a student of his.

BS: Cheri told me to start teaching.

PD: So you made it into The Groundlings.

CS: We were in a class together. I said, "You should really write that idea," and so . . . I don't know, did you say, "Let's write it together," or did I say, "Let's write it together"?

BS: I'm going to choose [that] you said, "Let's write it together." I have no idea. No, it just seemed like a good idea.

CS: We wrote it and then we gave it to our neighbor, Xander Berkeley, who is an actor, and he forgot to read it. And then one day his girlfriend Seana read it. She was cleaning the house and she found it, and she made him read it and he liked it. And then that night we were standing out on the corner. We were doing our improv show at the Déjà vu Coffee House on Vermont and Hollywood Boulevard. The owner had just obtained a theatre right down the street. And we said, "What are you going to do in the theatre?" and he said, "I don't know, you got anything?" And I said, "Yeah." And he said, "Can you have it ready in two weeks?" "Yeah." He had a theatre, he had a barn. And so we said to Xander, "Do you want to direct it?" And we got all of our friends together, and we just put it up—and this was during the L.A. Olympics, the Arts Festival—and because it was celebrating Los Angeles, it became sort of a *go-to* play.

BS: It was fun!

CS: And later we moved it to a theatre on Melrose.

BS: It's basically a long-form parody of *Our Town*.

CS: It was called *Our Place* because the big Olympic slogan was, "L.A.'s The Place." It was really fun. Basically, it was a long exploration of why we lived in L.A. when all of our friends were moving to New York. It was our excuse for an appreciation of Los Angeles.

BS: I thought the funniest thing was, we went on a radio show to promote it, and the guy said, "Why don't people call in and say what they like about L.A." Ninety-eight percent of the callers said, "I like the weather." And that was it. "I like the weather!"

CS: And it's true. What's not to like?

PD: Do either of your families have a show business background?

CS: Not even a little bit.

BS: Only our kids.

CS: We're definitely a theatre family.

BS: A couple of years ago, Cheri said, "I think they're all going to be old people in the business."

PD: Were your families funny?

BS: [*To Cheri*] Your mom is funny.

CS: My mom is funny. And my dad's a little bit funny.

"I'm legendary in my own family."

BS: Nobody in my family's particularly funny. I was the funniest person in my family. I'm legendary in my own family. My brother was telling me things that I said as a kid, and I said, "Oh, that's pretty good." Completely forgotten.

JD: Let's see—you did *Our Place*, and then what happened?

CS: Some people saw it. It got a little bit of attention, and I think Chuck Schnabel, who was at CBS at the time, said, "You should do something." And somebody else said, "You should do late night."

BS: Then one night when we were on *Cheers*, I said I would do the warm-up, which is insane. I shouldn't have done it. The reason you shouldn't do it is, about three seconds in, you realize, "Oh, they hate me because when I'm talking, they're not filming, and they're not seeing what they came to see." So I said to the audience, 200-plus people, "You know, my wife and I are partners. Does anyone here work with their husband or wife?" Nobody. Zip. Then I say, "Oh, then we're freaks." But back then we were freaks, and we're still freaks. In later years, we've known more people who actually work with their husband or wife.

"... when we had a fight at home, the animals would go under the couch. So all the guys ... went under the chairs."

BS: The only time we actually had a husband-and-wife tiff was when we were on *The Jeffersons*. We got into some argument, it was my fault, and we couldn't get out of it. It kept spiraling down, and we were just like baby writers at the time, we shouldn't have even been talking, and it spiraled down and down, and we had told these guys—they were great guys, Peter Casey and David Lee—that when we had a fight at home, the animals would go under the couch. So all the guys around the table went under the chairs.

JD: Did you like the Writers' Room?

BS: I liked the Room.

CS: He loved it. It gets in my way.

BS: She just wants to get the work done, and everybody else is willing to talk and, "Blah, blah, blah." And that's what I like.

Bill likes the Writers' Room and Cheri doesn't . . . at least, she didn't once she had kids. We've heard stories from writers about good Rooms that were fun to work in and bad Rooms that were competitive and hostile, but the opinions of the Rooms always depended on the quality of those rooms themselves—except for Michael Elias (see page 89), who just didn't like writing by committee. Cheri's take is a new one. While she is very friendly and socially skilled, she didn't like the Rooms because the writers spent too much time talking about everything but the script. They kept her away from her kids. She just wanted to get the story done and go home.

CS: I wanted to get home and be with the kids. But sidetracking is one of Billy's special talents. It's at the bottom of his résumé.

BS: Yeah. "Able to lead conversations down avenues and in directions not conceived of."

CS: I don't know if you've noticed, but he's good at it.

BS: Everybody needs a skill.

CS: And I have learned to appreciate that skill in you.

BS: Here's my impression of Cheri: "Alright, alright, we're on page . . . line . . ." It's a much more valuable talent to have.

CS: Well, if you want to go home. If you *don't* want to go home, then it's good to sidetrack. I was not well-suited to it once we had children, which was very early in our career.

BS: Most people have a late night, but once we took over a show, because of Cheri, we just got stuff done. And we did rewrites and I worked on other shows as a consultant, and I'd call Cheri and say, "They just spent two and a half hours on one joke, and it's not even a very good joke." We'd just go, "Boom!" and if it was like, "Eh, we'll leave it there, and we'll come back and get it, we won't come back and get it . . . whatever." We went to Warner Brothers and we did an act, and we'd say, "Oh, we're going to go home and do the other act in the morning." They went berserk, they panicked.

CS: We said, "We will have it before the actors get to it."

BS: "We'll have it in the morning."

CS: "It will be in front of them before they're ready."

BS: That's why we were lucky to work on *Cheers* all those years.

JD: Did you come in after Shelley Long left?

CS: We did two Shelley and five Kirstie Alley years.

JD: Was it *Pee Wee's Playhouse* you developed?

BS: Yeah, the stage show.

CS: The original *Pee Wee Herman Show.*

BS: Yeah, the *Pee Wee Herman Show.* It went to the Roxy.

PD: Television has evolved to the point where the writer/producer/creator has the real power. What skills do you need for such a comprehensive job?

"Here's the key phrase to remember: 'Well, one of them has to be the worst episode of the season.'"

CS: Well, there are a lot of skills you need when you set out to be a writer, but you don't necessarily think, "Oh, some day I'm going to have to be looking at blueprints and making decisions on set design. They're going to wheel in a rack of costumes and ask me to make a choice. I'm going to be casting." You just don't know that. If you're successful, you're going to become the decision maker, because you're the one who's still standing when everybody else falls away. Not the director.

BS: Here's the key phrase to remember: "Well, one of them has to be the worst episode of the season."

JD: Do you think having smaller staffs and giving out fewer assignments the way they used to has made television better?

BS: I don't know. They do all this rewriting, and a lot of the rewriting seems to just go sideways, as opposed to the old days. They would just write it and that's it!

CS: And I don't understand that whole "parceling out" method. The way that works is different people are working on different parts of a script. I know they do it on a lot of shows. They do it on *Desperate Housewives*. Doing it this way, how can they know that all these different parts of a story are going to work together? How can they know it's not going to have to be cobbled together at the back end?

BS: How many things in life work when the committee is working on them? Not many.

CS: That's why I think—though God knows you get stretched so thin, like Larry David, he must be losing his hair—but there's such consistency to his stories. The stories on *Curb Your Enthusiasm* are so intricate, and you know that any little detail he lays in at the beginning is going to pay off at the end. And I don't know how you would do that when you have five Rooms going.

"We would always say, 'Boy, if only we could have shown the reading, it would've been great.'"

BS: Oh, that would be impossible.

JD: Does tabling always make a script better, or does it just get different?

BS: Sometimes in TV, we used to think the reading was the best. We would always say, "Boy, if only we could have shown the reading, it would've been great."

CS: Unless you've got trained theatre actors who are going to be able to recreate that discovery—that spontaneity that comes with saying it the first time—sometimes they get a little bored. They get a little stale. And so you've got to think of some new jokes. And they don't want to say the same thing to the audience twice, because it's just not going to have the same effect the second time. So you've got to think of something new, and sometimes it just doesn't come off the top of your head. We had actors on *Cheers* who could hit it precisely every time, and that joke was gold from day one until shooting. But there were other actors who you just kept having to feed new material and then it got so you'd have to retake it and retake it, and retake it, and set up the shots. It's a long process.

". . . one day we watched a scene between the first A.D., the second A.D., and the prop guy. And the prop guy's doing a pretty good Woody."

BS: With a successful show, the actors start to get movie work, so they're not there, and so then the prop guy will fill in for Woody Harrelson during the run-through. And then one day we watched a scene between the first A.D. [assistant director], the second A.D., and the prop guy. And the prop guy's doing a pretty good Woody.

CS: That's why we *love* working with people who come out of the theatre. Because they're used to recreating a performance, working it, honing it, and getting it right.

BS: And working off other actors.

CS: And listening. And precision. I mean, talk about Christine Baranski, who we're so stuck on. Her precision is just crystal.

PD: You started at The Groundlings. Where did you learn the rest of the craft?

CS: On the job. In the Rooms, and by reading a lot of scripts. There may have been classes you could take, but we were already out of school and we didn't know about them.

BS: Lowell Ganz, who was on *Laverne & Shirley* and *Happy Days* as a writer/producer and wrote movies like *Parenthood* and *City Slickers*, taught a class at Sherwood Oaks. Lowell Ganz was good. He would say things like, "TV is not radio." And suddenly you were like, "Oh, yeah."

CS: Yeah, except then later on, when we got to *Cheers*, the Charles brothers said, "We want yours to be a radio show."

BS: Actually, TV *is* radio. Sure, you do some physical stuff, but very often, physical stuff will get lost and you always need someone to say something. Always.

CS: It has to be radio because people are multitasking while they're watching. They're not watching TV, it's just sort of *on*, and you need to be able to look up and catch it.

An Interview with
Leonard Stern

A partial list of Leonard Stern's credits as a creator, show runner, and writer includes: *I'm Dickens, He's Fenster; He & She; The Steve Allen Show; The Good Guys; The Honeymooners; Get Smart; The Phil Silvers Show; Operation Petticoat; McMillan & Wife;* and *The Jackie Gleason Show.*

Leonard Stern was there at the birth of situation comedy on shows like *The Honeymooners* and *The Phil Silvers Show.* For nearly sixty years, he enjoyed an unbroken string of successes in TV, film, theatre—and even publishing, as co-founder of Price Stern Sloan, the inventors of the *Mad Libs* books. And yet, for all his accomplishments, his humor about himself and his work is sometimes self-effacing and always witty and enthusiastic.

While Leonard Stern admires the talented writers in this book whose humor springs from a deep well of anxiety and hostility, he is proud of making comedy in which conflicts arise from good intentions between people who genuinely care about one another—intentions that have unintended consequences. Of the writers we've interviewed for this book, some like to start by asking questions about structure, while others talk about characters. Leonard, a consummate professional, gets right down to work, dimensionalizing characters and developing story. As he works and re-works the Premise, we watch it evolve and deepen. And remarkably, it all comes from love—which makes Leonard Stern unique among comedy writers.

Leonard passed away in 2011, having contributed his talents to dozens of shows and winning two Emmy Awards during his career.

PD (Peter Desberg): As we've explained in our Premise [see page 9], how would you go about developing the show's plot lines?

LS (Leonard Stern): I generally find something that would amuse and interest me and have some subtext of currency. Right away as I read this, I said, "Do the parents live better than the child?" because even though the child makes more money today than they ever made, the world has changed and economics are dramatically different. You can own a house that you bought for 10 percent of what you would pay today, and you have security. The daughter Sarah, if she were married, I have a feeling she and her husband would both work, because it would be a requirement. And they never catch up to the parents. They'd be dependent upon the parents—in this case, Molly.

So my tendency is to have the daughter have a husband, as opposed to a single's existence. It would appeal to me because I feel television has noticeably ignored this tremendous life situation that is probably taking part in one or more family's relationships. The father, and the mother, and the daughter, and the son, and their lifestyles are not compatible. And I would want them to mesh.

So I would see Molly becoming a business partner of the daughter Sarah, so that it brings it to another level. She's not a meddler, she's not interfering. They're just a generation or two apart in thinking. So their concepts of music are radically different. And when I started to think like that, I said, "What kind of business would I put them in?" Something where they would be polarized in taste. And as a consequence, Sarah would be much more the business woman; the mother, much more the social animal in the Premise, and the mother contemptuous of contemporary music. "Where is the melody? Where are the rhymes?" And discouraging sales by telling people not to buy that. And so you start to have a dramatic Premise, if they have to go home together, and what if indeed Sarah's separated from her husband and now living with her mother, it's . . . how do you separate your office life from your home life? And suddenly, you're not in a clichéd situation. You're off on an experimentation, which is, I believe, a true reflection of what is happening today in our society, certainly in the middle class. Now if you want to ask questions, you're certainly welcome to . . . if you're still awake!

PD: I love the way you set it up. What kind of business would you put them in?

LS: Well, I would have them own a video/DVD and CD store on a college campus. And also they'd have a little version of Starbucks going. And then the mother . . . I would give some kind of background that she had a moment in her life where she knew celebrities. So suddenly, she has an importance in a college community. And she also decides to take classes. And suddenly, Sarah realizes where she got her drive from. It wasn't the father, as she suspected. It was her mother. And then Molly is trying to apply everything that's new, except taste. Her taste stays rooted in the past. And so you get a paradox, and you get a conflict. But it's a fun conflict. It isn't demeaning to either person. And that, to me . . . I think I can say with equanimity and conviction that most of the times, the shows I developed were based on liking, not negativity, not putting someone down. Consequently, it's harder to write comedy of love and caring.

One of the few things that Freud got right was that most humor that gets laughs is rooted in hostility. Comedy writers must have read this paragraph in his book, because most TV and movie comedy is mired in hostility. That makes Leonard Stern even more remarkable. He acknowledges the need for conflict, but finds it in love. He will have two characters who deeply care for each other—each with a goal to help the other—but the two sets of goals collide, producing major conflicts. Each character has the best of intentions, leading to the worst of outcomes.

It's . . . what's the word, "spritzing" is much more acceptable, and you get more writers capable of that. Affection is somewhat of an embarrassment to most comedy writers, and not to be revealed unless you break the glass.

JD (Jeffrey Davis): Why do you think that is?

> ## "I was kind of handicapped. Most of the people I know who were successful writers had dysfunctional families. Everybody in my family liked each other."

LS: Because comedy writers are at war with society, I think—innately, not intentionally, it's there. I was kind of handicapped. Most of the people I know who were successful writers had dysfunctional families. Everybody in my family liked each other. I had to forgive them . . . it handicapped me. Others had this marvelous head start. I think it's also social . . . a way of fitting in, by being the odd one out. The paradox is of minor significance.

PD: When you're writing more positive comedy, is it more difficult to find conflict?

LS: Not necessarily, because the conflict can come out of caring. *He & She* was a show I did and I think we did thirty-two episodes, and it received every nomination for a writing award in comedy from the Writers Guild, and the same from the Emmys. Four different writers on the shows . . . teams competed with each other. And that was the ultimate compliment. That show was a very prideful hug of each other. There was inordinate respect that they had. They were bright and eccentric, and they made it permissible.

I think we introduced the first fop [a character who acts foolish] in television in a character Jack Cassidy played, who was both their best friend and greatest irritant. So that . . . I just love that show, and it's radically etched in my mind.

JD: How would you bring conflict into a happy mother/daughter relationship?

LS: It's working already because there's a difference, as I said, primarily in taste, and then there's the belief: "But how could you feel this way when you're my daughter?" And that could be a discussion; it doesn't have to be spiteful or hateful to be funny. I know if the daughter needed a dress for an occasion and it doesn't fit into the budget at the moment—the store had a bad month—the mother says, "Wear this." And she says, "Mom, thank you, but it's not me." And suddenly, that's enough of a reason to have a problem when she learns that her mother was offering her the dress in which she was married. Then, Molly says, "You look terrible." But the mother feels good about it. And yet, you've had a problem. It's much more fun because you go on an untraveled road. It's much easier to do pejoratives and put-downs.

PD: You structured it so you have at least three generations working here because you've got the mother's generation, the daughter's, and then they're on a college campus, which is still younger.

LS: I thought because you're always out of step, no matter how long . . . when you're marching, you find yourself occasionally out of step, let me say, and that would be part of this. And I love the fact that the mother's strong opinions affect business. Some people won't come in because she's there. "They're free to do what they want, but this is my feeling about that."

JD: Does that come from something in your life?

LS: No, probably gestation. I said . . . the professor suddenly is smitten with the mother. That, in itself, is interesting. But he's ultra-conservative. That's the one thing she can't stand about him. And yet, he's interesting. So you're dealing with a political situation, but an important one—to make the recognition that conservatives can be lovable.

PD: Rather than just having a conflict between two people who don't get along, you're saying they don't get along with this *part* of a person. You're looking at the traits as what's causing the conflict.

"I received a fan letter from Stan Laurel. I didn't believe it, because everybody . . . knew how I loved Laurel and Hardy, so I figured it was a prank."

LS: I'm glad you're making these distinctions. Most good comedy is character-oriented. There can be eccentricities, or exaggerations, or hyperbole. I was a great admirer of [comedy duo Stan] Laurel and [Oliver] Hardy, before it was fashionable to be, and the very first show I did on my own was *I'm Dickens, He's Fenster*, the wellspring of which was Laurel and Hardy, and to my great astonishment, I received a fan letter from Stan Laurel. I didn't believe it, because everybody who worked with me on *The Steve Allen Show* knew how I loved Laurel and Hardy, so I figured it was a prank. But ultimately, Steve Allen said to me, "Have you ever heard from Stan Laurel?" So I figured now I know who wrote the letter. It turned out he was doing a book, *The Funny Men*, and he had interviewed Stan Laurel, and Steve had said, "Is there any show you like very much?" And he said, "I'm enjoying one tremendously; it's called *I'm Dickens, He's Fenster.*"

As Steve was about to say, "I know who wrote it . . . he was my head writer," Stan said, "I even wrote the creator and never heard from him." And so Steve said, "That can't be." So he told me the story that Stan had written me, and at the time I thought it was Steve who had written me. And right then and there Steve had his little book, and we called Stan Laurel, and he became a critic of the show, and critiqued it every Monday. It was on Friday night. And we became friends. He was slightly paralyzed in the face, but I almost talked him into coming to the show, and [at] the last moment he felt uncomfortable. A remarkable human being, and this was an endorsement of what I believed. We had great fun with paranoia.

But Laurel and Hardy had that . . . they were against each other, unless somebody interfered with the team, and then they were beautifully wedded and welded together. And this was exciting. And they had the world in microcosm, beautifully etched. I remembered Stan would do something like that, he'd be able to do something remarkable with his fingers [*Leonard does a gesture with his fingers*]. I don't know if this is on camera, but anyway, he'd be able to do something adroit with his fingers, and throughout the movie, Hardy would try and do it unsuccessfully through most of the film, and then he'd turn around and hit Laurel. Then you understood it. And it's marvelous. And they remained friends because Laurel understood it as well. At worst, he'd get tearful.

PD: As you were looking at Molly and Sarah, is there a particular way you go about looking at their traits?

LS: Well, there I probably borrow from life, because I was a collaborator for many years, I worked with Marty Ragaway in the beginning, then Sid Zelinka on *The Honeymooners*, and of course, your dad, Jeffrey, on *The Good Guys*, and so that you learn how to tolerate—I'll use a euphemism—eccentricities of your partner, and adjust to it, but it doesn't leave you completely unscathed, because ultimately, it's the paranoia. You always assume the other one's plotting against you. So you always have to be on the lookout. So it's a sustained truce.

PD: So here we have mother and daughter. Give me some ways you might flesh out the characters to bring out the conflict.

LS: Well, we have the foundation of a woman, the daughter gave up a job, I assume we're staying with the format that she was formerly working for a man, and she recognized that there was no promotion. The mother and she had to raise a loan to justify the investment of their new business. So the daughter looks like she'd be the one to be concerned with making the payments. And the mother would decide to enchant the person to whom they owed money. So this is reprehensible until you realize it's done in major corporations. So you're starting to see it be dimensionalized. And suddenly, the mother's wearing something low-cut, and so there's an argument: "We're not doing that; we're not stooping that low," Sarah says. "I'll just bend over once," Molly says. And you can see . . . the minute you start thinking, jokes emerge unknowingly. The foundation is right, and survival is at the bottom of this, always. I don't think we ever did a *Honeymooners* show where the problem wasn't money. But I don't know if most people's problems aren't the lack of funds. And so that's always painful, and it's difficult to contemplate.

And also suddenly, I see the mother preparing a list of donations she's going to make, and things she's going to give away, and they don't have any money. And I love that premise, because it doesn't mean we won't have it, and "If I should die suddenly, I want to have this distribution of wealth," and then of course, it's imaginary wealth. If you imagine it long enough, it will exist, it'll be palpable.

PD: You mentioned the nice, normal family you grew up in. Were they funny people?

LS: No, they were extraordinarily prideful. My father was an extremely gregarious man. He talked to anyone, and he had that persona that people would talk to him. But it was an embarrassment to me. He'd stop the mayor of New York, and he'd be talking to him. I'd feel embarrassed for the mayor. But here's a marvelous example of my father's personality. It took me a long time to understand it and his ways.

We did *The Honeymooners* in a huge theatre; it sat 3,000 people, so it was enormous, and it was live. So it was opening night every week, and my parents came to every show, same theatre. Sid Zelinka and I, it was one Saturday, and it was raining torrentially, and we had to get back to the theatre, we'd broken for lunch. And the front entrance was closest, so we knocked on the door, and said, "Writers," and the usher said, "Stage Entrance," we said, "It's raining out," he said, "Stage Entrance," we said, "Come on, it's pouring, you've seen us here . . ." and we're making no progress whatsoever. And suddenly the head usher came up and as he opened the door, he said, "That's okay, that's Mr. Stern's son."

PD: How did you learn to do what you do? How did you learn your craft?

LS: That was something I wanted to do. I almost had no choice. I wrote my first play, strangely enough, when I was thirteen in a French class. Mrs. Blankenstein—we always called her Frankenstein—decided to put it on, she would direct it. I loved the response it got, and it was humorous. I was very fortunate to go to a high school that had a strong drama department and did musicals twice a year, and original musicals with a sixty-piece orchestra, thirty-five people in the choir, and I wrote three of those in a period of a year and a half, while I was in my last half a semester of junior year and then the full senior year.

And then when I went to college, I automatically wrote the varsity show; even if they didn't have one, I wrote it, and talked them into it. So I was very comfortable in that. And I wrote the humor column, and edited the yearbook, and I met Marty Ragaway in college. He was doing a very humorous college magazine with extraordinarily high standards. So we were of similar interests. And then the War came, and I went into the service, and then when I came back, Marty had established himself as a writer doing occasional radio material. And he and I, through his connections, got to write a show, which fascinates me to this time.

It was for a man named Jimmy Edmondson, who was [known as the character] Professor Backwards. He could write words backwards on the blackboard. It's a good field, except if you're on radio. It diminishes rapidly. So we had to create a story for him, and the only person who didn't emerge from that show was Jimmy Edmondson. But Nanette Fabray was the vocalist, The Ames Brothers, who then were The Amery Brothers, a trio; and a very gifted actor, Ed Begley, was the heavy, the boss. So that was our cast. Most went on to do many, many things. I don't know what happened to Jimmy.

JD: Who mentored you early on?

LS: I think the plays I attended were an enormous influence on me. When I became a screenwriter, I was indebted to a man named Frank Davis, a remarkable human being and one of the founders of the Writers Guild. I had come to Hollywood to do the twenty-sixth version of the second *Jazz Singer*, which starred Danny Thomas and Peggy Lee, and it couldn't find a more incongruous casting, unless you went to the Irish Abbey Players. And Frank, I didn't know him, knocked on my door, and he said, "I know this show's been a problem for everybody who's on it, and I've been sort of the recipient of all the complaints of the writers. I've been the analyst on this show, and I'm just offering my service to you, because I'm well aware of the history and the strife, the internal problems." And suddenly I had somebody to take care of me and guide me. I think it was the first thing I had done without collaborating. He was invaluable. In a sense, he became a collaborator from a distance.

JD: Of all the people you've mentored, who are you the most proud of?

LS: I don't think I mentored. What I did is function in the job I was supposed to do, and I guess that's rare. So I hear things like, "I owe so much to you," and all I did was fulfill the function of the director that I was hired to do. I did the job I was supposed to do. But I've been lucky in all my associations. Dick Benjamin and Paula Prentiss are a superb example. Gloria, my wife, had seen a play in Chicago—I think *Barefoot in the Park*—and she called me from there and she said, "I've just seen an actor. Go put his name down. Dick Benjamin. He's marvelous, and he's your type. You'll love him." I said, "Thank you." Now I go to CBS and pitch the idea for *He & She*, and Mike Dann, who's in charge of creativity or programming—they're not necessarily the same thing—said, "If you can get Paula Prentiss, you've got a go-ahead."

Well, I didn't know Paula Prentiss, and I didn't have my father's personality to get to know her. I was at a card game and the man next to me happened to be her manager. It was the only time I ever played in that game. And it was astonishing. So he said, "I'll talk to Paula," and I gave him the premise, and he came back and said, "She loves it, but she'll only do it with her husband," and I said, "Who's her husband?" and he said, "Dick Benjamin." My eyes lit up. And I said, "Oh, my God, by coincidence, I'm perfectly willing to, let me get the go-ahead from CBS." And I called CBS, and said, "I have the couple, I've got Paula Prentiss," and Mike Dann said, "You've got a commitment." I said, "There's a kicker. She wants to work with her husband." He said, "Who's that?" And I said, "Richard Benjamin," and he said, "That's okay."

And so we went and developed the show together. They were on the road traveling, and I would send them notes, and I'd ask them to define their character so I could incorporate it in the script, and it was very exciting. About four weeks later, I get a phone call, a message to call Mike Dann in New York. I call him, and he says, "Leonard, did you sign Paula Prentiss and her husband?" I said, "Yes." And he said, "Is he an actor?" He didn't know what he did, they were just so anxious to make the deal that they agreed, and so . . . that's the history of the show. And it reflected that kind of absurd beginning.

JD: You alluded to this earlier . . . the idea that television ignores an element of life these days that perhaps in the past it didn't. Why do you think it ignores women in their fifties like Molly?

"This show is 100 percent correct 3 percent of the time."

LS: Because they're victimized by statistics and research, which is essentially organized guesswork. What they've done is surrendered. What they've been empowered to do and don't recognize any longer is respond viscerally, and go with that instinct. Remember, we're all instinctual, and then it's wedded to our experience. You can be formidable, but everybody didn't want to get blamed, so they encouraged research: "Now, hey, I love it, but they don't." Or some malleable statistic, you know, they started to play games. This show is 100 percent correct 3 percent of the time.

Mark Twain had a marvelous saying. I'm paraphrasing: "Facts are hard, statistics are pliable." And there are lies . . . "damn lies and statistics," another Mark Twain quote. So he was carrying the banner a long, long time ago.

JD: Is there any question in your mind that a show with a daughter and mother in her fifties could find an audience?

"My grandchildren have been victimized by the laugh track. They assume that 'Hello' is funny."

LS: If it's good and fun, it will. But it has to be fun, and it has to not use a laugh track; it has to earn its laughter. It has to be done live. It's abysmal and subversive what's happened. My grandchildren have been victimized by the laugh track. They assume that "Hello" is funny. And if you add a curse word behind it, that's insurance. There was a marvelous sketch in a Writers Guild award show that was brilliantly written by Carl Reiner and Mel Brooks. They did a sketch where they were two guys who sweetened a show, did a laugh track, added it, and by error, they've gotten Lincoln's Gettysburg Address. And they start to edit, judging what "four scores" were, and played back the laugh track. And it's the best indictment of the absurdity that has been happening now for too many years.

JD: What's going on with the *Get Smart* movie? [Note: This interview was done a year before the movie was cast. The movie was released in 2008.]

LS: I'm subject to the same rumors you are. I have no idea. This is common indictment of the thinking when they do a remembered or revered television show. They don't hire any of the original writers, even as consultants. And they change the characters, or lose the essence. If you're going to make *Get Smart*, why not do *Get Smart?* *Bilko* was a good example. The essence of Phil Silver's character, that was the support for the whole show, the pillar that held it up, and they changed that, and it's frightening to me. We sold *Get Smart* for a movie, and we had what we thought was a marvelous premise. It was a gay, autocratic designer, who wanted to own the world so he could dress it. And that premise, you laugh, and that's how you have to follow it. But the studio decided to do it in an entirely different way. And I kept saying, "Why? Why are you doing it this way?" And they said, "We don't want to do the television show." And I said, "Then why did you buy it?" And then they added a title, *The Nude Bomb*, they thought that would draw.

"'We don't want to do the television show.' And I said, 'Then why did you buy it?'"

It was our premise, but it wasn't our script. As I said, the premise appealed to me, and I thought, "You don't need an established person." It came as a result of Jack Cassidy playing "Jet Man" on *He & She*. He flew, literally and figuratively, and I figured he'd be marvelous. Jack could be sinister, if he so desired. And I thought he'd have substance and he could be camp through this, and that this is the kind of frightening person, because he at least has a purpose. Most dictators don't have one. So that's why the governments maintain armies, 'til they think of something they should do. And here he had. He needed to conquer the world. Put his designer label on the map.

PD: Can you tell when your stuff is funny?

LS: Pretty much, because it's character-oriented. I know the character will work. I don't know if everything the character will say will work. But that led to a series of remarkable characters for the show, and led to catch phrases. I think there were probably more catch phrases on the shows I did, because they were reflective of a character. *Get Smart* had seven or eight. We probably tried forty, but it was a pretty good percentage.

JD: How did that work? Did you, Mel Brooks, and Buck Henry sit in a Room together?

Sherwood Schwartz, creator of *The Brady Bunch,* and Leonard Stern, co-creator of *Get Smart,* had similar Hollywood experiences. Major studios bought the rights to make a movie of each of these iconic shows. The studios didn't use any of the original writers on the movie scripts. Sitcom writers develop uncanny ears for the consistency of character and dialogue of their characters. When you have a few free hours, read *A Martian Wouldn't Say That,* compiled by Leonard Stern. This book illustrates, through real memos, how executives develop television programs and films at the expense of consistent characterization. The studio executives lost the *voice* of the characters, along with their consistency of action. To replace these crucial factors, they compensated by taking these wholesome shows and heading them in a salacious direction. In the initial studio version of *The Brady Bunch* movie, the kids grew up to be pimps and whores. Sherwood said, "Not my kids." He insisted that he be involved in the movies. The subtitle for the *Get Smart* movie was *The Nude Bomb.* The Schwartzes were approached by a major studio for a *Gilligan's Island* movie as well. They vowed not to relinquish creative control.

LS: No, no, Mel and Buck wrote the first draft of the pilot show, and ABC turned it down. And a rewrite was done, and Danny Melnick said, in selling it, "If you don't like it, you can have your money back." Within twenty-four hours, they asked for their money back. So we were stuck with the script. And miracle of miracles, it was post-pilot time, but NBC had Don Adams under contract and was desperate to use him in this given year. And so, we had a meeting with them, and [NBC chairman and CEO] Grant Tinker responded favorably to the idea, and I agreed to adapt it for Don, with whom I had worked on *The Steve Allen Show.* So I did the dialogue changes to his cadence and rhythm, and I added the secret doors, and things like that, so that the final version, I guess Mel, Buck, and I worked on. And then Mel got a movie, *The Producers,* shortly after that, and the show sold, so Buck remained as the story editor, and Mel went on to glory. And the next year, Buck got *The Graduate* [he co-wrote the screenplay].

PD: Have you done any performing yourself? Stand-up?

LS: No, no. I'm quite self-conscious. I've been asked that question a couple of times. Sammy Kahn, before he hired me to write the musical version of *The Man Who Came to Dinner*—he was the producer and the lyricist—said to me, "You're not an actor," and I said, "No," and we talked, and he said, "I like you very much, are you sure you're not an actor?" I said, "No."

JD: What happened to that project?

LS: It was finished and cast, and the specter of television interfered. The movies didn't see any compatibility with television and were panicked. And so it had Clifton Webb, Doris Day, Gordon MacRae, and the Ritz Brothers in the principal roles. I had a great experience on it. When I was hired by Sammy, he introduced me to Vernon Duke, they were doing the music together, and at that meeting I said to him, "If my job requires my commenting on the music, I'm not qualified, and that may be very disturbing to you, but I'd just as soon not start, because I'm relatively tone deaf, and so it's your option, but at least you'll know this. I can discuss the lyrics." And they said, "It's okay."

Alright, I went to work and I like them, and I had something good for three or four weeks, and suddenly one morning my doorway's filled with Vernon and Sammy, and they're looking anxious, and I become apprehensive, and they say, "Come with us." And I said, "Oh, God, I hope this is not where they're going to play something for me . . . they've forgotten." So all the way down the hall, finally I said, "Remember, I'm tone deaf, I can't hear," and they're ignoring me, and sure enough, they go into a room with a piano and Vernon sits down, and Sammy says, "Listen," and they play a little song, they turn expectantly to me, and I said, "I'd have to hear it another hundred times to be able to tell you anything that would be meaningful to you." He said, "We'll play it again," he had a little ire in his voice, "Okay, play it again," and I say, "I'm sorry," and he said, "Okay, okay, okay." And I'm dismissed. And so I'm feeling, "Okay, I got this over . . . had to go through it, but thank goodness it's done and it's behind me." Four days later, there they are in the doorway again, and he said, "Come with us, we fixed it." The power of negativity.

JD: Well, I love what you did with this mother/daughter Premise. I think you're the only person who said you could derive conflict from love.

LS: You've met with hostile people. I had a good time. And thank you.

Zen and the Art
of Tongue Thrusting

In an ancient Zen parable, after just three months at a monastery, a novice approaches an elderly monk and asks him if he is on the one true path to enlightenment. The elderly monk smiles patiently and replies, "Tuesday will never come if the rose doesn't grow straight." This is precisely why we didn't interview any Zen monks.

This parable reminds you to beware the next time you hear a writing guru preach that *"The one true way* to write comedy is . . ." What you should do then is thrust your tongue out in her direction. If you're enrolled in a university writing class, and worried about your grade, you should cover your face with your heavy, overpriced textbook—and *then* thrust out your tongue.

But don't take it from us. Listen to two comedy masters on the subject:

Some years ago at the Paley Center in Los Angeles, Larry Gelbart (creator of *M*A*S*H, Tootsie,* and *Oh, God!*) and Mel Brooks (creator of practically everything else) were participating in a panel discussion about *Your Show of Shows,* the legendary 1950s weekly series where they developed their comedy writing chops and where the Writers' Room was invented.

The evening ended with a Q & A session. Lines formed on the left and right of the auditorium, facing the stage. Someone moved to a microphone and asked, "What's the difference between a joke and wit?"

Mel Brooks picked up the glass of water at his elbow and poured it over his head. "That's a joke," he said, as water dripped down his forehead like Niagara Falls.

When the laughter died down, the audience member asked, "So what is wit?"

Without missing a beat, Larry Gelbart answered, "Wit is dry."

At the same panel discussion, Gelbart was asked how many rules of writing comedy there were. "Fifty-five," he said. "Unfortunately, nobody knows what they are." The interviews in this book prove that there are as many ways to create comedy as there are writers who do the creating.

Parting Can Be Sweet Without Sorrow

Nobody likes finishing a good book. We find ourselves slowing down, savoring every chapter or rereading them, trying to delay the inevitable moment when we'll have to put it back on the shelf or close our Kindle. We delighted in every moment of participating in and editing the interviews in *Now That's Funny!*. The sad part was not having enough space to leave every word of them in. Publishers are strangely reluctant to publish 1,200-page books these days.

But we are not quite ready to say goodbye. In the Introduction to this book, we mentioned that we have created a website, www.nowthatsfunny.lol. This site will house occasional blogs and videos. There will be short video excerpts from the interviews so you can get a feel for who these writers are as people, what their work space looks like, and watch them work in real time.

It will also be a forum for your ideas and insights about comedy. We also hope that you will be inspired to create your own developed version of the Premise. The website will be home to an area for you to post it. We want www.nowthatsfunny.lol to be the beginning of a community based around comedy writing.

Glossary

arc. The evolution of the plot and characters of the story or series.

beat. An important joke or moment in a story.

coverage. A summary report of the contents of a script or project with an evaluation of its viability.

four-box demographics. Basic age groups of the audience. Filmmakers and show runners strive to make their story appeal to as many demographics as possible.

The Groundlings. Los Angeles-based improv group and improv/comedy school. Graduates include *Saturday Night Live*'s Kristen Wiig and Phil Hartman.

heavy. A villain.

high concept. A TV show or film that is largely based on a simply-stated premise, rather than a more complete character development and broader story.

house number. A substitute for a joke that specifies its characteristics. It is used in scripts to mark the location of a joke that will be created later.

Humanitas Prize. An industry award for enriching human understanding dealing with important social issues.

hybrid pilot. A pilot in which some scenes are filmed on location, and others on a soundstage.

lock. A defined situation or relationship in the script.

malapropism. A type of joke in which a character misuses a word that sounds similar to the word he actually meant to say.

middle-slice pilot. A pilot that provides introductory information about a series, but takes place as if the series were ongoing.

multi-camera show. A TV show performed live in front of a studio audience. It uses three or even four cameras to catch all the different actions in real time.

omega dog. One of the lowest-status members of a Writers' Room.

pilot. Typically the first and premiere episode of a television series. It must provide backstory, establish a franchise and premise, and also entertain the audience.

pipe. An industry term for the backstory; background information on the characters and the relationships between them.

post-production. Sound and editing enhancements made to film or video after filming.

premise pilot. Introduces a series, giving the necessary background and presenting the characters.

punch up. Adding comedy to an already written script. Often done by specialists, although sometimes done in the Writers' Room.

Room Monkey. A member of the Writers' Room whose function is to provide energy, often using a broad approach to comedy.

show runner. A writer-producer who runs the Writers' Room, and is involved with every aspect of the show.

single-camera show. A TV show shot like a movie, using only one camera. Not performed live with an audience.

spec script. A speculative script written with the intention of selling it or getting work as a writer.

spritzing. A comedy term for spitballing ideas.

table reading. Actors sitting around a table reading a script. An initial step done to see how the script works.

tabling. This is done by a group of writers in the Writers' Room to develop stories and punch up scripts.

tummler. A social director or comedian, who stimulates audience participation.

turnaround joke. A type of joke in which a scene completely contradicts the scene immediately before it. (e.g., A character says, "I absolutely do not want Chinese food," and the scene then cuts to that character sitting in a Chinese restaurant.)

Writers Guild of America. The union that represents writers in contract negotiations and other services.

Writers' Room. The room in which script writers gather to create, discuss, and write stories for a series or film.